THE CHILD'S RIGHT TO PLAY
A Global Approach

Edited by Rhonda L. Clements and Leah Fiorentino

Published under the auspices of Hofstra University

Westport, Connecticut
London

Library of Congress Cataloging-in-Publication Data

The child's right to play : a global approach / edited by Rhonda L. Clements and Leah Fiorentino.
    p.   cm.
    Includes bibliographical references and index.
    ISBN 0–275–98171–1 (alk. paper)
    1. Play—Psychological aspects.   I. Clements, Rhonda L.   II. Fiorentino, Leah.
BF717.C44   2004
155.4'18—dc21   2003046963

British Library Cataloguing in Publication Data is available.

Library of Congress Catalog Card Number: 2003046963
ISBN: 0–275–98171–1

First published in 2004

Praeger Publishers, 88 Post Road West, Westport, CT 06881
An imprint of Greenwood Publishing Group, Inc.
www.praeger.com

Printed in the United States of America

The paper used in this book complies with the
Permanent Paper Standard issued by the National
Information Standards Organization (Z39.48–1984).

10 9 8 7 6 5 4 3 2

Contents

Contents

Figures and Tables

FIGURES

TABLES

Acknowledgments

The editors are greatly indebted to the many professionals who have contributed their works to this book. Special thanks are extended to Margaret Maybury and Sylvia J. Giallombardo for their valuable criticisms and helpful suggestions concerning the editing process, as well as Alexej Ugrinsky, Natalie Datlof, Athlene A. Collins, and the entire Hofstra Cultural Center staff for their continued advice and support throughout the project. Recognition is given to the outstanding efforts of the Adelphi University Graphic Design Studio students (Julie Beale, Lawrence Bilello, Jessica Calderon, Kimberly Hollenstein, David Martin, and James Roberts), under the direction of Professor Dale Flashner, for their graphic contributions. The illustrations are the creation of Kimberly Hollenstein from the Adelphi University Graphic Design Studio. Acknowledgment is gladly given to John Beck, production editor, and to Terri Jennings, who performed the typesetting and design of the book.

Finally, the editors thank Sylvia, Tom, Logan, and Kendel, who contributed the time, effort, energy, and love necessary to keep the creation of this book . . . a playful activity.

Introduction

*Rhonda L. Clements and
Leah Holland Fiorentino*

Life should be lived as play.

—Plato

Play exists at the very heart of childhood. It is the fundamental means through which children learn about themselves, their family members, their local communities, and the world around them. The freedom to explore, experiment, make believe, and make one's choices is a key ingredient in the healthy development of every child. Play also fosters the child's creativity and curiosity and enhances the child's ability to cope when confronted with events out of the child's control. It is the right of every child to experience the joy and developmental benefits derived from play.

This book offers the reader contemporary thoughts from more than sixty national and international specialists in the areas of early childhood and play leadership, brain research and educational psychology, as well as playground specialists, child life specialists, and movement and physical educators. All works reflect the authors' deep commitment to the belief in "education through play" or "play for its own sake." The book also confirms the belief that play, along with the basic needs of nutrition, health, shelter, and education, is vital to develop the potential of all children.

To assist the reader in obtaining this understanding, we have divided the book into five distinct parts. Part I addresses topics of special interest to parents and caregivers concerning definitions and the importance of play. Among other issues, the chapters will show how play has been and can serve as a vehicle for the young child's increased language development, imagination, social competence, cognitive awareness, and coping strategy. Part II offers information concerning curriculum development, programming, and several academic teaching issues. Teacher trainers and child-care directors will find this content useful to facilitate change in their own educational settings.

When children play they draw upon previous experiences, such as things they have done, seen others do, read about, or viewed on television, and they use these experiences to play scenarios and engage in creative activities. Topics reflecting the child's props, playthings, and play environments are blended together in Part III to expand the reader's understanding of the value and use of objects and play spaces that can have a profound effect on the child's physical and emotional development. Failure to make adequate provisions for the child to play can result in bored, disaffected children with little to occupy themselves during holidays and after school. In contrast, the usage of age-appropriate toys of different textures and colors, and safe play facilities, awakens the child's exploration.

Part IV offers several in-depth chapters linking the most current research connecting brain and learning with play. Like the three previous parts, the information is expansive and yet very comprehensible for those readers viewing brain research for the first time. The information shows how play arouses the child's learning, social interaction, quest for adventure, and ability to role play and communicate. The role of play as an aid for the child's decision-making and problem-solving process is stressed.

Part V contains an overview of the importance and right of all children to play. The content is derived from a written declaration from the International Association for the Child's Right to Play. It summarizes definitions of play, identifies trends affecting childhood, and gives proposals for action to protect, preserve, and promote the child's right to play as reflected in Article 31 of the U.N. Convention on the Rights of the Child (adopted by the general Assembly of the United Nations, 20 November, 1989). Article 31 states that the child has a right to leisure, play, and participation in cultural and artistic activities. This right is the thread that runs through all of the book's chapters, and is the primary rationale for the book.

PART I

PLAYFUL ISSUES FOR
PARENTS AND EDUCATORS

Part I opens with Lisa Hermine Makman discussing some early British and American viewpoints toward the child's right to a work-free childhood. The chapter skillfully examines children of different social classes between 1830 and 1930 and confers the legislation that limited child labor and enforced school attendance. Specific legal developments and educational theories are included to assist the reader in learning when and why society began to view childhood as a time of learning and play. Similarly, Nancy K. Freeman and Mac H. Brown explore some of the moral and ethical dimensions of controlling children's play by focusing on the works of Vivian Paley's *You Can't Say You Can't Play* (1992) policy. It looks at how we use adult power to control and shape the young child's social learning skills. It also describes possible implications when adults mediate disputes and forbid aggressive or exclusionary activities. Brian Ashley identifies four principles that parents, teachers, and community leaders should consider to foster expressive play in the young child's play environment. He stresses that theory and research favor the need for children to control their own spaces. He asserts that parents may be the greatest obstacles to their child's self-discovery, even when efforts are made to offer creative play environments. Raquel Ary-De Rozza and Joanna Payne-Jones address the importance of fantasy play as a leading factor in the child's social development. Attention is given to sound educational theories that describe the therapeutic benefits of fantasy play for all children, including those that are disabled. Children empowerment issues are also included. Janice H. Patterson conveys strategies for parents and teachers to use when building resilience through play. The work considers internal characteristics of resilient children, as well as environmental factors that support resilience in many parts of the world. Special attention is given to situations involving the child's participation in creating classroom rules, playground safety, and cooperative play groups. Jerome L. Singer, Dorothy G. Singer, and Amanda E. Schweder investigate the value of play training as a means to enhance preschool children's school readiness through imaginative play with parents and teachers. An in-depth discussion of procedures, implementation, and outcomes are presented in this original research piece. Findings clearly indicated how play training led to increased vocabulary scores, which are a critical measurement of school readiness. Roisin McCooey explains the value of using audiovisual recordings to observe common peer interactions in preschool settings. The information retrieved from the research was reviewed by early childhood specialists to consider the socialization themes that normally occur. Knowledge gained from the audiovisual data assisted each teacher in identifying which children could most benefit from additional sharing and negotiating experiences for optimal prosocial development. More important, the data helped the teachers learn when it was most appropriate to intervene or not intervene.

Part I continues with three chapters reflecting an international perspective on play. To begin, Ivana Lisul offers information on how play can serve as a viable coping mechanism for children who have been exposed to war. Six- and seven-year-old children were interviewed fourteen months after the 1999 NATO bombing on Yugoslavia. Results showed that many children had never discussed their fears with their parents, and often used aggressive imaginative play and drawings to relieve their fears and stress. Marilena Flores Martins summarizes key characteristics of the Brazilian culture and emphasizes the need for the government to provide greater resources for existing and new play initiatives. The need for trained play workers and a heightened number of leisure activities is highlighted. Similarly, Rikuko Okuda of Japan speaks frankly about the Japanese culture and the need to update their child-rearing methods and parent resources to include the child's need for play. The work identifies common parenting practices that are aimed at academic learning and obedience at the earliest possible age. She urges greater sensitivity toward the young child's interests versus cognitive development.

Yvonne E. Keairns, Janet Edwards, and Christina Calucci report on a fifty-year program located at the Arsenal Family and Children's Center in Pittsburgh, Pennsylvania. Founded in 1953 by Dr. Benjamin Spock, the Center's research clearly shows the importance of active learning through play, and the value of play as a means to reconcile traumatic situations between young children and their parents. A schedule of events and responsibilities is included to assist the reader in better understanding the implementation process.

Part I of this books ends with Charlie McCormick's challenging the reader to think of play as a contemporary rite of passage. This rite of passage focuses on the individual's interactions with parents, peers, and society as a whole. Those readers interested on cultural anthropology will greatly enjoy this skillfully written debate on popular culture.

1

The Right to a Work-Free and Playful Childhood: A Historical Perspective

Lisa Hermine Makman

Return to the beginning: become a child again.

—Tao Te Ching

The late nineteenth century is a pivotal point in discussing the concept of child's play. In the first half of that century in England and in America, work was generally understood to be morally good for children, and most books produced for them promoted this good. Child's play was not generally discussed, actively encouraged, or theorized. This began to change as new legislation increasingly limited child labor and enforced school attendance. At this time in both England and America there were three main groups that lobbied for the reform of laws connected to children's activities: progressive reformers, who opposed child labor for being inconsistent with children's interests; educators, who viewed school as the proper place to socialize children; and economists and labor activists, who argued that child labor took adults' jobs and depressed their wages. In England, as a result of this lobbying alliance, legislation was introduced limiting child labor, beginning in the 1830s. The Factory Acts of 1833 and 1834, harbingers of a broad new conception of childhood, set a minimum age for employment and made provision for part-time schooling for those under thirteen.

Commencing in the 1840s, the government appointed Children's Employment Commissions to investigate children's working conditions (Children's Employment Commission, 1842a, 1842b, 1843). Their investigations led to further restriction of child labor in a variety of occupation, throughout the century. The first report of the Children's Employment Commission, in 1840, took mining as its subject of investigation. The commissioners found that children as young as three or four were working in mines, and that a common age for starting this work was six or seven. Investigators described the appearance of these child miners, using such terms as "disgusting" and "unnatural." The reports and especially the images accompanying them attracted much public attention. As more types of children's work came to be seen as "unnatural," play came to increasingly be viewed as children's "natural" activity. Between the 1830s and the turn of the century, the idea that work is morally good for children, especially poor children, slipped into its opposite: Labor came to be seen as corrupting. By the 1860s, school, not work, was commonly understood as the ideal place to socialize poor children.

In America, child labor was first regulated in 1813, when Connecticut became the first state to require factories to set up schools for their workers and to limit the child's workday. Regulation continued to be effective only at the state level, well into the twentieth century. By 1930, thirty-eight states required educational qualification for children to work. In 1938, Congress enacted the Fair Labor Standards Act, which has a provision prohibiting "oppressive child labor."

One of the results of these legal developments (and, to an extent, a cause for them as well) was that poor children ceased to be perceived by the culture at large as workers and came to be viewed instead as pupils, consumers, and, above all, players. The idea of an economically worthless but emotionally "priceless" child gained prominence in discussions of children and childhood (Zelizer, 1985). Children came to be valued for their inner qualities; in fact, these qualities were increasingly represented as "treasure" or "wealth." Children also came to be valued for their playfulness, and this playfulness was imagined as an inner and inherent quality as well. During this period, organizations devoted to the study of children's mental activity—the study of their playful nature—burgeoned and flourished. By the turn of the century, the nature and significance of child's play had become a topic of much lively public discussion. After being introduced to the work of G. Stanley Hall at the World's Fair in Chicago in 1893, British "child-lovers" established the Child Study Association, declaring children the "wealth of all nations." Two years later, Francis Warner established the Childhood Society for the study of children. Gradually, a carefree, labor-free childhood came to be characterized as a fundamental right of all children, regardless of their social class. By the 1890s this idea was widespread. At the International Labor Conference in Berlin in 1890, a "universal" minimum age for work was declared for the countries of northern Europe.

By the end of the century, imaginative, scientific, and pedagogical writings for and about children expressed new ideas about their social roles. In such works, childhood was represented with increasing frequency in spatial terms, as a protected place removed from the adult world of politics, commerce, and work; a protected place for play. Such descriptions were prescriptive; they suggested that children *should* be set apart from the adult world of work. During this period, for the first time, institutions appeared in England and in America that shaped the lives of children in accordance with the idea that childhood constitutes a self-sufficient sphere, a sphere for freedom and play. These institutions, including municipal playgrounds and game clubs, sought to preserve children—especially poor children—from a grown-up realm understood to be corrupting and containing "unruly" impulses. Municipal parks and public playgrounds were created or redesigned to supply young people with enclosed and supervised play spaces. Nurseries and kindergartens were opened to encourage and safeguard the play of children too young to attend government schools. Vacation schools and game clubs were established to provide children, especially children of lower classes, with organized activities when school was not in session. Private nurseries were set up by prosperous parents to isolate and supervise children within homes. Often these places and programs replaced gainful employment in containing and managing the activity of poor children. Although they commonly served children of the poor, they reflected beliefs that were held at the time with regard to children of all social classes. For the most part, these institutions offered play as the rightful occupation of the young. Play was coming to be understood as the decisive activity for children, activity that would cultivate and preserve the natural treasure perceived to be hidden within them.

These new institutions functioned as "preserves" for children in two divergent senses. First, they were believed to shelter children from an unseemly adult world, to shield them from corruption and thus to nourish their internal childish nature. Second, they provided a means for corralling children into closely monitored environments in which, it was hoped, the proper sort of childhood would be preserved. This twofold idea of "preservation" expresses a somewhat paradoxical view of children and their play. Whereas children's play activities were perceived as inherently salutary, even pointing toward or bringing about a utopian future (as writers such as Maria Montessori suggested at the time), they were also perceived as anarchic and consequently as threatening to society. For example, Nora Archibald Smith (1902) pointed to the potential in play for both a positive "freedom" and a negative "lawlessness." Discussing the sort of play that caretakers at a community center for children (a "neighborhood house") should aspire to cultivate in children, she asserted that "spontaneous bubbling is just what we want, but at the same time, it must be guided. . . . We want the play spirit first and foremost, freedom and relaxation, but *not* confusion and lawlessness" (145–146).

Many educators and psychologists at the turn of the century emphasized the crucial role played by environment in shaping children's physical and psychical "play." They believed that the environment could help to channel children's raw and chaotic play into productive, organized activity. Maria Montessori, for example, claimed that children will learn "naturally" in their play if they are placed in a properly organized environment. Similarly, W. R. Jordan (1902) stressed "the immense importance of the most careful regulation of the environment of the young" (232). This emphasis on the fundamental significance of surroundings for children originated in romantic educational theories that had been known in England and America for over a century but became particularly popular at the end of the nineteenth century. The appearance of institutions designed to shape children's play paralleled the revival of these theories. Specifically, the last decades of the nineteenth century saw a renewed interest in the educational theories of Jean-Jacques Rousseau and his intellectual heirs, Johan Heinrich Pestalozzi (1746–1827) and Friedrich Wilhelm August Froebel (1782–1852), who invented the idea of a "kindergarten." These thinkers stressed the importance of the child's self-directed activities (play) and emphasized the impact of environment on the child's development. Furthermore, they associated the child with the natural world and viewed the child's development as an organic process. In *Emile* Rousseau (1762), argued that the child, a "young plant," should be enclosed and isolated in a "natural" environment—free from the contaminating influences of human culture—in order to achieve the ideal, "natural education" (38). Froebel, whose ideas became particularly widespread in England, developed Rousseau's conception of the child as a plant, arguing that what children needed above all was a "garden" in which to flourish. Froebel used the term "garden" not only to denote a specific location appropriate for a child's schooling (as in the "kindergarten"), but also as a symbol for the child itself, a figure designating the child's particular relationship to its environment. The child, like the literal garden, was of nature but not raw nature; it was a nature cultivated, pruned by the social world—the wild and the tame combined in a perfect balance. By the time the Froebel Society was established in London in 1874, Froebel's theories about child development and education were already widely discussed in popular magazines for parents and teachers and in child-care manuals.

Froebel's work was discussed and developed in the forum provided by a new genre of child psychology journals that began to appear between the 1880s and before the turn of the century. In these journals, child's "play" was increasingly the focus of discussion. These periodicals, journals such as *Child Life* and *The Paidologist*, defy current disciplinary boundaries. They attracted a broad audience composed of both specialists and nonspecialists. They were child psychology journals in that they shared an interest in exploring the inner life of children. *Child Life*, for instance, was "A Magazine for Kindergarten Teachers, Parents, and all Interested in the Education and Development of Young Children." *The Paidologist: The Organ of the British Child-Study Organization*, aimed at appealing to "the world-wide circle of lovers of children." In these journals, child's play was often described as an essential prelude to and aspect of work. It differs fundamentally from work in that it is noninstrumental; its value is not connected to a function in the everyday world. The child's play, a spontaneous and noninstrumental activity, was commonly construed as a model for adult work. As a writer for the journal *Child Study* insisted, "Men are slaves unless they carry into life-work the spirit, the life, the freedom with which a child flings himself into his so-called play; [otherwise] we are not men but slaves, drudges" (Murray, 1901, 169). It was the inner state of the child, its "spirit" and "freedom," that the adult was here encouraged to emulate. The only hope this writer held out for the "enslaved" adult laborer was to imitate the playfulness of youth. The idea of play as a prelude to work is expressed in the work of Karl Groos, whose books, *The Play of Animals* (1898) and *The Pay of Man* (1901), suggested that the play of young humans, like the play of young animals, was predominantly a preparation for necessary adult activities.

In these writings the emphasis was on child's play as a preparation for adult life. Play was an activity in which people developed a creative or free relationship to the outside world. Such a relationship seemed to many of the writers who contributed to these journals to be endangered by modern conditions of labor. Therefore, an early life engaged in play was seen as a possible antidote to the drudgery of work. Yet during this period a different notion of play developed, the notion of play as an activity for its own sake. This idea corresponded to the notion of childhood not as a temporal stage in human development so much as an alternate space. Turn-of-the-century discourses on childhood were often characterized by what Johannes Fabian (1983) in his discussion of emergent anthropology had called *"allochronism,"* or "the denial of coevalness" (32). Not unlike such figures as the "savage" and the "primitive," children were understood to inhabit a temporal realm separate from that of adults. In this sense, they were thought to exist outside of history altogether. Children were imagined in this way as childhood came to be associated with the private, subjective world of the imagination, a world that was not subject to the rules of time.

The children's literature that developed in the second half of the nineteenth century displayed this association between childhood and the space of the imagination. We see this connection very clearly in the classics of children's literature, such as George MacDonald's *At the Back of the North Wind*, Lewis Carroll's *Alice* books, and J. M. Barrie's (1904, 1930) *Peter Pan*. In all of these works the realm of childhood is not posited as a prelude to a productive adulthood so much as the alternative to such an adulthood. Each of these works contains an imaginary realm that is for the most part inaccessible to adults. Peter Pan, the boy who will not grow up, embodies this idea of a life of perpetual play. In Barrie's drama, Peter cries, "I just want to be a boy and to have fun" (85). The emphasis in these works is on play for its own sake, play as autonomous activity.

Play was viewed by many as noninstrumental and thus more exalted than actual work. Its value was understood as being disconnected from function in the everyday world. H. L. Withers (1902) wrote in *Child Life*, "Work is an expenditure of energy in pursuit of a required end, an object outside itself. . . . Play has no further intentional end than the action itself, like the gambols of a kitten or the running and jumping of boys let loose from school" (38). The play of children is here construed as a *natural* activity, like the play of animals. In this natural play, "self," or "self development," replaces the imperative of a "required end" (such "required ends," the writer suggested, might include those set forth by school). Withers continued, "in discussing the supreme value [of play], . . . we are not thinking of play in antithesis to work, but rather of play as the most convenient name for the total sum of self-activity in the child. This self-activity resembles play in that it is pursued for its own sake as the expression of inner impulses; but it resembles work in so far as it is quite earnestly carried on" (38). Withers argued that play comprises the "total sum" of the child's self; it is in play that the child's "total" identity becomes manifest. This idea that all of a child's disparate activities cohere to form a totality became the basis of a conception of childhood as a discrete, unified space.

The central contention in this chapter is that the idea that play is both what children primarily do, and what they should be encouraged to do, did not become a prevailing cultural assumption until the late nineteenth century. Moreover, the notion that institutions need to provide a special forum to foster children's play developed during this period. These ideas about child's play emerged in tandem with new conceptions of childhood itself. New understandings of childhood at this time were conditioned by children's changing social roles and by the spread of romantic ideas about education. Throughout the nineteenth century, the pervasive idea that children are essentially corrupt and that work will help to make them good was gradually displaced by the romantic idea that children are closely associated with a beneficent nature and the idea that a child's inner nature is not inherent but generated by and potentially perfected through education. The development of the Evangelical movement in the nineteenth century also played a key role in conditioning attitudes toward children. As Catherine Robson (2001) has pointed out, Evangelical Christianity reinforced romanticism's "tremendous emphasis on the care of the child," and understanding of "the world as a continual source of moral danger [to the child]" (7).

This historical perspective allows us to see that both the idea that all children have a right to a relatively work-free and playful childhood, and the widespread idea that the playfulness of children has inherent value, emerged only at the end of the nineteenth century; these ideas are historically contingent. We thus can see that concepts regarding childhood are part of a larger social framework. At the end of the nineteenth century, when the concept of a playful childhood gained prominence, childhood came to be seen as a separate sphere. This separateness was championed, perhaps, because it offered the promise of a secure world within our insecure world.

REFERENCES

Barrie, J. M. (1904, 1930). *The Works of J. M. Barrie*. Vol. 10. New York: Charles Scribner's Sons.

Children's Employment Commission. "First Report." (1842a). Parliamentary Papers X.

Children's Employment Commission. "Second Report." (1842b). Parliamentary Papers XIII.

Children's Employment Commission. "Second Report." (1843). Parliamentary Papers XIV.

Fabian, J. (1983). *Time and the Other: How Anthropology Makes Its Object*. New York: Columbia University Press.

Groos, K. (1898). *The Play of Animals*. New York: Appleton.

Groos, K. (1901). *The Play of Man*. New York: Appleton.

Jordan, W. R. (1902). Heredity. *The Paidologist* 4(1): 232–236.

MacDonald, G. (18) *At the Back of the North Wind*. New York: Random House.

Murray, E. R. (1901). On Kindergarten Games. *Child Life* 3(Suppl. 1): 169–171.

Robson, C. (2001). *Men in Wonderland: The Lost Girlhood of the Victorian Gentleman*. Princeton, NJ: Princeton University Press.

Rousseau, J. J. (1979). *Emile*. A. Bloom, Trans. New York: Basic Books.

Smith, N. A. (1902). The Alfred Corning Clark Neighborhood House. *Child Life* 4(15): 145–146.

Tenniel, J. (1982). *The Complete Illustrated Works of Lewis Carroll*. London: Chancellor Press.

Withers, H. L. (1902). The Distinction between Work and Play. *Child Life* 4(13): 32–40.

Zelizer, V. (1985). *Pricing the Priceless Child*. New York: Basic Books.

2

The Moral and Ethical Dimensions of Controlling Play

Nancy K. Freeman and Mac H. Brown

Play defines childhood. It is protected in the U.N. Convention on the Rights of Children, supported in early childhood educators' professional literature, and the cornerstone of quality programs serving young children. The following explores the moral and ethical dimensions of adults' involvement in children's play, paying particular attention to the rules they create and the policies they enforce that implicitly or explicitly control children's freely chosen activities.

A postmodern social constructivist position is taken here to problematize how teachers encourage, condone, or prohibit play and consider the effects of their actions on children's personal agency and efficacy. The Code of Ethical Conduct, developed by the National Association for the Education of Young Children (NAEYC) (Feeney & Kipnis, 1989/1998), is particularly reliable for the guidance, advice, and support it offers teachers who are mindful of the moral and ethical implications of the decisions and policies they routinely make; and for justification in challenging the conventional wisdom that puts control of children's play in adults' hands.

This discussion is put into the context of the work of Vivian Gussin Paley, specifically the authoritative statements she made in her widely acclaimed book, *You Can't Say You Can't Play* (Paley, 1992). The purpose is to explore the moral dimensions of seemingly routine policies that teachers create in an effort to make their classrooms physically and emotionally safe, inviting, engaging, and educational for the young children in their care.

THE ROLE OF PLAY IN EARLY CARE AND EDUCATION

Play is in vogue. Mainstream literature directed to pre-service and in-service teachers promotes a child-directed play-centered curriculum (Bredekamp & Copple, 1997; Chaillé & Silvern, 1996; Gestwicki, 1999). Advocates for play are constructivists who understand that children learn through active engagement with the people and things in their environment. They contend, in short, that "play is the work of children."

The literature describing quality programming in the terms of a play-based curriculum puts the power and responsibility for controlling children's play in the hands of adults, for they determine the schedule, select materials, and create expectations about what is permitted and what is not during the play times they plan for children in their care. They are, in fact, the most powerful players in the classroom. Adults' voices are heard and their influence felt inside in the housekeeping center, block corner, and at the water table, as well as outdoors in the sandbox, in the playhouse, and on the swings. Adults set the stage and control the players, taking responsibility for keeping a watchful eye on all corners of the classroom as the days, weeks, and months unfold.

THE ROLE OF ETHICS IN PLAYFUL CLASSROOMS

The NAEYC Code of Ethical Conduct (Feeney & Kipnis, 1989/1998) established childhood educators' primary responsibilities to young children in the context of core values that "express central beliefs, a commitment to society, and a common purpose," ideals, that "point the individual in the direction of desirable and exemplary professional behavior," and principles, "practices that are required, those that are permitted, and others that are prohibited" (Feeney & Freeman, 1999, p. 18).

It is important to think about the role that this code plays. It reminds teachers and caregivers that they should be guided not only by their personal idiosyncratic beliefs, but also by the ethical standards adopted by their largest professional organization. One role that the code plays is in helping early childhood educators answer the difficult question, "What should a good teacher do?" The chapter explores a variety of seemingly routine decisions teachers and caregivers frequently make that, upon deliberation, have important moral and ethical dimensions. The code can be used to bring these considerations of adults' power and control to the fore.

PLAY IN VIVIAN PALEY'S CLASSROOM

Vivian Paley spent a long career as a kindergarten teacher. She has written a shelf-full of popular books describing her classroom and the students who populated it over the years. One group of students made her particularly concerned about individuals who were routinely excluded from their classmates' play. After careful reflection she posted this sign: "YOU CAN'T SAY YOU CAN'T PLAY," announcing the establishment of a new social order. Paley's pronouncement presented an interesting perspective from which to explore issues of morals and ethics, power and control in the classroom. Paley (1992) explained that when she talked with her kindergarteners and older children about its implementation, she asked them, "Is the new rule fair? Can it work?" (p. 33). But was she asking the right questions? How should teachers define *fair*? How can they balance the conflicts created by their responsibilities to and relationships with each of their students? What is the difference between a rule that *can* work and one that *should*? The heart of this dilemma has to do with the rights of the individual child and the tension that always exists when the needs of the group are in conflict with those of individuals. Do we preserve the individuals' rights of self-determination, or those of the group?

DEVELOPMENT AND PLAY

We begin by considering the developmental issues related to children's sociodramatic play. First, we know that make-believe thrives when children have the opportunity to form small groups of players who share particular skills, abilities, and dispositions. Some children can sustain dramatic play with just one other child. Children are limited by their maturational level, experience, interests, cognitive abilities, and/or skill when working with abstractions. Others are more sophisticated, able to manage complex fantasies with multiple continually transforming and evolving roles. Noticing these variations in ability and children's success playing reminds us that rich dramatic play is fragile and can be ephemeral. It exists, to a large extent, in the minds of the players, and the play frame can be easily broken or destroyed by players themselves when they violate the rules, by outside intruders, no how well-intentioned, or by any distraction that pulls the players out of their fantasy (Bateson, 1955). Sustained dramatic play depends on the existence of complex, carefully negotiated personal affiliations; it cannot be sustained by a large group of children whose connections with each other are simply their membership in a class or adult pronouncements of who will play with whom.

Adults' agendas are unavoidably privileged in the classroom. One example of how a teacher might use her power would be assigning an immature child to play with a more sophisticated player. In doing so she is upsetting the natural pattern of affiliation and jeopardizing the satisfaction that children can derive from their fantasy play. While there might be occasional benefits to this kind of intervention, artificial externally imposed arrangements are more likely to be frustrating for both, limiting the complexity of the play for the more able partner and stretching the less able child beyond the limits of what Vygotsky (1978) would call his Zone of Proximal Development. Enforced affiliation suppresses sociodramatic play, for group experiences are reduced to the lowest common denominator, the skill level of the least developed child. In situations like these, children are likely to be stuck reenacting familiar and comfortable themes rather than creatively exploring the uncharted territory of creativity and spontaneity.

PLAY AND FRIENDSHIPS

The sophistication of the social play children can engage in is also determined by their ability to sustain friendships. Paley, like all experienced teachers of young children, realizes that children will form exclusive groups or cliques. Adult concern should be not whether these alliances will form, but rather how to make friendships constructive and how to temper the trauma that comes when friendships come and go. By enforcing this mandate, Paley is privileging inclusion. She is doing what she can to ensure that her students will come to see that rejection is not permissible, for she has judged that inclusion has precedence over sustained play or children's license to select their own play partners.

Usually, when exclusion becomes a classroom concern, teachers work with the frequently rejected child, coaching him or her so that he or she can become a successful being accepted by the group. Teachers who take this approach demonstrate that they appreciate that satisfying play requires intersubjectivity, and they help the excluded child extinguish behaviors that are barriers. More often than not, when children are helped in getting along with others, they are strongly motivated to join in social play. Paley's rule reduces this intrinsic motivation by putting the attainment of inclusion in adult control. Children lose ownership, the issue is out of their control, and the satisfaction and learning involved in overcoming hardship has been taken out of their hands—for better or worse. Instead of pushing the excluded children to reevaluate their interactions with peers, Paley shifts the responsibility for getting along from the individual to the group. That means that the group is forced to change its expectations and attitudes.

Paley's policy is tampering with relationships, denying the reality that friendship is, by definition, an exclusionary relationship, with insiders and outsiders, players and nonplayers. Teachers who critically reflect on these dimensions of classroom relationships are likely to appreciate the value of creating classroom affiliations, as well as dealing with incidents of rejection, as part of the explicit curriculum. We believe that being explicit about these social issues, so important to children, is more helpful than haphazardly dealing with isolated incidents of rejection as they occur. Teachers who make the decision to include discussions of children's experiences with acceptance and rejection as part of the classroom curriculum give children control over their play by openly examining acceptance and rejection instead of hiding the problem (relegating it to the null curriculum) or taking control (quashing autonomy in the name of adult-imposed expectations).

WHAT IS THE ROLE OF ETHICS?

When considering dilemmas like the one created in Paley's classroom, it helps to evaluate how the early childhood educators' Code of Ethics applies to policies like "You can't say you can't play." Is Paley honoring her commitment to "base [her] practice on knowledge of child development"? This is, after all, one of the field's core values. Does she reflect her respect for children? How about "appreciating the special vulnerability of children" or "creating settings that foster children's social, emotional, intellectual, and physical development and respect their dignity and their contributions"? There are not clear-cut answers to those questions, and prescribing solutions is not, with a very few exceptions, the purpose of the code. Its most important contribution is the guidance it provides, leading the way toward ethical practice. It is a compass pointing practitioners in the right direction, not a road map showing the one best course of action.

Like adults turning to the code for guidance, children benefit from having guidelines to help them reach decisions that are fair and respectful to all but leave room for individuals to weigh their conflicting responsibilities and consider the likely consequences of various courses of action. Clear-cut, mandated solutions help neither children nor adults internalize standards of behavior, nor do they foster autonomy to do what is right in the face of conflicting pressures and preferences. The job of teachers and teacher educators alike is to nurture students' (of all ages) abilities to participate in a democracy with confidence, competence, and fairness.

PLAY AND DEMOCRACY

Finally, Paley's policy appears to support democracy because of its emphasis on the inclusion and furthering of democratic ideals such as tolerance. Like Corsaro (1997), however, we might wonder if this rule might not be a powerful adult's unwarranted intrusion into the children's hard-won community.

Paley (1992) introduced this issue when she asked Sarah, "Can the classroom be made to feel like your backyard?" The child's insight was poignant, when responding, "At home the children come and go at will. Here we're stuck with each other all day" (p. 57). Corsaro (1997) questioned whether it was realistic and developmentally appropriate to expect fifteen to twenty children to be able to get along. This raises the issue of our responsibilities to children who spend most of their waking hours in public spaces, for the hurried childhood Elkind (1988) saw on the horizon is now a reality. Parents' demanding work schedules often require them to create comprehensive child-care arrangements, placing their children in out-of-home settings for ten to twelve hours a day. Opportunities for informal, spontaneous, unstructured play with self-selected neighborhood playmates have been eroded by the schedules imposed by parents' workday responsibilities. Children more often than not find themselves in the care of a series of nonfamilial adults who routinely make decisions about which toys are appropriate, which play themes are acceptable, and how and when adults should direct, interrupt, or interfere. We challenge the notion that adults should be licensed to tamper with the private spaces children manage to carve out and sustain in the name of advocating equal access for all.

ANOTHER WAY

We do not mean to create the impression of disagreeing with early childhood educators who believe it is their responsibility to help children develop the social skills they need to gain entry into groups and sustain group activities. The existence of moral imperatives should be recognized, and letting children bully each other physically or emotionally should not be advocated. In addition, it is worth-while to help children develop the ability to negotiate from a personal, individual perspective. Suggested, however, is a corollary to "You can't say you can't play," and that might be, "I won't play that way." Paley justifiably believes that children need to learn to resist pressures to exploit, exclude, and reject, and, importantly, that the habit of exclusion is a destructive one. Children must be prepared to func-tion as a member of the group; maintaining egalitarian relationships, leading peers in constructive pursuits, tapping into each person's potential and abilities. It is problematical, however, that she puts the power in the adults' hands rather than leaving children in control of their play space and their private relationships. We wonder if giving children opportunities to solve problems by themselves, letting them control classroom incidents of inclusion and exclusion, might not better pre-pare them to define respectful personal relationships and the true meaning of com-munity. This process would help children become members of an equitable society by redistributing responsibility from the powerful and controlling adult to the col-lective of voice of fully participating equals.

Paley (1992) seemingly challenges basic principles of democracy, for she privi-leges individual rights in favor of majority rule. Furthermore, democracy requires individuals to recognize and accept self-imposed restrictions on their personal powers. Children who have to "play nice" do not get these opportunities to develop autonomy, a sense of their place in the community, and the skills necessary to be-come self-governed in an egalitarian society. Challengeable, however, is Paley's elevation of exclusion and rejection to the level of moral imperative. We believe that exclusion from play offers an appropriate setting for children to hone the skills, abilities, and dispositions of getting along. By making inclusion a moral im-perative, Paley has usurped children's rights to privacy and agency, rejecting their protestations that if they are not free to control their play then "what's the whole point of playing?" (p. 4). Has she not turned her back on what characterizes play—freely chosen, self-directed, pleasurable activity? Paley struggles with this issue, for she herself wonders if the desire to form exclusive groups is "in the same category as, say, biting others" (p. 73), but her resolve is unshaken, and her man-date stands.

As we confront these issues we turn to our professional Code of Ethics. It is a re-minder that there are not easily reached resolutions to this or most other real-life teaching dilemmas. "It depends" is likely to be the most appropriate response when an outsider is asked to help teachers puzzle out what they should do. "It de-pends" should also be the teacher's response to incidents of exclusion and rejec-tion in the classroom.

ANOTHER WAY

Is enforcing the rule "You can't say you can't play" the best way to help children create a moral compass that will serve them well when there is no controlling adult to take that responsibility from them? Is it the best way to prepare children for their participation in our democracy? Can it be that Paley's rule is communistic or

Marxist? Her "you can't say" policy could be interpreted this way, for she has taken a stance that privileges community over individuality. Perhaps, however, rather than trying to raise Marxists, Paley is trying to show us a way that democracy can evolve to create truly inclusive communities, alleviating some of the injustices found in our current form of "me-first" capitalism. This perspective would represent a radical departure from popular Western, individualistic traditions and would be one postmoderns would find appealing to explore.

Perhaps Paley's most important contribution is leading children to embrace as their own a social order where inclusion is the norm. Her intervention would be highly laudable if it were to have the effect of prompting children to internalize values that make the imposition of the rule "You can't say you can't play" no longer necessary. If that were to be the case, her children might well be the ones to lead a social reformation, creating a world where inclusivity is the dominant value, racial, gender and other quotas are forgotten, and we could rest assured that affirmative action of all sorts would have outlived its usefulness. Is that too much to ask as one of the benefits of well-planned kindergarten experiences?

REFERENCES

Bateson, G. (1955). A Theory of Play and Fantasy. *Psychiatric Research Reports* 2: 39–50.

Bredekamp, S. E., & C. Copple (eds.). (1997). *Developmentally Appropriate Practice in Early Childhood Programs* (rev. ed.). Washington, DC: NAEYC.

Chaillé, C., & S. B. Silvern. (1996). Understanding through Play. *Childhood Education* 72(5): 274–277.

Corsaro, W. A. (1997). *The Sociology of Childhood.* Thousand Oaks, CA: Pine Forge Press.

Elkind, D. (1988). *The Hurried Child: Growing Up Too Fast Too Soon* (rev. ed.). Reading, MA: Addison-Wesley.

Feeney, S., & N. K. Freeman. (1999). *Ethics and the Early Childhood Educator: Using the NAEYC Code.* Washington, DC: NAEYC.

Feeney, S., & K. Kipnis. (1989/1998). *Code of Professional Ethics and Statement of Commitment* (rev. ed.). Washington, DC: NAEYC.

Gestwicki, C. (1999). *Developmentally Appropriate Practice: Curriculum and Development in Early Education.* Albany, NY: Delmar.

Paley, V. G. (1992). *You Can't Say You Can't Play.* Cambridge: Harvard University Press.

Vygotsky, L. S. (1978). *Mind in Society.* Cambridge: Harvard University Press.

3

Adults: An Obstacle to Children's Self-Expressive Play

Brian Ashley

Man does not cease to play because he grows old;
man grows old because he ceases to play.
—George Bernard Shaw (1856–1950)

In modern urban society children require but do not get adequate physical space and space in time to express their own intrinsic needs. Unfortunately, it is adults who have the responsibility to ensure that children have that opportunity, but often are the greatest obstacle to children's achievement of that opportunity. For a child's full development, play activity should be freely chosen by the child to meet needs arising from within him- or herself, and should be directed toward goals chosen by the child. Children's needs for self-expression are restricted by the intervention, direction, and control of adults. Parents, if they used their great opportunities in time and contact, especially in the child's earliest years, could counteract this tendency. But unfortunately they lack the confidence to challenge the power and influence of the professional view that the important developmental process is that which takes place within institutions. Facing such weighty opinion, parents feel themselves deskilled, and they become brainwashed to support the professional views and to subscribe to the same aims and methods.

The following focuses on a specific community need that is clearly emerging in modern society, where this professional view can be shown to have failed and where noninstitutional measures are needed. In meeting this community need, the role of the parent and the role of other understanding adults can be seen to be crucially important. This will require measures to support parents and build up their confidence.

THE DISAPPEARANCE OF INFORMAL SUPPORT
SYSTEMS WITHIN COMMUNITIES

The deskilling of parents is part of the influence of social change. The increasing spread of large-scale urbanization is removing the institution of the traditional extended family, where there was no strict boundary between a family unit and the surrounding social system and there continued to be a support and relationship resource. Children had close relationships with children from other families within the wider social system. Children were encouraged to develop within a child culture in which they learned from each other with a minimum of adult interference or supervision. This traditional family is being rapidly replaced by the so-called nuclear family, often established far from family and friends, separated from the wider social system, and becoming inward orientated. It is difficult for wider social networks to develop, and this modern unit lacks the informal support and advice available in the traditional system. Current research suggests that, as a result, most parents in society today require support in developing their parenthood on a firm basis. This need is not confined to parents with financial problems. The support required is in meeting the uncertainties and questions of normal everyday life. This kind of support is not readily available in today's complex and swiftly changing society. The absence of such support can quite easily lead to the development of problems costly to society. The provision of such a simple support system, readily available to all and easily accessible from the home, could prevent or alleviate such problems.

There are two other important reasons why such a support system for parents should be given more attention; the first involves the importance of brain stimulation in the earliest years. Recent research, that electronically maps the brain's neurological development from or even before birth clearly demonstrates the importance of stimulative social activities between the mother/mother substitute and the child in creating within the brain the neurological network necessary to receive learning and to facilitate new learning. If this network is not stimulated from the earliest age, the child is less able to receive and respond to future learning experiences. The development of this brain network is not a simple physiological process but is dependent on continued appropriate stimulus within these close interpersonal relationships in infancy. If appropriate stimulation is delayed, the undeveloped network hinders the learning capacity long into later years and it is increasingly difficult to repair the deficiency. This explains why children who, for family, cultural, or environmental deficiency reasons do not respond at an expected level to institutional learning, can rarely be helped by institutions to reach the normal level of response. Even compensatory programs using special additional resources within institutional learning have not succeeded in repairing the deficiency. It is particularly difficult for institutions to offer the individual stimulus within the close inter-personal relationships necessary for such reparation. Programs have increasingly had to be orientated outside the institutions, emphasizing family support programs from the earliest age.

Second, educational and early years learning research has established the amount and importance of early learning accomplished within the normal family and home.

Measurement of the child's capacity to understand the basic precepts necessary for developing institutional learning shows that most of these precepts are already learned at an early age within the home and family and that the normal child has this capacity when beginning institutional learning. Comparing the extent of this capacity with the comparatively short period of time taken to achieve it leads experts to the conclusion that this process of home learning is the most effective learning process offered by modern society at any age or stage of development. The judgment of researchers is that the effectiveness of this home learning is due to the fact that it is largely child initiated within a personal relationship and context familiar to the child, which the child can influence. It also differentiates itself from institutional learning in that it is based upon questions emerging from the child, rather than, as in institutional learning, from questions prompted by the adult.

This evidence provides the argument for an adequate family support system to be developed to work with the parent and child from birth rather than waiting for problems to emerge within institutions and then trying to take remedial action. Of course, it will be argued that many countries already have an excellent system of prenatal care and have advice and support for parents of newborn children. The tendency, however, is for such advice and support to concentrate upon health and physical care and for this support to reduce in extent gradually during the child's first year, and later to be more orientated to any specific health problems that emerge rather than upon ongoing readily available general support. Early learning research, however, points to a need for support less specialized than these existing support health services. It requires a support service to help all families with the important home early learning function. This support needs to be available near the home to all families, be easily accessible and responding to parent or family initiated questions, and not be directing or controlling. It requires being able to offer the same kind of professional help and knowledge that home early learning experiences offer to children. Because it is being offered to parents and not children, it requires expertise in facilitating adults as equals in the process of learning how to help their children's development.

THE SWEDISH OPEN PRESCHOOL: A MODEL
FOR FAMILY SUPPORT

The author's views are based on conclusions from a four-year development project in Sweden involving the forms and methods of "open preschools" used in Sweden to support parents who are at home with their young children. The research included a questionnaire survey of all parents using twenty-four open preschools in five different local authority areas, and was published in Sweden as part of the report of the government-supported project (Ashley, 1989). In this model the community authority provides a local meeting place where parents and their children can attend and meet with other parents and children in a supporting developmental environment. The authority usually provides one or two trained childcare staff members who work with the parents, helping them to work with their own children. The parents and children attend voluntarily and decide on the frequency and length of the visit, depending on their needs. The parents attend as much to their own needs for social contact with other adults as to the needs of their children to play with other children. Strong evidence of this need of the adults to meet and support each other is shown by the fact that an increasing proportion of those who attend are parents with very young, even newly born children. Many open preschools have started special "baby cafes" for this need group. Parents have an advantage in learning more about their new babies. They are the obvious group to be provided with knowledge about the advantage of "early learning" for their children, gaining support in developing their own capacity to help their children. They can be helped to facilitate the self-expressive play of their children and to observe and learn from that expression so that they can provide wider opportunities for the child to explore further. Their increased self-esteem and confidence in this parental role can then enable them to provide the essential basis for the future self-confidence and independence of their children. By learning the importance of self-expressive play and its results in infancy, they can prepare themselves for ensuring that their child continues to get the opportunity, space, and time, even when the child enters and becomes engaged in the institutional process. Parents who have been helped and made aware of the importance of these self-expressive opportunities can, in the future, present a challenge to institutions to change their practice toward more self-expressive learning for children.

For these "open" units to work as a parent-support model rather than a child-care model, the staff needs special training. Its members are mostly recruited from child-care centers and bring that training and experience with them as an important basis. But they need retraining from being child focused, as in child care, to being adult/parent focused in the open preschool. They need to change from the role of adult directors of development and learning processes with children to the role of facilitators/supporters of other adults (parents) as facilitators of their children's development.

It is a long and difficult learning process for both the staff and the parents. The process has to support self-expressive learning by adults in order that they can learn to facilitate it in their children. The process has to provide a nondirective and supportive environment in which adults can explore and develop their own potential. In one such developmental project directed by the author, it took three years before the participating staff and parents really began to understand the process in which they were involved. When they succeeded in understanding the process, however, the results of the mutual support provided by parents for each other and by the staff as background facilitators were immense. Parents increased an understanding that facilitating their child's self-directed learning is an investment that has full-time effects throughout the child's future.

It is not easy for the official system to accept the principles upon which the process is built, because these principles often question the basis of that system itself. The long preparatory staff training and parent learning process to achieve these results is not often easily understood and appreciated by decision makers or by supervisory personnel. Often this lack of understanding leads to impatience for quick results and attempts to force or direct the developmental process. If this happens, the benefits of this hopeful model can be frustrated and it can be distorted into repeating the inadequacies of institutional education. Having worked as a facilitating consultant in developing the model, the author has found that his main role is in trying to "protect" the development process from being too much affected by these extraneous pressures, and in trying to create understanding and tolerance in the external system to allow development to proceed. Doing so helps to produce sufficient discerning people in positions of authority who are willing to extend the patience and toleration necessary to allow this support model to prove itself.

REFERENCE

Ashley, B. (1989). *The Open Pre-School as a Centre for Families and Children in the Neighborhood.* Stockholm, Sweden: Nos-Konen Project, Norstedts.

4

A Brief Look at Fantasy Play

Raquel Ary-De Rozza and Joanna Payne-Jones

Fantasy play, pretend play, make-believe play—all of these are aspects of the same type of cognitive and affective processes. In such processes, children (and adults) deliberately enter a world where the mind's inner landscapes become the playground, where external objects are used as symbols for internal images. In different expressions of fantasy play, children reenact day-to-day experiences, experiment with behaviors and roles that reflect their inner needs, wishes, and fears, and develop problem-solving and self-regulating capacities. It is important to recognize that fantasy play is never frivolous or silly. On the contrary, it is a most serious business with a most serious purpose. Fantasy play gives us a lifeline to the important parts of our psyches. That is one reason that we adults will never willingly relinquish our right to fantasy play anymore than we did as children.

Children are capable of mental representation at approximately the age of two, when they begin to engage in fantasy play. At first the child plays alone, but at about three years of age playing with a friend is preferred. However, if the child is alone an imaginary companion is still available. By the age of four or five, sociodramatic play becomes important and children engage in role-enactment of a story or are capable of having a plan of action or focusing on a role identity.

Research by Sutton-Smith (1967), Rosen (1974), and others revealed that sociodramatic (make-believe play) helps children develop increased problem-solving skills, not only in social interactions but also in cognitive tasks; increases personal competence and self-image; helps children learn to negotiate their impulses, with themselves and with others; helps children learn to delay gratification; and helps children understand the perspectives and opinions of others. Studies by Piaget (1962), Erikson (1963), and Bettelheim (1975) revealed that imaginative fantasy play permits children to intellectually respond to situations through fantasy, consolidates learning and memory through practice and continuous testing on both emotional and intellectual levels, strengthens autonomy and initiative against forces beyond the child's control, increases emotional stability since the child can manipulate the circumstances, and allows the child to "out-power" fears that seem menacing. Children can safely engage in role play, character play, regression, risk, adventure, nonsense, silliness, and humor—they can "be" fantasy creatures of all types. This kind of activity fosters self-awareness, planning ability, and role-taking capacities. Vandenberg, Singer, and Pauls (1968) stated that fantasy play is a "critical cognitive skill—a form of organizing and reorganizing the meanings and action possibilities of one's experiences that enhances the flexible and varied uses of one's capacities for daily problem solving" (p. 195). Singer and Singer (1979) commented that "by re-playing and re-shaping schemas, a sense of control and power is gained over a small part of a vast and impenetrable universe" (p. 195). Children who engage in fantasy play early in life exhibit more imagination and creativity when they become older (Vandenberg, 1971; Singer & Singer, 1979; Sutton-Smith, 1967).

Children enter into fantasy play as easily as they enter into the events of a story or movie. As adults we continue to become similarly involved because the reasons are still valid: There is a definite healing or therapeutic benefit in many forms of fantasy. We can visit strange, unknown places, converse with magical beings, or do battle against powerful adversaries. At some level these can become representations of our everyday lives: the stories we hear, the interactions with other people, the things that frighten or delight us, and ways of recalling events and changing situations.

Vygotsky (1976) considered fantasy play a leading factor in development. He believed that in fantasy play a child creates an imaginary situation where he or she can grapple with desires, postpone or deny gratification, and learn to control impulses. Piaget (1962) observed that unfamiliar themes in fantasy play require more planning and more language exchanges and also develop intersubjectivity—the understanding of another's perspective. In fantasy play children can put situations and relationships into manageable parts that can be assimilated or accommodated. In this way they are able to practice and develop self-discipline.

In fantasy play children can create an inner world, that may be very challenging or even frightening at times, but it is not nearly as overwhelming as the outer world. In story dramatizations, theater, dance, pantomime, theme, and folk festivals we are joined by a common bond on a universally understood stage of human experience. When children (and adults) engage in role play, pretend to be human or animal characters through masquerades, and so on, they reach into aspects of their own psyches. These aspects may be good, bad, wild, gentle, mysterious, outrageous, very vulnerable, or very powerful. These layers of our own personalities often are not as accepted by others in the "real world," yet they need an outlet that is safe for the self as well as for others around us. This is what fantasy offers, and it can be repeatedly performed and re-formed.

Fantasy teaches personal and social ways of coping and surviving. Because the real world is often unpredictable and uncertain, with elements of adventure, risk, and danger, there is a need to imagine confrontations with adversaries and rehearse our escape to safety, to those who will love and protect us from harm. According to Singer and Singer (1979) and Sutton-Smith (1967), children who become adept in make-believe play show an ability to concentrate better for longer periods of time; have a greater ability to follow adult guidelines and rules when alone; are more resourcefulness; exhibit greater self-control; have greater flexibility, including divergent solutions to tasks and problems; demonstrate the ability to recall, manipulate, recombine, and extend associations of previous experiences with persons, objects and actions; and show greater facility in abstract thought problems.

In children with special needs and children with learning disabilities who are guided and encouraged in fantasy play (i.e., imitative role play, make-believe actions and situations), research has shown an improvement in all developmental areas (e.g., language, visual/auditory perception, gross/fine motor, cognition, and social–emotional). Progress was noted in symbolic representation tasks, problem-solving skills, verbal communication, and interactive persistence.

Advancements were made in waiting abilities, in delaying impulse gratification, and in lowering incidences of hyperactivity, distractibility, and short attention span. Such improvement blends very well into a form of play often used with children. Creative Dramatics is a very interactive experience—a "play within a play" sort of thing. It uses forms of literature to foster growth in all developmental domains and stimulates greater collaboration between both brain hemispheres. Five such domains exist: (1) creative development—self-expression through interpretation of the storyline and characters and experimentation with plot and characters; (2) social–emotional development—cooperation, role play, and identification with story characters; (3) cognitive development—sequences of actions in story, synthesis of meaning, symbolic representation using props and costumes, connection between thought and action; (4) language development—articulation, timing, verbal and nonverbal expression of emotion with both receptive and expressive modes greatly engaged in thought/words/gestures; and (5) physical development—large/small muscle action, balance, movement through space directionality, gestures, and timing.

Because it compels a high level of involvement from children and adults alike, creative drama teaches important things about self-discipline: sharing of power; waiting for turns; respecting others' ways of doing things; giving and taking guidance/direction from others (adults and peers); allowing time to carefully listen to others and to observe others; appreciating abilities of each individual according to what each one is capable of doing; appreciating the cooperative efforts of all; trying, retrying, persisting in efforts; and negotiating, solving problems through collaborative means. This helps to develop self-discipline at two different levels. First, through processes of self-regulation, self-talk, self-negotiation, and management of impulses, and second, through self-acceptance, self-confidence, and self-recognition. These aspects of self-understanding support the development of personal competence conducive to achievement.

Personal growth is a learning process and is the most positive process for learning. A key part of "process" is that it belongs to the person doing it. He or she is allowed to control the action, to decide how, how much, when to repeat, whether and when to stop, and so forth. Many children are not permitted to spend much time in truly gratifying play, and often they are given limiting or "educational" directions about how to play. This takes on the flavor of a "control" issue between adults and children and immediately changes the entire ambiance, where children are not equal players. Surely, there are times for adult guidance, but there must also be many moments when children "take over." When we allow children to engage more freely in "process," we are sharing power. This teaches something important about sharing and it lays the foundations for self-discipline, management of impulses, and self-regulation. We might do well to show respect for their process by what children do as they find ways to use materials and asking questions, questions that make children think about possibilities with materials and equipment; and suggestions in implementing children's ideas, but allow children to discover the moments of success personally, through their own efforts, in their own time. Researchers call this method "scaffolding" (Beck & Winsler, 1995). Scaffolding involves making comments or suggestions and asking questions in such a way that children are supported—not pressured—in taking steps that will bring them to the appropriate conclusions in solving problems on their own.

As young children we begin to learn self-regulation of behaviors and the ability of delay gratification of desires. This learning involves very complex, personal processes that each of us must manipulate and control from an individual perspective. In order to understand the process, children need to explore issues.

There is also a way of explaining and/or demonstrating a procedure or process at a level of communication so that someone who has not yet done it can grasp the idea and move forward in achieving the result. Vygotsky (1976) described this as engaging the "zone of proximal development." He stated that "all higher mental functions—those that are unique to human beings—are initially created through collaborative activity."

Vygotsky's theory stressed the importance of the social–cultural context. The "special connection" that fosters optimal learning is an aspect of the relationship that develops between people in a social–cultural context. The teacher must have an awareness and a sensitivity to the learner. When this interplay is in balance, something special is communicated by the adult to the child: It is not exactly "taught," but rather is received and acted upon by the child. The teacher and learner share an interactive experience, but the learner must be given a great deal of the power. This creates a social–cultural bridge. This type of "give and take" or guided assistance is a supportive, positive way of teaching. It occurs in all cultures, in many different interactive styles, and in all social–cultural contexts. It is always used in teaching the young and inexperienced, and it is not only a human experience—animals do it, too. Haight and Miller (1993) showed that pretend play with parents or adult caregivers resulted in children taking over more and more of the leadership role in the play as they became more competent, and this skill extended to later peer relationships.

BIBLIOGRAPHY

Beck, Laura E., & Adam Winsler. (1995). *Scaffolding Children's Learning: Vygotsky and Early Childhood Education*. Washington, DC: AEYC.

Bettelheim, B. (1975). *The Uses of Enchantment*. New York: Random House.

Bruner, J. S. (1972). Nature and the Uses of Immaturity. *American Psychologist* 27: 687–798.

——— . (1986). *Actual Minds, Possible Worlds*. Cambridge: Harvard University Press.

Erikson, E. H. (1963). *Childhood and Society*. 2d ed. New York: W. W. Norton.

Fein, G. (1981). Pretend Play: An Integrative Review. *Child Development* 52: 1095–1118.

Haight, W. L., & P. J. Miller. (1993). *Pretending at Home: Early Development in a Sociocultural Context*. Albany: State University of New York Press.

Johnson, J. E., J. F. Christie, & T. D. Yawkey. (1987). *Play and Early Childhood Development*. Glencoe, IL: Scott, Forsman.

Nickerson, E. (1973). Applications of Play Therapy to a School Setting. *Psychology in the Schools* 10: 362–365.

Piaget, J. (1962). *Play, Dreams and Imitation in Childhood*. New York: Norton.

Rosen, C. E. (1974). Effects of Sociodramatic Play on Problem-Solving Behavior among Culturally Disadvantaged Preschool Children. *Child Development* 45: 920–927.

Schaefer, C. E. (1985). Play Therapy. *Early Childhood Development and Care* 19: 95–108.

Sheridan, M. D. (2001). *Play in Early Childhood: From Birth to Six Years*. Rev. ed. New York: Routledge.

Singer, J. L., & D. G. Singer. (1979). The Value of the Imagination. In B. Sutton-Smith (Ed.), *Play and Learning* (pp. 195–218). New York: Gardner Press.

Skellenger, A. C., & R. Hill. (1994). Effects of a Shared Teacher–Child Play Intervention on Play Skills of Three Young Children Who Are Blind. *Journal of Visual Impairment and Blindness* 88(5).

Smith, P. K., M. Dalgleish, & G. Herzmark. (1981). A Comparison of the Effects of Fantasy Play Tutoring and Skills: Tutoring in Nursery Classes. *International Journal of Behavioral Development* 4: 421–441.

Sutton-Smith, B. (1967). The Role of Play in Cognitive Development. *Young Children* 22: 361–370.

Vandenberg, S. G. (1971). What Do We Know Today about the Inheritance of Intelligence and How Do We Know It? In R. Canero (Ed.), *Intelligence: Genetic and Environmental Influences*. New York: Grune and Stratton.

Vandenberg, S. G., S. M. Singer, & D. L. Pauls. (1968). *The Heredity of Behavior Disorders in Adults and Children*. New York: Plenum.

Vygotsky, L. S. (1976). Play and its Role in the Development of the Child. In J. Bruner, A. Jolly, and K. Silva (Eds.), *Play: Its Role in Development and Evolution*. New York: Basic Books.

Zeigler, E. F., & M. F. Stevenson. *Children in a Changing World*. Pacific Grove, CA: Brooks/Cole.

5

Play and Imagination as Tools for Building Resilience

Janice H. Patterson

In the International Resilience Project, Edith Grotberg and her colleagues in thirty countries studied the resilience of children and determined it to be a universal trait. Resilience is "a universal capacity which allows a person, group or community to prevent, minimize or overcome the damaging effects of adversity" (Grotberg, 1995, p. 2). Play provides an integrative context essential for the development of a resilient child. Discussions of play focus on (1) sensorimotor play, in which infants and toddlers experiment with bodily sensation, motor movements, objects, and people; (2) pretend play, in which children carry out action plans, take on roles, and transform objects as they express their ideas and feelings about the social world; and (3) games with rules, which generally involve two or more sides, competition, and agreed-upon criteria for declaring a winner. The following information offers specific strategies that adults can use to promote resilience through sensorimotor, pretend play, or games with rules.

PLAY AND RESILIENCE

Vygotsky (1978) contributed to our understanding of the central role of play in the development of a resilient child. He asserted that every function in a child's development occurs first at the social level and then at the individual level. This makes the social context in which the child lives and plays critical to developing resilience. Vygotsky's view of how children develop an understanding of rules offers guidance in understanding research that shows that boundaries and high expectations are key characteristics of resilient people.

Vygotsky (1978) believed that all play has rules and that as play becomes increasingly complex, rules become more explicit. Therefore, dramatic play with its implicit rules is the foundation for games in which the rules are more explicit. The implicit rules of dramatic play guide children in determining roles and behaviors. Children follow these rules until conflict arises among the players. Once the conflict occurs, the child will assert his or her view of the rules that should govern the character's behavior. As the child confronts others' views, he or she learns that there are rules different from his or her own. The child begins to negotiate the rules of play, especially those differing from his or her views. The child learns that others do not want him or her to throw sand in their eyes or take the bubbles away when they are blowing them. Developing the ability to set expectations for self and others cannot happen without the presence of others.

Parallel to setting expectations for self and others is the development of both giving and receiving care and support. In play, children learn to get along with others (Aldridge, 1993, p. 61) and to practice loving and being loved. I watched as four-year-olds Sabrina and Monica interacted in the housekeeping corner. Monica lay on the floor in a fetal position and Sabrina gently covered her with a blanket. Sabrina began to sing, "Hush, little baby, don't say a word, Mama's going to buy you a mocking bird." Monica smiled and snuggled down into her make-believe bed as Sabrina pretended to turn out the light and tiptoed out of the area. Sabrina demonstrated her view of loving behavior from parent to child, and Monica was able to happily receive that love as the "baby." Playing at caring and giving support helps build the child's self-esteem and assures her that she is loving and loveable.

One of the most important studies of childhood resilience reported on the role of a caring adult in the life of a resilient child. Emmy Werner, a University of California child psychologist, studied a group of students on the island of Kauai from 1955 to 1985. Werner (Werner & Smith, 1982) found that students who emerged from childhood to adulthood without major problems "had at least one person who unconditionally accepted them as they were." She also found that resilient children had at least one skill that gave them a sense of pride and acceptance with their peers. It is important that even children who began school without these traits were able to develop them with appropriate intervention.

Bernard (1993) reported that children who had someone in their lives who communicated high expectations, set boundaries, and helped them learn appropriate behavior were more likely to be resilient than children who did not have this support in their lives. Resilient children have had caring relationships, and they know they can love and are loveable. Self-esteem develops in resilient children because they have opportunities to participate in play activities where they can receive rewards and recognition for their efforts. In Bernard's work, children who lived with high expectations, had caring relationships, and participated in meaningful activities demonstrated resilience. The work of Bernard and other researchers represents a dynamic new paradigm that cuts across disciplines of psychology, psychiatry, education, and sociology to establish that children can bounce back from adversity and heal themselves. In the sections that follow, specific strategies are presented in each of the salient areas for childhood resilience: caring and support, high expectations, and meaningful participation.

CARING AND SUPPORT

For a child to be resilient, there must be at least one person in that child's life who provides support for the child and his or her positive development. Werner and Smith (1982) found, in their forty-year study of "at risk" children from the island of Kauai, that the most frequent positive support for the child outside the family was a teacher. The teacher not only provided educational guidance but also was a positive, supportive role model for the child in other areas of life. One way an adult can promote caring and support is to provide a safe environment for play.

Children need to know that they are safe from outside forces and that the adult will protect them if needed. Adults who promote resilience are alert to any signs of bullying or mistreatment among children at play. They will not allow any child to be treated with disrespect. Many of these teachers believe in a "community" of learners in which children are encouraged to support each other, to listen effectively to others, and to honor points of view that differ from their own. Savvy adults know the value of actively teaching such conflict resolution strategies as those promoted through the "Don't Laugh at Me" program (Roerden, 2000). Adults who protect children are alert for any signs of abuse or neglect and actively seek to support the child if the situation warrants it.

In a recent school visit, two children, Eddie and Anthony, were tussling on the floor because Anthony had a truck that Eddie wanted. Eddie grabbed Anthony by the neck and said, "I'm going to choke you if you don't give it to me!" After Mrs. Williams, the teacher, stopped the fight, she talked with the children separately about strategies for solving problems other than physical ones. She asked Eddie, "What else could you do to have a turn with the truck besides choking Anthony?" She asked Anthony, "What can you do when someone starts to hurt you?" After private conversations with the children, she brought them together and asked them to "play" how they would handle the same situation about who gets the truck. Eddie looked at Anthony and said, "Can I have a turn with the truck?" Anthony replied, "Not yet, wait until I finish building a garage and then you get a turn."

Mrs. Williams didn't stop there. She called the two boys over and praised them for solving their problems. In fact, she said, "You are good thinkers and know other ways to solve problems besides hitting each other." Adults who protect children are alert for any signs of abuse or bullying and actively prevent it; they set boundaries that keep children safe. This is not to imply that the adult must always physically intervene, but the adult does set limitations and model-appropriate behavior. Positive, personal attention from the teacher can help the child develop self-esteem and reinforce positive aspects of the child's behavior. A teacher like Mrs. Williams will also find opportunities to interact with the children as a player.

An often overlooked, critical aspect of developing resilience is learning to ask for help when needed. Adults may wrongfully assume that children know how to ask for help. If a child has not been valued or allowed to express needs or is just very shy, he or she may have trouble understanding that expecting a lot of yourself does not preclude asking for help when needed. The child may not know how to ask for help. It is important that teachers and other adults model asking for help and practice it with children in a play setting. Even very young children can be taught to ask, "Will you help me?"

For instance, in the "fight" described earlier, the adult felt the need to intervene in the children's play without being invited. Skillful teachers can sometimes adopt the script of the children in the play setting as they suggest opportunities for problem solving. If the teacher assumes the role of a third player entering the fight scene, he or she can "play" different alternatives in the setting to demonstrate alternative strategies. Some would argue that this is ultimately a more powerful approach than that taken by adults who interrupt the play episode and replace the children's plans with their own. It is important for adults to provide opportunities for children to set goals and decide what they are proud of and what needs to be strengthened for themselves.

HIGH EXPECTATIONS

Children can be taught to expect survival in the face of adversity. As children enter middle childhood, adults can actively teach children that they have inner strength and are resilient (Wolin & Wolin, 1994). For far too long we have taken pity on children who face challenges and treated them as victims of circumstance. By openly admiring their skills in coping with the problems they face, we can help them see that they are strong and can handle problems that develop. They can also be taught strategies to get what they need. If children perceive themselves as victims, they will act as victims. Play allows children to learn the expectations for effective social interaction. For example, Emma and Mia both expressed an interest in being the "teacher" during free time in their kindergarten. As they bantered back and forth, jockeying for position of teacher, they realized that to be a teacher, they needed a student. They decided to take turns being teacher and student. Emma even suggested setting a timer so that it "would be fairer." By negotiating their time in each role, the girls learned important social rules in a safe way.

It is instructive to reflect on the work of Kamii (1985) and her thesis on the purpose of moral autonomy in classrooms for young children. Moral autonomy means being governed by yourself and not by others. If teachers continually intervene, children will not develop the moral autonomy necessary to help them decide what is fair or unfair. In the following example, the teacher did not intervene; she only watched from a distance.

Caitlin and Mollie were playing in the housekeeping area as mother and little girl. Caitlin, the "mother," was washing dishes with real water and soap in the sink and talking to Mollie, playing the "child." They were clearly having fun and enjoying having the housekeeping corner to themselves when Robert walked up and wanted to play in the water. Caitlin responded with, "I know. You be the Daddy and it's your night to wash the dishes while I put the baby to bed." Through such social dilemmas, children develop autonomous thinking that supports resilience.

OPPORTUNITIES FOR PARTICIPATION

Teachers who provide children meaningful opportunities for participation in the classroom and play community help students build resilience. Participation in a meaningful way is a basic human need. Without opportunities for meaningful involvement, children feel alienated and alone. Too often meaningful involvement is limited to sports and academics in schools.

One of the most important categories for participation is student involvement in creating classroom rules, including the consequences. Teachers can guide a discussion that targets the needs of children by asking such questions as, "What makes you feel safe at school?" or "How do you want other people to talk to you?" When a child responds, "I feel safe when nobody pushes me or when they ask me to play," the responses become the basis for classroom rules. A positive, structured (but not too structured) play environment with fair rules is an important aspect of a safe environment.

Harriet M. Glick, an instructional integration specialist in the Minneapolis school system, reported a different kind of meaningful participation. When she first went to Hiawatha Elementary School in Minneapolis, she asked students what they did best. Many children could not answer the question without coaxing, but those who did respond most frequently said, "fight." The school began to use what they learned from resilience research and developed additional local strategies. Five years later, when Glick asked the same question, children responded, "I share well," or "I can read well," or "I'm a good listener." The school made deliberate choices in honoring talents and skills beyond sport or academic achievements. Children were involved in the school community in meaningful ways and were connected to that community (North Central Regional Laboratory, 1994).

Meaningful participation can be stimulated in a variety of ways. Adults can provide opportunities for children to play in cooperative groups. In classrooms where cooperative playgroups are used, teachers report that children develop sustaining relationships with peers that they would not have approached in other settings. Cooperative play must include teacher recognition of the importance of each child in the play session's success, including the idea that each one brings a unique perspective to the group. Teachers can support resilience by encouraging cooperative play among peers, stimulating them to generate new ideas, and to helping resolve problems. A cooperative play environment provides a natural arena for the teacher to reinforce taking turns, listening to others, asking for help, and giving and receiving help.

Children also need time to play alone. When a child plays alone, he or she can gain an opportunity to feel good about participating in the world. Because a child playing alone has no preconceived ideas about "the right way to play," the child can have a positive experience that influences self-concept. For example, Juan, age nineteen months, was playing with a set of nesting blocks in the corner of the living room. He experimented with the blocks, stacking them up to build a tower. Although the tower fell the first time and, again, on his second try, he kept playing with the blocks until he had a tower of five blocks. His pride was evident in the huge smile. He felt quite good about himself at that moment.

CONCLUSION

The adult intent in promoting children's resilience recognizes the importance of providing a classroom environment that generates resilience through play. When teachers provide a caring environment, consistent and realistic high expectations, and opportunities for meaningful participation, students have a better chance of gaining a productive place in society. The strategies offered here were gleaned from classrooms where teachers believe that all children can thrive by using play as the medium.

BIBLIOGRAPHY

Aldridge, J. (1993). *Self-Esteem: Loving Yourself at Every Age.* Birmingham, AL: Doxa Books.

Bernard, B. (1993). Fostering Resilience in Kids. *Educational Leadership* 51(3): 44–48.

Grotberg, E. (1995). *A Guide to Promoting Resilience in Children: Strengthening the Human Spirit.* The Netherlands: Bernard Van Leer Foundation.

Kamii, C. (1985). *Young Children Invent Arithmetic: Implications of Piaget's Theory.* New York: Teachers College Press.

North Central Regional Educational Laboratory. (1994). *Resilience Research: How Can It Help City Schools?* Portland, OR: North Central Regional Educational Laboratory.

Oxley, D. (1994). Organizing for Responsiveness: The Heterogeneous School Community. In M. C. Wang and E. Gordon (Eds.), *Educational Resilience in Inner City American: Challenges and Prospects* (pp. 179–189). Hillsdale, NJ: Lawrence Erlbaum.

Roerden, L. (2000). *Don't Laugh at Me.* Video and Teacher's Guide. New York: Operation Respect.

Rutter, M. (1979). Protective Factors in Children's Responses to Stress and Disadvantage. In M. Whalen-Dent (ed.), *Primary Prevention of Psychopathology.* Vol. 3: *Promoting Social Competence and Coping in Children* (pp. 49–74). Hanover, NH: University Press of New England,

Vygotsky, L. S. (1978). *Mind in Society: The Development of Higher Psychological Processes.* Cambridge: Harvard University Press.

Werner, E., & R. Smith. (1982). *Vulnerable but Invincible: A Longitudinal Study of Resilient Children and Youth.* New York: McGraw-Hill.

Wolin, S., & S. J. Wolin. (1994). *Survivor's Pride: Building Resilience in Youth at Risk: Voices from the Front: James's Story; Voices from the Front: Tanika's Story.* (Films). Verona, WI: Attainment Company.

6

Enhancing Preschoolers' School Readiness through Imaginative Play with Parents and Teachers

Jerome L. Singer, Dorothy G. Singer, and Amanda E. Schweder

> If we keep the child in us alive, we get along and children help us most in doing that.
>
> —Edward Sandord Martin

A reasonably impressive body of literature going back to Smilansky (1968) and Freyberg (1973) supported the feasibility and value of play training procedures in early childhood (Singer & Singer, 1990). Yet it remained important to demonstrate that play training for socioeconomically disadvantaged families can produce gains in children's school readiness skills after parents or other caregivers engage in imaginative play training for a minimum of two weeks with their preschool children.

STUDY 1: TRAINING PARENTS

This project's initial study focused on parent training groups conducted in five different day care centers in New Haven, Connecticut, serving the lowest socioeconomic levels of inner-city families. Three of these preschool centers are Head Start affiliated, two are independent, and one is church affiliated but nonsectarian. One of the five settings drew heavily on a Latino population; most communication in that school was conducted in Spanish, although signs and notices were uniformly bilingual.

DEMOGRAPHIC CHARACTERISTICS OF THE FULL SAMPLE AND OF EXPERIMENTAL AND CONTROL FAMILIES

One hundred and three children participated in the study. Of these, fifty were boys and fifty-three girls. Thirty-four children were three-year-olds, sixty-three were four-year-olds, and five were five-year-olds. Ethnically, thirty-three were classified by parents as Caucasian, thirty-three as African American, eighteen as Latinos, four as Asian American (Chinese, Japanese, or Indian), and twelve as of mixed backgrounds or unspecified.

The children were described by the preschool setting as eighty-two solely English speaking, nine as Spanish-speaking (but with enough English for testing), three as bilingual in English and Spanish, and the rest as speaking another language (e.g., Chinese, Hindi, Russian) but with enough English for participation. Our critical groups (experimental and control) showed no overweighing of non-English focused children in their constituents. Three-quarters of the parents in our experimental and control groups were primarily English speaking, with fourteen primarily Spanish speaking and the balance bilingual. Again, none of our findings concerning training response could be attributed to parental language differences for children in the groups.

Parental marital status analyses indicated that forty of the children's parents were currently married, five were divorced, and fourteen separated. In thirty-five instances the child was being reared by an unwed parent or another single relative. More than half of these preschool children were being reared by a single parent, most often by the mother. Again, with random assignment to the experimental and control groups neither group showed an overweighing of two-parent or single-parent-reared children at the outset.

With respect to family socioeconomic status (SES), we based our scoring primarily upon parental (or other caregiver) occupations. When both parents were child rearers, we chose the higher score of the two as an estimate. On a scale of one for the highest SES (managerial, professional, etc.) to seven for lowest (unemployed, part-time employed in minimum wage jobs), our children's parents clearly ranked well below the middle of the scale, with 57 percent of families at levels six or seven and with a group average of six.

We carried out extensive analyses of the role of SES in predicting various children's scores regarding initial play behaviors, scores on the school readiness measures, and the frequency of game play by parents. While it is clear that lower SES is consistently associated with lower performance by the children, our random assignment avoided any systematic distortion in relative SES weighing for the experimental and control groups.

A final demographic measure was the age of parents. The average age for mothers was thirty-one and for fathers thirty-five. For most of these families the children in our study were among the youngest of a group of children. Our inquiries led to the conclusion that on the whole, parents' comprehension of the value of early child care or parents' commitment to a program like Head Start emerged over time. Our inquiries of parents during training sessions made it clear that this sample was unaware of the value of imaginative play. Almost unanimously, they reported that their own parents had not played with them when they were children (except for sports).

MATERIALS AND GAMES EMPLOYED

The play techniques serving as a basis for the parents' engagements with their children were derived from methods described in Singer and Singer (2001). These procedures included video demonstrations for the two training sessions and a printed manual for parents' subsequent use during the two weeks of monitored play engagements with their children that included the following games:

Restaurant game. A story about a birthday party at a pretend restaurant, designed to enhance preschoolers' skills in sequencing, planning, politeness, sharing, cooperation, counting, color and shape recognition, and fine motor skills (pretend writing).

Submarine game. A travel game about a pretend submarine trip to the ocean floor to find a sunken treasure, designed to enhance children's vocabulary, language usage, counting skills, color and shape recognition, and fine motor skills.

Bus to the Zoo. Another travel game about a pretend bus ride to the zoo to help a monkey find his lost banana, designed to enhance children's vocabulary (e.g., names of animals), language usage, politeness, color recognition, large motor skills, and familiarity with local educational resources (e.g., library).

Seasons: The spring game. A spring story about a bunny who eats a gardener's carrots, designed to enhance children's understanding of emotions and how one's actions affect other people's feelings, sequencing, politeness, vocabulary, language usage, color recognition, large motor skills, imagination, and basic science.

The training video consisted of the following:

Introductory and concluding messages to parents of preschool children. Overviews of the benefits of highly motivating imaginative play for enhancing children's ready-to-learn skills, illustrated with live-action excerpts of children engaging in the program's learning games.

Demonstrations of how to play the four learning games. Live-action sequences of "parents" of various ethnicities playing the four learning games (Restaurant, Submarine, Bus to the Zoo, and Spring) with three- to five-year-old children. Each sequence demonstrated easy ways to play a particular game using common household items and included a spoken narration to highlight specific learning activities occurring at key points in the game.

Computer-generated 3D animation. Playful, computer-generated 3D graphics introduced each game, provided transitions between games, and created the program's tone and "signature." Still frames from the 3D animations were incorporated into the printed manuals to create a unified style and approach in the training materials.

Both the training video and its accompanying printed manuals were revised extensively on the basis of feedback from experimental group parents. The revised materials were later used in training control group parents.

The printed training materials consisted of two booklets, one pertaining to game instructions, the other to materials employed:

Instructions: Games to Play with Your Child. These clarified the goals and directions for the four primary learning games and four additional games (another travel game, "Spaceship to the Moon," and three more seasons games), as well as an introduction to skills-enhancing play and a resources list. To help parents focus on fostering the critically important skill of language usage, we underlined each use of new vocabulary words in the instructions.

Materials: Things to Use for Playing the Games. These consisted of printed pages of "props" for playing the learning games: numbers (1 to 10); pretend money; colors chart; happy, sad, angry faces; shapes (circle, square, and triangle); animal pictures (for Bus to the Zoo); and a Submarine game picture (underwater scene).

PARENT WORKSHOPS

All parents attended two training sessions on consecutive weeks. These were conducted in most cases in the early evening when parents arrived to pick up their children at the participating day-care centers. After a pizza dinner, the children were moved to another room and were monitored by day-care staff members while the parents were engaged by the workshop's staff members. African-American and Hispanic graduate students, as well as the senior researchers, introduced the concepts and then used the videos and the printed manuals for further elaboration. Free discussion by parents was encouraged and proved lively. Following the training sessions, lasting approximately one hour to ninety minutes, parents were taught how to keep daily records of their play activities and of children's responses. These "logs," critical for analyses of parent compliance and children's responses, served as the basis for subsequent data analyses. During the two-week period, regular phone calls were made to parents to learn of their involvement, to deal with any questions they had, and to explain further the maintenance of their records.

RESULTS

Initially, the experimental group (N = 39) and control group (N = 47) had not differed significantly on any of our measures following random assignment to these groups. However, after experimental group parents were trained and engaged their children in the learning games for just two weeks, there was a clear trend for higher scores on the Total Score Readiness Measure for the experimental group children, who attained an average score of 66 (SD = 16) compared with 59 (SD = 15) for the control group (see Figure 6.1).

When we examined the effects of the intervention on the subcomponents of the school readiness measure, we found that the experimental group showed higher average scores for almost all of the subtests, notably effectiveness in vocabulary,

Figure 6.1
Total Scores on Accumulated School Readiness Variables for
Control and Experimental Groups

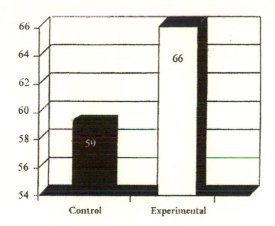

knowledge of colors, general information, nature knowledge, and good manners knowledge. Improvements in vocabulary were especially important, since vocabulary and language usage correlate best with general intelligence measures and have been shown to be particularly relevant to school readiness. Children showed measurable but less significant gains in counting skills and recognition of emotions, despite the inclusion of these skills in the games and parent-training materials. For ethical reasons, after training and testing the experimental group we offered play training to parents in the control group. Our data from testing the children in that group indicated comparable improvements.

Study 1 testing also included measuring four types of behavior by the children prior to and following their parents' exposure to training. These variables were imaginativeness of play, positive emotionality (smiling, laughing, interest, curiosity), persistence at tasks, and cooperation with peers and teachers. We carefully trained the raters and observers to ensure their reliability in scoring children's overt behaviors. Two independent raters blind to group status conducted at least two ten-minute observations of each child on separate days in their day-care centers.

Observational data also indicated an important consideration for further training in Study 2. The play protocols recorded by our observers indicated that when children were in the day-care settings they did not seem to be playing the learning games (Restaurant game, Submarine game, etc.) they had played at home with their parents. One possible explanation is that just two weeks of exposure to play with parents who had themselves no personal experience of parent–child imaginative play may have been too limited for children to assimilate these specific games that were played at home into their repertoire of activities in the school. Our earlier training studies with children had involved far more intensive parent training

(Singer & Singer, 1990). However, a more important implication relates to the training of day-care staff. For experimental purposes, day-care teachers in our study were purposely kept "blind" to our parent-training procedures, and it was our impression that most of the workers in these day-care centers did not appreciate or utilize imaginative play as an avenue toward school readiness. A good deal of earlier research clearly indicated that direct training of day-care teachers in imaginative play techniques could lead to gains in children's school-readiness skills. Therefore, we can conclude that the revised program we will produce in Study 2 should include training components for day-care workers so that activities in the preschool setting could work in synergy with at-home play activities to enhance children's read-to-learn skills.

In addition, we scrutinized factors that might predict children's gains after parent training by conducting very extensive further analyses using multiple regression statistics to determine what combinations of demographic, intervention, and game-playing features best predicted gains on our school readiness measures. What clearly emerged from these statistics was that older children did better than younger ones, and that children whose mothers were somewhat higher in socioeconomic status performed better after training. Of special significance was the sex of the child. When we conducted multiple regression analyses separately for boys and girls, what emerged clearly was that girls showed more gains than boys. For example, the combination of variables of older age (four-year-olds), higher SES for fathers, and parent training yielded an R-square (adjusted) of .64 as a predictor of postintervention scores on school readiness for girls. Similar results emerged for general information, good manners, and vocabulary.

Both boys and girls showed postintervention gains in school-readiness skills; however, since girls showed greater gains than boys, this suggested that we should modify our training approaches and materials to include elements that can prove more effective with preschool children of both sexes.

As to parent reactions during training, despite some of the stresses faced by parents in attending our sessions (e.g., rearranging work schedules, obtaining transportation, several heavy thunderstorms), their reactions were almost unanimously positive. For most of the parents the importance of imaginative play for preschool children came as a kind of revelation. They realized the importance of such activity, for most had missed out on it or developed it only at later ages. There were frequent spontaneous remarks about the novelty of this concept and its relevance in developing school-readiness skills.

The parents were quite receptive to our printed manuals, *Instructions: Games to Play with Your Child* and *Materials: Things to Use for Playing the Games*. Some parents—especially those for whom English is a second language—had initial problems with particular words in the manuals, but they quickly overcame these obstacles during the training sessions.

The training video was extremely well received. Parents were totally caught up in following the narration and clearly enjoyed viewing the real children in the play segments. Parents were also quite helpful in suggesting modifications for a revised training video. For example, some parents suggested that they would prefer a less formal, more "playful" presentation by the on-camera narrator.

While the overall reaction to the training was excellent, it was clear from our subsequent analyses of the parents' reports of their weekly play with children that certain games were more extensively used than others and that cultural backgrounds played some role in game choices. While the parents were generally quite candid during training sessions, they did not refer to ethnic differences in these sessions.

Such differences did emerge clearly from the weekly logs of the games they chose to play with their children. At the first training session parents received forms to record their daily play activities during the next week. Follow-up phone calls from the staff encouraged them to bring the completed forms to the second training session. At the second training session, parents were asked to describe their play experiences during the first week, and they also received a new set of log forms with stamped, addressed envelopes. Phone calls were again made to parents. Eventually, two sets of logs were received from nearly all participants in the first phase of training and then from the prior control group once they had received training. Parents' verbal reports about their play experiences and their comments when receiving reminder phone calls were scored and provided quantitative data for statistical analyses.

These data indicated that practically all of the parents made serious efforts to play with their children using the games suggested in the training video they had watched and the written materials they had received. The almost unanimous response was surprise and delight at how much enjoyment their children showed by the opportunity to have imaginative play initiated by the parent(s). Parents were pleased that children readily engaged in the games, wanted to play them often, tried to involve siblings or friends in the play, and seemed to "catch on" to the cognitive and social skills embedded in the games.

Many parents showed resourcefulness by using the travel games (submarine, bus) in actual transportation situations: for example, as they drove the children home from day care or sat on a public transport bus.

Parents also reported that children introduced their own variations into the games and sought to relate games to actual events. A number of children tried to relate the restaurant game to actual visits to diners or fast-food settings. Others tried to extend the submarine game to a pirate episode, or the zoo game to an aquarium trip. After playing the bus game, which includes visiting a pretend library, several children actually asked parents to go to a "real" library, where they obtained library cards and were amazed to find the wealth of resource material they could freely borrow.

The training sessions evoked other useful talk about times and places for play. One mother from a Head Start center who had missed the first training session angrily reported that her stress in getting to and from work and settling her children in day care, plus household maintenance, precluded her opportunities for play. Several parents pointed out to her how easily she could play the submarine game at bath times and incorporate other games as part of bedtime rituals. In her subsequent log report and phone conversations, this woman reported how delighted she had been by her child's response to the mother's initiating play and how she had found a number of occasions for enjoyable play interactions.

Some parents called attention to the fact that the games opened the way to discussions of safety (which was not emphasized in our training materials). The bus game especially encouraged parents to incorporate references to safe behavior (e.g., seat belts, not running or pushing while on a bus, and watching one's entrances and exits).

The amount of time spent on play varied widely. The time spent ranged from ten to forty-five minutes a day. From a quantitative standpoint, the frequency or actual time spent playing with children was not of itself a significant predictor of higher experimental group scores on the school readiness measures. Variations by ethnic groups and the qualitative intensity of play seemed more predictive of higher scores. In general, English-speaking parents played games with more frequency than did Latino parents. Certain games seemed more attractive to different families.

STUDY 2: TRAINING PARENTS AND TEACHERS

Objectives for the second year of study consisted of two phases. The first entailed a replication and extension of the previous study, with the specific goal of determining whether the focused training of day-care teachers or of both teachers and parents of a new sample of children would yield even stronger results than the training of parents alone. We produced new versions of the video and manualized program, from four to six games, including revised versions of two games (Bus to the Zoo and Spring, now called "Camping"), and two new games ("Mirror," "Puppet") to address specific skills (feelings, counting) that seemed to require additional training. The second phase meant extending the work in the New Haven area to two other cities, Atlanta and Los Angeles, to determine if reports from those settings would further support the findings of the Study 1 experimental research. This second phase involved the training of day-care center directors to provide the play workshops for teachers, and if possible, parents. Data were collected from directors and teachers about the usefulness of the revised video and its apparent effect on the children in the day-care centers.

THE DESIGN OF STUDY 2

We had obtained reasonably good results in a relatively short time (two to four weeks) with children whose parents had received play training and had extended play to their children. We wondered if our highly stressed parents' limited opportunities for play might have precluded sufficient generalization of the children's play from the home to the more relaxed atmosphere of the day-care centers. We designed this study to determine if there would be advantages in just training day-care center teachers, or whether, as seemed most likely, offering play training to both the child participants' parents as well as to their teachers would yield the strongest impact. Accordingly, we set up four conditions for evaluating the revised and expanded training video and printed materials: (1) parent training only (a replication of the previous first-year study), (2) teacher training only, (3) joint parent and teacher training, and (4) control group training (only after concluding the observation and testing of the children in all four groups). Based upon our experience in the training of parents and data from earlier studies, we hypothesized that our results would be strongest for combined parent–teacher training. We assumed that while parent-only training *ought* to be the ideal situation, the combination of home-life stress and limited play opportunities reported by parents in our first study might mitigate such an advantage. Presumably the day-care center workers and teachers would be more prepared to engage the children in pretend play, and of course the more flexible free-play opportunities in the day-care settings might permit more play practice for children.

PROCEDURES

Logistical constraints precluded a completely random assignment of children to one of the four groups. Four separate but very similar day-care settings were employed. In several instances, for reasons of failure of parent attendance at training workshops, children were reassigned to the control condition. Parent training was offered to all of the control group parents after the completion of the pre- and postdata collection.

The following were carried out: An approval of the procedure and informed consent steps by Yale University's Human Investigation Committee, a participation approval from each day-care center's director, and an informed consent from participating children's parents.

The project's format included two weeks of observation and testing of the children at their day-care centers by trained teams of paired observers and testers, and two evening workshops for parents, for teachers, or for combined parents and teachers on two occasions, a week apart. Following the first workshop the parents and teachers began playing with the children and were trained to keep logs or records over the next few weeks of how often and what games they played with the children, and how the children responded. At the second workshop we obtained feedback on parents' and teachers' reactions to training materials (video and written), to their use of play with children, and to children's responses. First-week logs were turned in. Parents were provided with stamped, addressed envelopes to send in logs following the second week of play. Follow-up telephone calls were made by the staff to ensure parents' and teachers' comprehension and compliance with training and log maintenance. At the end of the two weeks of play training by parents, teachers, or both, the children were retested and reobserved over a two-week period. Training of the control group parents and teachers followed, but practical constraints precluded further formal data collection afterward.

SAMPLE CHARACTERISTICS

A total of 107 children were studied in Year 2, Phase 1. Their mean age was 4.0 years; boys made up 48 percent of the sample, girls 52 percent. Mothers' ages averaged 30.5 years. With respect to ethnicity, 81 percent were non-white, predominantly African American, with just a few Hispanic, Asian, or mixed ethnicity. The primary language for 99 percent of the children was English. A majority of the parents (54 percent) were unmarried. With respect to socioeconomic status, 67 percent of the fathers held positions at the clerical, manual, semiskilled, or unskilled levels, while 66 percent of the mothers worked at these levels. Our sample of participants for Study 2, Phase 1 reflected a much higher percentage of African-American children than Study 1, with considerably fewer Hispanic families, and with a generally comparable SES level to Study 1. In Study 2, as in the earlier study, almost the same percentage of parents were unmarried. Socioeconomic levels were quite comparable, though the effects of the change in the welfare law were reflected in a somewhat higher percentage of parents who were employed (at manual, semiskilled, or unskilled levels). Again, as in Study 1, we were reaching on average a somewhat older group of parents, perhaps because gaining entrance to day care often required a greater degree of parent maturity and effort.

RESULTS

With some minor refinements, essentially the same observational and school-readiness testing measures were employed in Study 1, Phase 1. The Cronbach Alpha levels (0.81 pre, 0.78 post) indicated fairly satisfactory internal consistency of the individual subtests and the total score. Factor analyses suggested, however, that the vocabulary measure was the dominant score, a finding comparable to our earlier study.

Unfortunately, the comparison value of counting measures was compromised by the fact that the control group in the day-care center instituted an intensive training in counting and matching written numbers to number names during the same period as our experimental groups were undergoing play training. We learned of this only at the study's completion. This training yielded sizable improvements in the control group's counting scores and prevented our inclusion of counting as a feature of a school-readiness total score, so our subtests were analyzed individually. It should be noted, however, that for our three experimental groups the greatest gains in counting from pre-to posttesting were registered for the parent–teacher combined training group.

Color naming and shape naming showed no special effects across all four groups (perhaps because all the children scored high in starting, producing a "ceiling" effect). There were, however, gains over the control group on general information, especially for the parent–teacher combined group. A similar result emerged for animal identification scores, again favoring the parent–teacher combined group. A similar result emerged for labeling emotions, with a sharp increase for the parent–teacher combined group. In the case of the nature awareness measure only, the parent-only training group registered an appreciable gain. In general, the combined parent–teacher training condition yielded the most consistent improvement in children's scores.

There were many positive qualitative reports from parents and teachers about improved courtesy from the children after play training with the adults. Our experimental group children did not score higher in the posttest than did the controls for the good manners identification measure. Despite this seemingly disappointing result for our purely verbal good manners score, we had more direct evidence of the children's incorporation of the prosocial behavior demonstrated in the various make-believe games that they had played. Both before and after the adults received play training the children's natural behavior had been observed, recorded, and rated by pairs of observers unfamiliar with the experimental conditions into which the children were grouped. These observations were rated for cooperation, a variable reflecting sharing and assisting activities with other children or day-care teachers. These observed cooperation scores reflected improvements for the three experimental groups from pre- to postperiods, with especially strong evidence of gains for the children whose parents and teachers had both received the play training and offered these games to the children. By contrast, the control group children showed a decrease in cooperative behavior over the same time period.

Our most impressive data (as in our first study) came from the gains made by our parent–teacher combined and parent-only training groups on the key variable of vocabulary. Here our three experimental groups in these three cities clearly surpassed the control group in the order of combined training, parent-only training, and then teacher training. These results were statistically reliable, not only in terms of raw scores, but for analyses with standardized scores.

We reexamined quantitative scores through transformation of absolute scores to normalized scores and examined the predictive power of such combined variables as age, gender, mother's SES level, as well as experimental condition. While some of our dependent variables predictors, such as gender or SES, had some role, they still supported the findings already described. Girls showed some advantages over boys on such variables as labeling emotions, and lower SES children were scored as being less cooperative by observers, but with these findings our results still held. There was consistent evidence that the training of both parents and teachers combined led to surpassing scores for that group over the control group, and that the training of parents alone, while not as strong, also showed trends in the same direction.

In summary, the general thrust of our results showed gains after play training by our experimental groups, in particular the combined parent–teacher training group, on variables of general information, animal labeling, and nature awareness. While quantitative scores for gains in knowledge of good manners were not better than for the controls, actual observational scores in the field showed that experimental group children from combined parent–teacher training increased in cooperation with peers and teachers compared to the control group, who showed a decline in such behavior over the measurement period. Of greatest importance was our finding that the play training led to improved vocabulary scores, since this variable is so critical for school readiness.

FEEDBACK SESSIONS

Teachers and parents gave us their reactions during the second workshops. We had asked for these opinions before we began the training session and had asked the teachers and parents to keep logs of the games played during the two weeks. These records gave us information concerning the games played and the length of time a parent or teacher played with the children each week.

The teachers and parents were extremely positive in their reactions to the video, manual, and handouts. Many of the teachers were able to use materials they already had in their classrooms.

Teachers were most enthusiastic about the Restaurant game, which was often played. They noted that the children used vocabulary from the games and enjoyed ordering from the menus they had made in the Restaurant game and taking turns as they played. The teachers generally played the games with small groups of about five or six children at a time. Teachers also noted that children were counting and beginning to learn shapes and colors. Teachers in one New Haven preschool did some reading about the games' topics. Some parents played suitable games in the car on the way to school or to shop, such as counting and naming colors or animals, or playing Bus to the Zoo, enabling them to point out interesting things to their children on the way. In terms of time, parents averaged about fifteen to twenty minutes a day playing the games. The game played the longest time in all groups was the Restaurant game. Materials were "helpful," and only one parent reported that her child did not want to play any of the games at home. One mother found that to encourage her child to count she played a game of "What would you like two of? What would you life three of?" and then she would make pictures of what he wanted. Some parents were able to incorporate the Mirror game into the other games as they played, using emotions as part of a game.

In summary, our data from the two studies support the value of play training for adult caregivers, enabling them to make imaginative gains with inner-city preschoolers. Considering the many practical difficulties especially confronting the parents, it seems evident that fostering imaginative play can lead to increases in children's school readiness. We are encouraged that our training videos and written materials were well-accepted and led to effective parent–child and teacher–child interactions. Our research continues; we are now training other parents, day-care teachers, and private home day-care workers with a new set of videos and written materials.

NOTE

The research described here was supported by a grant, number R307F70031, to the Media Group of Connecticut, Inc., from the U.S. Department of Education Early Childhood Institute. Harvey Bellin was the principal investigator and served as the producer of the video and manual. Our research assistant, Tamara Sharpe, aided in preparing statistics for the first of the two studies. Inquiries concerning the research report should be sent to Jerome and Dorothy Singer at the Department of Psychology, Yale University, P.O. Box 208205, New

Haven, CT 06520-8205. Inquiries concerning the videotape and manual should be sent to the Media Group of Connecticut, 7 Maple Street, Weston, CT 06883-1026.

REFERENCES

Freyberg, J. T. (1973). Increasing the Imaginative Play of Urban Disadvantaged Kindergarten Children through Systematic Training. In J.L. Singer, *The Child's World of Make-Believe*. New York: Academic Press, pp. 129–154.

Singer, D. G., & J. L. Singer. (1990). *The House of Make-Believe: Children's Play and the Developing Imagination*. Cambridge: Harvard University Press.

——— . (2001). *Make-Believe: Games and Activities for Imaginative Play*. Washington, DC: Imagination Press, American Psychological Association.

Smilansky, S. (1968). *The Effects of Sociodramatic Play on Disadvantaged Preschool Children*. New York: John Wiley and Sons.

7

Using Audiovisual Recording to Observe Play in Preschool Settings in Northern Ireland

Roisin McCooey

In the little boy . . . see the final man.

—Chinese Proverb

The following highlights the enormous benefits of the use of audiovisual recording in the preschool for the analysis and understanding of peer interaction during play. The videotaped episodes provide an insight into the intricate details of play from different perspectives. An estimation of the validity of the interpretation of audiovisual data can be made by involving professionals from early years education in the analysis process. This can help practitioners in early years education develop strategies to improve peer interaction and advance play to its optimum potential.

Interactions with peers during early childhood are of major importance for development, since they are the contexts within which basic social skills emerge and are enhanced. Children in modern society are experiencing social interaction with peers at a younger age and for longer periods of time, as more mothers are joining the work force. Therefore, peers are having a more significant influence on a child's social development. When children start preschool, they need to learn to interact with many unknown peers. To learn to do this successfully depends in part on the effectiveness of the program implemented by the educators. Kratcoski and Katz (1998) believed that a teacher's ability to plan activities that provide varied linguistic experiences and that result naturally in meaningful communicative interactions is important for the development of effective social skills. There is an increased interest among teachers, parents, and other professionals in ensuring that the group peer experience during play is a positive source of growth for all children.

The investigation in inner-city Belfast covered 150 children in eight preschool centers: two playgroups, two nursery schools, two private day nurseries, and two reception classes. Children were followed through one academic year, October 1999 to June 2000. In Northern Ireland the Labor government made a commitment to provide a good-quality preschool education place for every four-year-old as part of the national child-care strategy. Northern Ireland has distinctive educational arrangements, in particular a lower school starting age than in England and Wales and a single entry date to compulsory schooling in September each year. Some children can be as young as four years, two months on entry to compulsory education. Although the investigator used a range of research techniques, the main focus here is on the audiovisual data collected.

Audio and video recording equipment were used, both to capture and reproduce for analysis the complexities of peer interaction during play in preschool settings. Many studies have implemented the use of audiovisual recording for the analysis of peer interaction. (e.g., Hazen & Black, 1989; Schober-Peterson & Johnson, 1991; Anderson, Clark, & Mullin, 1994). Audiovisual data are far more versatile than other forms of data and can be viewed by researchers from diverse backgrounds and disciplines, who can bring fresh perspectives to the data analyses. The children's play in preschool was videotaped because a recording device captures much of the complexity and interconnectedness of naturally occurring talk and action (Mehan, 1979), permitting analysis of nonverbal behaviors as well as talk behaviors. Audiovisual data collection has the capacity for completeness of analysis and comprehensiveness of material, reducing the dependence on prior interpretations by the researcher. When recording the children's play, a broad range of activities, with different children interacting with no adult intervention, was recorded. Thus, important intricate details of what happens during play are available for analysis.

The researcher estimated the validity of interpretations from the data, and was able to do this by involving others in the analysis. Conclusions regarding patterns in the data needed to be checked. Leading on from the data collection, a group of early years experts interested in exploring their attitudes and thoughts on peer interaction in play were brought together. The participants were chosen to represent an interesting and diverse range of expertise: advisory and inspection professionals, teachers, and academics. Excerpts of the play episodes, which were videotaped in preschool settings in Belfast, were shown to the early years experts; using a schedule, they offered their interpretations and judgements. The group was asked to consider the socialization themes appearing in the excerpt of play they viewed. When watching the excerpts of video, it was important that these participants attempt to free themselves from adult conceptions of children's activities and enter the children's world. The participants' reactions were audiotaped and later compared to my own interpretations, which had been recorded prior to the meeting. This is an important methodological technique for estimating the validity of interpretations of qualitative data, providing a way to calibrate judgments made during the analysis of the video data. The researcher's judgments were therefore calibrated against early years experts. Upon completion, a rich and stimulating discussion about the children's play took place. Some of the main issues that were discussed follow.

Specific excerpts of audiovisual data can provide a breadth of knowledge of peer interaction during play. Peer interaction is just one area this research focused on, for the audiovisual data can be used to analyze a range of criteria relating to children's play. Play attentively observed by a number of individuals, such as curriculum planners, inspection professionals, academics, and teachers/practitioners in the early years arena, can provide an effective overview from various perspectives. This approach will provide early years practitioners with additional information, that could increase their ability to decide on appropriate assistance for each child in groups of children when working together. Preschool educators have stressed social interaction as a primary objective (Tizard & Hughes, 1984), requiring children to cooperate. Social training should not be left to chance, but planned to maximize children's potential for developing social skills (Quilitch & Risley, 1975). Knowledge gained from the audiovisual data can help practitioners ensure that every child becomes a fully participating member of the group during play. Hill (1989) pointed out that if teachers of young children do not promote play, then children with limited social skills will continue to play alone, while those with well-developed social skills play in groups. Preschool children do not always engage in cooperative conversation during free play; however, they appear to view the situation as a social one in which talking together is a desired goal. Young children are aware of and interested in their peers as conversational partners during play.

Early years practitioners can use the audiovisual data as an aid in encouraging children to develop the necessary social skills to express how they feel about what their peers are doing during play. It can also help children deal with the range of scenarios they may face: being a bully, being a victim, and being part of a cooperative group. Children should experience play, which is enjoyable, and it is our responsibility to help children develop play to its optimum potential. Hazen and Black (1989) suggested that interventions to help socially rejected preschool children may include helping children start and maintain conversation and helping them to adapt their talk to the needs of the particular social situation. Shared discussion with a focus group might provide solutions for difficult situations in the preschool setting, which are part of everyday interactions between children. Hill (1989), in his study of socially rejected and neglected children in schools, revealed that behavior problems (often with boys), nonparticipation (often of girls), and exclusion of children with physical disabilities can intensify if intervention by the adult does not occur.

Early years practitioners should aim to help children use language to solve problems independently. Analyzing audiovisual data may help practitioners develop strategies to use when interacting with children. Therefore, in a situation involving a dispute between two children, by focusing on the victim, children can learn strategies for using language to fulfill their needs, enabling them to teach themselves and other children that they are not victims. McNamara (1995) also pointed out that experience shows that regular "sharing" times, in pairs and in a circle, can help in reducing such bullying, especially when combined with an open discussion about "what it feels like to be picked on." The group of early years experts in the researcher's study agreed that they wouldn't directly teach preschool children social problem-solving skills or negotiation skills. However, they suggested bringing these skills into circle time to reinforce and show sharing and negotiation strategies. That time provides an ideal opportunity to bring children together to share their play and learning with each other. The group emphasized that adults have a crucial role in ensuring that the play environment is free from bullying and intimidation. Other skills need to be developed to help children deal with feelings and provide them with alternatives to aggression. Early years practitioners need to realize that aggressive behavior is a skills deficit area and can have a detrimental effect on the development of play. Audiovisual data can be used as a tool for behavior management to encourage prosocial behavior and help prevent antisocial behavior. Disruptive play episodes could be shown to the child and the child's parents, and with the early years practitioner they could talk about it together and work out how best to deal with it. Alternatively, Wittmer and Honig (1994) suggested videotaping children who are behaving prosocially to facilitate sharing and to help promote good behavior.

Gender orientation is also important to consider. In preschool settings it is normally free choice for children as to where they sit; adults rarely position children for play according to gender. Smith and Inder (1993) believed that promoting successful cross-gender interaction over collaborative activities is a useful way of developing common interests and skills in boys and girls, teaching them about their similarities and differences, and helping them to share future roles. Ramsey (1991) pointed out, however, that teachers who attempt to organize nonsexist classrooms and convey the idea that boys and girls can be friends are often frustrated by the children's resistance. Simply placing children in groups and telling them to work together does not in and of itself produce a cooperative effort. There are many ways in which such unstructured group efforts can go wrong; for example, seating children together can produce mutual competition or individualistic learning.

Another aspect to be considered is adult intervention. When adults intervene in children's play they need to base their actions on knowledge and understanding, which audiovisual data can help provide. Early years practitioners can plan programs to anticipate children's needs in order to provide the appropriate play environment. In the design and setting up of children's play environments, adults can orient the arrangement of the play area toward improving the progress of play. Audiovisual data also provided a way for practitioners, researchers, and policy makers to share ideas and perspectives so that they can learn from each other, for the children's benefit. Sheridan (1999) believed that the adult needs to have a clear understanding of when it is appropriate to intervene in children's play and when it is appropriate to stand back and observe unobtrusively. In preschool settings where adults solve the problems for the children all of the time, children are not learning to use their words to help them. Therefore, the children are not learning to respond to the language of their peers and they are dependent upon the adult. In preschool settings where the children are left to solve their problems without adult support, some children learn that they can dominate without considering the feelings of others, and others learn that they are powerless in the presence of leaders. In neither situation do children feel as safe or as competent as they could, and so it is important for the adults in preschool to consider the effect of their intervention or nonintervention. Attention given to skills of negotiation, listening, turn taking, and social problem solving will create a group of children who not only have fun but also help each other to learn.

Early years practitioners work with children during a period of great intellectual, physical, emotional, and social growth. The use of audiovisual data provides teachers and parents in the early years arena with information about play that has the capacity to sharpen and enrich their ability to decide upon appropriate assistance for children in preschool. Meeting with early years professionals helped to highlight the important contribution that in-depth analysis of audiovisual data and discussion make in understanding peer interaction, play, and the overall socialization of preschool children.

REFERENCES

Anderson A., A. Clark, & J. Mullin. (1994). Interactive Communication between Children: Learning How to Make Language Work in Dialogue. *Journal of Child Language* 21: 439–463.

Blakemore, C. (2001). The Lessons We Really Need. *Nursery World* 34 (March).

Hazen, L. H., & B. Black. (1989). Preschool Peer Communication Skills: The Role of Social Status and Interaction Context. *Child Development* 60: 867–876.

Hill, T. (1989). Neglected and Rejected Children: Promoting Social Competence in Early Childhood Settings. *Australian Journal of Early Childhood Education* 14(1): 11–16.

Kratcosti, A. M., & L. G. Katz. (1998). Conversing with Young Language Learners in the Classroom. *Young Children* (May): 30–33.

McNamara, S. (1995). Let's Co-operate! Developing Children's Social Skills in the Classroom. In J. Moyles (Ed.), *Beginning Teaching: Beginning Learning in Primary Education* (pp. 158–172). Buckingham: Open University Press.

Mehan, H. (1979). *Learning Lessons: Social Organisation in the Classroom.* Cambridge: Harvard University Press.

Quilitch, H. R., & T. R. Risley. (1975). The Effects of Play Materials on Social Play. *Journal of Applied Behavioural Analysis* 6: 573–578.

Ramsey, P. G. (1991). *Making Friends in School: Promoting Peer Relationships in Early Childhood.* New York: Teachers College Press.

Schober-Peterson, D., & C. J. Johnson. (1991). Non-Dialogue Speech during Preschool Interactions. *Journal of Child Language* 18: 153–170.

Sheridan, M. D. (1999). *Play in Early Childhood: From Birth to Six Years* (rev. ed). London: Routledge.

Smith, A. B., & P. M. Inder. (1993). Social Interaction in Same and Cross Gender Preschool Peer Groups: A Participant Observation Study. *Educational Psychology* 13(1): 29–42.

Tizard, B., & M. Hughes. (1984). *Young Children Learning.* London: Fontana.

Wittmer, D. S., & A. S. Honig. (1994). Encouraging Positive Social Development in Young Children. *Young Children* (July): 4–12.

8

Play as a Coping Strategy during a Time of Bombing and Destruction

Ivana Lisul

Play empowers children and reaffirms their individual right to develop at their own pace.

—IPA/USA

For the normal development of a child, a life without highly stressful unpleasant
events that create the feeling of uncertainty and defenselessness is necessary. Yet
no life is risk-free, not even a child's. Children often deal with equally stressful situations as adults: They get to know hunger, injustice, violence, death, and extreme
fear, and deal with it the best way they can. If the experience exceeds the limit of
general human experience and at the same time is highly intense and sudden, we
call it a traumatic experience. A child has no ability to assimilate such an experience in his or her own basic picture of the world that includes beliefs and schemes
of functioning people, space, and oneself. This basic picture is being shattered by
the traumatic experience, and a child has to change it. Because of its great intensity, this traumatic event will cause suffering in almost every child who is exposed
to its effects.

A child's reaction will depend on his or her age and cognitive and emotional capacity. A preschool child is almost totally dependent on parents and is able neither
to cope with danger nor to think of a way to change the situation, and due to that,
helplessness increases. A child of this age will ask for constant physical contact
with the parents (or a trusted person), and will show a highly developed fear of separation. This fear can be detected in a child's problematic behavior: sleeping disorders, waking up in the middle of the night, asking for someone to sleep with him or

her. All other fears can get stronger and more generalized. New fears could be related to a real situation, but could also be the result of confusion or imaginations.

Regressive behavior is also very common. A child of this age cannot accept a full concept of death. The death is reversible—the dead one can come back. Therefore, the death of a relative or a person close to the child could be misunderstood as abandonment. Some children will seem peaceful and quiet despite the traumatic experience. This, however, does not necessarily mean that a child is not hurt by the situation, and if we give that individual an opportunity to express his or her feelings, teachers can gain a great insight. A special type of repetitive (traumatic) play often occurs among children of this age. The characteristics of this kind of play compared to creative play are seen in Table 8.1.

As adults, children will respond to stressful situations highly individualistically. That is why some children will react strongly even to very low stress intensity, and some will react minimally to traumatic experiences. The factors determining the reactions to stressful events are called resilience factors (see Table 8.2). Some of these factors are individual characteristics of a child, such as temperament, adaptability, self-respect, positive self-concept, inner locus of control, extraversion, activity, and sociability. A basic strength of personality that is created by parents' responsiveness to child's needs—the quality of interaction between the parent and the child—is also very important. Previous experiences can provide different effects: Sometimes they can be used as a preparation for other stressful situations, but can also make dealing with a stressful situation harder by wasting a child's capacity for dealing with stress.

A child's perception of the event, especially regarding his or her own reactions, is very important. An impression that one's own fear is inappropriately strong could cause a feeling of shame and helplessness and therefore could lower self-es-

Table 8.1
Usual (Creative) Play and Repetitive (Traumatic) Play

Usual (Creative) Play	Repetitive (Traumatic) Play
• is always played for fun • is characterized by the emotional distance • has a hedonistic quality • is spontaneous • is dynamic and full of movement • has flexible roles • has a tranquilizing effect on anxiety and helps in problem solving • provides togetherness among children in a playing group	• causes anxiety • has no emotional distance • has a hedonistic quality that is basically dark • is compulsive, not spontaneous • is stereotypic and static • has inflexible roles, there being no creativity • does not create possibilities to solve the problem and easily becomes regressive • causes distance when among children in a playing group

Table 8.2
Resilience Factors

Individual Characteristics
- age
- basic personality strength
- previous similar experiences
- adaptability
- temperament
- self-respect
- positive self-concept
- inner locus of control
- extroversion
- activity
- sociability

Characteristics of a Traumatic Event
- type of event
- sudden/expected event
- exposure length

Child's Assessment of an Event
- child's own reactions
- parents' reactions
- parents' responsiveness to child's needs

Family Support
- preserved family
- financial status

---

teem. A child's perception of parental reactions and, even more, parental responsiveness to a child's personal needs will provide great affect to a child's ability to deal with the situation. It is therefore necessary to give a child the opportunity to express his or her feelings, to give support, and to provide adequate protection.

One of the most painful experiences that a war can bring is bombing, especially the ruination of home or school. These situations increase anxiety in children and develop different fears and phobias. The necessity for a separation between a parent and a child often occurs in situations of war, and a child can feel extremely alone when left alone to deal with the danger. Although parents can provide necessary protection to a child and help in overcoming fear and confusion, they usually do not actually know what their child is experiencing. Unfortunately, children rarely speak of their feelings, and parents almost never ask.

In dealing with stressful situations, children use a variety of different coping strategies. Coping strategies are different mechanisms used to overcome fear and anxiety caused by a stressful event and provide control over the situation, as well as over emotional reactions that may lower the efficiency of a person's cognitive and emotional functioning. The coping strategies of a preschool child are developing. If a coping mechanism is subjectively assessed as functional, it is being kept in a child's behavior. A model that is given by parents or by persons a child loves and respects is very important as well. Not all coping strategies are equally functional. Some are constructive and help regain balance, but some are inadequate and might even damage the recovery process.

Much research has been done in Yugoslavia during and since the bombing in the spring of 1999. The research presented here was accomplished with a group of children in a primary school damaged in a May 1999 attack. At the same time, two boys from the group lost their homes. Results shown here, similar to the results of other investigations, can provide a picture of the abilities of preschool children in coping with war traumas.

Although this investigation was done fourteen months after the bombing stopped, the memories of the children were alive and full of details and emotional reactions. Eighteen of twenty-three children assessed their fear during the bombing as "great." Fourteen said that their parents did not talk to them about the situation and their feelings; seven had been separated from their parents; and ten had spent the time of the bombing with relatives, outside their homes. Other ways of support, besides conversation, were missing as well. Most of the parents considered talking about feelings unnecessary. Innocent lies, such as talking about thunder instead of a bomb, were common as well. Among these children there were many who were overprotected, not allowed to go out from the house to play or obligated to stay in front of the shelter most of the day, often only with adults. These children today assess their fear of war even greater than during the bombing. Six of seven children who were at their grandparents' or relatives' homes during the bombing claim that they felt safe there, but that they often remembered the sound of bombs and planes and were scared of them. Still, they cannot think of any other possible way to deal with another stressful situation but to "escape" to these "safe places."

However, nineteen of the twenty-three children had an active and positive attitude to the traumatic situation (see Figure 8.1) and therefore processed the readiness and ability to fight their own fear and confusion. Thirteen of these nineteen children used play as a coping strategy, five used drawing, and one used both drawing and playing (see Figure 8.2). The children also said that sometimes the content of play was not as helpful as being with friends, talking to them about what they know, feel, and usually do during the day. Eleven of the thirteen children who used play as a coping strategy used war as a topic of the play. These games are described as "fighting among the groups," "fighting together against pilots using plastic bombs," "killing each other with water guns," or "killing boys and girls from another shelter." Most of the children told us that they had not always liked the game, and that they had often. Only three of these children still play "war games." All of the other children are playing, as they call them, "normal games." The reason for this, however, is that the "war games" remind them of the fears they felt during the bombing. Still, all the children who used play as a coping strategy consider it very helpful, and they recommend it to all children experiencing stress, fear, danger, or confusion, as they had.

Seven of the twenty-three children considered the possibility of having their home ruined as the most terrifying experience, five thought the ruination of their school,

Figure 8.1
Attitude toward the Truamatic Experience

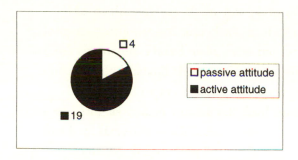

Figure 8.2
Coping Strategies (Active Attitude)

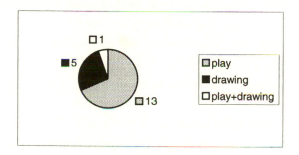

five thought terrifying the rocking of the building, five feared for the life of parents, six thought the sound of the planes and bombs, and three thought the ruining of bridges (see Figure 8.3). These attitudes were expressed in play or drawings, or both.

Two years after the bombing, eighteen of the twenty-three children assessed their fear of war as being less than it was during the onslaught, but fourteen still described it as "quite great." Yet the fear was less intensified because nothing stressful or disturbing was happening. All of the children from this sample were sure that no one could do anything to prevent wars.

WHAT CAN WE LEARN FROM THIS?

With the children from this sample that had been involved in the study for more than three months, this was the first time that they showed disapproval and unwillingness for cooperation. Although it was quite clear that the topic of conversation was difficult, none of children refused to take a chance and tell about his or her feelings and experiences. No one else talked to them after the bombing ended, so this was the first time they actually talked about it. Unsatisfying communication between parents and children leads to the conclusion that, overall, parents do not realize the extent to which their child feels and thinks about the situation that they are dealing with. This has been proven by the different kinds of "white lies" that parents told to their children in order to "calm" them, refusing to talk and understand the feelings of their children. Parents had actually tried to find the safest possible place for their children, primarily thinking of physical safety. Being afraid themselves and worried about the future and well-being of their families, they neglected their children's need to be protected in other ways, to be supported in efforts creating a full picture of what was going on. This aspect is very important in coping with the situation. Children need to improve their self-respect, to feel adequate. Talking to them would help them in these efforts as well.

In addition, the data showed that some children felt overprotected. They had been obligated to spend a lot of time with adults, listening to their conversations or television programs, so the confusion and new fears that appeared were probably influenced by these indirect forms of communication. The children had heard too much information, which they, having no other proper explanation, interpreted the best way they could using their own isolated knowledge and experiences, often mixing a lot of things together with things that had nothing to do with war itself. That is the reason why, for example, one boy thought that a tornado was a part of the war, terrified by the fact that it might "arrive" and take him and his loved ones to a place unknown where none would be able to find them. He still had nightmares with this topic. Confusion and the feeling that they did not know the situation probably resulted in increased fear and the feeling that they would certainly not be able to deal with any similar experience ever again.

Still, a positive attitude was noticed in most of the children. That attitude assisted the investigators in learning how children deal with traumatic experiences. An active, positive attitude gives a child the impression that he or she could change the situation, and that is exactly what these children were doing: writing letters of protest and sending peace pigeons made of paper to the world. Some of these children had support from their parents in their activities, but some did not. Yet for all of these children their activities helped them to feel brave, needed, useful, and, most important, control over their feelings and behavior. For thirteen of these children, the most frequently used coping strategy was play. Most of these plays were "war games," full of fights and anger, but children were able to think of reasons for war and solutions that would stop it through those games. In some of them children observed some characteristics of traumatic play and they were very precise in pointing out and explaining them. This is very important, because traumatic war games increased some problems and fears, and the children's ability to find solutions helped in their recovery. A very interesting fact is that one could actually notice elements of play in drawings of the children. These drawings showed a lot of activity and emotional involvement, and one could actually feel that the child was living through the objects and things being drawn. This gave the investigators the opportunity to talk to the child and to receive information about the child's perception of the situation, which is very important for a child's well-being and is very much different from those of an adult. Children think very seriously about what is occurring around them. To understand this better, just think of the definition of war given by a seven-year-old boy from the sample: "A war is a situation when you can lose everything that you ever had."

These results helped the children's teachers to learn what kind of education should be provided for parents, teachers, and caregivers to make their life more complete and successful. Proper education on the topics of crisis and traumatic experiences and children's abilities in coping with them is extremely important in cases of children whose parents are separated or tend to be overprotective.

REFERENCES

Kapor-Stanulovic, N. (1999). *How to Help Children in Crisis*. Belgrade: UNICEF.
————. (1999). *Organization of Psychosocial Help*. Belgrade: UNICEF.

9

Play Initiatives in Brazil

Marilena Flores Martins

The Brazilian people came from very different origins, with the immigration of more than 5 million people from all continents. Brazil is geographically divided into five regions, each having a very different landscape. Sixty percent of the population lives in urban areas, a percentage that grows each year. Rural migration comes mainly from the Northeastern states and from the countryside in the Southeast to big cities, such as São Paulo, Rio de Janeiro, Belo Horizonte, and Brasilia. Consequently, this internal migration overloads the public health, housing, and education systems in these urban environments. On the other hand, it enriches the cultural life in these centers.

Brazil is a multicultural country, inhabited first by native Indians and discovered in 1500 by the Portuguese, who began to colonize the East coast. The official language is Portuguese, but this is spoken in different accents throughout the country, an outcome of the initial mixture of Portuguese and the indigenous Indian language Tupi-Guarani. Later the mixture increased with the influence of African words and expressions from the English, French, German, Italian, and Japanese languages.

The fact that we have inherited our cultural background from an Iberian nation is very significant. Spain and Portugal bridged the European exploration of the new world. Therefore, the formation of the Brazilian people is due to the fusion of Portuguese, native Indians, and Africans who were brought to the country as slaves. This explains the cultural wealth of our people being linked to all forms of art expressions, food, clothing, and mainly leisure activities.

This cultural fusion is very apparent in the people themselves. The miscegenation of the races has been supported and stimulated since the time of Portuguese colonization. They promoted marriages among native Indians and Caucasians, and their descendants with Africans. Since then, Brazil has become a nation of "mulatos." Albert Einstein, who visited Brazil said of the people, "The ethnic mixture I spot in the streets is delicious. The Portuguese, the native Indians, and the Africans, were blended spontaneously, like plants, subdued by the heat."

Spontaneity and creativity have been the strongest elements of the Brazilian culture and they have permeated all of our play and cultural activities. The first half of the twentieth century brought immigrants from many nations north of the Equator, including Iberia, Italy, Germany, Japan, Poland, and China. The Brazilian culture incorporated their new habits and traditions, influencing the people's leisure and play activities. Thus, typical Portuguese and Spanish religious celebrations merged with Italian and German gastronomic festivals. The native and African habits of promoting gatherings where dance, body painting, and percussion music are present, allied with Portuguese street dance, led to the greatest form of Brazilian expression in play and leisure, referred to as Carnival. Equally important is another form of play and leisure expression, which was brought by the British, incorporated into Brazilian daily life, and identified as part of the national psyche: football. A multitude of Brazilians are football team supporters. The communists described this extreme fanaticism as "the opium of the people."

In Brazil the human body plays an important part in peoples lives, in dance and expression at Carnival, and in the social importance of the beach and climate at leisure time. In short, the outdoors is a Brazilian way of life. In urban centers this physical expression plays a less prominent role in people's daily lives; it is more restricted to indoor provisions or socioeconomic opportunities. One finds health clubs in countryside towns, but these act more as meeting points for youngsters and other generations. In the small towns, grandparents have more opportunities to play with grandchildren in the public squares and parks, opportunities not always available in urban settings.

The lack of leisure opportunities in the urban centers affects the quality of life, resulting in more stress to citizens. Local communities have identified these problems and have been organizing themselves into committees in order to fight for a better quality of life. All citizens want improvement. Public space is no longer protective and safe. Instead, it has become a place for the exercise of violence and preventing pluralist and multicultural manifestations. This country could be a model in the use of outdoor public spaces for play activities due to the favorable climatic and multicultural characteristics, but circumstances have been causing serious deviations in children's personalities and youngsters have very little opportunity to play freely in public spaces. Adolescents have to start working early in their lives, and only recently has a national plan for the creation of sports spaces been outlined. Even if this constitutes progress—play and leisure activities, free play, and play for the pleasure of play—it still does not have proper attention from the government. This is a favorable moment for the establishment of toy libraries. The positive side is that these libraries are safe environments. On the other hand, they became exclusive to a minority group.

In this context, the Brazilian Association for the Child's Right to Play assumes a role of fundamental importance in Brazil because it reinforces access to culture and the right to play, for the child as well as for the whole family. The Brazilian Association for the Child's Right to Play has developed a community project in partnership with various sectors of society—Rotary Club, Scouts, private organizations, NGOs, and volunteers—in order to express sound principles with concrete action. This project is called "Brincandando," or "Playwalk," and is organized annually in one of the public parks in São Paulo. Last year we were partners with the SIFE (Students in Free Enterprise) in a great event that started in the United States called "Make a Difference Day." The Brazilian Association for the Child's Right to Play published a manual on the SIFE Web site, on how to organize a Brincandando activity. The Brazilian Association for the Child's Right to Play has branches in the states of São Paulo in the Southeast, Pernambuco in the Northeast, Paraná and Santa Catarina in the South, and Minas Gerais in the central region.

The association is also concerned with training courses for play workers. It is not possible to have an effective policy for play activities without capable play workers to implement such a policy. The training courses are for people with different backgrounds, professionals to community leaders, managers, parents, and volunteers. Hence, the association created the Ludens Center project. The center has already organized the first postgraduate/extension course in partnership with a private university in São Paulo. Finding enough resources to sponsor students has been the greatest obstacle. There is the desire to expand the training courses to other communities, but currently the association is limited by available resources. There is not a national policy to provide training for play workers, which emphasizes the important role that the Brazilian Association for the Child's Right to Play has in developing and offering training programs. Government educational policies do include toy libraries in their curriculum, although very few public schools can offer play environments.

This is a moment when politicians need to awake to the necessity of violence prevention and social development. The Brazilian Association for the Child's Right to Play is a vital organization that leads the way by offering programs where the main focus is the human being. This organization fosters the right not only to health and education, but also to the joy and pleasure of living through play for all children and young people.

REFERENCE

Einstein, A. (1988). *Ideas and Opinions*. New York: Bonanza Books.

10

The Status of Child's Play in Japan

Rikuko Okuda

There are serious problems with young parents who did not have enough opportunities for play during their childhood. Japan is still a Confucian country—its influence has lessened a bit recently—and so it remains a *tate-shakai* society, or top-down orientated one, very hierarchical, rigid, and male oriented. Parents, especially fathers, have the strongest power in a family. It is quite natural for children to obey their parents, and furthermore, they have no right to raise any objection to their parents. The same usually happens at school. Japanese sentiment is deeply influenced by Confucian thought, which has in fact prevented the Japanese people from establishing a democratic society in its true meaning. For those parents with this self-restricted mentality, it goes without saying that they expect their offspring to follow the same social rules.

In 1997 the Nationwide Center for the Promotion of Boys and Girls Organizations reported to the United Nations that the rapid economic growth, material wealth, and competition of children to get into better schools, starting in the 1960s, have brought various distortions to the health and life of Japanese children (Juvenile Center, 1997). The truth is that this, in turn, gave birth to the problems of human rights unique to Japan. With this competition, education started earlier and earlier. Its educators included Shoichi Sekimoto (1989), who wrote a book advising mothers to educate their babies still in the womb. It covered mathematics, geography, biology, and so on, and is still read by mothers who hope that the fetus will absorb the knowledge. Some infants in diapers, sometimes under the age of two, attend classes. Instructors teach *kanji* characters using flash cards. Some children who cannot speak Japanese well are sent to English classes by their mothers, while others are encouraged to learn by rote difficult phrases and passages of classical Japanese literature, which puts these children under pressure.

There are also many parents who grew up without having sufficiently played in their childhood. Some of them find it difficult to get on with others because all they had to do in their childhood was study and get good marks. They did not have to help their parents with chores, and they were unable to spend time with peers, preventing the learning of many social skills.

So, when people become adults and have babies they suddenly realize they do not know anything about how to deal with their infants and think that child-rearing books have all the answers. This fact has caused some extreme results, such as child abuse or negligence. Many young mothers firmly believe that only manuals or other written material can tell them the truth about the right way to bring up their children. We cannot blame such mothers, because their teachers in school demanded their complete obedience. As a result, young mothers find it hard and survive without any given hints, or manuals, because the education system had not encouraged them to think for themselves.

Masami Oh-Hinata (1999), a psychologist who has studied these child-rearing books, concluded that they are not helpful. In one such book a mother is timing how long her baby cries. The book says, "When your baby cries for more than fifteen minutes, you should take your baby into your arms and soothe. If he or she stops crying before 15 minutes, don't worry, so you should let the baby cry for 15 minutes before doing anything." Mothers like these are often highly educated, and they want to be perfect and ideal mothers. If their babies do not grow up exactly following the stages written in the manuals, they panic, not knowing what to do. They can suddenly turn into hysterical, harsh, and unforgiving mothers, leading to abuse. There are other young mothers who have dropped out of school. Some have no confidence in themselves, no self-respect. They often cannot bring up their babies properly. Consequently, this causes child abuse, negligence, and even abandonment of child care.

When people lived in larger family groups there was more support for young mothers, with the extended family living under one roof; now, with the nuclear family, there is less support from the extended family and this is not corrected with the help of social services or government institutions, as in other countries.

As mentioned before, the education system doesn't teach mothers to rely on themselves. Another problem lies in the working routines of men in Japan; they often work very long hours and so do not help with child rearing; although this is changing slowly, many men do not see themselves as having to help in this area.

As far as public and private facilities for child care is concerned, in 1999 I had a chance to engage in research on what would be the most desirable community for child raising (Okuda, Kino, Yamada, & Yamamoto, 1999). We focused on public, private, and voluntary organizations for child care. For example, we explored hospitals, nursery schools, facilities for disabled children in the public and private sectors, and of course the people who work there, and in the voluntary sector we studied such things as local children's associations and sports and culture clubs. Many of these organizations were staffed by volunteer parents. Some of the problems we found are as follows: Although the people working in these areas were committed and motivated, they were often too focused on their specialty, institution, or the children they worked with. There were not many interactions between these organizations. Moreover, the local government failed to coordinate their own activities with those of private and voluntary organizations. The Japanese Association for the Child's Right to Play felt that it was very important for there to be more interaction and more exchanges of information among these groups, from which the children could benefit. Therefore, we began a network between these people.

On the positive side, there recently has been interest in Roger Hart's book, *Children's Participation: The Theory and Practice of Involving Young Citizens in Community Development and Environmental Care* (1997). In Japan there are many children who feel hostile to the adults around them but do not and cannot show this, so superficially at least they are obedient, for reasons already mentioned. Thus, in Japan many people have started to pay attention to and study Hart's book, which discusses the uniqueness of individuals and cooperative group participation. Among them are study groups that have begun reporting and exchanging information found in their communities.

We have seen that some of Japan's problems with child rearing are being shared with other countries, but other problems stemming from our social system, education system, and so on are more unique to Japan, or at least to northeastern Asian countries. A great need exists for training programs in child rearing to contain information about the importance of play and how ordinary citizens can rear their children in more sensitive and playful ways.

REFERENCES

Hart, R. A. (1979). *Children's Experience of Place*. New York: Irvington.
———. (1997). Children's Participation: The Theory and Practice of Involving Young Citizens in Community Development and Environmental Care. Sterling, VA: Stylus.
Juvenile Center (1997). *The Convention on the Rights of the Child* (Preliminary Report). Tokyo: Collection of Basic Reports to CRC from NGOs and Citizens.
Oh-Hinata, M. (1999). *Kosodate to deau toki* [When Mothers Have Their Babies]. NHK Books 852. Tokyo: NHK.
Okuda, R., H. Kino, S. Yamada, & K. Yamamoto. (1999). *What Would Be the Most Desirable Community for Child-Rearing: A Research in Nagoya City*. Submitted to the Nagoya Urban Institute.
Sekimoto, S. (1989). *Taikyo=Akachan wa tensai desu* [Prenatal Training: Babies Are Geniuses]. Tokyo: Chobun-sha.

11

Play of Reconciliation: Play between Parent and Child

Yvonne E. Keairns, Janet Edwards, and Christina Carlucci

Arsenal Family and Children's Center (Arsenal) has since 1997 implemented reconciliation programs between parents and their children. The fundamental premise on which these programs are founded is that children and their parents can be reconciled through play.

Arsenal was founded in 1953 by Dr. Benjamin Spock as a place where children could thrive through programs based upon respect for the child and the parent. From its inception, Arsenal has believed in the child's right to play. Based on nearly fifty years of observation—careful study and work with young children—we know that two things are essential to their healthy development: opportunities for active learning through play and the passionate involvement of at least one adult in the life of each child. We organize all of our programs and services around these essential elements.

Therefore, when designing the Supervised Parenting and Play Program (SP&P) and the Individual Parent/Child Mentoring Program (Mentoring), it was a natural progression to use play as a medium of reconciliation between a parent and child who have for a variety of reasons been estranged from each other. The parents who attend our reconciliation programs represent those suffering from various forms of addiction, mental illness, or bitter custody battles, those who have been neglectful and/or abusive, and those who simply wish to strengthen their relationship with their offspring. Referrals are made by families, judges, lawyers, mediators, pediatricians, social service agencies, and court-appointed Special Advocates (CASA). For many of the children, the only time they are with a parent is when they are attending our play program for weekly two-hour group visits or forty-five-minute individual mentoring sessions with their parent.

The play of reconciliation programs begins with the staff modeling respect, careful listening, appreciation for what is truly done well (not empty praise), and setting and maintaining limits in order to keep everyone safe. What an outside observer sees in the play of reconciliation programs is deceptively simple. The staff member provides a safe space with a range of play activities appropriate to the child's age, which may include play materials requested by the parent or child. In any particular play session the child is simply invited to play as he or she wishes, with the mentor and parent following the child's lead.

Arsenal promotes play experiences that invite children to explore, create, manipulate ideas and objects, and negotiate relationships that are important to them. This active participation with toys, materials, and people, as well as with the natural environment, permits young children to grow in a personally meaningful way that includes their parent.

Two broad goals guide our work with the children as they play: first, developing the entire child while paying special attention to such skills as self-awareness, impulse control, persistence, zeal, self-motivation, and empathy; second, transmitting essential human values, including respect, compassion, and honesty. When children experience these values they are better able to integrate and live them out as they develop relationships throughout life.

Four qualities characterize the environment established and maintained by the staff mentors: *time*—to be a child, to practice repeatedly and without hurry each developmental task, to discover at their own pace who they uniquely are; *care*—that keeps them safe, that encourages and delights in their play, that permits making mistakes and taking risks; *calm*—in the midst of a sometimes frightening world, in the face of angry feelings, in a way that makes control and mastery seem possible; and *control*—of those parts of their lives that they should manage (i.e., age-appropriate choices and decisions), and our assurance that we will remain reliably in control of the rest.

Arsenal also extends children's opportunities for reflective and inventive play in our unique Garden for Children. Grounded in our knowledge of young children's need for space, unhurried time, well-defined limits, and a certain sense of inner quiet, the Garden for Children provides a safe haven in which to discover the world with their bodies and their imaginations. Rather than a collection of static playground equipment, the Garden for Children includes places to investigate, challenges to climb, secret nooks in which to hide, flowers to nurture and enjoy, and spaces for crawling, digging, performing, and contemplating.

Fundamental to Arsenal's reconciliation programs is the protection of the child's right to play. While these programs may be experienced as therapeutic, they provide opportunities in which play serves as the point of departure for new and enjoyable ways in which children are integrated, within one's self, with the world, and with the parent.

In the Mentoring and SP&P programs at Arsenal the play of the child is the foundation upon which we nurture reconciliation between a parent and his or her child. As the child plays and the parent follows the example of the mentor in attending to the child playing, the relationship between them begins to be renewed, refreshed, and rebuilt. Play draws the parent onto the child's ground, where the two can encounter and embrace one another by playing together. The joy of playing together draws from the parent and the child what is inherent within them but can become muddled or twisted; that is, their love for one another. There is a quality in play that lends itself to this renewal and reconciliation, a communication between child and parent that can happen on many levels without any words spoken. There is the opportunity through play for the child imbedded in the adult to come forth.

Perhaps most important, in both programs it is the child who leads in play. The more able the parent is to attend to the child's focus, becoming engaged as the child desires, the more successful the sessions are. When the parent is able to engage in this way, the strength of the child to call forth the parent's love is unleashed. The strength of the child to evoke love from the parent is encouraged and supported by the mentor and the simple yet often difficult parameters of the program. Reconciliation happens when the child dares to be himself or herself in play and the parent dares to follow.

The SP&P and Mentoring programs work with parents and children (from birth to ten years of age). While the programs have the same philosophy of reconciliation through play, each program's format is unique.

SP&P was designed to meet the needs of noncustodial parents who are required to have supervision when visiting with their children. These weekly two-hour visits take place on evenings and weekends in a group setting. At least twelve sessions are recommended; however, families may stay in the program as long as necessary. Up to six families are in each room with two staff members. The warm and inviting rooms are carefully designed with child-size furniture and appropriate play materials for the ages of the children in the group.

Initial contacts for SP&P are directed to the program coordinator, who gathers the necessary personal data (including brief background information and how much time has passed since the last contact with the child) for the noncustodial parent, the custodial parent, and the child or children who will be participating in the program.

The noncustodial parent is required to receive an orientation (see Appendix to this chapter). It is during this time that the program's history, philosophy, and structure are reviewed with the parent. Parents are instructed to arrive fifteen minutes before their children and to stay fifteen minutes after their children leave (this extra time insures that there is no contact between noncustodial and custodial parents, and it allows the staff members and noncustodial parents to discuss how the sessions are progressing and the parents to document reflections on their visit). The noncustodial parent is then asked to sign program related forms that include program guidelines, attendance guidelines, and audiovisual permission. At the conclusion of this process a date is set for the first visit, typically two weeks after the orientation.

The week following the orientation the child and his or her custodial parent are invited to attend a preview visit of the center. During this time they have an opportunity to meet the staff, play, and thereby acquaint themselves with the SP&P environment.

Also at this time the custodial parent is required to sign program-related forms, including emergency contact information and an audiovisual permission form.

When visits begin, the noncustodial parent arrives and signs in with the security officer and proceeds to the classroom to await the child's arrival. After the child's arrival, the SP&P staff supports both the child and parent by creating a comfortable setting for play. During the visits the SP&P staff members observe and assist when necessary. These members also encourage, identify, and praise positive parenting when they see it occur. After each visit, the parents meet with the staff and complete a journal entry. Staff members document visits through weekly progress notes. On a monthly basis, the noncustodial parents confer with the staff to allow parents to reflect on progress, and the staff provides parents with feedback and helps set goals for future sessions. Throughout this process the program coordinator keeps in contact with individuals and groups that had referred the children. It is a goal of the program that the noncustodial parents will eventually no longer need supervision when visiting with their children.

The Mentoring program is similar to the SP&P program, with a few key differences. While SP&P serves only noncustodial parents, Mentoring is designed to strengthen parenting skills and to reconcile *any* parent–child relationship. This is done through weekly forty-five-minute individual sessions with one parent, one child, and one staff mentor. Just as in SP&P, Mentoring begins with a parent orientation. There are ten parent–child sessions to follow, with a midway parent conference with the mentor. Mentoring follows a systematic approach. It begins with the mentor interacting with the child the entire first session, with the parent observing. Each week the parent interacts with the child increasingly, while the mentor slowly pulls back and interacts with the child decreasingly. By the halfway point the mentor only interjects and provides feedback when necessary. Through these individual play sessions, communication between the parent and child is improved, parents gain effective parenting skills, and parents and children discover enjoyable and constructive ways of being together. Both SP&P and Mentoring strengthen relationships and extend beyond the playroom to the home, school, and community.

APPENDIX A: SUPERVISED PARENTING AND PLAY PARENT ORIENTATION OUTLINE

Schedule

Staff arrives at 8:30 A.M. (Saturday) or 4:30 P.M. (Thursday)

Visiting parents arrive at 9:15 A.M. (Saturday) or 5:15 P.M. (Thursday)

Children arrive at 9:30 A.M. (Saturday) or 5:30 P.M. (Thursday)

Play Time (free choice)

Snack

Parent/Child(ren) read together

Outdoor Play (or upstairs gym, depending on the weather)

Goodbye
Parent Journal Entry

Parent Responsibilities

Read with your child

Help your child feel important to you

Support and take part in your child's play

Help your child follow program rules and routines (for example, clean up after play in each area)

Use appropriate language with your child

Use positive discipline

Monitor your child's safety and provide necessary help

Participate in monthly parent conferences

Seek child development and parenting information from the staff

Staff Responsibilities

Provide child development and parenting information to parents

Make program decisions

Report suspected child abuse

Ensure children's safety from verbal and physical harm

Parent Record Keeping

Weekly journal entries

Parent conferences/self-assessment

Staff Record Keeping

Attendance/arrival and departure times

Weekly notes

Weekly journal responses

Parent conferences

Children Youth and Families (CYF) referrals only: weekly safety assessments and monthly progress reports

Final reports: objective, descriptive, and without recommendations; given only in response to a court order or CYF request

12

The Child's Rite of Play: The Consequences of Taming the Liminal Stage in Contemporary Rites of Passage

Charlie McCormick

It is rare that popular culture, the mass media, and scholarship concur with each other, but they tend to agree when it comes to contemporary rites of passage. In short, they perceive rites of passage in contemporary society to be in a sorry state: they are either dysfunctional (Grimes, 2000, p. 94), absent (Grof, 1996), or trivialized (Christopher, 1996). D. M. Dooling (1976), former editor of *Parabola*, was one of the earliest individuals to articulate this position when she asked, "What have we done to our rites, and what are they doing to us?" (p. 2). The implicit answer to Dooling's question is "nothing good." But the best way to fix these rites continues to be debated in popular culture, the mass media, and scholarship. The following information participates in this debate by theorizing the practice of two types of rites of passage: those that foster individual capability (those that provide individuals with a glimpse of who they might be) and those that foster individual competency (those that teach individuals who they must be). In doing so, this chapter argues that even though contemporary American society tends to sanction rites of passage, facilitating competency, we can re-create rites of passage fostering capabilities by ritualizing play.

As indicated, many writers and thinkers agree that the idea of rites of passage resonates in contemporary American society. The interest persists, a long line of ritual scholars tells us, because of rites of passage's sociocultural significance. They can transform the lives of individuals and communities. For example, the ethnographer and comparativist Arnold van Gennep (1909, 1960)—who literally wrote the book on rites of passage—compiled cross-cultural evidence in support of his position that rites of passage were transformative. Van Gennep discussed this transformation in terms of a spatial metaphor: Individuals move from, through, and back toward the social group in rites of passage as their social position (their social status) changes. Beyond just speaking in metaphors, van Gennep developed a tripartite model of rites of passage (that he presumed was a universal model) of separation, transition, and incorporation (or reintegration), in which the neophyte was removed from his or her community, reeducated (i.e., transformed), and placed back into the community into his or her new role or status.

Similarly, Victor Turner, a cultural anthropologist of the mid-to-late twentieth century who conducted most of his fieldwork among the Ndembu of Zambia, found rites of passage to be transformative. Focusing his intellectual energies on van Gennep's middle stage of rites of passage (the transitional or liminal phase), his analysis revealed that during this liminal phase novices were able to rid themselves of the norms that usually governed their lives. As they did so, argued Turner (1969, 1995), "we may catch glimpses of the unused evolutionary potential in mankind which has not yet been externalized and fixed in structure" (p. 128). Turner perceived the liminal phase as having immense liberatory potential for individuals; it made them into something new. Interestingly, though, Turner finally saw the initiate's transformation less important than the social group's transformation into a cohesive unit. He wrote that, after the liminal phase, "The ritual subject . . . [returns to] a relatively stable state once more. . . . He is expected to behave in accordance with certain customary norms and ethical standards binding on incumbents of social position in a system of such positions" (p. 95).

While the scholarly literature confirms that rites of passage have transformative potential, there is much less agreement as to whether the location of this significance is the individual's liberation (the individual's development of capabilities) or the social group's cohesion (the individual's development of competency). There is evidence—evidence van Gennep and Turner acknowledged but ultimately found problematic—from many ethnographies that less complex societies locate the significance of rites of passage in the individual's liberatory transformation, that rites of passage transform individuals in ways in which no one could anticipate. It provides a betwixt and between moment wherein individuals discover who they might be rather than who they must be. In short, it makes individuals into men and women (Grimes, 2000, p. 109) who are capable of independent thoughts, actions, and beliefs. The Native American "vision quest" is one of the most frequently referenced examples of a rite of passage that develops the individual's capability. Among the Crow, the vision seeker would induce the vision during the liminal phase through mutilation, fasting, forced insomnia, or hallucinogens. Who or what the supernatural visitant might be could not be anticipated, nor could the visitant's gift—a song, a symbol, a dance, knowledge, or a taboo (Oswalt, 1988, pp. 234–235). The high drama of these experiences—the gore, the grief, the sexual, and the macabre—were not irrelevant. It was useful because, unless forced to, individuals will tend not to push themselves past their presumed capabilities. Jack Kornfield (1996), who was trained as a Buddhist monk, explained why capability resulted from a dramatic liminal period. He quoted his Buddhist teacher as having said,

I'm always asking my students to do difficult things. The food is unpredictable and poor; we sit up all night; it's freezing cold and you only have these simple cotton robes; it's boring here; it's demanding, it's lonely; and you do things that are fearful, like sitting alone all night in the forest. Yet all of it has the purpose of leading you to a freedom in yourself, to something greater than that which you knew to be true. (p. 43)

Contemporary American society also has rites of passage that develop individual capability, but these are in the vast majority of cases considered unofficial rites of passage. As such, they tend to be dysfunctional due to the lack of recognition that these are transformative moments, that these are rites of passage (Foster, 1996).

Though Turner clearly identified the individual's development of new capabilities during the liminal phase, this development confused him. He knew the individual grew as an individual during rites of passage, but the community—seemingly despite the individual's growth—was strengthened too. Even Barbara Myerhoff (1982), one of the most important rite of passage theorists in the late twentieth century, would finally characterize this situation—so confusing to Turner—as a paradox. She stated, "Transformation is the ultimate goal in life-crisis ceremonies" (p. 131). This is not to suggest, however, that social integration is absent or irrelevant in her conception of the activity. On the contrary, social integration is integral to the activity; she notes: "Rites of passage certainly do not *cause* social integration, rather they reflect and enhance it" (p. 128). Neither van Gennep, Turner, nor Myerhoff had an appropriate model through which they could unravel this seeming paradox of an experience that generated innovative individuals who were then seamlessly affiliated with and subjected to the prevailing and normative social structures. Lacking this model, van Gennep and Turner could only assume that the cohesion of the social group finally ascended over the liberated individual as the outcome of rites of passage. Social structure triumphed over individual will (Weber, 1995). It is a conclusion that has been embraced by contemporary American society, given the influence of Joseph Campbell (1988), Clarissa Pinkola Estés (1992), and Robert Bly (1990), all of whom wrote best-selling books invoking the idea of rites of passage or initiation and were influenced by the work of van Gennep and Turner.

Because contemporary American society regards as official those rites of passage that develop competency, our rites have little of the high drama associated with the liminal stage in less complex societies. We are not trying to scare initiates or expand the limits of their physical, mental, and emotional beings, so the drama is largely unnecessary. Instead, we are trying to get youth, in particular, to accept normative modes of conduct and belief (see Howe and Strauss, 2000, for a full explanation of the motivations surrounding this effort). For example, American youth experience the rite of receiving the driver's license and more social privileges only after they have proven themselves competent at following driving rules. Steven Zeitlin (1992) verified that this process of enculturation and cultural reproduction is foregrounded in contemporary rites of passage when he stated, "Contemporary customs of passage stress incorporation more than separation or transition" (p. 10). Of course, Zeitlin invoked the idea of incorporation rather than competency, but incorporation only works when individuals are competent enough in the organizational structure to act cooperatively. Zeitlin's position on the orientation of contemporary rites of passage was supported by the Christian author Martin Marty (1989), who clearly identified that whatever is happening with rites of passage today, rites of passage are not developing youth's capabilities. He wrote, "Modern life undercuts the ordeals, the liminal experiences, the rites and the reintegration. . . . Many Christians don't learn catechism, endure public examination, pass through terror and get confirmed in the vivid ways our generation did" (p. 703).

Contemporary American society tends to be an impersonal, bureaucratic world that encourages following rules rather than making reflective moral decisions. We thrive in this environment when we are competent adults. The term's association with responsibility, maturity, citizenship, and clear-headedness is intended. Therefore, rites of passage that are oriented toward competency are essential. What seems less necessary are the potency and uncertainty that accompany rites of passage oriented toward competency. Instead, individuals must become competent in everyday life and content with this competence. In fact, they should valorize it. That is what being an adult is all about.

To be fair, it is not just the contemporary world that seeks to develop competent—rule-governed—individuals. Anthropologists Schlegel and Barry (1980), for instance, noted that rites of passage for girls predominated in simple societies, where females played a more important role in food production, while in middle-range societies rites of passage for boys predominated, since most communal activities were carried on by men. In other words, there appeared to be a correlation between rites of passage and adult responsibilities.

It was argued earlier that contemporary American society's decision to make official rites of passage that develop competency—and unofficial rites of passage that develop capability—is a decision influenced by a popular culture that was itself influenced by perplexed researchers. This is not meant to imply, however, that rites of passage that are oriented toward competency lack worth. On the contrary, the benefits are clear. The best result of this orientation is greater group cohesion. Presumably, if the individuals understand the organizing structure and rules, then a community can take shape. In addition, the contemporary American context demands that individuals have a precise understanding of, aptitude for, and performance ability in a specific set of skills and situations. After all, we are able to control—however limitedly—the environments in which we live. Therefore, we do not need to be able to prepare for the unknown (or do we?); we need opportunities to learn competency in our structured environment, to value this environment, and to accept it as natural. Finally, in the absence of competency rites, coming of age can quickly devolve into a violent, peer-driven initiation that becomes progressively more dangerous (Grimes, 2000, p. 94).

These benefits notwithstanding, something is lost when rites of passage are oriented toward competency rather than capability. Perhaps most important, youth are not provided with the opportunity for autonomy, and they therefore cannot be asked to assume responsibility for this autonomy. This is a perpetual problem in all teaching and learning situations, of which rites of passage is one variation. Teachers constantly fight against the idea of "letting go," of letting learning happen through trial and error, which includes the chance to make mistakes. Rites of passage that have as their end competency—like other learning situations—deny the child the opportunity to question the status quo—sometimes mistakenly—and to realize the extent to which his or her values, beliefs, and behaviors are constrained and influenced by sociocultural forces.

Interestingly enough, there is evidence indicating that as rites of passage develop individual capability, the community becomes stronger. This seems, of course, counterintuitive. Certainly, van Gennep, Turner, and to a lesser extent Myerhoff found it counterintuitive. But it happens nonetheless. Martin Marty (1989) wrote, "The more water churches use for baptism, the more they restrict baptism to adolescent or older people, and the more they have an ordeal, a liminal stage before integration into community, *the higher their growth rate*" (p. 345, emphasis added). He is suggesting that as individuals experience growth, the community grows too. Arguably, this process need not be perceived as counterintuitive when it is imagined as a gift exchange.

The idea of a gift exchange seems to be the theoretical model (a model that postdated van Gennep and Turner) necessary to reconcile the paradox of rites of passage that both liberates the individual and strengthens the social group at the same time. Lewis Hyde (1979, 1983), author of *The Gift*, describes gift exchange in this way:

The gifts we give at times of transformation are meant to make visible the giving up we do invisibly. And of course we hope that there will be an exchange, that something will come towards us if we abandon our old lives. So we might also say that the tokens we receive at times of change are meant to make visible life's reciprocation. They are not mere compensation for what is lost, but the promise of what lies ahead. They guide us towards new life. (p. 44; see also Anttonen, 1992)

What this means is that individuals with capability can "gift" their communities, can bring their potential powers to their communities, if the community "gifts" the individual with a higher social status and an understanding that this individual has been transformed with capabilities. The exchange reconciles the paradox.

The ritual solution that D. M. Dooling (1976) was looking for now seems apparent. Contemporary American society should reorientate its rites of passage toward fostering individual capabilities. But a major obstacle remains. If this is done, somebody is going to be hurt. The liminal phase in rites of passage that develop capability seems too dangerous not to be tamed. Thomas Leemon (1997), commenting on George Harley's work with the initiation of the Poro of Liberia in the 1930s, clearly illustrated this danger when he wrote, "Some neophytes do not survive [the rite of passage]. . . . Should death result, the neophyte is buried and he is never mentioned" (p. 8). Today there would be a lawsuit. While taming liminality seems a rational enough response, logic indicates it may not be. After all, why does our culture think pain is so shameful, that it is to be avoided at all costs? Why do we think that postponing pain in childhood postpones it indefinitely? Why do we assume that hurting is easier to handle when it hits us later rather than earlier? Why do we assume that physical scars are worse than psychological or developmental scars? These are tough questions, and they go a long way toward showing that culture tends to trump logic in everyday life almost every time. Adults do not want their children to get seriously hurt, but they do want their children to know what their capabilities are. Adults want their children to know who they might be, not who society thinks they should be. This may sound like a great idea, but if this realization can only accompany a potentially dangerous situation, then most adults in contemporary American society are going to assume it should stay an idea.

Fortunately, it is possible to theorize a situation in which this realization could occur that is not brutal at all. Indeed, it need only be playful. More specifically, it needs to be ritualized play. To ritualize play, adults must (1) establish ritual opportunities—but not outcomes—for transformation to occur to the individual initiate, (2) mark this transformation externally (so that the initiator has a tangible marker of the internal transformation), and (3) implicate this play in a relationship based on gift exchange (so that the initiators are cognizant of the initiate's transformative moment).

It is possible to imagine as least two types of ritual play opportunities that would facilitate individual transformation and the development of capabilities. The first type would be rough, hard play. This would be a complement to (not a replacement for) imaginative, creative, and/or nice play. Rough, hard play is not the same as playing disturbing video games or watching action–adventure movies. There are no consequences to that sort of mediated play. Rough, hard play with presumed (though never final) consequences puts youth in a situation in which they must—or at least have the opportunity to—find out what they are capable of. Absent this situation, a child might never know his or her capabilities unless there was a moment of real crisis—not play crisis—or unless this individual could afford one of the extreme vacations that are now available. To heighten the experience of this sort of play, the elder involved in the ritual should resist the child's performance of the rite even as this adult organizes it. Like the presumably threatening play itself, the resistance of adults to the performance gives the ritual play a transformative dimension.

The other type of ritual play opportunity facilitating capability would be disenchanting play (Grimes, 2000, p. 136). Disenchanting play is play where people fail, where they get hurt, where they learn there is no Santa Claus. Syndicated columnist Bob Greene (1984), writing in *Esquire*, described the importance of disenchanting play about, in his case, the importance of being cut from the team. He wrote that when he was twelve he tried out for the seventh grade basketball team. One day he walked into the gym and discovered the "cut" list that the coach had posted without warning, indicating who would remain on the team. His name was not on the list. He wrote,

I held myself together as I walked out of the gym and out of the school, but when I got home I began to sob. I couldn't stop. For the first time in my life, I had been told officially that I wasn't good enough. . . . All these years later, I remember it as if I were still standing right there in the gym. . . . I don't know how the mind works in matters like this; I don't know what went on in my head following that day when I was cut. But I know that my ambition has been enormous even since then; I know that for all my life since that day, I have done more work than I had to be doing, taken more assignments than I had to be taking, put in more hours than I had to be spending. I don't know if all of that came from a determination never to allow myself to be cut again—never to allow someone to tell me that I'm not good enough again—but I know it's there. (p. 10)

People need moments of disenchantment for their capabilities to emerge. But these disenchantments must be marked as rites of passage, as tranformative moments that grow the individual rather than shrinking the individual.

In addition to establishing play as a transformative opportunity, the experience must be marked externally to call the initiate's attention to the internal transformation. Without this marking, the significance of the moment may very well be lost by the initiate, and transformation will not happen or it will be only temporary. This marking does not have to be on the order of tattooing or circumcision; it could be a simple pin or henna design on the arm, anything to indicate that a threshold has been crossed and that the individual should recognize this even as others have.

Finally, whether hard or disenchanting play, if play is to transform the individual without incurring the wrath of the social group it must become implicated in a gift exchange; this play must become a gift that is reciprocated. In other words, initiation must become as much for the initiators as it is for the initiates. Initiators must welcome the capable individual into the social group as a changed individual who is deserving of greater rights and responsibilities: This is the group's gift to the initiate. The individual's gift to the social group will perhaps never be fully realized, since it was his or her willingness to experience and endure the transformative moment that provided this individual with creative capability and potential (Turner, 1982, p. 28; Sutton-Smith, 1997, p. 221).

Rites of passage have long been constructed and reconstructed because of need, sociocultural trends, strategic manipulation, and dumb luck. This is indisputable. It is a misguided and ultimately hopeless exercise to try to establish which of these is the "authentic" rite of passage (Bendix, 1997). None of these variations are entirely perfect, and none are entirely lacking in worth. It is important, however, to theorize the differential impacts associated with different practices of rites of passage. This chapter has theorized the differential impacts of rites of passage that foster individual capability and rites of passage that foster individual competency. By analyzing the impacts associated with each of these orientations, it has questioned what—if any—benefit there is in perpetuating contemporary rites of passage that tame liminality, engendering competencies instead of individual capabilities. It has argued that the benefits are minimal and the possibility of damage to the individual's development great. It has also theorized a practice of rites of passage that builds the individual's capability without undermining the cohesion of the social group. This happens through ritualized play. But enough theorizing and words—our children have a rite to play.

REFERENCES

Anttonen, P. (1992). The Rites of Passage Revisited: A New Look at van Gennep's Theory of the Ritual Process and Its Application in the Study of Finnish–Karelian Wedding Rituals. *Temenos* 28: 15–52.

Bendix, R. (1997). *In Search of Authenticity: The Formation of Folklore Studies*. Madison: University of Wisconsin Press.

Bly, R. (1990). *Iron John: A Book about Men*. New York: Vintage Books.

Campbell, J. (1988). *The Power of Myth, with Bill Moyers* (Betty Sue Flowers, Ed.). New York: Doubleday.

Christopher, N. G. (1996). Service as a Right of Passage. In L. C. Mahdi, N. G. Christopher, & M. Meade (Eds.), *Crossroads: The Quest for Contemporary Rites of Passage* (pp. 125–131). Chicago: Open Court.

Dooling, D. M. (1976). Focus. *Parabola* 1(4): 1–2.

Estés, C. P. (1992). *Women Who Run with Wolves*. New York: Ballantine Books.

Foster, S. (1996). Bunny Bashing into Manhood. In L. C. Mahdi, N. G. Christopher, & M. Meade (Eds.), *Crossroads: The Quest for Contemporary Rites of Passage* (pp. 339–352). Chicago: Open Court.

Greene, B. (1984). Cut. *Esquire* 102 (July): 10.

Grimes, R. L. (2000). *Deeply into the Bone: Re-inventing Rites of Passage*. Berkeley and Los Angeles: University of California Press.

Grof, C. (1996). Rites of Passage: A Necessary Step toward Wholeness. In L. C. Mahdi, N. G. Christopher, & M. Meade (Eds.), *Crossroads: The Quest for Contemporary Rites of Passage* (pp. 3–15). Chicago: Open Court.

Howe, N., & W. Strauss. (2000). *Millennials Rising: The Next Great Generation*. New York: Vintage.

Hyde, L. (1979, 1983). *The Gift: Imagination and the Erotic Life of Property*. New York: Vintage Books.

Kornfield, J. (1996). Buddhist Monastic Traditions. In L. C. Mahdi, N. G. Christopher, & M. Meade (Eds.), *Crossroads: The Quest for Contemporary Rites of Passage* (pp. 41–50). Chicago: Open Court.

Marty, M. E. (1989). Rites of Passage II. *The Christian Century* 106 (July 19–26): 703.

Myerhoff, B. (1982). Rites of Passage: Process and Paradox. In Victor Turner (Ed.), *Celebration: Studies in Festivity and Ritual* (pp. 109–135). Washington, DC: Smithsonian Institution Press.

Oswalt, W. H. (1988). *This Land Was Theirs: A Study of North American Indians* (4th ed.). Mountain View, CA: Mayfield.

Schlegel, A., & Barry, H. (1980). The Evolutionary Significance of Adolescent Initiation Ceremonies. *American Ethnologist* 7(4): 696–715.

Sutton-Smith, B. (1997). *The Ambiguity of Play*. Cambridge: Harvard University Press.

Turner, V. (1982). *From Ritual to Theatre: The Human Seriousness of Play*. New York: PAJ.

———. (1969, 1995). *The Ritual Process: Structure and Anti-Structure*. New York: Aldine de Gruyter.

van Gennep, A. (1909, 1960). *The Rites of Passage* (Trans. Monika Vizedom and Gabrielle Caffee). Chicago: University of Chicago Press.

Weber, D. (1995). From Limen to Border: A Meditation on the Legacy of Victor Turner for American Cultural Studies. *American Quarterly* 47(3): 525–536.

Zeitlin, S. (1992). The Life Cycle: Folk Customs of Passage. In P. B. Nelson (Ed.), *Rites of Passage in America: Traditions of the Life Cycle* (pp. 8–23). Philadelphia: The Balch Institute for Ethnic Studies.

PART II

PLAY TIME

Part II opens with Bruce D. Grossman providing a foundation for understanding play as conceptualized by Piaget, with particular attention on the belief that play is critical to the child's intellectual growth. Grossman supports Piaget and has further contributed to the documentation of the case in favor of preserving play's valuable role in the early development of children. With a clear view of the reality of play in Taiwan, Pei-Yu Chang presents a meaningful case study of a traditional Taiwanese, academically oriented kindergarten with respect to the cultural and political forces that deprive children of play experiences. Specific research findings are shared and suggestions for change are included to reinforce the basic tenet that play provides the context for children to learn, to explore, to express their ideas, and to have fun. The international perspective continues with Mei-Chun Lin, James E. Johnson, and Karen McChesney Johnson discussing Montessori-influenced kindergartens in Hsin-Chu, Taichung, Taiwan, and Beijing with consideration for play environments, special events, and dramatic play centers and props. This chapter directs the reader toward findings targeted at the context of early education globalization and specific cultural contexts and argues for equal status accorded to academic and playful activities. The authors summarize their chapter with a list of suggestions for culturally grounding new Early Childhood Education programs.

Carolyn M. Patterson incorporates the theories of Piaget and Vygotsky with exploration and hands-on learning to view an alternative perspective on how children construct their own knowledge bases. The chapter continues with a comparison of Piaget and Vygotsky to Howard Gardner's multiple intelligences and the importance of interactive play with peers and adults. Several original activities are shared that support the argument for increased play opportunities to promote growth in early years as a foundation for lifelong learning. Monica McHale-Small and Tabatha A. Uhrich outline the use of play, movement, and fun to motivate students as they learn beginning literacy concepts and convert even the most reticent of emergent readers. Several samples of innovative movement activities are provided that clarify the need to reinforce early reading skills while meeting the needs of kinesthetic learners. Paramvir Singh identifies the inextricable relationship between play and sport. In this chapter he compares the basic needs of children in developed countries with the needs of children in developing and undeveloped countries. He raises the question of the impact of hunger, economy, malnutrition, and inactivity on children in underdeveloped countries and contrasts this with the impact of overtraining, technological innovations, and medical manipulations on children in developed countries. Lynda Reeves examines how individuals with motoric diversity can easily become "active" participants through developmentally appropriate pedagogy. She proposes that developmental appropriate pedagogy enables all children to play successfully in an inclusive environment, not merely those children previously labeled. Attention is called to the collaborative relationship between children and their teachers that is fostered when developmentally appropriate pedagogy is facilitated in the learning environment. Marianne Torbert examines how children become active learners and critical problem solvers through the creation of a productive and cooperative learning environment where children explore divergent movement possibilities and generate possible solutions to movement problems. Connections are made in this chapter between the constructivist approach and traditional methods of teaching physical education. A strong case is made to consider the individual differences that are perceived among children and require an approach to education where differences are celebrated and used as positive contributing factors within the growth process.

Anne M. Rothschadl and Christopher M. Nunes share information on developmentally suitable sports programming for ages three and up, with a focus on the means for creating activities appropriate for four distinct age groups. A commitment by adults to consider the need for active play and successful models of youth sport programming are highlighted in this chapter. Beatriz Pereira identifies research findings collected from over 2,300 children in public schools in Portugal and the significant differences concerning gender and bullying behaviors. This chapter describes an intervention program for reducing bullying behaviors in school settings, especially on playground facilities. An interesting literature review contains an overview of the most recent research data on bullying behaviors. Eva Peterson shares an interesting perspective on social relations as a dominant feature of young children's play activities, whereby actions on a playground affect the way that children learn to treat each other. The expectations of adults and the influence adults have over the play environment dramatically impact the policies and rules that come to govern the traditional playground context. Susan Hudson and Donna Thompson introduce the readers to the work of the National Program for Playground Safety and address the current statistics regarding the maintenance of a safe and inviting school and community playground. Their overview of unsafe conditions and unsafe actions associated with playground risks is insightful and offers suggestions to minimize risks while maximize playful opportunities. Finally, Leah Holland Fiorentino looks at a unique approach for integrating assessment tools into the play environment. She encourages play professionals to ensure accountability in their programs by keeping records of formal observations using new hardware and software and connecting the world of play to the world of technology.

13

Play and Cognitive Development: A Piagetian Perspective

Bruce D. Grossman

Children and people. They grow into tomorrow only as they live today.
—John Dewey (1859–1952)

The spontaneous activity of play, a universal characteristic of healthy infants and young children, appears to be under increased attack in many industrialized nations. This chapter briefly assesses developments in the battle against play occurring during the past forty years in the United States. Particular emphasis, however, is placed on the research and theories of Jean Piaget, which have contributed to the documentation of the case in favor of preserving play's valuable role in the early development of children.

In the late 1960s, when the Johnson administration initiated "Head Start," those of us involved in early childhood education were concerned that, in an effort to hurry so-called disadvantaged children, the traditional play atmosphere of nursery schools would be abandoned in favor of a more structured, pre-academic curriculum. Indeed, the professionals involved in educating three- and four-year-olds from poverty backgrounds debated about just how much didactic recitation should replace the more relaxed free play environment favored by the National Association for the Education of Young Children (NAEYC). At about the same time, the Children's Television Network was producing *Sesame Street* and the *Electric Company*, both of which seemed to embrace a more didactic, formal approach to teaching letters and numbers to young children at home, using a speedy format borrowed from advertising.

Meanwhile, American psychologists and educators became aware of the research of a Swiss philosopher named Jean Piaget. Piaget described himself as a "genetic epistomologist." He was less interested in the application of his research than in studying how the human mind developed—specifically, how we know what we know as we grow and develop. Ironically, even when there was national pressure to structure and evaluate the performance of preschool children, early childhood educators were armed with the findings of Piaget and his colleagues at the Rousseau Institute, who argued that allowing children to play freely with a variety of objects was in fact the best way to promote their cognitive growth. Piaget's thesis was especially well articulated in his book, *The Construction of Reality in the Child* (1954), where he described how the young child builds or fashions a mental picture of his or her world out of the experiences that child has while moving about in it.

Of course, maturation plays a significant role here. Unlike such behaviorists as Jerome Bruner (1977), who tend to believe that anything can be taught to a child at any age if it is presented properly, Piaget insisted that the child must be neurologically ready to really understand what is being taught. Otherwise, the concept or idea being taught is an affectation at best. A good example is the concept of number. While a child of three or four may be taught to count, it is not until at least age five, when "conservation" is possible, that the child has an actual sense of number. So, even after counting a series of objects that are lined up with space between each, when the space between the counted objects is eliminated and when these objects are suddenly lumped together, a preoperational child will maintain that there are now fewer objects. Counting, then, does not give a child a constant sense of how many a group of objects represents, since the number changes with appearance.

What affects a child's intellectual growth—maturation or experience? In effect, Piaget maintained that you need both, which is hardly surprising, but it supported the notion long held by teachers who worked with young children that experience alone is not enough. In a recent article, Leonard Sax (2001) offers a brief review of the so-called kindergarten movement. He reminds us that the eighteenth-century French philosopher Jean-Jacques Rousseau argued against attempting to teach children to read at an early age. Two hundred years before Piaget published his research, Rousseau maintained, as Sax put it, "Children must first learn to develop their own minds free of adult influence" (p. 3).

Influenced no doubt by Rousseau, as well as by Swiss educator Johann Pestalozzi, Friedrich Froebel created the first "Kindergarten" in Germany in 1837 (Brosterman, 1997), where the emphasis was not on teaching reading and other academic skills, but literally on gardening and other first-hand experiences. In the 1940s, a well-known American pediatric researcher, Arnold Geselle, popularized the concept of "readiness," exhorting parents and teachers to hold off instruction until their children were biologically "ready." (Geselle & Ilg, 1943). Geselle was also waging a struggle against the behaviorists, such as John Watson, who maintained that it was never too early to begin a child's training. That was the era when experts recommended "scheduled feedings" of infants (i.e., every three hours), rather than on demand.

For the following twenty or so years, early childhood educators, as represented by the NAEYC, were still trying to keep the pressure off preschool-age children. They promoted curricula stressing creative, social, and, especially, hands-on activities. They also advocated choice, describing the teacher as a facilitator rather than as a director of children's activity or an authority on learning. These teachers regarded the young children's sense of wonder and boundless energy as both evidence of the intrinsic appeal of self-directed learning and as a source of power to accomplish this exciting exploration.

As noted previously, in the 1960s educators and the general public were being told, more insistently than ever, that in the modern industrialized world there was no time for play in the natural sense. Play was justified only when described as the child's "work," and, as such, needed to be scheduled and directed for the optimum performance level, especially for so-called culturally deprived children, meaning poor minority children. At best, free play was a luxury only rich and middle-class children could afford (Grossman, 1968).

In response to this renewed pressure for early childhood to enter the academic mainstream, Piaget was embraced as the scientific white knight who had suddenly appeared on the academic horizon shouting, "Don't push those children. Give them an exciting, encouraging, safe environment and let them play." Although his writings had been published for over two decades (mostly in French), suddenly his researched-based findings helped to affirm and legitimize what teachers of young children had observed in the classroom. Specifically, Piaget regarded the child's mind not as being like a camera taking a picture that is an exact replica of what exists in the world outside, but as being a painter's brush creating a personal, unique interpretation of reality.

Piaget posited stages of cognitive growth that imposed limitations on how children could view the world, which in turn accounted for their perceptions being different than those of older children and adults. Certainly, adults could get around these limitations by telling their children what the world looked like and could even provide labels for these ready-made perceptions, but according to Piaget and most early childhood educators, while this may make those children appear to be smart, this process is not the same as knowing for themselves. Most important, by repeating what adults told them was so, the children did not really understand what they had supposedly learned. In that case they were either likely to lose this information more readily or at least relinquish the ability to evaluate the material or to actually think about it beyond mindless repetition.

The type of learning that interested Piaget was markedly different from the behaviorist view dominating American psychology. It was not simply a matter of strengthening connections between a stimulus and response, as B. F. Skinner contended. Piagetans maintained that true learning involved integrating new experiences into children's existent mental structure by a process he termed "assimilation" and "accommodation." In effect, when confronted with a new experience or bit of data, all humans, adults as well as children, initially react by attempting to fit the new event into what they already know (assimilation), but if their action or understanding is not successful, they experience a tension (disequilibrium) and are then likely to change their behavior or their perception (accommodation). In this case, the event leads to a new or altered mental structure (schemata) (Piaget, 1954).

An important point here should be considered before discussing one's own experiences and views related to the learning process; the role of maturation. Behaviorists were not much concerned with this natural growth except as it restricted children's response capability. They usually attempted to get around this limitation when training animals or young children by breaking down more complex responses into smaller units ("successive approximations") that could then be combined to produce a desired outcome. Piaget, like most early childhood educators, took the process of maturation more seriously. He advised postponing certain learning tasks until children were biologically ready: Two good examples are toilet training and reading. In both of those cases it has been established that, ironically, premature training can result either in a delay or an unfavorable outcome for these skills.

Piaget also offered some very specific notions about how experience affects intellectual development. He focused on two types of direct experience that are likely to influence how individuals view the world and, consequently, how they know what they know: (1) through physical activity (i.e., seeing, touching, manipulating objects, etc.) and (2) through social activity. Added to this mixture of experience is the child's and ultimately the adolescent's or adult's ability to think logically and use abstract reasoning. Even during the child's earliest years, what Piaget termed the "sensory-motor period," there is evidence of an increasing capacity to perform mental operations ("logical mathematical") on concrete experiences. For example, Piaget noted that during the second year of life an infant can begin to take an already acquired action and invent new variations or uses. He argued that this baby is thinking, even before he or she has acquired language (Piaget, 1954).

Piaget did less research on social activity. Nonetheless, he regarded the admittedly arbitrary version of the world attained from observing and talking with others as playing a very significant role in mental development. Much of our knowledge, including language and moral behavior, is derived from what we are told or see, but while this information may go unquestioned at first, as we acquire the mental capacity to think we are increasingly able to put this information to the test of logic and reason and essentially compare this socially derived information with our own direct experience (Wadsworth, 1996).

How do these Piagetian ideas conform to early childhood educational practice? First, they support the value of social play—characteristic of an early childhood classroom. Traditionally, programs for young children have emphasized the importance of encouraging social interaction in the form of cooperative play and group time discussions. Typically, there is far less time devoted to social interaction among the children in a pre-academic classroom. Second, consistent with Piaget's ideas about the process of accommodation leading to new mental structures, social interaction provides a challenge to children's preexisting way of seeing or doing things. So, in the free play atmosphere of the early childhood center, children have the opportunity to learn for themselves about the physical world, with the assistance of teachers. They also have to deal with the intellectual challenges presented by interaction with their classmates and the important rules and routines of the classroom.

Given Piaget's contention that children naturally create their own personal cognitive structures, it might well be asked what an adult's role is in this model. As indicated earlier, Piaget believed that children's general experience in a setting filled with opportunities to explore is most beneficial. The materials and the opportunities to explore them is of course provided by teachers, but the structure and meaning comes out of each child's interaction with this physical and social world. Play is, by definition, spontaneous and free, rather than adult directed. Ideally, the children create the rules and make their own conclusions about what has taken place. For the most part, in the early years that Piaget called the "preoperational period" the process is intuitive. Children at this stage are unable to explain why they are reacting as they do, but their actions suggest that they are learning or adapting to the physical and social requirements that they encounter.

Seemingly, most teachers of young children and most programs in the United States cannot completely follow the Piagetian model. Even when these educators agree with Piaget's theoretical position, in practice they feel the need to provide some structure and direction to children, usually in the form of coaching or guiding activities. Structure for play is also evident in the selection of materials and their arrangement in the classroom. Teachers are predisposed to taking into account the children's age, as well as their specific interests, or they might actively demonstrate a crafts project, for example, or choose to point out certain environmental features on a walk with the children. Most would regard this type of intervention as potentially helpful to a child's construction of his or her cognitive map, as long as it was not excessive and allowed for restructuring by the child. Lev Vygotsky (1978), the Russian developmental psychologist, called this form of adult support "scaffolding," allowing children to "climb higher," metaphorically speaking. Vygotsky agreed with Piaget's stages of cognitive development, but argued that it is appropriate for adults to gently guide children to the next developmental level when the opportunity arises.

Likely as not, Piaget would say, "What's the hurry? Children will get there on their own," but Americans tend to be impatient. In that regard, I would recommend reading David Elkind's (1988) book *The Hurried Child* for an awareness of the dangers of pushing children too fast. Clearly, most people have not heeded his warning. We need to make some allowance for the demands of our fast-paced society. Children need time to enjoy play that is not competitive or subject to adult judgment. Most important, they need to have fun.

REFERENCES

Bruner, J. S. (1977). *The Process of Education*. Cambridge: Harvard University Press.
Brosterman, N. (1997). *Inventing Kindergarten*. New York: Harry Adams.

Elkind, D. (1988). *The Hurried Child: Growing Up Too Fast Too Soon* (rev. ed). Reading, MA: Addison-Wesley.

Geselle, A., & F. L. Ilg. (1943). *Infant and Child in the Culture Today*. New York: Harper and Bros.

Grossman, B. (1968). The Academic Grind at Age Three. *Teacher's College Record* 70(30): 227–231.

Piaget, J. (1954). *The Construction of Reality in the Child* (M. Cook, Trans.). New York: Basic Books.

Sax, L. (2001). Reclaiming Kindergarten. *Psychology of Men and Masculinity* 2: 3–12.

Vygotsky, L. S. (1978). *Mind in Society: The Development of Higher Psychological Processes*. Cambridge: Harvard University Press.

Wadsworth, B. J. (1996). *Piaget's Theory of Cognitive and Affective Development: Foundations of Constructivism* (5th ed.). White Plains, NY: Longman.

14

Academia versus Child's Play: A Cultural Conflict in Taiwan

Pei-Yu Chang

Education is not the filling of a pail, but the lighting of a fire.
—William Butler Yeats (1865–1939)

Play as an important vehicle for children to learn has been supported by historical experts and current researchers. Its early supporters included Rousseau, Dewey, Piaget, and Vygotsky. Rousseau (1977), in *Emile*, clearly indicates that children should be allowed to play. Dewey (1916) believes that children should learn from real-life experiences and emphasizes the value of constructive play and make-believe play. Piaget's constructivism reveals the importance of self-regulated play (Forman & Kuschner, 1983). Vygotsky (1978) considered play as the main source for children's development because it creates a zone of proximal development. Current research also provides substantial evidence supporting the value of play. According to Johnson, Christie, and Yawkey (1999), play reflects, reinforces, and results in children's development. In addition to the developmental value, Johnson (in press) indicates that play also has educational values and expressive values. Play provides the context for children to learn, explore, express their ideas, and have fun. As a result, a play-based curriculum is recommended as a developmentally appropriate practice in fostering children's learning and development (Bredekamp & Copple, 1997).

Play is children's innate language and favorite activity around the world. However, its nature and meanings vary in different contexts. King (1992) asserts that the meaning of human behavior derives from the context in which it occurs. To adequately interpret children's experiences and understand the learning process therein requires the investigation of cultural and societal contexts where the actions occur. To understand children's play, the impacts of contexts cannot be ignored.

Though play has been considered an important component of early childhood program in western countries, it is not a sanctioned school activity in some private Taiwanese kindergartens. This chapter presents a case study of a traditional Taiwanese kindergarten class (Class Dragon in the Efficient Learning School), one demonstrating the submission of children's play in an early childhood program to a cultural emphasis on academics. Adult beliefs and the arrangement of activities for their children are responsive to the requirement for successfully surviving in the cultural and social context of Taiwan. The sources and rationales for the influences of parental beliefs on children's learning and play are evidenced by inspecting the cultural impacts and societal forces in Taiwan. An analysis of them yields a more complete contextual understanding of children's play (or the lack thereof) in traditional private kindergartens serving lower-income families in an urban setting in Taiwan.

The Efficient Learning School was a private kindergarten located in Chufong, a northwestern city of Taiwan. There were over 300 children enrolled in this school. Unlike most of the private kindergartens in Taiwan, this school had a policy of waiving the registration fee and lowering the monthly fee. This policy was one of the main features attracting parents in enrolling their children in the school, because over 70 percent of the parents had a low monthly income.

Class Dragon had thirty-five children and one regular teacher who helped children learn basic math, use the abacus, do mental math, use computers, and recognize and write both Chinese characters and phonics. Textbooks and worksheets were the main learning materials. Children were expected to be quiet, sit well, and work hard on workbooks all of the time. As a result, opportunities for social interaction were not given. In addition, written homework were assigned every day. Each semester, two paper-and-pencil tests were administered for evaluating children's acquisition of academic skills and concepts. Along with the learning of academic subjects, there were English and arts classes taught by itinerant instructors: two English teachers, an art teacher, a music teacher, a dance teacher, and a physical education teacher. There was no playground or free playtime provided. The only toys and play equipment available were a basket of small blocks, two slides, and some tricycles. Children seldom played with these toys and play equipment; they were allowed only when there was extra time left from structured lessons or when children behaved well.

One of the main criteria parents used in choosing a kindergarten was the curriculum or activities provided. It was quite clear that most parents sent their children to the Efficient Learning School because they expected them to master academic skills (e.g., recognition of Chinese phonics and characters, basic math, etc.), so as to well prepare them for elementary school. Parents' preference of academic excellence causes an emphasis on work over play. This phenomenon reveals that the role of play in early childhood programs is related to the purpose of early childhood education and parents' expectations. Although both the teacher and parents indicated that play was helpful for children, their understanding of learning through play seemed to be limited. The teacher's articulation of learning through play was concerning the use of toys to capture children's attention (e.g., the English teacher threw a ball to a child and required him or her to repeat a vocabulary word after the teacher). Likewise, parents seemed to have little understanding about the value of play in children's learning. Most did not believe that children could learn solely through play. Their perception of learning meant providing structured lessons using textbooks and practice worksheets. Play had no relationship with learning, and children could not play until they had finished their assignments.

Bronfenbrenner's (1979) ecological theory of human development showed that development is the interaction of a growing person with the changing environment. As discussed earlier, children's rights to play are related to parental beliefs of the purpose of early childhood education. Parents' expectations or selections of schools for their children are influenced by the traditional Chinese culture and the societal force operative in Taiwan. In traditional Chinese society, scholars were greatly respected and education was highly esteemed (Chen & Teng, 1995). Consequently, possessing higher education was strongly valued. The importance of education is still valued. Parents do their best to support their children's education because higher education ensures higher income, more prominent social status, fine clothes, and luxury living conditions. On the other hand, the belief of malleability valued in traditional Chinese culture is another force that affects children's learning. Chinese children are viewed as moldable clay; thus, training and didactic instruction are regarded as effective teaching methods. Children learn from imitating more skillful adults instead of through explorations or play (Gardner, 1989).

The exam-oriented educational system in Taiwan causes parents to judge children's success or failure based upon their performance and achievement in school-related tasks. Parents seem to have a narrow definition of success, since they tend to believe that failure in school is failure in life (Chen & Teng, 1995). Parental demands on children to be successful in their school work begins in the early years of schooling. As a result, a large percentage of parents favor schools that focus on the acquisition of academic skills. Direct instruction rather than play is believed to be a more effective way of helping children to master academic skills.

REFERENCES

Bredekamp, S. E., & C. Copple (eds.). (1997). *Developmentally Appropriate Practice in Early Childhood Programs* (rev. ed.). Washington, DC: NAEYC.

Bronfenbrenner, U. (1979). *The Ecology of Human Development*. Cambridge: Harvard University Press.

Chen, H.-M., & H. F. Teng. (1995). No Longer Just an Academic Question: Educational Alternatives Come to Taiwan. *Sinorama* 20(3): 8–20.

Dewey, J. (1916). *Democracy and Education*. New York: The Free Press.

Forman, G. E., & D. S. Kuschner. (1983). *The Child's Construction of Knowledge: Piaget for Teaching Children*. Washington, DC: NAEYC.

Gardner, H. (1989). The Key in the Slot: Creativity in a Chinese Key. *Journal of Aesthetic Education* 23(1): 141–155.

Johnson, J. E. (in press). Developmental Theory and Research and Child's Play That Is Educational. In C. Y. Chien with J. E. Johnson (Eds.), *Developmental Play Applications to Early Childhood Education Curriculum*. Taipei, Taiwan: Psychological Publishing.

Johnson, J. E., J. F. Christie, & T. D. Yawkey. (1999). *Play and Early Childhood Development*. White Plains, NY: Longman.

King, N. R. (1992). The Impact of Context on the Play of Young Children. In S. A. Kessler & B. B. Swadener (Eds.), *Reconceptualizing the Early Childhood Curriculum: Beginning the Dialogue* (pp. 43–61). New York: Teachers College Press.

Rousseau, J. J. (1977). *Emile* (B. Foxley, Trans.). New York: Dutton.

Vygotsky, L. (1978). *Mind in Society: The Development of Higher Psychological Processes*. Cambridge: Harvard University Press.

15

Dramatic Play in Montessori Kindergarten in Taiwan and Mainland China

Mei-Chun Lin, James E. Johnson, and Karen McChesney Johnson

> Formal academic skills acquire meaning and urgency when they are taught in the context of culture and expression. The issue need not be cast as alternatives: as either academic or playful activities. Rather, playful activities, storytelling, story reading, drawing, and painting, embedded in an imaginative cultural curriculum, evoke and extend core symbolic competencies without which academic proficiencies cannot be attained. (Fein, 1992, pp. 34–35)

Do children have a right to play in kindergarten? Do children have a right to engage in make-believe play in a Montessori classroom? What happens when model early childhood education programs, such as Montessori, are fused with different cultures? How do we integrate and transform theory into practice? What are teachers' responsibilities? How does the value of play become understandable to the parents? These are some of the questions raised in the context of discussing provisions for dramatic play in Montessori Kindergartens in Taiwan and Mainland China. Observations were made of programs in Beijing as well as Tainan, Taichung, and Taipei during the spring of 2000.

ECE MODELS

Model or "brand name" programs or approaches to early childhood education (ECE) are well known and have provided an assortment of theory-based practices and policies to the field for decades (Day & Parker, 1972). Currently, prominent models seen in many developing countries include Bank Street, the Project's Approach, High/Scope, and Montessori (Roopnarine & Johnson, 2000). ECE curriculum and teaching approaches emanating from these models vary considerably but can be ordered along two key dimensions: philosophical goals and conceptions about childhood.

In ECE a concern about the quality of the learning experiences and the children's well-being underpins the selection of events and activities in the center, on the playground, or in the gym. There are, or should be, purposes behind each and every decision about how time, space, materials, and human agency will mix, in different play corners or in different project or activity areas. A useful way to think about the philosophy of a program is to ask, "What is the purpose of the purposes?" When this question is raised, not only is the level of abstraction elevated, but also core values must be confronted. What is the image of a particular child—past, present, and future? Are children at school honored for who they are, or only for who they might become?

Constructivism as an educational philosophy assumes that children are outreaching by their very natures, "budding scientists" who are intrinsically motivated to learn. Children are constantly engaged in thinking and problem solving, forming hypotheses and revising them with positive and negative feedback from the environment. Knowledge does not reside outside, experiences are not given to the child; rather, experiences are had by the child, knowledge is constructed and exists in the dynamic and reciprocal relationship between the child and the social and physical world. A teacher's valuing of children's autonomy in an intellectual sense, set free within an educational setting prepared to afford children the opportunities to learn, to realize, and to have insights is the critical defining characteristic of a teacher who believes in constructivistic education.

Maria Montessori (1964) also believed in freedom with limits, with a concern for the collective interest and will. The learning environment has to be conducive to peace, quiet, and order so that children can achieve independence and mastery, and a sense of self-efficacy. Children are intrinsically motivated toward ordering their environment and learning; personal hygiene, cleanliness, and manners are integral parts of the school day. Montessori concentrated on what children need to fulfill their potential, remaining mindful of the well-being of children in the here-and-now. In the mid-1980s the National Association for the Education of Young Children (NAEYC) came out with its policy on Developmentally Appropriate Practices (DAP). These guidelines were the result of members of NAEYC who were Montessorians working together with members who were Piagetians. DAP is constructivistic education in its orientation.

Nevertheless, there are questions about just how constructivistic Montessori actually is, especially in underrating the importance of play in the curriculum, pretense play in particular. Typically, Montessori ECE programs do not have a make-believe play corner, for instance, and in general reject the incorporation of fantasy into the daily curriculum. Still, Montessori ECE is clearly a developmental approach.

Montessori viewed children as having "sensitive periods," windows of opportunity for learning and growth, for qualitative and positive change along their developmental trajectory. Education must be sensitive to these sensitive periods, an idea that is akin to our current notion of readiness. Language is best taught between birth and three years, for instance. Imagination is best encouraged between six and twelve years. Accordingly, fantasy and sociodramatic play are not part of Montessori ECE, which is targeted toward the under-sevens. However, interestingly, children over six years should have dress-up clothes for some role play, as they engage in occupation-type activities or imagine living in another culture or region of the world learning about climate, customs, and the like during geography and social studies lessons.

TEACHERS' ROLES

Maria Montessori about a century ago used a "timely" analogy of a mechanical clock to illustrate how teachers should work with children. While traditional didactic teachers would literally move the hand on the clock face along with their fingers, the Montessori "directress" would wind up the clock to make it work. Teachers set the child in motion: "Our educational aim . . . must be to aid the spontaneous development of the mental, spiritual, and physical personality" (Montessori, 1964, p. 17).

The roles of the directress included preparing the environment ("keeper and custodian"), child observation (directress comparable to an "astronomer" gazing at the stars and recording observations), demonstrator showing a child one-to-one how to use materials correctly, and leaving the child to use materials without teacher interference (Wolfe, 2000). The "prepared environment" was critical for responding to the sensitive periods of childhood and absorbent minds. Materials and activities were self-correcting and graded according to difficulty. They were labeled "didactic," as they were designed to teach the child to be an increasingly capable and independent worker. Toys were "pedagogical devices."

PLAY IN ECE AND IN MONTESSORI

Play is the "gasoline" that makes the DAP "engine" go; but only high-quality super-grade fuel can get the engine really revved up (Johnson, 1994). Although the idea that play is at the center of the ECE curriculum is widespread, it is not uncritically accepted. For example, Trawick-Smith (2001) has delineated four distinct approaches to play in ECE that can be combined in various ways in a given program's schedule and curricular organization: (1) a broad-based developmental approach aimed at all areas of child development, such as seen in the Bank Street model; (2) narrowly focused play intervention aimed at a specific dimension of development, such as creative drama, literacy play, group games, or sociodramatic play; (3) free play or "hands-off" play curriculum inspired by psychoanalytic theory, with the teacher as an attachment figure nurturing socio-emotional development; and (4) nonplay intervention, such as seen in didactic teaching or drill and practice (e.g., Distar, Behaviorism).

Another more affirmative variant of the last approach, constructivistic in its orientation, might be the use of classroom investigations or projects in which exploration and imitation are the processes (accommodation) applied by the child, more so than is the process of play itself (assimilation). This kind of approach would not be incompatible with Montessori's methods of teaching and views on play. Montessori stressed reality adaptation and nature, and she eschewed fantasy. Imagination develops from a sensory base and a foundation in real-world experiences. Montessori didactic materials are generally made of sturdy hardwoods, glass, and now high-quality plastics. Authentic as well as high quality materials are used (e.g., child-proportioned brooms and dustpans). Plants, animals, and small gardens are standard in Montessori classrooms as children are drawn to the cycles, rhythms, and inherent order of the natural world (Torrence & Chattin-McNichols, 2000).

CULTURAL VARIATION AND ECE

A current major challenge in this era of the globalization of ECE is to determine what aspects of mainstream thinking about ECE or DAP or children's play—thinking arising out of such professional organizations as NAEYC in developed countries—represent culture-bound ideology or represent moderate universals based on a common biology and psychology across cultures. This determination is a prerequisite for deciding a possible prescription for some aspects of ECE or DAP or play that would then become "universal ECE practices and policies," even as other aspects of ECE may vary widely from one culture to another.

Another burning issue is more descriptive in nature. Since the expectation is not for ECE to change a culture but rather a culture to change ECE, just how does a culture such as Taiwan or Mainland China apply appropriate ECE practices and policies imported from abroad? In just how many diverse ways within a given culture does this adaptation get played out? Is the way it gets played out related to educational levels and background experiences of those in ECE who are doing the borrowing? How is the way it gets played out related to other factors within the cultural context, such as religion, history, politics, economics, or national government educational examination policies? How is the way it gets played out related to geography and ecology, such as tight spaces (crowding, congestion in urban areas) or inordinate durations and/or intensities of very warm or very cold weather?

OBSERVATIONS OF MONTESSORI KINDERGARTENS

Visits were made to several Montessori kindergarten classrooms in Taiwan (three programs in Tainan, one in Taichung, and one in Taipei) and to several classrooms of two Montessori kindergartens in Beijing, Mainland China. Informal conversations were also part of these visits. The teachers in Beijing made it clear that they were not Montessori in actuality, but were "on the road" to becoming Montessori.

The main impression of these visits was just how Westernized the kindergartens were and how affluent or elite they were, depending on the social status of the middle- and upper-middle-class families enrolled at the sites. The Taichung program, for example, had elaborate and expensive equipment not ordinarily seen in Montessori classrooms, including a playland with plastic balls for children to dive into and an expensive climbing wall in the playground. In fact, the first kindergarten seen in Tainan was even called the "Elite Kindergarten." This program's entrance room had a puppet theater set up; otherwise the program's layout and materials in the regular classrooms and its daily schedule were Montessori. Interestingly, the two kindergartens seen in Beijing also had provisions for pretense play, but in this case the make-believe play materials were in the classroom, with dress-up clothes and dolls, a pretend kitchen area, and teachers willing to engage the children in pretense. All of this represents a departure from Montessori.

The kindergartens purporting to be Montessori in Taiwan and Beijing were similar in that didactic materials were present in all cases. However, only in Taiwan were the rooms clearly recognized as Montessori in flavor. Another important difference was that in the Tainan, Taichung, and Taipei kindergartens the directresses were trained for one or two years; the teachers in Beijing made it clear that they wanted to convert to Montessori but had only one month of training so far. They expressed a need to better understand the underlying philosophy. Nevertheless, a sense of orderliness pervaded all kindergartens seen in Taiwan and Beijing.

Evidence of cultural adaptation of Montessori was also seen in the practice of using itinerant teachers for learning English as a second language, for gym or physical education, and for music and art. In the United States, for instance, the same teachers are usually responsible for these subjects. Even though Westernized, these kindergartens also had Chinese characters on display and character stamps (for verbs) ready for use with the children who were from four to six years of age.

COMMENTARY

Chinese child-rearing beliefs help to explain why Montessori programs appeal to Chinese educators and parents alike. In comparing Chinese and Montessori beliefs and practices in education, overlap exists but there are important differences that often are not recognized.

Central Beliefs of Chinese Culture

Most Chinese have grown up within the Confucian heritage. Confucianism, although not a religion in itself, has had a profound impact on Chinese and other Asian people, comparable to that of Christianity in the West. The Confucian ethics system has been observed for more than 2,500 years. Along with this belief system, "the ethic of filial piety" is most influential in guiding family life and in shaping the educational beliefs of the Chinese. The ethic of filial piety means that children have to follow whatever the parents say, want, or expect. Generally speaking, there are three duties that need to be carried out (Ho, 1994): (1) *to the self*—taking care to avoid harm to one's body because it is such a precious gift from parents that no one would want to harm it and risk hurting the feelings of parents, (2) *to the parents*—obeying and honoring one's parents and providing for the material and mental well-being of one's aged parents, and (3) *to the family*—conducting oneself so as to bring honor and not disgrace to the family name, performing the ceremonial duties of ancestor worship, and ensuring family-line continuity.

From these descriptions one can understand that what grounds Chinese culture is a collectivist tradition or interdependence within the family. Children achieve for their family in the collectivist-based society, while children achieve for themselves in the individualist-based society (Greenfield, 1994). Another aspect of Confucianism is the belief in maintaining interpersonal harmony and peace through good conduct, good manners, and emotional restraint. Parents, especially traditional ones, tend to express their feelings, thoughts, and emotions covertly. In order to maintain harmonious relationship with others they expect themselves, as well as their children, to conduct themselves with emotional restraint, politeness, and tact. Taking good care of one's body helps to take away parental worries; conducting oneself with emotional restraint, politeness, and tact as well as maintaining harmonious relationship with others are all important and are valued by parents.

Basic Beliefs about Child Rearing

Traditional Chinese beliefs influence child-rearing practices. For example, since taking care of one's body is important, some Chinese parents think that a good life habit is important and should be trained earlier on. Some children begin toilet training around the age of six months. Many parents hope that their children can acquire the habit of neatness, that everything can be orderly, and that every behavior can be in routine. Parents reinforce these traits and do not believe they will develop internally from within the child.

Socially, parents also expect their children to conduct themselves with emotional restraint. In consequence, a major goal of socialization is impulse control. Instead of encouraging toddlers to engage in active and exploratory behaviors, some parents want them to restrain themselves from active or aggressive games. Some parents also discourage their older children from rough and tumble play. Occasionally you will hear some Chinese parents say to their children, "Don't play too wild!" Some will even stop children immediately when they think play is getting out of control.

Another example illustrating the child-rearing belief in impulse control is when a guest comes to visit. If children receive gifts from the family guest, they are expected not to open the gifts right away because it is considered "impolite" to unwrap gifts in the guest's presence. Children must wait.

Since the collectivist viewpoint is adopted by the Chinese, children are encouraged to show their "good behaviors" in public in order to honor the family or parents. Chinese parents usually like to receive praise from others for their children's decent manners. Otherwise, they will feel "loss of face" (shame) in front of other people. In the case of a child's misbehavior, many times the parents will provide instant feedback to the child. Most parents believe that "errors" indicate that the child has not yet learned proper conduct and that the duty of adults is to provide quick correction for the misbehavior, thus avoiding further confusion or mistakes in the future. The Chinese believe that children need to learn to take criticism because that is the way a mature person grows. For the American, giving criticism to a child usually brings the concern of impacting the child's self-image. This is a very different viewpoint in terms of belief in forming a person. The Chinese are described as being self-critical; Americans are described as self-affirming (Miller, Wiley, Fung & Liang, 1997).

Belief in Education

Education is highly valued in Chinese cultures, because education was considered the only way to achieve upward mobility in society (Sue & Okazaki, 1990). There is an old Chinese saying: "No other walk of life is as prestigious as that of being a scholar." Accordingly, education holds a very important place for the Chinese. Parents place great importance on education.

Parents, especially mothers, take their roles seriously as their children's teachers. Parents and children spend a lot of time in doing homework and in mastering academic skills, about fifty-five minutes of focused practice on a task. To achieve success in academics, parents expect children to learn to "concentrate" for a long period of time. Essentially, teaching children to concentrate is an important primary goal of early childhood education.

In educating young children, Chinese parents hold one concept similar to traditional parents in the United States. Many parents believe that a child is like a piece of white paper. Adults can choose whatever color they want to paint on the paper. If you color it red, it will turn red; if you color it black, it will turn black. Another analogy is the example of the empty vessel. Chinese adults think that children are like empty vessels, and many adults in the United States, as well, like bottles full of water. Teachers and parents, being repositories of knowledge, see children as vessels to be filled (Ho, 1994). This image of the child is reflected in preferred ways of guiding children's work. There is adult-directed learning and adult selection of learning experiences. They think that children's early mastery of impulse control helps them be receptive to adult-directed learning.

Gaps between Chinese and Montessori Educational Beliefs and Practices

Of all the early childhood program models in Taiwan, the Montessori program is recognized as one of the most popular. This popularity is a result of the illusion created from the learning environments and classroom atmosphere in Montessori programs. From appearance, parents are led to believe that the Montessori philosophy and pedagogy about educating young children are the same as their own. However, there is a serious gap between what the parents think and what the program really is. The following descriptions are intended to give some examples of these gaps.

In the Montessori program, as part of practical life experiences, there are different tasks, such as buttoning, lacing, zipping, and so on, on dressing frames. From the parents' point of view, this is seen as a wonderful chance for children to learn about taking care of one's own body. Parents fail to see that the Montessori emphasis with these practices is on the sensory materials and their use in providing daily experiences for children. Another misconception about Montessori's program is the concept of order. Parents are fascinated by the orderly environment of the Montessori program. Parents are convinced that children will learn to maintain their play materials and space neatly through what appears to them as constant efforts exhibited by the Montessori teachers to this end. Parents fail to appreciate that Montessori believed that the internal sense of orderliness comes from the child, who is the optimal resource in keeping the environment in good order. The adult's job is not to provide constant prompts from external guidance, but to secure the sense of orderliness from the child within.

Another aspect attracting Chinese parents to the Montessori program is the social order in the classroom. In contrast to the play-based curriculum, children stay quiet and talk gently when they are working. Few aggressive or even assertive or active behaviors are observed; nor does rough-and-tumble play exist in the Montessori program. Once again, parents think that this particular program matches their educational goal that children should learn to control impulses, to conduct themselves with emotional restraint, and to display politeness and tactfulness in public. Some parents even misinterpret Maria Montessori's idea about the child's social life, presuming that children learn only on their own, that pure learning evolves from the individual child's efforts rather than from being in the group. On the contrary, Montessori was one of the earliest advocates to suggest providing children with specialized group settings outside families to assure better stimulation for growth and learning.

In addition to the social and life aspects of the Montessori program, the academic learning materials—such as math, language, and other content—also fascinate Chinese parents. When parents see Montessori teachers constantly demonstrating with different materials, teaching academic content with specialized tools, they are thrilled with the idea that their children are learning "a lot" by being in this kind of program. Moreover, when seeing that children can concentrate on their tasks for such a long period of time, parents are even more delighted because this is just what they want from their children. Once more, parents are preoccupied with the thought that concentration is very important in young children's learning, but most parents do not really understand the "absorbent minds" concept, whereby, from the Montessori perspective, persistence on a task derives from the child's intrinsic motivation. Children are born with the desire to ask questions, explore alternatives, formulate and evaluate hypotheses, and conduct trials to test their ideas.

TRANSPLANTING THE MONTESSORI MODEL

The transportability of a model ECE program is always a potential problem, even within the same culture. The "blueprints" of the designer might not be fully understood by the builder or teacher in the classroom. This is especially an issue when models are transported across national borders. Some departures from Montessori were seen, especially in Beijing. Fidelity of ECE model implementation requires understanding the program's philosophy, which in turn means sufficient levels of training and education. Clearly, one month is not enough, as was the case in the kindergartens in Beijing. However, even with sufficient training in Montessori ECE, as was the case with the teachers seen and interviewed in Taiwan, some slippage from or adaptation of "the Real McCoy" is expected. The use of itinerant teachers is one example of this. Professional educators make the model fit the culture.

The cultural gap is more obvious when comparison is made between the model and parental perceptions of the model. Deep-seated values and culturally based priorities stand in the way of a clear view. Parents assimilate and distort or bend the reality of the model to fit their preexisting biases. However, even if parent education cleared up the misperceptions, problems would remain. Parents may understand correctly the theory of the ECE model or why play is theoretically a valuable way for young children to learn at school, but still reject the idea because of opposing values. Hence, a major challenge exists for play advocates to explain the theory and to convert people in other cultures over to the play way in ECE. For both teachers and parents, what is required first is a culturally relevant remake of the model. The imported model must be fused with the culture without either losing its integrity.

How do we transplant a model program to a different culture? How do teacher educators train teachers? How can parents be instructed? Here are some suggestions:

- Examine cultural belief systems with respect to education. For example, teachers in Taiwan need to examine their own cultural belief system to see how it relates to early childhood education and child-rearing issues with both teachers and parents.

- Examine the ideology of the transplanted program. Identify the basic beliefs of Maria Montessori and compare these beliefs with the beliefs that seem to underpin existing practice in the classroom.

- Compare and contrast cultural beliefs and practices with the model program beliefs and practices. Interrogate the features of the national educational and child-rearing beliefs and practice. Then compare with Montessori programs.

- Combine the ideas to form a new whole that fulfills the needs of the culture, of the parents, and, most important, of the child

- Ask national teachers to think of factors influencing their practices within their cultural and ecological context. Consider factors within the cultural context, such as religion, history, politics, economics, or national educational examination policies. Consider geography and ecology, such as tight spaces (crowding, congestion in urban areas) or inordinate duration and/or intensities of very warm or very cold weather.

- Develop ways to implement the "new" ECE program. For example, ask teachers to find alternatives when considering space, materials, time, and instructions. Using a nearby community park could be one response.

ADVOCATING THE CHILD'S RIGHT TO PLAY

To conclude, advocacy for the children's right to play in Taiwanese and Chinese kindergartens can be effective by following these steps:

* Help parents realize that young children's play is different from older children's play. Children's educational play in kindergarten, for example, is not the same thing as a teenager's "goofing off."
* Help parents realize that only certain kinds of play are encouraged in the kindergarten curriculum. Play that is educational is "in," while play that is merely for fun is "out." After all, ECE and play theories have been in existence for many decades; ECE and fun theories are nonexistent.
* Help parents realize that overly stressful exams for educational placements should not ruin ECE; two wrongs do not make a right. Argue that developmentally appropriate practices using play in the ECE curriculum will bring the same or even better performances by their children, meeting parents' expectations.
* Help parents to see the connection between the process and the product of play. Explain how certain kinds of play can bring about certain kinds of learning and development, and overall well being in their children.
* Help parents be more aware of the beliefs and expectations governing their own child-rearing practices. Ask parents to compare their beliefs with Montessori or other ECE beliefs and find commonalities in order to form a new perspective and understanding that meets the needs of the social context, the parents' expectations, and the child's development.

REFERENCES

Day, M., & R. Parker. (1972). *The Preschool in Action: Exploring Early Childhood Programs* (2d ed.). New York: Allyn & Bacon.

Fein, G. (1992). Play and Development. In V. Dimidjian (Ed.), *Play's Place in Public Education for Young Children*. Washington, DC: National Education Association of the United States.

Greenfield, P. M. (1994). Independence and Interdependence as Developmental Scripts: Implications for Theory, Research, and Practice. In P. Greenfield & R. Cocking (eds.), *Cross-Cultural Roots of Minority Child Development* (pp. 1–40). Hillsdale, NJ: Erlbaum.

Ho, D.Y.F. (1994). Cognitive Socialization in Confucian Heritage Cultures. In P. Greenfield & R. Cocking (Eds.), *Cross-Cultural Roots of Minority Child Development* (pp. 285–313). Hillsdale, NJ: Erlbaum.

Johnson, J. (1994). The Challenge of Incorporating Research on Play into the Practice of Early Childhood Education. *Journal of Applied Developmental Psychology* 15: 603–618.

Miller, P. J., A. R. Wiley, H. Fung, & C. H. Liang. (1997). Personal Storytelling as a Medium of Socialization in Chinese and American Families. *Child Development* 68: 557–568.

Montessori, M. (1964). *The Montessori Method* New York: Schocken Books.

Roopnarine, J. L., & J. E. Johnson (eds.). (2000). *Approaches to Early Childhood Education* (3d ed.). Columbus, OH: Merrill.

Sue, S., & S. Okazaki. (1990). Asian-American Educational Achievements: A Phenomenon in Search of an Explanation. *American Psychologist* 45: 913–920.

Torrence, M., & J. Chattin-McNichols. (2000). In J. L. Roopnarine & J. E. Johnson (Eds.), *Approaches to Early Childhood Education* (3d ed.) (pp. 191–220). Columbus, OH: Merrill.

Trawick-Smith, J. (2001). Play and Curriculum. In J. Frost, S. Wortham, & S. Reifel (Eds.), *Play and Child Development* (pp. 294–339). Columbus, OH: Merrill.

Wolfe, J. (2000). *Learning from the Past: Historical Voices in Early Childhood Education.* Mayerthorpe, Alberta: Piney Branch Press.

16

Play-Based Curriculum: A Strong Foundation for Future Learning

Carolyn M. Patterson

Children have to be educated, but they have also to be left to educate themselves.

—Ernest Dimnet

Play, the work of children, is a phrase we hear quite frequently in early childhood education. What does this mean for children in the sense of their learning growth? What does it mean for educators of young children in how they prepare and design their learning activities? How can educators justify the decision to establish play-based activities in the classroom? These are questions that will be explored throughout this chapter to discover answers that strengthen the philosophy for educators of young children, thus allowing for the provision of opportunities that promote growth in the early years and lay a foundation for lifelong learning.

Fred Rogers, creator of *Mister Rogers' Neighborhood* on WQED in Pittsburgh, Pennsylvania, emphasizes the importance of play very clearly: "Child's play is one of the most misleading phrases in our language. We often use it to suggest something easy to do, something trivial, but it's not—not by any means. When children play they are working. For them, play is both a serious and a necessary business, and it is one of the most important ways children learn and grow" (Dimidjian, 1992, p. 13). For educators like Fred Rogers, who believe so strongly in play's positive effect on children, historical research strongly supports this philosophy. This goes as far back as Plato, who proclaimed, "do not use compulsion but let early education be a sort of amusement; you will then be better able to find out the natural bent" (Armstrong, 1994, p. 49), and continued with philosophers who are more familiar to early childhood educators.

In his famous book *Emile,* Jean-Jacques Rousseau emphasized that children learn not through words but through experience (Armstrong, 1994). Johann Heinrich Pestalozzi and John Dewey had a genuine belief in positive teacher–student relationships and that the process of learning should develop all facets of every child, including interpersonal relationships (Downs, 1975). Dewey believed that "education is a cooperative transaction of inquiry engaged in by independent human beings which quantitatively and qualitatively enriches life" (Dewey, 1966, p. 116). Dewey firmly believed in the importance of the individual: "The goal of education for children and society's goal for adults should be to supply each individual with whatever he or she, personally and uniquely, needed for full development in all dimensions. Education must include a student's physical and moral well-being as well as intellectual development" (Dewey, 1966, p. 116).

Friedrich Froebel stressed that the child was the important part of the education system and gained experience from his or her own activities (Butts, 1947). Susan Blow, closely following Froebel, felt that children should learn through play, singing, hands-on experience, and physical activity. Parental involvement played a large part in her curriculum (Fein, 1981). As early childhood moved into the early twentieth century, Erik Erikson and Jean Piaget based their educational foundations on psychosocial theory and appropriate staff development. Erikson believed that (1) a learner should be actively engaged, (2) a learner negotiating his or her own goals is most motivated, (3) working in teams provides good educational experiences, (4) consideration needs to be given to both conscious and unconscious affects and motivation, and (5) individual needs and differences must be considered in planning (Elkind, 1987). Piaget-based classrooms are characterized by their activities and by the cooperative understanding that both the children and the teacher have of what they are working to achieve. Piaget had a solid base in social transmission—children learning through action with peers and adults (Bringuier, 1980).

Truly meaningful education actively engages the physical, mental, verbal, and social/emotional domains. For a young child, the body functions completely in the acquisition of knowledge, best gained through a process of moving, speaking, doing with others, discovering for oneself, and mastering new challenges in an environment where play and work dominate (Dimidjian, 1992, p. 13). In play, children control the rate and manner in which they acquire new knowledge, free of tension. Play is a self-initiated and open-ended process with internal motivators that provide positive emotions and allow children to solve self-imposed problems. Researchers distinguish particular forms: functional play, rough and tumble play, constructive play, pretend play, and games (Pellegrini, 1986; Rubin, Fein, & Vandenburg, 1983). Often these types of play blend together, but they also serve different functions of social engagement, symbolic expression, and motor activity. Each form contributes to children's development.

Vygotsky (1967) suggested that childhood spontaneous play may be where children function at their highest level of competence. Vygotsky made a distinction between what a child could accomplish under the best, most supportive circumstances and what the same child could accomplish when these supportive circumstances were not present. The spread between unsupported and supported performance is called the "zone of proximal development" (ZPD). Scaffolding (an adult knowing when to support and when to withdraw assistance) is an integral part and allows us to help a child reach toward his or her potential rather than be hampered by what some consider unreadiness (Scales, Almy, Nicolopoulou, & Ervin-Tripp, 1991, p. 199).

Howard Gardner (1993) helps to interconnect these philosophical ideas through his theory of multiple intelligences that supports play-based curriculum. Gardner contended that the purpose of school should be to develop intelligence and to help people reach goals that are appropriate to their particular spectrum of intelligences. Gardner points out that one needs to use several different developmental maps in order to understand the seven intelligences. Piaget provided a comprehensive map for logical–mathematical intelligence, but one may need to go to Erik Erikson for a map of the development of the personal intelligences, and to Noam Chomsky or Lev Vygotsky for developmental models of linguistic intelligence (Armstrong, 1994, p. 5). Key points of the multiple intelligence theory are (1) that each person possesses all seven intelligences, (2) that most people can develop each intelligence to an adequate level of competency, (3) that intelligences usually work together, and (4) that there are many ways to be intelligent in each category.

The multiple intelligence theory emphasizes the rich diversity of ways in which people show their gifts within intelligences as well as between intelligences. The seven intelligences are (1) linguistic—the capacity to use words effectively; (2) logical–mathematical—the capacity to use numbers effectively and to reason well, including a sensitivity to logical patterns and relationships; (3) spatial—the capacity to perceive the visual–spatial word accurately and to perform transformations upon those perceptions; (4) bodily–kinesthetic—an expertise in using one's whole body to express ideas and feelings and/or facility in using one's hands to produce or transform things (specific skills include coordination, balance, dexterity, strength, flexibility, and speed); (5) musical—the capacity to perceive, discriminate, transform, and express musical forms, including sensitivity to rhythm, pitch, or melody, and timbre or tone color of a musical piece; (6) interpersonal—the ability to perceive and make distinctions in the moods, intentions, motivations, and feelings of other people; and (7) intrapersonal—self-knowledge and the ability to act adaptively on the basis of that knowledge (Gardner, 1993).

Viewing these seven intelligences in relationship to the developmental areas of growth—social–emotional (interpersonal and intrapersonal), physical, fine and gross motor (bodily–kinesthetic, spatial, and musical), cognitive (linguistic, logical–mathematical, spatial) and language (linguistic, spatial, and musical)—that children need to develop, one can see how important it is to develop all areas and allow for an overlap of activities, promoting multidevelopment. By identifying both the strengths and weaknesses of children, experiences can be designed to enhance growth and/or to plan alternative methods of teaching to support difficulties. Children who are given early opportunities to develop all areas of intelligence learn to operate from their strengths and to assess how to approach new learning situations (Kagan & Kagan, 1998). Assessment becomes a central feature of the educational system, as educators observe and determine strengths and weaknesses and appropriate activities to support these: "Children's play shows us how well they are developing and is also the means for further development. It helps children develop knowledge, social skills, and motor skills. It also helps them express feelings appropriately. Thus play is the basis of developmentally appropriate programs for young children" (Sawyers & Rogers, 1994, p. 57).

Play can be supported in our classrooms and provide the most optimal learning experiences for children if (1) children choose activities, (2) children determine how long to play within the framework of classroom guidelines and a warning system for clean-up, (3) activities and materials are provided that challenge various levels of skills, (4) a safe physical environment is provided, (5) interruptions are minimized by well-designed usage of space, (6) choice in how objects and materials are used is encouraged so children can try out new skills in unusual ways, and (7) a schedule is planned that allows maximum usage of playtime. By using these simple guidelines, all aspects of the day, including conversations, reading, transitions, and group time, can be made more playful (see Figures 16.1 through 16.4 for examples of play activities for different areas).

Early childhood education is a foundation and should be child oriented and sensitive. If an individual has a strong foundation, his or her abilities can complement and build upon each other, providing a successful growth for all children involved. Individuals cannot contribute successfully to society it they are lacking self-worth, value, and positive skills. In order for education to provide individuals with a positive growth toward self-actualization, it must allow diversity and different methods of exploration, and view varying manners of acquiring knowledge as an asset, not a detriment. The uniqueness of the individual must be preserved within the framework of a successfully functioning group classroom. Accomplishing this requires the teacher to be a facilitator who has organized an aesthetically pleasing classroom that fosters hands-on experimentation, opportunities for group problem solving, fair routines and procedures arrived at cooperatively, and choice making. The assessment of the learning environment must provide an avenue for positive growth. Assessment is valuable and valid only if students, teachers, and parents gain insight into how accurately knowledge is being applied in practical situations. Assessing informally and expecting high standards allows educators to view the whole student. The premise of education touching the whole student has to begin early and continue throughout life. If we as adults would allow ourselves to become more actively immersed, as children do, maybe our deep sense of wonder would be sparked more consistently.

REFERENCES

Armstrong, T. (1994). *Multiple Intelligences in the Classroom.* Alexandria, VA: Association for Supervision and Curriculum Development,

Bringuier, J. C. (1980). *Conversations with Jean Piaget.* Chicago: University of Chicago Press.

Butts, F. R. (1947). *A Cultural History of Education.* New York: McGraw-Hill.

Figure 16.1
Play Activity: "What's the Password?"

Materials:	Objectives:
• Oaktag • Markers • Laminating Film	• Recognize letters, colors, shapes, and numbers • Use group cooperation

Activity:
　　　This is a very simple daily or weekly way to reinforce concepts. It can be used at the entrance or center areas. Tape up one card with a concept you want children to work on. As children enter the area to play, have them tell each other and/or a teacher what color, shape, letter, or number it is. Change when you feel they are recognizing and reinforcing easily.
　　　If you set up activities and areas to allow only so many children in at a time, you could place that number card near whatever you use to help students know how many children are allowed in the area.

Figure 16.2
Play Activity: "What Is Missing?"

Materials:	Objectives:
• Five or six real items (from the classroom) or use flannel board cutouts • Tray or flannel board	• Visually discriminate objects • Name objects • Use memory skills • Use language skills

Activity:
　　　Place the selected objects in full view of all students. Discuss and name the objects. Have one child at a time hide his or her eyes while the teacher removes one object and then has the child try to remember it. Ask the class to hold off giving any help to their friend until the friend asks for some.

Variation (for older children):
　　　Keep all the objects, but change the order or arrangement, then have the child replace the objects in their original order.

Dewey, J. (1966). *Dewey on Education* (Reginald D. Archambault, Ed.). New York: Random House.

Dimidjian, V. J. (ed.). (1992). *Play's Place in Public Education for Young Children*. Washington, DC: NEA Early Childhood Education Series.

Downs, R. B. (1975). *Heinrich Pestalozzi: Father of Modern Pedagogy*. Boston: Twayne.

Elkind, D. (1987). *Early Childhood Education* (ERIC Document ED 326 311), University of Illinois, Urbana-Champaign.

Fein, G. (1981). Pretend Play: An Integrative Review. *Child Development* 52: 1095–1118.

Gardner, H. (1993). *Multiple Intelligences: The Theory in Practice*. New York: Basic Books.

Figure 16.3
Play Activity: "Friendship Match"

Materials:	Objectives TSWBAT:
• Camera • Two matching photos of each child • Oaktag, rubber cement, permanent marker • Laminating film • Ziploc bag	• Recognize their classmates • Match similar pictures • Count the number of cards they match

Procedure:
        The teacher takes a picture of each child involved in a classroom activity (be sure it is a face picture and is as close-up as possible). After the film is developed (be sure to have doubles made), glue each picture on a piece of oaktag (4" x 6" for 3" x 5" pictures, or 5" x 7" for 4" x 6" pictures). Print each child's name below the photo and then laminate. Place in a Ziploc bag and mark "Friendship Match Game." Have a small group of children play as a "Go Fish" game or a memory game, making their matches and naming their classmate friends. Each child can then count his or her number of cards after all matches are made. Place the game in a game activity area.

Figure 16.4
Play Activity: "Flower and Seed Match Game"

Materials:	Objectives:
• Eight to ten different packages of flower and vegetable or fruit seeds (buy 2 of each kind—look for inexpensive deals at Wal-Mart or similar stores) • Two sheets of white posterboard • Black permanent marker • Glue/tape • Index cards • Two baskets	• Use visual discrimination to match a variety of seeds. • Begin to name some flowers and vegetables or fruits.

Activity:
        Prepare one game board for flowers and one for fruits/vegetables. Open one package of each kind of seed carefully. Glue some seeds in equal spacing on the poster board, which has been labeled "Flowers" or "Fruits/Vegetables" at the top. Allow seeds to dry thoroughly, then tape correct seed envelope over the top of each seed pile (tape at top so that children can bend upward and see seeds, and then look at the picture on the seed packet. Prepare index cards of seeds in the same way as above for each type, so their individual index cards can be placed in baskets and then matched to the seed chart. This game is suitable for a garden shop area, discovery area, or game area.

Kagan, S. & M. Kagan. (1998). *Multiple Intelligences: The Complete MI Book.* Washington, DC: Kagan Cooperative Learning.

Pellegrini, A. D. (1986). Communicating in and about Play: The Effect of Play Centers on Preschoolers' Explicit Language. In G. Fein & M. S. Rivkin (Eds.), *The Young Child at Play: Reviews of Research*, vol. 4 (pp. 79–92). Washington, DC: NAEYC.

Rubin, K., G. Fein, & G. Vandenburg. (1983). Socialization, Personality and Social Development. In P. H. Mussen & E.M. Hetherington (Eds.), *Handbook of Child Psychology*. vol. 4 (pp. 693–774). New York: Wiley.

Scales, B., M. Almy, A. Nicolopoulou, & S. Ervin-Tripp (eds.). (1991). *Play and the Social Context of Development in Early Care and Education.* New York: Columbia University Press.

Sawyers, J., & C. Rogers. (1994). *Helping Young Children Develop through Play: A Practical Guide for Parents, Caregivers, and Teachers.* Washington, DC: NAEYC.

Vygotsky, L. S. (1967). Play and Its Role in the Mental Development of the Child. *Soviet Psychology* 12: 62–76.

17

Simon Says . . . "Reading Is Fun!"

Monica McHale-Small and Tabatha A. Uhrich

The following describes a collection of movement-based games and activities that have been developed to teach beginning reading skills, and argues for the inclusion of such activities in the classroom and the gym. *Simon Says . . . "Reading Is Fun!"* (Uhrich & McHale-Small, 2002) is a compilation of activities that developed as a result of work with a multidisciplinary team of educators as they sought to intervene with first graders struggling to learn early reading skills (for example, see Figures 17.1 and 17.2). The games and activities grew in number, complexity, and skill level as new groups of students, some older and some younger, were invited into the activity. The original intent was to develop activities to reinforce early reading skills while meeting the needs of kinesthetic learners. What we have found is that our games are enjoyed by all types of young learners, kinesthetic or not, because "fun" is the keyword in *Simon Says . . . "Reading Is Fun!"*

Many activity books and instructional aids aimed at early literacy skills attempt to incorporate all of the learning styles in their approach to instruction. However, the bulk of tactile/kinesthetic activities continue to involve sitting, with hands-on activity designed more appropriately for the tactile learner than the kinesthetic learner. Few activities are geared toward the child who is fidgety and wishes to move about the room while learning. We make no claims that these games and activities will revolutionize the teaching of reading, nor that the games are going to corner the market on innovation and creativity; however, the assertion is made that *Simon Says . . . "Reading Is Fun!"* fills a distinct void when it comes to strategies to reinforce beginning reading skills while meeting the needs of kinesthetic learners.

The *Simon Says . . . "Reading Is Fun!"* activities vary in terms of the skills being taught or reinforced, the materials used, and whether the activity is or is not an

Figure 17.1
Movement Activity: "Jumping Jellybeans and Elephants"

Equipment: Hula-hoops, (rubber discs, empty boxes).	Area: Classroom, gymnasium, or outdoors
Number of participants: 1+	Grade: Preschool–3

Activity:

The name for this activity refers to Project Read's terminology for one-syllable and multisyllable words. Single-syllable words are said to be jellybean words because, like jellybeans, the whole word fits into your mouth at once. Elephants, however, are too big to fit into our mouths. If we wanted to eat an elephant (a proposition sure to emit gleeful "Yuck's" from young children), we would have to slice it up into pieces. Multisyllable words, like elephants, don't fit into our mouths all at once either. This activity helps children to hear, see, and feel the size of various words.

Typically, we have the children use their own names for the initial practice with this activity. Using our own names first, we clap our name using one clap for each syllable. We count the claps and then lay out one hula hoop for each syllable we clapped. We then jump into the lined up hoops, pronouncing each syllable as we jump. The children can be partnered or they can work alone. When working with a partner, one child can say and clap the word while the other child counts and places the hula hoops in a line. To reinforce left-to-right progression, we have the children place the hoops in a horizontal line with the first syllable "placed" on the left. This means the jumping will start at the left on the line of hoops.

This activity can quickly become a competition to see who can think of the word with the most syllables. There are countless ways to extend and modify this activity. Sometimes we have the students get letter cards and spell each syllable inside the hoop. This works best with their names or other words they can already spell easily. They can spell their names with the letter cards and then determine which letters make up which syllable.

Instead of hula hoops, empty boxes (shoe boxes or, for bigger fun, packing boxes) can be used to "build words," stacking one box for each syllable. Left-to-right progression is not reinforced, but kids still have a blast trying to think of the tallest words they can.

This activity can be adapted and used for breaking words into individual phonemes. It is a good idea to use something smaller than hula hoops when breaking words into phonemes. This helps the students to get a better understanding of phonemes as the smallest sound parts in words. In the gym we have some pink rubber discs that fit inside the hula hoops and can be used to represent the phonemes. A final "layer" consists of placing letter cards on top of the "phoneme discs."

Note: Reprinted with permission of the authors and Scarecrow Education.
Source: Uhrich and McHale-Small (2002).

actual game. Movement is the thread that runs through all of the activities, and movement is what makes these activities so appealing and engaging for all young children, whether or not they are or will become kinesthetic learners. Children engaged in *Simon Says . . . "Reading Is Fun!"* are moving about the classroom or gym searching for various letter cards, making words, or experiencing spatial con-

Figure 17.2
Movement Activity: "Mystery Writer"

Equipment: Alphabet letters	**Area:** Classroom, hallway, gymnasium, or outdoors
Number of participants: 2+	**Grade:** K–2

Activity:
  Each student has a partner. One partner selects a letter from the box and "writes" that letter on a partner's back, using a finger. The partner tries to guess what letter was drawn. If the student is unable to guess, the mystery writer may give a clue by telling what sound that letter makes. The mystery writer can also write the lower-case version of that letter if the partner has difficulty guessing the upper case, or vice versa. Once the child guesses the correct letter, the partners should switch roles.
  This activity is most effective if tailored to the particular needs of each child. Choose partners ahead of time and give each pair a bucket or box of letters selected just for them. A mix of letters that have already been mastered plus a few that have recently been introduced works best.

Note: Reprinted with permission of the authors and Scarecrow Education.
Source: Uhrich and McHale-Small (2002).

cepts with bodies. Sometimes they run, sometimes they ride scooter boards. At times they may be working alone, simply matching letters or finding the letters they need to spell their names. Sometimes they are working with partners, writing sight words with letter cards, jump ropes, or chalk. Sometimes they are using their bodies to form the letters. At other times they are listening hard for the sounds of the letters in their names as their cue to run or chase or find a new spot on the floor. At all times, they are moving, laughing, shouting, and experiencing letters, sounds, words, and other concepts with their whole bodies.

  Fitting teaching strategies to the learning styles of students certainly has intuitive appeal. There is also a growing literature that suggests that addressing the individual learning styles of students can indeed boost academic achievement (Braio, Beasley, Dunn, Quinn, & Buchanan, 1997; Dunn & Dunn, 1993; Spires, 1983; Stone, 1992). In working with first grade and kindergarten students who are below level academically, a quick discovery was made that these were often the same students who "couldn't sit still" in the classroom. These experiences seems consistent with Dunn and Dunn's (1993) contention that kinesthetic learners, students who learn and think in terms of somatic sensations, make up the majority of those students labeled "at risk." It is as if these children use up all of their energy just trying to keep themselves still or seated and then have little left over to devote to the task of learning.

  In our own work there have been a number of children who were able to demonstrate skills in the gym—an environment where they are free to move as much as they like while working—that they were unable to demonstrate consistently in the classroom. One five-year-old boy, unable to focus sufficiently to demonstrate competence on a letter-identification assessment in the classroom, easily named every letter and sound when he was allowed to run, pick up a letter card, name it, make the sound, and drop it in a bucket. By allowing him to move freely while practicing his letters, he was engaged and he gave the task his full attention to completion. Having found the task pleasurable and fun, rather than a chore, he will be more likely to engage in similar activities. Of course, this child will eventually need to be able to use these concepts in a more traditional setting, but as we work toward that goal he is getting meaningful practice, experiencing success, and having plenty of fun.

While the games and activities encompassed in *Simon Says . . . "Reading Is Fun!"* may well be essential for those kindergarten and first grade students who simply cannot master their letters and sounds without ample opportunities to move, the activities can be a fun motivating reinforcement for all students. All children, especially young children, love to move and play. It has been shown that the movement and fun of *Simon Says . . . "Reading Is Fun!"* activities can keep a whole classroom of children actively engaged in what is essentially a spelling and vocabulary lesson for the better part of a class period. With little direction, the children adapt the activity or game to fit their own needs. "Mystery Writer" is an activity used to teach letters to kindergarten and first grade students. It simply involves using one's finger to "write" a letter on a partner's back so that that person can guess the letter. When this game was played with a first grade class, the more capable students quickly asked for word cards instead of letters. When a partner readily guessed the word, they moved to longer and more difficult ones.

Another class of first graders quickly became engrossed in a relay type game involving teams of players traveling one at a time on a scooter board to retrieve needed letters from a collection of alphabet cards encircled by a hula hoop at the other end of the gym. The goal was to take turns finding the letters needed to spell a given word. Once the team read their word and used it in a sentence, they were given a new word and the relay was repeated. At no time was the class told that a winner would be declared or that helping was or was not allowed. The children made the game fit their needs. The competitive teams of students zoomed across the gym, cheered their teammates to move faster, and acted as if they had just won Olympic gold when they completed their words. The less competitive teams shouted encouragement and some even assisted their struggling teammates by pushing them on the scooter board or helping them to locate the needed letter. Competitive or cooperative, all of the students were playfully engaged in academics and simply could not get enough of the activity.

The push for academic standards has swept across the country in recent years. What this has translated to in many school districts is more and more academics at younger and younger ages. Academic kindergarten programs are quickly replacing the more traditional developmental programs. In the quest for academic excellence, play has often been left out of the equation. It is our contention that this play versus academics dichotomy is a false one. Learning can and should be playful and fun if we are to gain the attention and stimulate the motivation of children. *Simon Says . . . "Reading Is Fun!"* is one example of how this can be accomplished. We have confidence and hope that truly child-centered educators will continue to create ways to make learning playful and fun.

REFERENCES

Braio, Ann, T. Mark Beasley, Rita Dunn, Peter Quinn, & Karen Buchanan. (1997). Incremental Implementation of Learning Style Strategies among Urban Low Achievers. *Journal of Educational Research* 91: 15–25.

Dunn, R., & K. Dunn. (1993). *Teaching Elementary Students through Their Individual Learning Styles: Practical Approaches for Grades 3–6.* Boston: Allyn and Bacon.

Spires, H. A. (1983). Learning Styles: Achievement Gains through Learning Styles Matching. Retrieved May 3, 2001 from http://www.learningstyle.com/research.html.

Stone, P. (1992). How We Turned Around a Problem School. *Principal* 72(2): 34–36.

Uhrich, T., & M. McHale-Small. (2002). *Simon Says . . . "Reading Is Fun!": Movement-Based Activities to Reinforce Beginning Reading Skills.* Lanham, MD: Scarecrow Education.

18

Growing and Playing Naturally in India

Paramvir Singh

Play is a child's response to life—almost where life begins, play begins. Play—is the way the child learns what no one can teach him.
—Lawrence K. Frank (1890–1958)

Activity is the basis of life. Activity may be a movement born at the birth of living beings and life is characterized by it, or it may be a play that is an inherent quality in the germ plasma of each individual. Biologically, movement or play depends upon growth, proving the dictum "Move and Grow." Watch a kitten chasing its tail or a young child racing up and down the passageway of a familiar house and you will see that physical activity is a needed and inherent characteristic of a developing mammal.

Play, sports, and games are not synonymous, but they are inextricably related. Play is recreation or any activity done for amusement. It includes everything from playing with toys to participating in sports. Games are forms of play having set rules, or contests played according to rules, whereas sports are the organized form of play, again having set rules for each event. In play people impose their own wishes or fantasies on the cause of events, rather than subordinating themselves to the requirements of the external world. This is most true of children's play. Play is characterized by a "speeded-up" and simplified version of human events, for players feel that play events are vivid and exciting in a way that ordinary events usually are not.

In primitive cultures, play occasions were often regarded as sacred. Present-day societies regard play and games as a matter of free choice. According to many authorities, the "work ethic" that developed during the Industrial Revolution led to a reverence for endless productive work and a disdain for all forms of playfulness that would distract from such work. The rise of modern sports and increasing expenditures on entertainment and recreation reveal that the work ethic has lost some of its strength. Modern-day children, with their innumerable toys, practice the manipulative control of objects just as their parents manipulate autos, thermostats, dishwashers, and computers. Both adults and children live in a world where the control of machines is critical to survival. The philosophy of play should be studied carefully during each growth period. Various studies have shown that for the first eighteen months of a child's life, play is a sensory motor activity. During this stage children explore the nature of objects around them and experiment with their own physical skills of manipulating, crawling, standing, walking, climbing, and running. Beginning at about the age of two or three, children show increasing interest in playing with other children. After the age of six, the pretend play of children becomes increasingly imaginative, with imaginary or pretend companions and a great diversity of fantasy among familiar playmates. Later, adolescents become interested in an increasingly diverse range of recreational activities.

Children's play today focuses more on mental than physical activity. Thus, play is not the same everywhere, but changes to suit the circumstances of survival in different places, with different cultural inferences based on historical themes; however, there is some universality. Games with rules also seem to be universal. It is generally agreed that a wide variety of factors are at work in play.

The imitative nature of play, to a great extent, depends on the values of society. Play is an expression of self as well as an opportunity to test one's limits. During the last thirty years or so there has been an enormous increase in the provision of sports for children. Indeed, the age of performers at international athletic competitions continues to fall. It has been estimated that about thirty percent of these athletes were under the age of twenty (McKenzie, 1986). However, these are by definition exceptional cases. At the same time it appears to be part of the more affluent society in which we live, the growth in television and televised sport, and decline in the informal active play of children in the fields and streets. These days many children live in multistoried apartments and heavily trafficked areas, a concrete jungle militating against "natural" forms of play and physical activity.

Problems of play, play facilities, games, and sports are different for developed and developing societies. It has usually been assumed that children's play is practice for adult life. There is a considerable difference between what occurs in a game and what must happen in its direct adaptation. For this reason, there is some value in thinking of play as adaptive potentiation (i.e., play creates responses that are of potential value rather than direct value for ordinary adaptation). The simplest interpretation at present is that play is related to the development of skill, strength, and flexibility in the adult.

There are sharp contrasts among underdeveloped, developed, and developing countries regarding minimum required playing facilities due to the lack of infrastructure and economic debts. In underdeveloped and developing countries, findings note that the physical development of children has been stunted by malnutrition and disease, and many children commence heavy work at a very early age (Chepyator-Thompson & Ennis, 1997). A major boost in the economy of these countries is needed before all children have an equal chance of realizing their potential, using appropriate playing facilities for proper growth and development. In developed countries, the situations are reversed. Many children now spend thirty hours or more per week watching television, and much of their remaining free time is spent in automobiles. The long-term effects of such studied inactivity have yet to be evaluated, although some recent data suggest deterioration of overall fitness during the course of childhood (Petlichkoff, 1992). Selection for competitive sports should utilize all the predictive tools of modern sports sciences, physical education, and medical sciences. Thereafter, the student may be assigned vigorous daily preparations for excellence in international competition.

The question of hunger, economy, and malnutrition on the one hand and that of inactivity, overtraining, the impact of technology, and medical manipulations on the other hand must be answered for youngsters, whose souls must be integrated into the futuristic approach of the global community.

REFERENCES

Chepyator-Thompson, J. R., & C. D. Ennis. (1997). Reproduction and Resistance to the Culture of Femininity and Masculinity in Secondary School Physical Education. *Research Quarterly for Exercise and Sport* 68(1), 89–99.

McKenzie, T. (1986). Analysis of the Practice Behavior of Elite Athletes. In M. Pieron and G. Graham (Eds.), *Sports Pedagogy* (pp. 117–121). Champaign, IL: Human Kinetics.

Petlichkoff, L. M. (1992). Youth Sport Participation and Withdrawal: Is It Simply a Matter of Fun? *Pediatric Exercise Science* 4(2): 105–110.

19

Play Doesn't Need Any Labels: Inclusive Play for All Children

Lynda Reeves

It should be noted that children at play are not playing about; their games should be seen as their most serious-minded activity.
—Michel de Montaigne (1533–1592)

Sam, Cindy, and Richard are playing Poison Hoop (Cole, 2001) with their peers, shuffling their feet inside their twenty-four-inch hula hoops to move so that they can avoid being tagged by the "poison hoops." Sam moves his hoop with ease, while Cindy and Richard are stumbling over theirs. Would you tell Cindy and Richard to stop stumbling over them? Or would you quietly hand each a thirty-inch hula hoop, instructing them to try it? Using a thirty-inch hula hoop would seemingly be easier to control, allowing the children to move smoothly on the floor. Would you still respond the same way, however, if you were told that Cindy has cerebral palsy and Richard does not have a disability? Would you make the equipment modification only for Cindy because she has a disability? Developmentally Appropriate Pedagogy (DAP) makes the necessary modifications, enabling each child to successfully play Poison Hoop. This chapter's purpose is to explore how to use DAP with that intent in mind, whatever the activity. Inclusive play is a matter of creative pedagogy.

How can any child be expected to succeed without DAP? It is a prerequisite to successful inclusion. If we look closely at the children on the playground, we observe that a small percentage is either gifted or has severe disabilities, while the majority is in the center of the continuum. Many at the center have difficulty with all or some of the following: cognitive, motor, and affective skills.

A child does not have to be labeled with a disability to be behind peers in cognitive, motor, and affective skills. It is best to let go of being obsessed with labels and look at each child as an individual with unique needs. If the goal is to provide DAP to all children, then it is not necessary to question whether children with disabilities can be accommodated in the classes, because DAP will ensure success for all children, regardless of their diverse motor, cognitive, and affective skills. All children yearn to be successful; therefore, all children thrive in a DAP environment.

DAP fosters a collaborative relationship between children and their teacher, as the teacher becomes the facilitator of a play environment having little restriction. Four factors that determine the least restrictive environment (LRE_4) for a child are safety, success, satisfaction, and skill appropriation. These factors dictate how well a child participates in a specific activity. In creating a play environment that promotes the joy of movement, DAP is the first building block for multidimensional play.

A continuum of adult intervention for play needs to exist so that the dynamic needs of children can be met as their play agenda changes. This coincides with DAP. Children respond differently to a specific play approach (Marchant & Brown, 1996). A continuum of play, from directed to guided to nondirected, acknowledges that no two children approach play the same way.

LEAST RESTRICTIVE ENVIRONMENT

LRE_4 becomes the guideline in determining the degree of adult intervention for a child. The teacher moves back and forth along the continuum, using LRE's four factors as the criteria for the degree of adult intervention. For example, the class is playing The Glob (Charpenel, 2001), skipping away from the globs to avoid being tagged and having to join them. The teacher monitors the activity, scanning to make sure that all of the children are LRE_4. Gary is moving very slowly, hopping instead of skipping. When Roger tagged Jenny, she was supposed to have hooked elbows with him to become one big glob. But Jenny is yelling at Roger, "I'm not doing that." The teacher has to step in as the facilitator for all three. Upon reaching Jenny and Roger, she gives them one racing baton to hold with Jenny's right and Roger's left hand. Now they work as one glob, skipping along to tag their peers. Knowing that Gary has good galloping skills, she walks over to him and says, "Gary, let me see you gallop." He gallops quickly, avoiding the globs.

Knowing when and how to intervene is critical for the activity's flow. There is a need for balance between the spontaneous, child-directed teacher as the facilitator and teacher-directed play. Sometimes it is best to simply let the play scenario evolve, with the teacher observing to make sure that LRE_4 is occurring. If there is a safety concern, then intervention is needed immediately. For example, a child refusing to play The Glob (Charpenel, 2001) and sitting down in the center of the game would be a safety hazard. Experience and intuition are influential when the facilitator needs to intervene in matters concerning skill, success, and satisfaction. Understanding how each child functions is crucial in assessing the status of these LRE_4 factors. Knowing that Gary has good galloping skills allows the facilitator to quickly have him replace skipping with galloping. One's skill level is critical to the success and satisfaction of the child's participation in the activity.

DEVELOPMENTALLY APPROPRIATE PEDAGOGY

The class is playing Group Juggling (Krouscas, 2001). One group of six children has successfully juggled a rubber chicken and yellow juggling block. Now the children add a blue juggle bean ball. Scanning the activity to ensure all of the children are LRE_4, the teacher observes Gary dropping the juggle bean ball when it is tossed to him. What adjustments are needed to make sure that LRE_4 occurs? Does Gary have the skill to juggle a ball that is only 2¾ inches in diameter? What object could it be replaced with that matches his skill level?

What other factors need to be considered? In addition to the LRE_4 factors, the following DAP factors for the activity need to be applied: the size, shape, texture, weight, and color of the equipment. For Krouscas (2001), the developmental hierarchy for the size of the objects for Group Juggling was the rubber chicken (20 inches long), juggling block (7¼ inches long × 5¼ inches wide × 2¼ inches in diameter), and juggle bean ball (2¾ inches in diameter). An object 20 inches long is much easier to grasp than a ball 2¾ inches in diameter. The shape of the rubber chicken and juggling block makes them easier for Gary to grab than a ball only 2¾ inches in diameter.

The selection of the size and shape of an object is dependent on the child's proximodistal development. The motor development principle of proximodistal development is growth beginning at the midline and continuing toward the extremities. Development begins at the midline, to the shoulder, down the arms, and finishes at the fingertips. This is why children first catch a ball at their chest. As their proximodistal development continues, they catch the ball with their forearms, followed by their fingertips. If children have not mastered the pincer grasp (thumb and index finger) they will have difficulty juggling small objects that require fine motor-skill precision.

Awareness of what textures are more comfortable for a child is critical to how well the child performs the activity. The texture that is appealing for one child may be offensive to another child. Krouscas (2001) believed that the rubber texture of the chicken and the cloth of the juggling block were within the children's comfort zone.

The weight of the object also influences the child's success in this activity, as the weight of the chicken and juggling block makes it easier for one to feel these objects as they make contact with the hand. Children are attracted to bright colors such as the yellow chicken and juggling block. Maybe Gary would have caught the juggle bean ball if it were yellow instead of blue? Considering DAP factors may change the way children are grouped for a juggling activity. Maybe six children can be assigned to a group that uses these three objects, and Gary assigned to one that is successful with the chicken and juggling block.

The next time the children are practicing their throwing skills, arrange a diversity of throwing objects along the wall and instruct them to select one object to throw. After throwing, ask the children why they selected their object. Their responses will include at least one or more of the DAP factors. Repeat the activity with the children selecting a different throwing object, and again ask them why. Adaptability becomes the foundation of activities as children learn that they can experiment with different objects. Children, on their own, tend to select objects that will make them successful. This ensures that the activity is individually appropriate for each child.

The earlier DAP is presented to students, the sooner they will begin to apply it on their own. Children are very observant of teacher and peer modeling, so it is not surprising for a child to run to the aid of a peer who is struggling with throwing and say, "Here, try this spider ball." The more modeling and reinforcement from the child's peers, the easier it will become for the teacher to become less directive. DAP becomes the hub of the classroom curriculum.

This DAP approach in classrooms can be used so that all children can actively participate in a play environment that is safe, successful, and satisfying for their skill level. DAP recognizes that there is a continuum of diverse motor, cognitive, and affective skill levels within any group. Planning for inclusive play is not restricted to children with disabilities. Integrated play is in, segregated play is out. This is not just a philosophy or concept, but a contemporary approach to ensure that all children are provided a LRE$_4$ play environment. When the activity fits like a glove, then inclusive play works.

REFERENCES

Charpenel, T. (April 17, 2001). The Glob. *PE Central*. Retrieved April 28, 2001 from http://www.pecentral.org.

Cole, J. (March 16, 2001). Poison Hoop. *PE Central*. Retrieved April 1, 2001 from http://www.pecentral.org.

Krouscas, J. (March 17, 2001). Group Juggling. *PE Central*. Retrieved April 1, 2001 from http://www.pecentral.org.

Marchant, C., & C. Brown. (1996). The Role of Play in Inclusive Early Childhood Settings. *Topics in Early Childhood Education* 2: 127–139.

20

A Games Model for Facilitating a Constructivist Approach

Marianne Torbert

Play enhances the child's language development, social competence, and creative thinking skills.

—IPA/USA

Jean Piaget believed that children actively construct knowledge by assimilating and accommodating new experiences, or by reworking their previous experiences in new ways as they gain additional experiences. Said in a different way, this means that a child takes in new information and adapts it to past experiences and the perceptions derived from them. From this, the child constructs new knowledge, new perceptions, and perhaps a new perspective. This ongoing process is similar to the German gestalt theory, in which experiences become integrated structures or patterns that are not the sum of the experiences, but have specific properties that can neither be derived from the elements of the whole nor be considered simply as the sum of these elements. Thus, common experiences do not lead to common knowledge.

This leads to the individual differences that we perceive among children, requiring an approach to education in which these differences are not only considered, but also created into positive contributing factors within the growth process. Our present system, while giving lip service to individual differences, tends to be based upon a stimulus–response, behaviorist approach. This has caused many of our children to experience anxiety, boredom, failure, and blame, because the system does not fit their learning needs. To allay this, the Leonard Gordon Institute for Human Development through Play at Temple University developed play experiences in the form of games based upon three premises:

First, there are basic life skills that support a child's ability to interact with his or her environment and draw input from these experiences. An example would be perceptual motor abilities that allow an individual to gather input through the multiple sensory systems, interpret this input, and respond in order to test out the newly developing perceptions.

Other examples of relevant basic life skills would be memory, perseverance, and the ability to recognize patterns and discern similarities and differences. These and others can be further developed through carefully selected games. A developmental increase in these life skills allows an individual to construct learning from better input, based on a more complete interaction with the environment.

The second premise involves an increase in the quantity and quality of experiences. If children are going to have the greatest opportunity to grow from their experiences, then these experiences must be thoughtfully planned to allow each individual to be actively involved in the growth process. Many opportunities to revisit and retest experiences are needed. This means that experiences must be constructed so that there are plenty of turns—no one having to wait without a purpose or being eliminated from an experience. This further means increasing the number of turns available whenever it will enhance growth. The institute calls this "expansion" and constantly seeks new ways to increase the available turns and opportunities.

In relation to the quality of experience for the individual, each participant must be able to enter the experience at a point that is challenging to him or her. The institute calls this "equalization." Because of individual differences, this will require multiple ways to enter and multiple levels of entry. This gives each child an equal opportunity to grow. Our task is to find ways to make this possible. Research (Csikszentmihalyi, 1975) has demonstrated that when the task difficulty matches the individual's ability to overcome the challenge level, the participant will experience a sense of harmony, competency, euphoria, and "flow." These feelings are so pleasurable that an individual will become intrinsically motivated to experience this sensation repeatedly. Since this type of participation leads to growth, an individual must continue to seek higher levels at which to experience this "flow" phenomenon. Our responsibility is to find multiple ways and levels within a task and make these available to our children.

Piaget and the Leonard Gordon Institute believe that learning can reach a higher level when it becomes a social experience. Piaget stated that "decentering" (seeing something from another's point of view) would increase the generation of alternatives and thus the growth of knowledge. The institute believes that differences can become a source of mutual growth and that experiences can be engineered to make this possible. The development of these experiences can make individual differences valued rather than simply accepted or respected. The institute calls these experiences "interactive challenges." We have also found that an atmosphere that supports and facilitates "equalization" also creates an environment in which "interactive challenges" can more readily occur. The institute has labeled these (expansion, equalization, and interactive challenges) as "inclusion factors" because they tend to facilitate inclusion and reduce exclusion. The construction of game experiences that support the development of relevant life skills and the three inclusion factors of expansion, equalization, and interactive challenge has formed the basis for the work of the Leonard Gordon Institute for Human Development through Play at Temple University since its establishment in 1985.

The third premise upon which the Leonard Gordon Institute builds is that children can be self-motivating as well as self-determining and self-governing. This belief is based on the works of Robert W. White (1959) of Harvard University and Mihaly Csikszentmihalyi (1975) in behavioral science at the University of Chicago. From White's "Motivation Reconsidered: The Concept of Competence," it can be concluded that people are born with a desire to develop and master knowledge. From Csikszentmihalyi's *Beyond Boredom and Anxiety: The Experience of Play in Work and Games*, it can be concluded that, given an experience in which participants' present abilities allow them to overcome a challenge, children will experience euphoria and a sense of competency. These feelings support their desire to become competent and be intrinsically motivated toward experiencing this growth process repeatedly, thus creating their own energy (intrinsic motivation).

To this end, the Leonard Gordon Institute's mission is to develop games that increase relevant life skills, the number of opportunities to grow in these skills, the opportunity to choose to enter each experience at an individual's personal level of development, and social interactions in which participants both receive and contribute to the growth-producing experience. We believe that this work can facilitate a constructivist approach to learning by being both a tool to support a constructivist orientation and a model to help those who wish to try a constructivist approach. As Piaget believed, we learn best through actively experiencing. When experiences are made socially, emotionally, cognitively, and physically growth producing, and comfortable for all, then the joy and celebration of growing enhances the desire to actively participate and grow from these experiences.

REFERENCES

Csikszentmihalyi, M. (1975). *Beyond Boredom and Anxiety: The Experience of Play in Work and Games*. San Francisco: Jossey-Bass.

White, R. W. (1959). Motivation Reconsidered: The Concept of Competence. *Psychological Review* 66(5): 297–333.

21

Organized Play through Youth Sports: A Four-Tier System

Anne M. Rothschadl and Christopher M. Nunes

America's future walks through the doors of our school each day.
　　　　　　　　　　　　　　　　—May Lean LeTendre

An estimated 33 million children will participate in sports this year (Lord, 2000). According to an American Sport Education Program (2001) report, by next year about one-fourth will drop out. The research indicates that the primary reason these children play sports is to "have fun," and they drop out because playing ceases to be fun (Sachs, 2000). Changing the typical approach to sports can make a significant difference in keeping our children actively engaged in healthy physical activity. Putting the "play" back into sports can make participation fun and thus sustain participation throughout the school years and beyond. Coaches and parents can work together to create and support intrinsically rewarding experiences in and through sports. Positive experiences can help children continue to be physically active into adulthood. The purpose of this chapter is to introduce a four-tier system of developmentally appropriate sports activities with a focus on fun and play, discuss the role of parents and coaches, and suggest a sample activity period to illustrate how the system can be implemented at each level.

THE LIFELONG PHYSICAL ACTIVITY IMPERATIVE

The U.S. Surgeon General (U.S. Department of Health and Human Services, 1996) has estimated that nearly half of the adult population is overweight or obese. Moreover, 33 percent of our youth are also overweight or obese, and obesity is rapidly increasing among preschool-age children (Dietz, 2001). Excess weight places these children at a much higher risk of acquiring one of the top three killers in the United States: heart disease, cancer, and cerebrovascular accident (stroke). The statistics on obesity for these children do not bode well for a future healthy adulthood.

The research indicates that those who are not physically active as children will remain sedentary during their adulthood (Braunstein, 1999; Trippe, 1996). Play and recreation professionals have an imperative to keep these children active. To ignore this imperative means placing our children at higher risk for high blood pressure, high serum cholesterol, and diabetes (Braunstein, 1999). The risk of acquiring these disease-related conditions can be greatly reduced if our youth eat nutritiously and stay physically active throughout their lifespans. Additional benefits of physical activity include the development of fine and gross motor skills, learning teamwork and cooperation skills, improving self-esteem, and learning responsibility (DeGraaf, Jordan, & DeGraaf, 1999). However, by the time these children reach adulthood, nearly 90 percent of them will have dropped out of regular, consistent cardiovascular activity, such as sports (Sachs, 2000). The primary reason children give for dropping out is that "it's not fun any more" (American Footwear Society, 1990). So, how can play and recreation professionals keep children actively engaged throughout childhood and into adulthood? The solution may be found in using a four-tier system that gradually introduces children to competitive sports and consistently reinforces the intrinsically rewarding side of playing sports that will keep them active into adulthood.

THE ROLE OF INTRINSIC MOTIVATION: KEEPING CHILDREN INVOLVED IN SPORTS

Computer games, television, and other passive activities dominate the time and attention of our youth. Play and recreation professionals must strongly advocate for well-rounded youth, and physical activity must be a part of this development. Sports can provide a structured means of supporting physical, emotional, cognitive, and social development while sustaining cardiovascular fitness. But keeping children involved in sports is a challenge.

The current emphasis on competition at the beginning stages of sports participation sets our youth up for failure in achieving a lifelong commitment to physical activity. The most often-cited reason children give for dropping out of sports is that it stopped being fun. Too much emphasis on competition and winning are specific reasons they give for their attrition (American Footwear Society, 1990). Steven A. Henkel (1997), associate professor of sport psychology and author of "Monitoring Competition for Success," stated that traditional sports result in the success of one team reducing the success of the other team. The traditional reward—winning—is in limited supply. Winning is primarily an *extrinsic* reward, and extrinsic rewards do not sustain motivation to participate over a long period of time. *Intrinsic* rewards do. Utilizing a different approach in teaching recreational sports to children can reduce the extrinsic emphasis and increase intrinsic rewards, such as positive, enjoyable experiences that will sustain long-term involvement.

The tiered system requires a triad of support. First, the child must have an initial interest in and desire to play sports. Children develop differing levels of focus on competition, largely based on the influence of parents and coaches (Henkel, 1997); thus, parents and coaches are critical to the success of the program. Parents must make intrinsic rewards the focus of their support for their child's participation. Coaches must introduce, nurture, and focus on the intrinsic rewards of playing the sport: improved self-esteem, sense of accomplishment, and pleasure. If any side of this triad fails to keep this focus, participation may not be sustained, negating the potential benefits.

THE FOUR-TIER SYSTEM

When children are old enough to participate in organized play, agencies that offer play and sports programs can utilize a four-tier system to create activities that enhance the child's intrinsic connection to sports in developmentally appropriate steps. The four-tier system starts with children five years old, offers developmentally appropriate sports instruction and participation, and progresses through the early teen years when children typically choose competitive or recreational sports. The four-tier system is presented here sequentially, focusing on selected developmental characteristics of each level, the role of the parent, and the role of the coach. In addition, a sample "activity period" (as opposed to "practice") that deemphasizes competition and emphasizes enjoyment is suggested for each tier.

First Tier: Play Time, Ages Five to Seven

Five-year-olds typically love to run, hop, jump, throw, and be physically active in their play. They are aware of sports and their active imagination may even lead them to imitate sports stars or other characters in popular culture. In the United States, these icons include the Power Rangers, Pokémon, Harry Potter, Poo-Chi, wrestling stars, or whatever is popular at the moment. Gross motor development is a primary focus during this stage and should also be addressed in sports participation.

Parents need to keep in mind that developing the large muscle groups (such as biceps, triceps, and quadriceps) is more important than competing or winning. Winning at this stage should be deemphasized, and concentration should focus on the development of these muscles. Equally important for parents is to emphasize the joy of playing and to avoid overscheduling (Kirn & Cole, 2001). By reducing the number of activities in which children participate, the child is more able to focus, have fun, and develop skills to a higher level in each activity.

Coaches need to incorporate a lot of movement into activity periods to support gross motor development. Coaches also need to introduce basic sports skill development, such as throwing, running, catching, control of body movements, and spatial awareness. Moreover, coaches must build interest in the sport and physical activity in general at this age. One method of achieving these results is to build a large number of "touches" into each activity period; that is, ensuring that each player gets to handle or "touch" the equipment many times during the activity period. The number of touches can be increased by utilizing more equipment, playing two-on-two or three-on-three games, or using smaller boundaries.

Cognitive development at this age includes the initial stages of the ability to understand cause and effect. Skills that are used to cooperate with others are also developing. Coaches can foster the development of these abilities and skills by teaching sportsmanship and fair play. Coaches can also feed the cognitive development of the players by involving the imagination. For example, playing such games as "Capture the Flag" or "Shipwrecked" can teach the cause and effect of positioning and strategy in a fun, engaging way.

Second Tier: Fun Time, Ages Seven to Nine

During the second tier the very beginning stages of competition are initiated by introducing a loose game structure; however, the primary emphasis is still on having an enjoyable experience and continued skill development. Little or no emphasis should be placed on the final score, and structure in rules and regulations should be limited. In addition, children at this stage do not take criticism well. Perceptions of success or failure depend on adult responses. Thus, parents and coaches both continue to play critical roles.

Parents need to focus on the child's overall improvement in physical and social abilities rather than on winning. Parents should also encourage participation in multiple sports. Single-sport competition can lead to burnout (Lord, 2000), whereas multisport participation can lead to improved overall muscle development and more diverse social circles. Parents can also advocate for rule changes that would support the concept of many touches for the players. For example, in games such as soccer the number of players per team can be reduced from eleven to nine. The elements of the sport would remain fundamentally the same while the number of touches would increase.

Coaches need to teach sportsmanship at this age and focus on the respect shown toward officials, the other team, and teammates. Through the teaching of sportsmanship, the joy of playing can be enhanced. More gamelike activities (5-on-5, 8-on-8) can be instituted while still focusing on the number of touches. Everyone should have equal playing times; thus, if the team has fifteen players, then all fifteen should have a turn at bat. Soccer or basketball can be divided into sixths or eighths instead of halves or quarters so that players can be rotated into the game more often. This kind of rotation helps keep players focused on playing rather than on the score.

Increasing abilities in hand–eye coordination allow the coach to use more complex skill-development activities and use such techniques as pairing less-skilled players with the more-skilled players to continue overall development. Coaches should avoid drills from high school, college, or professional teams because these are training tools geared toward athletes with a much higher level of physical ability and cognitive processing, and are vocationally oriented. The emphasis for children must still be on having a positive sport experience.

Third Tier: Game Time, Ages Nine to Eleven

Continued skill development and continued focus on fun should be prominent. This stage allows for honing skills for plays and exploring player positions. The concepts of winning and losing can be introduced, along with leagues and standings, since gross motor skills are more developed and game structure has been initiated.

Parents must understand that their child plays a role on the team. The child may not be the star, but his or her contribution to the team, such as motivator or defensive specialist, is important. Continued positive encouragement, having fun, and making friends are more important than competing or winning. In addition, parents need to be aware of the relationship between intense sports participation and puberty. Growth spurts in boys and girls may make control of large muscles more difficult. Poor nutrition and overtraining can lead to or create such problems as the athletic triad—amenorrhea, osteoporosis, and anorexia (Estronaut, 2001)—in girls.

Coaches need to teach players to set goals for the individual and the team. Children at this stage of development may take more risks and can usually understand cause and effect well enough to begin to self-correct errors. Setting goals for their own development is an essential step forward in improving skills. For example, goals might include improving the ability to field ground balls, cutting two seconds off the fifty-yard backstroke, improving free-throw percentage by 5 percent over the course of the season, or passing the ball at least five times before shooting a basket.

Team development can also be fostered as players begin to understand the differing contributions of group members to a common goal. This development also allows the coach to introduce the ideas of most-improved player, most-improved offense, most-improved defense, best effort, best attitude, best team support, and so forth. Multiple recognition of differing roles needs to be acknowledged, and can help the coach focus on team goals of communication, teamwork, and positioning.

Coaches also need to stress the joy of playing over winning. Varying activities throughout the course of the season can sustain interest. Tie-dying team shirts, designing and painting a sheet for a team flag, playing backward (such as running the bases in reverse), and using a different size ball can help keep activity periods enjoyable rather than using repetitive drills. Many nontraditional activities can provide the same skill outcomes as the traditional drills. With nontraditional activities, children are kept active, challenged, and motivated to continue.

Fourth Tier: Playing Sports, Ages Eleven and Up

The fourth tier is critical for a number of reasons. Children tend to become less active as they grow up (Braunstein, 1999; Trippe, 1996), and peers may encourage other, more sedentary activities, such as computer games, television watching, and "hanging out." Therefore, it is essential to realize that when competition outweighs fun, the potential for dropout increases. With increased time spent on sedentary activities, negative health effects surface. At this point, the concepts of a championship and a most-valuable player are introduced. The children are ready to handle these concepts because they have developed physically, mentally, cognitively, and socially. Each tier had prepared them for this stage. Although the championship and the most-valuable-player award are perceived as extrinsic rewards, the children have been properly prepared to keep the consequences and outcomes in perspective.

Parents need to keep in mind that having fun and making new friends continue to be important. They also need to be aware of the possible outcomes of too much emphasis on competition. Parents can help their child keep sports from becoming all consuming and help keep winning and losing in perspective by discussing balance with such other life arenas as family, friends, school, and faith. Talking with their child after the game is a way to provide emotional support. Respectful behavior toward coaches, officials, and the other team provides essential modeling and diverts focus from competition to skill development and the experience.

Coaches also need to help players understand that sports are only one part of life and not life itself. Boys going through puberty can grow rapidly to 6 feet and still only weigh 130 pounds. At a stage when looking "cool" in front of peers is important, subsequent awkwardness and seeming loss of ability can be discouraging. Providing a sense of competence and control by involving the players in decision making can help keep them engaged. For example, coaches might ask the players to decide practice times, team colors, skill areas that need practice, plays to run, and new activities to keep activity times playful. Again, it is the fun that will provide the intrinsic motivation to stay involved. Activities such as a postseason game with parents are a way of carrying the pleasure beyond the season and keeping the "play" in playing sports.

SUMMARY

Play should be purposely incorporated at all levels of youth sports so that children can find the intrinsic rewards in sports participation. Children, parents, and coaches all need to keep the emphasis on fun in order to sustain participation throughout childhood and into adulthood. Increased participation can provide the physical activity necessary to reap such health benefits as lowered cholesterol and blood pressure and lowered risk for heart attack, cancer, cerebrovascular accidents, and diabetes. The four-tier system takes consistent cooperation among players, parents, and coaches. The system keeps enjoyment in sports to help healthy children grow into healthy adults.

REFERENCES

Athletic Footwear Association. (1990). *American Youth and Sports Participation.* North Palm Beach, FL: Athletic Footwear Association.

American Sport Education Program. (2001). Youth Sport Coaches. *American Sport Education Program.* Retrieved March 21, 2001 from http://www.asep.com/asep/coaches/youth.

Braunstein, J. B. (1999). Putting the Fun Back into Exercise for Our At-Risk Kids. *Diabetes Forecast* 52(11): 31.

DeGraaf, D. G., D.J.M. Jordan, & K. H. DeGraaf. (1999). *Programming for Parks, Recreation and Leisure Services: A Servant Leadership Approach.* State College, PA: Venture.

Dietz, W. H. (2001). The Obesity Epidemic in Young Children: Reduce Television Viewing and Promote Playing. *British Medical Journal* 332(7282): 313.

Estronaut. (2001). The Female Athletic Triad. Retrieved March 21, 2001 from http://www.womenshealth.org/a/athletic_triad.htm.

Henkel, S. A. (1997). Monitoring Competition for Success. *Journal of Physical Education, Recreation, and Dance* 68(2): 21–28.

Kirn, W., & W. Cole. (2001, April 30). Whatever Happened to Play? *Time*, 56–58.

Lord, M. (2000). When Cheers Turn into Jeers (and Tears). *U.S. News & World Report* 129(3): 46.

Sachs, M. L. (2000). Lighten Up, Parents! *USA Today* 129(2666): 62.

Trippe, H. (1996). Children and Sport. *British Medical Journal* 312(7025): 199–200.

U.S. Department of Health and Human Services. (1996). *Physical Activity and Health: A Report of the Surgeon General.* Atlanta: Centers for Disease Control and Prevention.

22

Bullying in Schools in the North of Portugal: What We Know about Children

Beatriz Pereira

Wonder is the beginning of wisdom.

—Greek Proverb

For this study we investigated the number of students involved in bullying in schools, who they were, and the site where this problem largely occurred. A diagnosis of the situation was made in three middle public schools with children from the fifth to the ninth grades (ten to fifteen years old). The results of this study prompted the development of an intervention program—a school policy program, mainly developed around the playground. The goal of this program was to reduce and prevent bullying among children in school, focusing on playground interactions. It was also oriented toward improving playground facilities and giving the students more opportunities for leisure activities, hoping that children would learn to make decisions and develop skills according to their interests (physical, intellectual, and social), while sharing in peer groups.

LITERATURE REVIEW

Smith and Sharp (1994) describe bullying as abuse of power between peers. There are some relevant characteristics to define it: (1) intentionality, (2) frequency (e.g., the same child is victimized many times, even weekly), and (3) physical strength—one child being more powerful than the other. Bullying is a form of aggression toward another person who is in some way less powerful than the aggressor; the act of bullying is intentional and takes place over time (Olweus, 1993).

Farrington (1993) described bullying as a repeated oppression, psychological or physical, of a less powerful person by a more powerful person. This was reiterated by Rigby (1997), who offered a concern over its malign intent and its deliberate exploitation of a power differential. Rigby listed six "bullying elements" to consider: (1) the initial desire to hurt, (2) the desire expressed in action, (3) the hurt individual, (4) that it is being directed by a more powerful person against someone less so, (5) that it is without justification, and (6) it is typically repeated, with evident enjoyment.

Research carried out to assess bullying in schools in different countries shows that it has been a widespread problem (Whitney & Smith, 1993; Olweus, 1989; Pereira, Almeida, Valenti, & Mendonça, 1996). In Portuguese schools a survey was conducted on children grades one to six, between six and twelve years of age (Pereira et al., 1996). The study included eighteen schools: twelve from the first cycle school (primary school) and six from the second cycle school (middle school), comprising 6,197 pupils. The results were as follows: The most common form of bullying was either direct verbal (name calling) or physical aggression (a hit, slap, or shove). Boys and girls experienced different types of bullying; girls were more often excluded and the subject of rumors spread by other children. Most of the bullying occurred on the playground; however, the majority of children liked the playground and said that there was enough space in which to play.

In Spain, descriptive data from a questionnaire designed by Ortega, Mora, and Mora-Merchán (1995) were given to teaching staffs during feedback sessions in thirteen schools situated in socially deprived areas in Seville and its surroundings. This enabled teachers to decide whether to be involved in a preventive action program to stop school bullying (Ortega, Mora-Merchán, & Fernández, 1996). The educational aspect of such a program worked with the democratic organization of school life, cooperative group work, and teaching feelings, attitudes, and values. This approach saw all sides of the educational community as having a shared construction of a culture for the school, along with negotiation of its routines, norms, and values (Ortega, 1997).

Ortega (1997) designed an intervention program called SAVE, with the purpose of reducing aggression in primary and secondary school. It had two facets: the diagnostic and intervention programs. The sample was composed of twenty-six schools in Seville, involving the participation of 4,914 pupils between the ages of eight and sixteen. The results revealed that 33 percent of pupils answered to having bullied others occasionally, and 33 percent reported themselves as having been victims. Furthermore, 5 percent reported bullying others frequently and 8 percent identified themselves as victims many times (Ortega & Mora-Merchán, 2000). Such cruelty was more frequent in the male gender; boys bullied others and were bullied more than girls (Boulton & Underwood, 1992; O'Moore, Kirklam, & Smith, 1997; Pereira et al., 1996). Boys were more often victims and, in particular, perpetrators of direct bullying (Olweus, 1993).

Pereira's (1998) three-year study concluded that bullying was more frequent at the primary schools. An intervention program was developed in both primary and middle schools. In the intervention schools (second to sixth grade), the levels of victimization dropped in three of five groups and the level of bullying others in one group. For the fifth and sixth grades no significant differences were found, but the results did suggest a reduction of being bullied on the playgrounds of the second cycle intervention (middle school). These findings suggested some success in the intervention, but its rather limited impact was also considered.

Recess is an important part of children's experience in school, especially in developing children's social competence (Pellegrini & Smith, 1993). Recess and lunchtime are fun. These are the moments when children could make their own decisions, define their own rules, and choose their own playmates (Evans, 1989). However, it is on the playground where there is more bullying (Whitney & Smith, 1993; Pereira, 1998). In a study of primary school children entailing a program of intervention at the playgrounds, Marques, Neto, and Pereira (2001) concluded that children prefer a playground with supervision and small equipment to play with (e.g., balls and ropes), and they also concluded that the bullying decreased more in this model of playground than if they had only supervision. The empty playground (no equipment) and the lack of supervision bred bullying. Olweus (1993) found a clear negative association between teachers' density during break time and the number of bully/victim problems. When the teacher/pupil ratio is low, there is an increase of bullying situations at school recess. A good diagnosis of this problem is the basis for defining an intervention program to reduce and prevent it. This diagnosis is made using methods developed to assess the incidence of bullying among children; observation that is both direct and indirect and information from students or teachers as to what is happening (their perceptions of bullying).

METHOD

The aim of this study was to describe what was happening in Portuguese middle schools about bullying in order to define an intervention program. In these Portuguese schools, the pupils have classes from 8:30 A.M. to 1:30 P.M. and, for two or three days, classes after lunch. They spend long periods of the day at the playground when they are at school without classes. They usually have a ten-minute break after each fifty-minute class. We chose three elementary schools (middle), from the fifth to the ninth grades (ten to fifteen years old), using an anonymous questionnaire (adapted from the Olweus, 1989, version) for all students in these public schools. The students were asked about being bullied and bullying others to make a diagnosis of the problem. This study included 2,366 students, 47.9 percent of whom were females and 52.1 percent males. The sample mostly included children from ten to fifteen years old; however, there was a small group of nine who were sixteen, seventeen, and eighteen years old.

RESULTS

The students were asked if they had been bullied and if they had bullied their classmates at school that term and how many times (see Table 22.1). Close to a quarter of the students (24.7 percent) had been bullied once or more, and 16.9 per-

Table 22.1
Being Bullied and Bullying Others in One Term
(Three Months)

Number of Occurrences	Being Bullied	Bullying Others
Never	75.3%	83.1%
One or two times	18.8%	12.5%
Three to five times	3.0%	1.7%
Six or more times	2.9%	2.7%

Note: The percentage was calculated for each place between the number of valid cases and the number of children that assumed they have been bullied in that place.

cent had bullied others. There were some persistent victims (5.9 percent) and some persistent aggressors (4.4 percent).

Regarding bullying and gender, we did a cross-table analysis and concluded that females were less involved in bullying; 81.7 percent never were bullied, and 91 percent had not bullied their peers. Males were more often victimized (30.6 percent) and more often the aggressors (24.4 percent). The percentage of boys who were never bullied was 69.4 percent, and of those who never bullied their peers was 75.6 percent.

Students were asked about how they had been bullied to identify the types or patterns of the abuse. Answers included physical abuse, taking their belongings away, threats, contemptuous words, spreading rumors or lies, rejection, and compulsively asking for money (Figure 22.1).

The playground was the place where bullying was most frequent (see Table 22.2). Students also mentioned the corridor, the bus stop, and near the main door. Although the restroom was the least mentioned, it necessitated our attention because violent types of bullying happened there.

When analyzing the percentage by age of children who bullied others, we concluded that those fourteen and fifteen years old bullied more than did the younger pupils, but that students between the ages of twelve and fourteen bullied others more persistently (six or more times). When comparing the percentage of victims by age, we found that students between the ages of ten and thirteen were significantly more often victimized than the fourteen- to sixteen-year-olds.

The percentage of children who bullied others increased with the number of retentions; there were significant differences. The Portuguese Education System allowed students with learning or behavioral problems to remain at the same level if they were unable to achieve the minimum skills for that grade. These pupils were then integrated with new, younger classmates. The average number of students who were retained was 0.52. This number is not only indicative of the one or two students who were retained for one year, but also the students with multiple years of retention. School success seemed to be related to the aggressive behavior of the students (Figure 22.2). For the group of students who never had retention, only 14.5 percent bullied a colleague during that term. This figure was less than the average (16.9 percent). For the students who had one, two, or three years of this

Figure 22.1
Types of Bullying (n = 2,332)

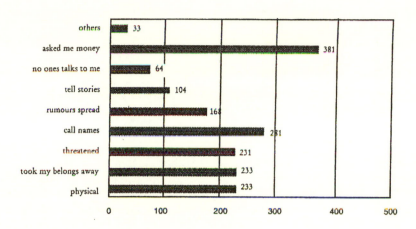

Table 22.2
Places Where Bullying Takes Place

Place of Being Bullied	Victim (Number)	Victim (%)
Playground	481	20.6
Bus stop	174	7.5
Main door	154	6.6
Restroom	58	2.5
Bar	115	4.9
Canteen	123	5.3
Corridor	205	8.8
Classroom	82	3.5
Other	95	4.1

Note: The percentage was calculated for each place between the number of valid cases and the number of children that assumed they have been bullied in that place.

underachievement at school, the percentage of bullying others increased. With four, five, and six retentions, this percentage also increased, although there were only a few cases to be considered.

DISCUSSION

The data show that most bullying behaviors occurred on the playground; however, the majority of children liked that area and said there was enough space to play. It can also be concluded that when pupils were not succeeding at school there

Figure 22.2
Number of Years of Underachievement and Bullying Others

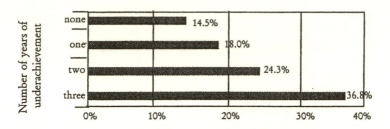

was a higher percentage of children bullying others; therefore, underachievement was related to the bullying of others. Interestingly, the percentage of students who admitted to having bullied others was different when they were asked if they had been bullied once or more during that term and when they were asked about specific situations, such as how they were bullied. In the first question, twenty-four children (7 percent) answered that they had been bullied, and in the second question thirty-six children (4 percent) admitted they had been bullied.

The results from this study confirm those from other studies (Boulton & Underwood, 1992; O'Moore, Kirkham, & Smith, 1997; Pereira et al., 1996) concerning gender differences; more boys were victimized by bullying and its perpetrators than girls. Concerning age, it was concluded that the younger children were more often victimized (ten to thirteen years old) than the older (fourteen to sixteen years old). About bullying others, the crucial age was fourteen or fifteen, with a lower percentage of younger pupils (ten to thirteen years) reported as perpetrators of bullying.

INTERVENTION PROGRAM

Having focused on the bullying problem at playgrounds, based on past survey results made in Portuguese schools (Pereira et al., 1996) and the intervention programs developed by Smith and Sharp (1994) in the United Kingdom and Olweus (1993) in Norway, we developed a program of intervention to reduce or prevent such abuse. In agreeing with the programs of intervention developed by Olweus (1993), Smith and Sharp (1994), and Pereira (1998), it was necessary to involve all staff members in developing an integrated program. The framework chosen for this study was the school's Educational Project (whole-school policy). The intervention plan had the following components: (1) involving and training the staff; (2) improving playgrounds by having different areas for play, offering different kinds of play equipment (e.g., balls, ropes), and supervising playgrounds; (3) improving leisure time at school and offering students a variety of activities according to their interest, including sport activities (e.g., volleyball, football, handball, dance, aerobics, swimming) and computer training, a language club, or chess club; (4) paying attention to victims and giving them opportunities to develop different skills; (5) stopping bullies without spending considerable time and effort with them; (6) defining specific rules about discipline, giving and working on them at the beginning of the school term, and having the students discuss them at a meeting with teachers and other school workers; and (7) developing a work group to coordinate support for the staff and students in dealing with bullying.

In these schools it was very common for 100 or 200 pupils to spend one or two hours on the playground together without adult supervision. To improve playgrounds and leisure time at school during breaks and holidays, we organized a training program for supervisors. The aim of this program was to develop playground observation skills, to learn to listen to and communicate with pupils, and to organize games or other activities in which support in resolving conflicts can be given.

This intervention program comprises a training period for the monitors, consisting of approximately twenty young people between the ages of sixteen and twenty-seven, who had finished the compulsory school and were unemployed. Some were taking one or two courses to finish secondary school. This group was trained to go to the playground and other places where children went during break time (including a chess club area, a toy library, or a computer room), observing what was happening with pupils and whether they would stay alone during breaks. They could suggest some activities or places where pupils could spend time. In some clubs or rooms they helped pupils learn how to play. They were also supervisors of the playground in middle schools (second and third cycle).

In conclusion, it is recommend that the Portuguese System of Education assume the responsibility to solve the considerable number of problems that students at compulsory schools (nine grades) have reported. It is also recommend that the head teachers and staff of schools develop intervention programs not only to eradicate bullying but also to give pupils opportunities to make their own decisions about what to do during their free time, about what they should learn (they should have an opportunity to choose some subjects), and about self-determination in playing and socializing (toward developing emotional, motor, and social skills).

REFERENCES

Boulton, M., & K. Underwood. (1992). Bully/Victim Problems among Middle School Children. *British Journal of Educational Psychology* 62: 73–87.

Evans, J. (1989). *Children at Play: Life in the School Playground*. Geelong, Victoria, Australia: Deakins University Press.

Farrington, D. P. (1993). Understanding and Preventing Bullying. In M. Tonry and N. Morris (eds.), *Crime and Justice: An Annual Review of Research*. Vol. 17. Chicago: University of Chicago Press.

Marques, A. R., C. Neto, & B. O. Pereira. (2001). Changes in School Playgrounds to Reduce Aggressive Behavior. In M. Martinez (Ed.), *Prevention and Control of Aggression and the Impact on Its Victims* (pp. 137–145). New York: Kluwer Academic/Plenum.

O'Moore, A. M., C. Kirkham, & M. Smith. (1997). Bullying Behaviour in Irish Schools: A Nationwide Study. *The Irish Journal of Psychology* 18(2): 141–169.

152 The Child's Right to Play

Olweus, D. (1989). Prevalence and Incidence in the Study of Anti-Social Behaviour: Definitions and Measurement. In M. Klein (ed.), *Cross-National Research in Self-Reported Crime and Delinquency*. Dordrecht, The Netherlands: Kluwer.

————. (1993). *Bullying in Schools: What We Know and What We Can Do*. Oxford: Blackwell.

Ortega, R. (1997). El proyecto Sevilla Anti-Violencia Escolar. Un modelo de intervención preventiva contra los malos tratos entre iguales. *Revista de Educación* 313: 143–161.

Ortega, R., J. Mora, & J. A. Mora-Merchán. (1995). Cuestionario sobre intimidación y maltrato entre iguales. Proyecto Sevilla Anti-Violencia Escolar, Universidad de Sevilla, Seville, Spain.

Ortega, R., J. A. Mora-Merchán, & I. Fernández. (1996). Working with the Educational Community against the Problem of Violence among Peers at School. The Seville Anti-Bullying Project. *European Conference on Educational Research*. Seville.

Pellegrini, A., & P. K. Smith. (1993). School Recess: Implications for Education and Development. *Review of Educational Research* 63(1): 51–67.

Pereira, B. O. (1998). *Estudo e prevenção do bullying no contexto escolar. Os recreios e as práticas agressivas da criança*. Dissertação de Doutoramento em Estudos da Criança, Braga. Universidade do Minho, Instituto de Estudos da Criança.

————. (2002). *Para uma escola sem violência. Estudo e prevanção das practices agressivas entre crianças*. Fundação Calouste Gulbenkian e Ministério da Ciência e Tecnologia (MCT). Textos Universitários.

Pereira, B. O., A. Almeida, L. Valenti, & D. Mendonça. (1996). O bullying nas escolas portuguesas: Análise de variáveis fundamentais para a identificaçao do problema. In L. Almedia, J. Silvério & S. Araújo (Eds.), *Actas II Congresso Galaico-Português de Psicopedagogia* (pp. 71–81). Braga: UM.

Rigby, K. (1997). *Bullying in Schools and What to Do about It*. London: Jessica Kingsley.

Smith, P. K., & S. Sharp. (1994). *School Bullying. Insights and Perspectives*. London: Routledge.

Whitney, I., & P. K. Smith. (1993). A Survey of the Nature and Extent of Bullying in Junior/Middle and Secondary Schools. *Educational Research* 35(17): 3–25.

23

Grounding the Players: Social Play Experiences Reflect School Playground Policies

Eva Peterson

The best preparation for school is to [enable] the preschooler . . . to experience widely and intensely what is relevant and appropriate to that stage.

—Lawrence K. Frank (1890–1958)

Playful behaviors are varied, complex, and constant. They happen continually, whether encouraged or forbidden. Young children express interest in stories, feelings, and ideas at play. They investigate, interpret, and react to themselves as well as everyone around them. They seek playmates to join them, asking, "Do you want to play?" and membership in a group, asking, "Can I play?" Sometimes a child or a group will focus on specific social attitudes. For example, a child acting like the "tough guy" may be welcome by other children who value that attitude. Social relations are a dominant feature of young children's play activities. During playground times, children select their own friends and groups. Their actions affect the way children learn to treat each other.

Adults' expectations for a playground context and the developmental needs of children are equally important but often invisible influences on the connections between play behaviors and how children learn to treat each other. These expectations provide the foundation for social implications that affect playground policies and they deserve the critical attention of the total school community.

The presence of adults on the playground influences the quality of children's social interactions, as well as the character of their play. They are models, mediators, and mentors who represent the cultural and social values of the responsible community. On the playground, supervisors mostly referee fights, umpire games, dry tears, scold stragglers, and expect children to form straight lines. Most of those adults report that they would prefer not to be on the playground, even though they understand the importance of supervision. Often, adults will either ignore or over-react to questionable activities. The predictable result is that children recognize the differences between how they are "supposed to" and how they are "allowed to" be-have. These double standards affect the way children learn to treat each other when they are making their own choices on the playground. For example, children are not "supposed" to tease each other, but everyone knows that children are "al-lowed" to take great advantage of the definition of that term. Maybe taking a hat looks like teasing but is really just a game of "catch." On the other hand, while some children love teasing games, others find them terrifying.

Children's choices of acceptable actions vary widely on the social "approval" scale. Actions also vary according to whether a child is acting alone or as a group member. When children realize the power their actions have to affect other people, they also begin to understand the differences between how people can, do, and should treat each other. Many forms of play help children connect and expand their own developmental interests, environmental opportunities, and emotional aware-ness. As they play, they mirror their experiences and sense of wonder. They ex-plore the future by traveling to Mars. They celebrate birthday parties. They enact heroic rescues. On the playground, children's social behaviors are reflected in play that helps them learn to do the following:

1. Discover and accept challenges (Piaget & Inhelder, 1964).
2. Structure and control relationships (Vygotsky, 1962).
3. Negotiate and cope with changes (Erikson, 1950).

DISCOVERING ADVENTURE: CHILDREN DEVELOP MOTIVATIONS AND IDENTIFY CHALLENGES AS PART OF SOCIAL PLAY

When children enter school, one new challenge is making friends. In the classroom the social rules are set and enforced by an authority figure. On the playground, how-ever, adults do not usually monitor how children try to make friends. Sometimes they dare each other physically, "Bet you can't catch me!" or "Let's jump off the swing!" Sometimes they try to attract attention by making demands such as, "I want to go first!" or boasting of special tricks, "Watch me go across the bars!"

Children also engage each other by acting out imaginary stories that incorporate their playground surroundings. Birthday parties are favorites for preschoolers and kindergarteners playing in a sand yard (Paley, 1988). Between first and third grade, rescue games are popular. For example, second graders might create a play-ground "rescue" filled with daunting challenges:

"Let's be firefighters! Did you see that movie on TV?"
"Yeah. But make the flames be coming from a house under the big slide."

"Yeah, and we have special equipment. So we can go in the flames!"

"No, you have the hose and first aid kit but I am trapped inside."

"Yeah, I have to go down the slide to get to you."

In addition to strategies for making friends and using the playground resources, children endlessly engage in characterizing their differences. Often this leads to confrontations, dares, and fights. Fights offer highly charged, exciting, and very easy opportunities for children to explore a wide range of social, intellectual, and physical challenges (Peterson, 1973). Learning to stand up for oneself is a necessary social skill that children practice at playground times. However, there are qualitative differences between the way children settle their differences on bare neglected playgrounds or on playgrounds that offer a rich variety of activities. Parents and teachers understand children's classroom learning benefits from a "rich environment." It is time to recognize that their playground learning also benefits from a "rich environment."

Any time children's play helps them learn social behaviors, it affects how they learn academic skills (Jarrett & Maxwell, 1999). We know that play and learning environments for young children are two sides of the same coin from which children work toward understanding their world (Piaget, 1962). Therefore, learning is not confined to the classroom and play is not confined to the playground. For example, whenever children play they also learn more about their world. They learn to

- Recognize complexities (Duckworth, 1987).
- Investigate using appealing materials (Edwards, 1998).
- Concentrate with more than one sensibility (Gardner, 1993).
- Enjoy good questions (Harlen, 1985).
- Create stimulating situations (Middlebrooks, 1998).
- Look for new challenges (Thompson, 1995).

Social Implications

The physical construct of the playground will affect children's social and intellectual behaviors. The fact that children are motivated to seek challenges in a variety of ways should be incorporated in planning strategies and playground policies. Children can be expected to use competitive actions to gain attention, increase skills, and promote themselves in a social group. Their actions reflect the common acceptable values they have observed in social situations. For example, children form teams and play games with a level of fairness and guided by rules that are defined by the group. Their activities range from dangerous to beneficial. One child may dare someone to jump from a swing, while another child may lead a larger group to jump rope for the benefit of the American Heart Association. The implication is that children need guidance in balancing their individual needs for attention and adventure.

Children can be expected to grow out of activities that no longer present a challenge. When they grow out of one set of interests they will look for others. The implication is that age-appropriate equipment for a play setting must meet safety concerns as well as different developmental, physical, and social levels. Children seeking challenges will use whatever materials they find appealing, whether dangerous or not. The implication is that the presence of age-appropriate, safe, and exciting materials invite children to play together, building a variety of positive, playful skills and social behaviors (Clemens, 2001).

TAKING CHARGE: CHILDREN INVESTIGATE CONTROL AND LIMITS OF POWER AS PART OF THEIR SOCIAL PLAY

An important early childhood job is to learn when, and to what extent, everyday situations can be independently managed. The extremes and difficulties of this mission are familiar to caretakers who contend with a nimble two-year-old crossing the street while ducking adult hands, or a willful preteen hiding phone calls after ten at night. Developmental issues of control are part of children's efforts to make sense out of their environment (Vygotsky, 1967). On the playground, children test both physical and social controls. For example, children imagining an exciting and dangerous adventure might want to climb to the top of a roof. That would be part of the physical challenge they create for themselves. In addition, they are challenging the caretakers' limits of control. Safety supervision is expected on playgrounds, but children's interest in taking charge are not always dangerous. Some children mimic the tone of voice and the demands of the supervisor as a means of controlling others. Other children envision a more independent status with their own project to manage and control, such as offering to make someone "pay" for "bothering" a friend.

The child who gathers errand runners or the pit boss who engages enthusiastic helpers are examples of children who take control of their own interests first. Children may also enjoy the power that allows them to define the vision and command the activities or supervise a story enactment. Often there are conflicts about who should be in control of whom, and someone complains about the "bossy" kid.

One compelling way for children to take control within a social situation is to start either a physical or a verbal fight. In most classrooms that is simply not allowed. However, if children are allowed to treat each other differently on the playground than in the classroom, an interesting dynamic emerges. The children may mimic language that teachers use, but they expect teachers to be in charge of how children act. Individuals do not see themselves as responsible parties to how other children treat each other.

Most curriculums expect kindergarteners to learn to control impulsive, immature behavior. Children are expected to "control themselves" and to obey the social expectations of the group (i.e., teacher). Three-, four-, and five-year-olds are admonished to "use your words" instead of hitting to express an idea. We want children to realize that words lead to control. Newly acquired social skills may then be incorporated into carefully supervised play in the dress-up corner or the block area. Kindergarten environments are supposed to help children learn to play by themselves, as well as have a positive outcome from their time together. As children get older, the attention directed toward social skills is overshadowed by concerns relating to academic skills. First graders who seek "a best friend," second graders who try to "belong," third graders who command a place as "gatekeeper," or fourth and fifth graders who squabble over contests for "good players" and "fair rules" are all still actively engaged in developmentally, age-appropriate learning about control issues and social skills. They are still learning how to treat each other.

Social Implications

Behaviors that seek control and power are healthy age-appropriate evidence that a child is becoming responsible for making decisions and eager to participate as a leader in a social situation. These needs also have implications for playground policies. Children learning to take control need support to become comfortable with the responsibilities of leadership. Children have very different ways of expressing interests, capabilities, and needs for controlling actions. Most school activities have a very limited range of leadership opportunities, and most classrooms accept a very narrow range of leadership styles. The child who can best imitate the teacher usually has the best chance of being allowed to exercise control and power.

Playground policies need to provide for many types of social leadership and teaching and learning styles. Adults provide leadership for teams of children to participate in activities such as ball games, jump rope, and tag that are governed by game rules. Traditionally, children who become leaders of playground activities are adept athletes, fast talkers, or bullies. They include, for example, the children who can pick a good dodge ball team, pick a good fight, coerce other children into being obedient, or buy acceptance by bringing candy. As long as playground policies continue to favor such stereotyped role behavior, there is an unspoken social implication: The success, recognition, and skills for managing peer groups is linked to some powerful athletic ability or personality trait that is out of reach for most children.

Children need opportunities to control many different types of activities and can be invited to be responsible for playground events that earn the respect of their peers in countless ways. Their leadership may not relate directly to playing at recess. How many children participate in decisions about purchasing equipment for the school? How many children attend public presentations concerning playground improvements? How many children help plan a group sing or an instrumental performance instead of setting up a car wash for playground improvements? These types of activities help the invisible or physically challenged children learn about power, command interest in play issues, and develop skills as socially respectful leaders. The most important implication is that each child needs to learn a positive leadership role related to playground activities and be accorded public respect. The focus must be on playground activities because it is the peer groups' most social platform. The playground is the place where children must earn independent social respect.

DARING TO BE FLEXIBLE: THROUGH SOCIAL PLAY CHILDREN LEARN SKILLS FOR COPING WITH CHANGE

In addition to using challenges and controls to measure their achievement, children must learn to anticipate and cope with changes in the world around them (Erikson, 1950). In many ways children prepare themselves for this task through playful scenarios that they enjoy. The two-year-old may take delight in changing a coffee cup into an imaginary cat dish simply by getting down on the ground and lapping from it as if the child had suddenly changed into a cat. The sixth grade girl may stick two great balloons in her shirt as if she had suddenly entered into an imaginary future.

Children's social groups have hierarchies and norms that change constantly in accordance with age-appropriate interests. Whether in or out of class, on or off the playground, children negotiate endlessly for rank and position. They are preoccupied with the social implications of their own actions independent of adult supervision. More often than not their social preoccupation is a nexus point between joy and sorrow, between competence and clumsiness, between playful actions and power-seeking positions.

Adapting to change is so important that it may well become a survival skill. Political, environmental, and technological changes are increasing in speed and intensity at an almost Malthusian rate (Gleik, 2000). Childhood is not exempt from the pressures of these changes. Academically, children are taught to seek out and predict change. It makes sense to teachers and parents for children to study mathematical problems that require changing fractions into percentages. It makes sense also that children have to be able to do those problems quickly.

The playground environment is not usually thought of as an important place for children to study change, but in fact it may be the best place to learn about changes in social and group dynamics. It is interesting to compare the modes and forms of play activities of today with those of fifty years ago. Roger Hart (1986) has focused on these kinds of changes:

There are dozens of accounts in the popular press about the demise of street games and chants. Such commentary usually seems superficial and nostalgic. However, if looked at together with the amazing records by Iona and Peter Opie (1959) on the history of children's street games one might conclude that this reflects an erosion of autonomous child culture. The streets have been a place where children could meet children on their own ground and create their own settings for play. Jane Jacobs (1992) considered the issue sufficiently important in her classic book on the Death and Life of Great American Cities to devote a chapter to it. She claims that children "need an unspecialized outdoor home base from which to play, to hang around in, and to help form their notions of the world." (p. 2)

There are equally important social implications involved in the constant jockeying for special social identities, such as the kids who eat lunch together, review their collections together, talk about birthday parties, become "club" members, or even join gangs. Inter- and intragroup adjustments result in constant tensions and competition. Skills in anticipating and managing these exchanges are critical and they engage every child everyday, both in every classroom and on every playground.

Children's natural urge to create and control change is unquestionably valuable to their health and development. The playground is a natural laboratory for their experimental changes in social interests. For example, it can be children's arena for changing their roles at play. Many special identities are classic and some children can change roles easily when offered equally respected choices. For example, many children who play the "bully" can learn to play the "leader" if given serious responsibilities. Also, children who find themselves as the "victim" can learn to play the "hero" if given a demanding problem.

The playground setting can offer children attractive opportunities to create many types of social roles away from adult expectations. However, the playground needs to offer more than just a space away from adults. It needs to offer a fascinating, inspiring environment for new opportunities before positive changes in social play dynamics will evolve. One way to do this is by obtaining apparatus that combines academic challenges with natural instinctive games. George Forman (1984) has been a pioneer in inventing equipment to offer children new ways of thinking about their actions and new ways to investigate physical phenomena. The National Science Foundation supported an effort to develop playground apparatus that would engage children in physical actions accompanied by symbolic representations at the same time. Two inventions that resulted, the Timer and the Light Track, have been very successful in terms of children's learning and social engagement, but they have only been built in a few places (Kimball & Peterson, 1996).

There are also many ways to inspire new leadership through programs for playgrounds. Inside the school, groups are often formed to run assemblies or present child-run school projects. The whole school becomes a closer community abuzz with excitement in preparing programs. Why not expand this approach to the playground? Children can become powerful agents for changing their playground environment.

A growing variety of projects are available for that purpose. Children can find safe, productive, and socially positive interactions with adults as well as other classmates in novel outdoor ventures. The explosion of schoolyard gardens and environmental programs across the country speaks to the evidence of success for integrated indoor/outdoor programs. Environmentalists have long been aware that working outdoors has important social implications for children. They have also been aware that outdoor activities provide a setting where the lines between social play and classroom learning are blurred. The Schoolyard Habitats program sponsored by the National Wildlife Federation is a valuable and successful example of purposeful, structured, integrated outdoor/indoor opportunities that combine learning and playful social interactions (see http://www.nwf.org/habitats/schoolyard).

Social Implications

Playgrounds require both structural and communal flexibility if children are to find more ways to be acceptable and responsible friends. For children who do not take traditional leadership roles, playground policies need to support them in advocacy roles and offer a variety of leadership opportunities that will help children earn the respect of their peers. Playground policies also determine the amount of time that children are allowed on the playground. Time is an important feature for constructive play. The implication is that children need supportive circumstances and an allowance of time to learn, practice, cope, and ultimately to play with the social changes that are part of learning how to treat each other (Jarrett & Maxwell, 1999).

CONCLUSION

The three sections of this chapter are grounded in classic theories of child development. The social implications suggest that the complex developmental needs of children must always be considered as the foundation for playground policy design, supervision, and desired outcomes or expectations. Children learn best in rich, variable, and age-appropriate environments. The playground is a valuable learning resource equally as important as the classroom. It provides the critical space and time for children to learn positive, independent, and social play skills that are imperative for every child's healthy development.

Playground policies have a vital role in the development of young children's physical, mental, and social health. Well-balanced, they provide for a setting where adults actively support creative play and positive conduct. An uninteresting play site promotes negative activities. A neglected site is a clear message of adult disinterest and disregard for children's needs. Children remember their play experiences as they grow into adults and memories of playground feelings remain vivid for their entire lives, for better or worse. The most important social implications of playground policies are hidden in those memories.

BIBLIOGRAPHY

Biber, B., P. Minuchin, E. Shapiro, & H. Zimiles. (1969). *The Psychological Impact of School Experience*. New York: Basic Books.

Clements, Rhonda L. (ed.). (2001). *Elementary School Recess*. Boston: American Press.

Duckworth, Eleanor. (1987). *The Having of Wonderful Ideas*. New York: Teachers College Press.

Edwards, C. P., L. Gandini, & G. Forman (eds.). (1998). *The Hundred Languages of Children: The Reggio Emilia Approach—Advanced Reflections* (2d ed.). Greenwich, CT: Ablex.

Elias, M., J. Zins, R. Weissberg, K. Frey, M. Greenberg, M. Haynes, R. Kessler, M. Schwab-Stone, & T. Shriver. (1997). *Promoting Social and Emotional Learning*. New York: Association for Supervision and Curriculum Development.

Erikson, E. H. (1950). *Childhood and Society*. New York: Norton.

Forman, George E., Fleet Hill (contributor). (1984). *Constructive Play: Applying Piaget in the Preschool*. Menlo Park, CA: Addison-Wesley.

Gardner, H. (1983). *Frames of Mind: The Theory of Multiple Intelligences*. New York: Basic Books.

Gleik, J. (2000). *Faster: The Acceleration of Just About Everything*. New York: Vintage.

Hammond, D. (1998). *KaBOOM! Playground Manual*. Washington, DC: KaBoom!.

Harlen, W. (ed.). (1985). *Primary Science: Taking the Plunge*. Portsmouth, NH: Heinemann Educational Books.

Hart, C. H. (ed.). (1993). *Children on Playgrounds: Research Perspectives and Applications*. New York: State University of New York Press.

Hart, R. (1986). *The Changing City of Childhood: Implications for Play and Learning*. The 1986 Catherine Molony Memorial Lecture. New York: Teachers College.

———. The Right to Play and Children's Participation. *Urban Parks Online*. Retrieved from http://www.pps.org/urbanparks/right_to_play.html.

Hawkins, F. P. (1969). *The Logic of Action*. New York: Pantheon Books.

———. (1997). *Early Years are Learning Years: The Value of School Recess and Outdoor Play*. Washington, DC: NAEYC.

Herron, R., & B. Sutton-Smith (eds.). (1971). *Child's Play*. New York: Wiley.

Jarrett, O., & D. Maxwell. (1999). Physical Education and Recess: Are Both Necessary? *American Association of Child's Right to Play* 55: 3–20.

Kimball, N., & Eva Peterson. (1996). Research Findings on National Science Grants: New Directions in Science Playgrounds. Paper presented at AERA National Convention, New York.

Leacock, E. B. (1971). At Play in African Villages. In E. B. Leacock (Ed.), *Play, A Natural History Magazine Special Supplement* (pp. 60–65). New York: American Museum of Natural History.

Loban, W. (1963). *The Language of Elementary School Children*. Research Monograph No. 1. Champaign, IL: National Council of Teachers of English.

McV. Hunt, J. (1959, February 27). *Experience and the Development of Motivation: Some Reinterpretations*. Eleventh Annual Institute in Psychiatry and Neurology of the Veterans Administration Hospital, North Little Rock, AK.

Middlebrooks, S. (1998). *Getting to Know City Kids*. New York: ASCD.

Moffit, M., & E. Omwake. (n.d.). *The Intellectual Content of Play*. New York: New York State Association of Education of Young Children.

Moore, Robin. (1990). *Childhood's Domain: Play and Place in Child Development*. Berkeley, CA: MIG Communications.

Nablan, G., & S. Trimble. (1994). *The Geography of Childhood*. Boston: Beacon Press.

National Education Association. (2000). Going the Extra Mile. In *NEA Today* (p. 30). Washington, DC: National Education Association.

Opie, P., & I. Opie. (1959). *The Lore and Language of Schoolchildren*. New York: Oxford University Press.

———. (1969). *Children's Games in Street and Playground*. Oxford: Oxford University Press.

Paley, V. G. (1981). *Wally's Stories*. Cambridge: Harvard University Press.

———. (1988). *Bad Guys Don't Have Birthdays: Fantasy Play at Four*. Chicago: University of Chicago Press.

Pelligrini, A. (1998). *Psychological Basics for Early Education*. New York: John Wiley and Sons.

Peterson, E. (1973). Letter from North Dakota: Inviting the People to See. *Urban Review* 7(4).

———. (1997). *Playful Behaviors and Play Opportunities as Partners in Environments for Children*. New York: Playground Environments.

Piaget, J. (1962). *Play, Dreams and Imitation in Childhood*. New York: Norton.

Piaget, J., & B. Inhelder. (1964). *The Early Growth of Logic in the Child.* New York: Norton.

Rosen, C., & H. Rosen. (1973). *The Language of Primary School Children.* Baltimore: Penguin Books.

Ruppel-Shell, E. (1994). Kids Don't Need Equipment, They Need Opportunity. *Smithsonian* 25(4): 79–86.

Stine, S. (1997). *Landscapes for Learning: Creating Outdoor Environments.* New York: John Wiley and Sons.

Thompson, D. (1995). *National Action Plan for Playground Safety.* Cedar Falls: University of Northern Iowa.

Vygotsky, L. S. (1962). *Thought and Language.* Cambridge: MIT Press.

———— . (1967). Play and Its Role in the Mental Development of the Child. *Soviet Psychology* 5: 6–18.

White, R. W. (1959). Motivation Reconsidered: The Concept of Competence. *Psychological Review* 66: 299–333.

24

Guidelines for Managing
Playground Risks

Susan Hudson and Donna Thompson

Playgrounds remain a fundamental area for children's play in America. Fortunately, these play areas have developed into more interesting and complex structures to meet the play needs of children. Unfortunately, the rate of playground injuries that occur on these public structures seems to have remained static through the 1990s (Hudson, Mack, & Thompson, 2000). However, according to industry reports it might be argued that the rate of injury is actually going down, since it would seem that more new playgrounds are built every year. Nevertheless, the fact does remain that a significant number of children (over 200,000 per year) are hurt on our nation's playgrounds (Tinsworth & McDonald, 2001). As such, it is incumbent upon play providers to understand the risk factors present in the playground environment and take appropriate steps to initiate injury-prevention measures to reduce the probability of injury to children on public playgrounds. This chapter will present a guideline for play providers in order that they may understand the risk factors inherent in the playground environment.

ANATOMY OF PLAYGROUND INJURIES

In order to develop a risk-management program for playgrounds, the play provider needs to understand how playground injuries occur. This includes a recognition of potential risk factors in the playground environment and how these risk factors can lead to playground injuries.

As shown in Figure 24.1, inherent in any playground environment are four major risk factors as identified by the National Program for Playground Safety. These factors are Supervision, Appropriate Development Design, Fall Surfacing, and Equip-

Figure 24.1
How Injuries Occur

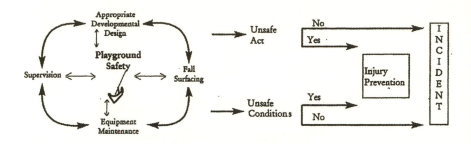

ment and Surfacing Maintenance. Each of these factors has two elements (unsafe actions and unsafe conditions) that, left unchecked, may lead to playground injuries. The rest of this chapter will provide basic information concerning both risk factors and elements for play providers to consider in creating a comprehensive risk-management plan to address those risk factors for public playground environments.

EXAMINING THE RISK FACTORS

Supervision

Research has shown that approximately 40 percent of all playground injuries involve the lack of proper supervision as a contributing factor (King, 1990; Frost & Sweeney, 1996). What are the unsafe actions and unsafe conditions inherent in the lack of proper supervision?

Unsafe Actions

There are two major people actions that contribute to playground injuries in the area of supervision. First is the lack of proper adult supervision. Adults need to supervise children on playground equipment, especially young children. Children do not always have the intellectual capacity to foresee possible hazards in the play environment. The authors have been called as expert witnesses in many cases where the lack of appropriate adult supervision has led to serious injury and even death of young children using public playground equipment. In the same light, children, while using the equipment, have a responsibility to stay within safety guidelines that have been explained to them. However, most public agencies just put new equipment into an area without providing any education to children concerning acceptable use. The problem is then compounded by not providing any signage or other educational material directing how to safely use the equipment. This is similar to buying a new car and ignoring the owner's instruction manual. With both the car and playground equipment, the lack of knowledge concerning how to do things in a safe manner can lead to disaster. As part of the opening celebration for a new playground, the play provider should furnish information to the general public about safe playground actions for both adults and children. In addition, every year during National Playground Safety Week they should reinforce ideas about playground safety for children in their communities.

Unsafe Conditions

Two physical items that contribute to unsafe supervision of playgrounds include: the physical layout of the playground structure and the avoidance of mixed play zones.

As noted in the U.S. Consumer Product Safety Commission's (CPSC) (1997) *Handbook for Public Playground Safety* (1997), all moving equipment should be at the edges of the playground. Thus, swings, merry-go-rounds, track rides, or any equipment that children are using to move through space should be located away from basic traffic patterns of the play area. Children using these pieces of equipment are not always in control of the equipment or their bodies. Likewise, attention should be paid to where children access and egress on specific equipment pieces to make sure that no blockage will occur with multiple usage. Avoid purchasing equipment that prevents adult supervisors from seeing children on the equipment. A supervisor should be able to see children from a minimum of two directions while standing in any one spot.

Finally, make sure that you have separated various play areas. A soccer field or other team sport areas should not be next to a playground area without a proper buffer zone. Mixed play zones can lead to unnecessary conflict between two different types of recreation users.

Appropriate Development Design

Playground equipment is designed for children ages two to five and five to twelve (U.S. Consumer Product Safety Commission, 1997; American Society for Testing and Materials, 1998). Yet the majority of public playgrounds in the United States are designed as if all equipment can be used by children ages two to twelve (Hudson, Mack, & Thompson, 2000). This fact leads to both unsafe actions and unsafe conditions in this risk-factor area.

Unsafe Actions

A two-year-old is not a twelve-year-old in terms of physical, emotional, social, or intellectual development. Thus, the mismatch of children's abilities with the requirements for safe use of equipment can lead to serious injury. This mismatch, coupled with the already-mentioned lack of knowledge of equipment used by children, can lead to an increase in the frequency of injuries on such equipment pieces as arch climbers, overhead ladders, and other challenges not recommended for young children.

Unsafe Conditions

By not physically separating equipment for children two to five and five to twelve years, play providers are setting up unsafe playground conditions. In addition, the absence of signs designating separate areas does little to educate the general public about the proper use of these areas.

It is also incumbent upon the play provider to insure that playground areas are designed with safety in mind and that the selection of equipment meets the play needs of children. In this light, the play provider must actively work with playground manufacturers and representatives in initial discussions regarding what the play provider's agency wants, rather than simply accepting the designs of the selected playground company and then having to renegotiate at a later date.

Fall Surfacing

Since 70 percent of all public playground injuries have the lack of proper surfacing cited as a major contributing factor (Tinsworth & McDonald, 2001), it is imperative that the leisure-service manager pay attention to the unsafe actions and unsafe conditions that are part of this risk factor.

Unsafe Actions

Two important aspects are inherent in this risk factor. The first, the inappropriate use of equipment by children, may or may not be able to be controlled, depending on the education program that the play provider has in place. However, the second, the proper and ongoing maintenance of the surface by adults, is a direct responsibility of the agency and should be a primary objective of any playground risk-management plan. Simply putting wood chips down one year and then adding some more five year later, when the budget allows, is not an appropriate or safe action to prevent playground injuries.

Unsafe Conditions

Play providers must pay attention to the selection of appropriate surfacing for all playgrounds under their control. This involves an understanding of suitable surface materials in relation to the height of the equipment, as well as the maintenance of any loose fill materials at the proper depth and the proper use zone (see Figure 24.2).

It is important to bear in mind the following safety measures:

1. Safe materials: Safe surfacing materials are comprised of either loose fill (e.g., sand, wood chips, pea gravel, chopped rubber, etc.) or unitary (poured-in-place rubber or rubber mats). Play providers should never place playground equipment over asphalt, cement, dirt, or grass. These surfaces simply do not have the shock-absorbing characteristics to cushion a child's fall.

2. Height: Equipment should be no higher than eight feet for school-age children and no higher than six feet for preschool children. Research has shown that the probability of injury doubles with equipment over the height of 6.7 feet (Laforest, Robitaille, Lesage, & Dorval, 2001; Chalmers, Marshall, & Langley et al., 1996). The play value (complex-

Figure 24.2
Safe-Surfacing Decision Model

ity of task) of a slide eight feet high is the same as one ten feet high. Thus, height does not add play value but does significantly raise the probability of risk (injury).

3. Depth: Loose-fill material must be at a proper depth to adequately absorb the impact of a child's fall. Minimum depth requirements can be found in the CPSC (1997, p. 5) *Handbook for Public Playground Safety*. The National Program for Playground Safety (Thompson, Hudson, & Mack, 2000) recommends that play providers start with twelve inches of loose fill material in order to give a cushion of safety for the children. Remember, not providing enough loose-fill material may be as dangerous as not having any shock-absorption material, since you give the child a false sense of security that the surfacing will be thick enough to cushion a fall.

4. Use Zones: It is of little value to have safe surfacing if it is not in the right place. Use zones refer to the area under and around equipment where a child might fall. For stationary equipment, the use zone extends six feet in all directions. Slides and swings have slightly different use zones. For slides, the distance is six feet, with the exception of the

area in front of the slide chute. Here, because children are moving off the equipment, the use zone is the height of the slide plus four feet. For swings, the use zone in front and back should be twice the height of the swing beam. Thus, if you have a swing beam that is eight feet high, you need the safe surfacing to extend sixteen feet in front of the swing and in the back of the swing. This is because children have a tendency to jump out of swings while they are in motion.

Equipment and Surface Maintenance

This last risk area is one that is often neglected. In a recent study of school playgrounds in Iowa, it was found that only 50 percent of the schools had regular inspections and maintenance of playground equipment (Bauer, Hudson, & Thompson, 2001). Equipment will not maintain itself. Steel rusts, wood splinters, and plastic cracks. Just like one maintains a car, play providers must maintain the play equipment in order to insure a safe play environment.

Unsafe Actions

The people elements in this risk factor include improper installation of equipment and lack of ongoing maintenance programs. It is important that any new playground area be audited after installation to make sure that pieces have been installed correctly and that the agency has a baseline safety check to use for evaluating future safety problems. In addition, an ongoing system of inspections and maintenance will insure that the area remains safe for use by children.

Unsafe Conditions

The play provider needs to be aware of any possible hazards in the environment (i.e., humanmade, such as roadways; natural, such as vegetation; and climatic, such as ice and snow) that can affect the safe use of equipment. In addition, the purchasing of equipment that does not meet U.S. Consumer Product Safety Commission (1997) guidelines or American Society for Testing and Materials (1998) standards for the playground area can lead to the development of unsafe conditions in the playground area.

This chapter has briefly outlined the risk factors and elements that leisure-service managers should address in order to develop a comprehensive plan to manage risks in playgrounds. By understanding these risk factors and underlying actions and conditions that can lead to playground injuries, play providers can begin to manage risks and insure safe playgrounds for children in their communities.

NOTE

It should be noted that both authors strongly support the provision of playground equipment to enhance a child's play and development. However, both authors think that many times the terms "risk" and "challenge" are misused in evaluating playgrounds. They contend that risk is the probability of injury, while challenge refers to the complexity of task that one asks of the child. It is the authors' belief that with careful planning and thought one can raise the play value or challenge of play equipment without increasing the risk of injury.

REFERENCES

American Society for Testing and Materials (ASTM). (1998). *Standard Consumer Safety Performance Specifications for Playground Equipment for Public Use* (F1487-98). West Conshohocken, PA: ASTM.

Bauer, H. (2001). Safe Supervision Practices in Iowa Public Schools. Unpublished master's thesis, University of Northern Iowa.

Chalmers, D. J., S. W. Marshall, & J. D. Langley. (1996). Height and Surfacing as Risk Factors for Inferring in Falls from Playground Equipment: A Case Control Study. *Injury Prevention* 2: 98–104.

Frost, J. L., & T. B. Sweeney. (1996). *Cause and Prevention of Playground Injuries and Litigation.* Wheaton, MD: Association for Childhood Education International.

Hudson, S., M. Mack, & D. Thompson. (2000). *How Safe Are America's Playgrounds? A National Profile of Childcare, School and Park Playgrounds.* Cedar Falls, IA: National Program for Playground Safety.

King, S. (1990). Developing a Safe Playground is Everyone's Responsibility. Paper presented at the Minneapolis Congress for Parks and Recreation. Minneapolis, MN.

Laforest, S., Y. Robitaille, D. Lesage, & D. Dorval. (2001). Surface Characteristics, Equipment Height, and the Occurrence and Severity of Playground Injuries. *Injury Prevention* 7: 35–40.

Olsen, H.,, S. Hudson, & D. Thompson. (2002). Children's Play. *American School Board Journal* 180(8): 22–24.

Thompson, D., S. D. Hudson, & M. G. Mack. (2000). Installing SAFE Playgrounds. *Play Book* (spring): 10–12.

Tinsworth, D., & J. McDonald. (2001). *Special Study: Injuries and Deaths Associated with Children's Playground Equipment.* Washington, DC: CPSC.

U.S. Consumer Product Safety Commission. (1997). *Handbook for Public Playground Safety* (Pub. No. 325). Washington, DC: CPSC.

25

Assessment as an Adventure Activity

Leah Holland Fiorentino

This chapter explains the role of recent technological advances as they relate to assessable components of play in open-movement environments. Recent advancements in the technological world have applications in all environments, and with a bit of imagination and courage, play professionals can approach their daily effort with a fresh perspective. The utilization of a wide range of resources encourages the use of technology to enhance a more authentic assessment and reflects a higher measure of public accountability. As the play professional is engaged in the design and development of assessable components to be observed, there is a natural engagement in creative thinking and a more critical analysis of the observable benefits of play for children.

If play is a vital contributor to the growth and development of children, then those professionals who provide play opportunities need to take advantage of these opportunities to observe and record developmental changes for each of the children in their charge. These observable developmental changes occur at variable rates, are bound to the individual strengths and needs of each child, and deserve to be recorded and celebrated as small victories in the pursuit of happiness.

RATIONALE FOR FORMAL OBSERVATIONS

The focus of professionals designing play opportunities should be driven by the strengths and needs of the children in the environment. Careful and thoughtful observations partnered with authentic assessment opportunities and formal record keeping place the play professional in a favorable situation to plan appropriate challenges for each developing child. Play professionals can now utilize handheld

Personal Digital Assistants (PDAs) to help with formal record keeping and collect data about individual and group dynamic changes over a prescribed period of time. Thereby, the play professional can store those observations for later discussions with the children, parents, and/or other play professionals.

Observation and assessment opportunities are never intended to interfere with the child involved in a play activity. The play professional's role is simply to note the activity and then either record a comment or assess a level of prescribed behavior. Once the notation is entered on the PDA, the play professional looks for other observable behaviors to record. Observations can be pre-set into specific categories or open to any observable behaviors, and the observation can focus on one child or many children interacting in a play environment. Play professionals need to be aware at all times that the observations and recorded comments are their perceptions of the child's behaviors; if questioned, the child may have different intentions.

CATEGORIES FOR OBSERVATIONS AND ASSESSMENTS

An assortment of observation and assessment categories exist that relate to the nature of play (both structured and unstructured) in a variety of contexts. Each category about which a play professional chooses to collect information can be assessed according to prescribed criteria or merely noted as present or absent. Play professionals can choose to observe specific prescribed categories to collect data about children that need additional attention, or play professsionals can observe and record observations on random children in the specified play environment. Play professionals can control the number of children they "plan" to observe, and play professionals can control the number of different categories they "plan" to observe for the children's behaviors.

A sample of different observation categories can be found in Table 25.1. These samples are based on categories derived from developmentally appropriate motor skills categories, cognitive development categories, social–emotional categories, and physiological fitness categories. The criteria levels are set based on currently accepted levels within each category. (Play professionals should be assured that each professional can determine criteria levels that best suit the children in their charge. The criteria levels need only remain constant across individuals within a group.)

One of the latest assessment hardware devices used to collect data about the fitness levels of children was developed by the Polar Heart Rate Monitor Company. The heart rate monitors consist of a watchlike device that is worn around the wrist and an adjustable strap that is fastened around the child's chest. The adjustable band contains a transmitter that sends a data record of the child's heart rate at regular intervals. The heart rate monitors are easy to use and collect important data about the changes in a child's heart rate as a result of different episodes of physical activity. The data collected from the heart rate monitors can easily be downloaded into a software program and then displayed graphically for parent conferences.

Table 25.1
Sample Observable Categories

Observable Category	High	Medium	Low
Use of Permanent Equipment	All equipment	< 1/2 equipment	None
Use of Manipulative Equipment	> 10 opportunities	5–9 opportunities	< 5 opportunities
Verbal Interactions	> 50	25–50	< 25
Parallel Play	> 5 opportunities	< 5 opportunities	Never
Social Contacts	> 5 other individuals	< 5 other individuals	Never connects with other individuals
Imaginative Play	Uses contextual equipment	Uses imaginary equipment	Never engages
Physical Activity Level	Low	Moderate	High
Activity Intensity Level	Low	Moderate	High
Fundamental Motor Skills: Gross Motor			
Walking	Initial	Elementary	Mature
Running	Initial	Elementary	Mature
Jumping: Horizontal	Initial	Elementary	Mature
Jumping: Vertical	Initial	Elementary	Mature
Throwing Overhand	Initial	Elementary	Mature
Striking: Two handed	Initial	Elementary	Mature
Kicking	Initial	Elementary	Mature
Catching	Initial	Elementary	Mature
Hopping	Initial	Elementary	Mature
Fundamental Motor Skills: Fine Motor			
Grasping	No opposition	Pseudo-opposition	True opposition

CONCLUSION

Not only does a child have a right to play, but the child has a right to have his or her play celebrated as he or she grows individually. This celebration of growth is easily initiated for the child, parent, and play professional when the changes in play behaviors have been documented over time.

If play is serious work—and, conversely, work could be serious play—then the children actively engaged in either process deserve a fair review of their efforts.

PART III

PLAYTHINGS AND PLAY SPACES

Part III opens with Pei-San Brown, Candra D. Thornton, and John A. Sutterby discussing several interrelated trends that are causing children to become "older" at younger ages, resulting in hurried childhoods. They explore this phenomenon through a critical look at the current toy culture, media strategies, parents' choices, and children's play. This chapter encourages child advocates to challenge society's assumptions about toys, marketing, media, and children's play. Elaine M. Van Lue explores the means by which traditional play and games are integrated to enhance learning. She encourages educators to incorporate games and play activities into their curriculums to help children become more physically fit, active, and well-coordinated, in addition to creating new opportunities for enhancing physical, social, emotional, creative, and mental skills. Joanne Hynes-Dusel shares innovative ideas for constructing and utilizing homemade equipment for various age populations. Specific directions and additional sources for the creative educator are included. Gustave Juhlin describes a special approach to four games and play activities that originated approximately 1,000 years ago during the Viking combative ages and have recently been revived in Scandinavian countries. The games and play activities are creatively linked to the traditions of the Viking culture to explain the game origins. Frederick Johnson integrates play and learning principles that can be used in all skill-based recreational settings while balancing structured practices with free play opportunities. The author cleverly contrasts the nature of play and practice for middle school children and suggests that middle school children may not be ready for competitive activities due to the required practice periods that precede a competition.

Lindsay C. Davis explains how creative intergenerational puppets can be made and discusses the commonalties between the child's right to play and the corresponding principles of older persons. The linking of the two generations offers the opportunity to transfer culture, knowledge, skills, and values from the older generation to the younger generation. Melissa Gemeinhardt introduces a unique facet of art education for children pre-k through grade 4, as well as a wide range of special-needs populations. The chapter focuses on the inclusion of Dada Movement elements into play activities using Developmentally Appropriate Practices. This approach encourages children to work independently in a safe context with unbiased encouragement designed to support learning and value individual choices. Gilbert W. Foley and John Castranova share an innovative program that utilizes open-ended or unstructured materials as an important addition to the many traditional school curriculums. These unstructured materials serve as a contrast to the present offerings for children and offer an array of educational materials and developmental toys. There is a discussion of the environments found to best develop the capacity for sustained attention, for making and testing hypotheses, and for expressing and understanding feelings and emotions. Vicki L. Stoecklin and Randy White examine the cultural development and operational issues in a 25,000-square-foot play and discovery center in Dubai, UAE, a society comprised of three cultures: Arab, Indian, and European. The authors address cultural challenges for both play leader staffing and the design of developmentally and culturally appropriate play events. The chapter concludes with a listing of many positive outcomes resulting from this innovative project.

Georgianna Duarte examines how the staff of the Texas Migrant Head Start Center, parents, children, and university students act as partners in play through a collaborative project. The collaborative effort of these professionals has created a unique approach to designing play areas. The chapter includes the successes of the project and suggestions for other design teams to consider. Kate Bishop identifies design features that provide sensory richness and reward, as well as educational tools and resources that can be utilized to design more complex environments. She carefully outlines the steps taken in a innovative project with the Royal Blind Society, and shares the collective wisdom of an expert design team. Finally, Lois A. Berggren explains the creation of a wall mural that was the collaborative effort of more than 250 participants of all ages and abilities in conjunction with the celebration of the 100th anniversary of Dorchester House. A discussion is included of how the participants engaged in a process of guided inquiry, evocative verbal imagery, creative movement, picture viewing, sharing of memories, and imaginative interpretation. The author presents art making as a truly sacred process in which young people explore and explain their world to themselves and others.

26

Kids Getting Older Younger:
The Adultification of Children's Play

Pei-San Brown, Candra D. Thornton,
and John A. Sutterby

Many authors have written about the ways in which adults infiltrate children's play boundaries and see children not as players, but as sophisticated consumers (John, 1999; Kirn & Cole, 2001; Steinberg & Kincheloe, 1998). Vandenberg (1990) suggested that toys had become a major instrument in the push to educate and adultify children. This accusation raises concerns about the way children are increasingly seen as a population to be manipulated by the adult world and that they are especially vulnerable as consumers. It is important to explore this adult manipulation of children's play by investigating the interplay between the media and toy industries and the potential adultification of children through such a relationship.

THE MEDIA

The media is often accused of being the largest transmitter of culture in our Western society. According to the *Frontline* episode titled "The Merchants of Cool" (Dretzin, 2001), five media conglomerates are presently responsible for the "selling" of almost all of youth culture. These five conglomerates are AOL/Time Warner, Disney, Viacom, News Corporation, and Vivendi Universal. Each of these entities own weblike networks of other companies that work together to sell youth culture. AOL/Time Warner is the largest media company in history. It reaches youth culture through film, the Internet, music, television, publishing, and recreation. Viacom, which merged with CBS Broadcasting, controls markets in radio, the Internet, film, television, publishing, theme parks, and other franchises (e.g., *Star Trek*). Disney is vested in film, the Internet, television, recreation, music, broadcasting, and publishing. News Corporation is involved in news, the

Internet, broadcasting, publishing, and sports throughout North and Latin America, Europe, Asia, and Australia. Vivendi Universal is the largest music company in the world. It is also involved in film, the Internet, television, publishing, and telecommunications.

The extent to which these conglomerates influence youth culture is evident when a few statistics are taken into consideration. Children spend an average of 3 hours per day watching television and an average of 6.5 hours per day with other forms of media (e.g., video/VCR/DVD, video games, computers) (American Academy of Pediatrics, 2001). Teens receive approximately 3,000 marketing messages per day, equaling over 1 million a year. By the time they are 18 years old, children have processed well over 10 million advertisements. Seventy-five percent of teens have television sets in their bedrooms and 33 percent have computers in their bedrooms, where they average over 2 hours a day on-line (Dretzin, 2001).

Currently, media advertisers are trying to brand and market products to younger and younger children. The recent trend is to target "tweens" (children ages eight to eleven) with products traditionally sold to older teens, like clothes, music, and food (TodÈ, 2001). However, the influence of these major media conglomerates on children's lives has not always been so pervasive.

HISTORY OF THE INTERPLAY BETWEEN MEDIA AND CHILDREN'S TOYS

Before the 1950s, toys were primarily advertised to adults. At this time adults were viewed as the main consumers of all goods, including children's toys and related products. In those days most of television consisted of shows directed toward families and adults. But in the 1950s *The Mickey Mouse Club* hit the airwaves as the first show created specifically for a child-only audience. Following this introduction of nationwide children's television came advertising aimed directly at children. Consumer and parent groups concerned about product placement and advertising to children pressured both government and the industry to protect children from advertising. From the 1960s to 1980, advertising on children's television remained self- and FCC-regulated (Federal Communications Commission), and toy-related shows were banned (Cross, 1997; Kline, 1993).

However, in 1980 Ronald Reagan was elected and the government began to deregulate children's television. In 1982 *He-Man and the Masters of the Universe* was the first television show with a toy tie-in. By 1984 the FCC no longer regulated the content of television for toy and marketing tie-ins, meaning that toys related to a show were available for purchase at the same time that the show was being aired. By the late 1980s toys and television shows were happily married and the number of toy-related and toy-based shows soared (e.g., *Transformers, Ninja Turtles, Power Rangers, Teletubbies, Powerpuff Girls*, and *Los Luchadores*). It is now common for shows to be developed around already-created toys. Children's television has become essentially nothing more than advertising for children's toys. Now, children are watching thirty-minute commercials instead of just thirty-second spots about their favorite toys (Cross, 1997; Kline, 1993).

MEDIA MESSAGES

Within their daily immersion in media of all varieties, children are constantly bombarded with glorified and enticing messages about adult and teen lifestyles. Toy-industry experts Levy and Weingartner (1990) described in explicit detail how toy designers looked at the types of television programs, movies, books, music, magazines, and clothing in which children were interested because they were aware of the power of media. Mary Pipher (1994), author of the book *Reviving Ophelia: Saving the Selves of Adolescent Girls*, believes that when children seek to emulate teen and adult life they choose the most salient images from the media on which to model that role. Unfortunately, to a large degree the images of adult and teen life depicted in the media consist of traditional gender and racial stereotypes, as well as stimulating images of sex, violence, alcohol, tobacco, and drugs.

As children's minds are saturated with these images, they seek to incorporate these adultified messages into their own worlds, first internalizing and then acting on the message that "growing up faster" and "acting older" is better. However, children do not distinguish between taking on adult/teen responsibilities versus taking on adult/teen roles in sex, violence, and so forth. When children are expected to behave in ways beyond their years, they will do so in all ways, not just in the ones selected by adults. If adult and teen life is glorified in ways that make stereotypes, sex, violence, and addictive drugs most salient to children, then they will incorporate those messages into their play and their relationships with others.

Children face a bewildering world of adult images, even to the extreme when in their play they encounter toys and playthings that reflect adult culture. Parents concerned about protecting their children's time of innocent childhood may be unaware that the toy and media industries carefully market images of violence, drug use, and adult consumerism directly to children. According to the CNN, in April 2001 a U.S. Congressional Committee voiced concern about the marketing of excessively violent games, toys, and movies to a younger and younger audience (Bierbauer, 2001).

One piece of tangible evidence of the occurrence of this type of marketing was found at the 2001 Toy Manufacturers of America Conference in New York. One of the toys being advertised was a tattooed, sneering, chainsaw-bearing doll/action figure/collectable based on the popular rap star Eminem. According to the Consumer Product Safety Commission's (1985) *Guidelines for Relating Children's Ages to Toy Characteristics*, dolls and action figures with realistic detail portraying real-life characters are most attractive to boys between three and eight years of age. While the consequences of having children play with dolls that are violent in theme is not clear, the fact that this aggressively depicted musician is packaged and marketed as a toy that appeals to children as young as three is a clear example of how variables of adult life gain entrance into children's play worlds.

As previously noted, one arena in which adult interference in children's play is highly visible is the movie or television show with toy tie-ins. The consolidation of media companies and the toy industry has created a market where the selling of toys knows no boundaries. This open season on children helps perpetuate a pushdown effect of consumer culture by acting on young children's desires to live the way they perceive teens and adults to live. Media gives them the ideas, toys give them the stage on which to act.

A number of toys, particularly action figures, videos, and video games, which are based on PG-13-, R-, and even NC-17-rated films or adult programs have been marketed to an increasingly younger segment of the population. For example, *X-Men* (PG-13) action figures were included in McDonald's Happy Meals for children earlier in 2001. In addition, *Charlie's Angels* dolls were placed on the market concurrent to the release of the PG-13 movie of the same name, just in time for the 2000 holiday shopping season. Similar arguments can be made about the movies *South Park* (R, NC-17), *Beavis & Butthead* (R, NC-17), *The Mummy* (PG-13), and *Josie and the Pussycats* (PG-13). Furthermore, the successful and violent entertainment sport of professional wrestling (which is usually only shown on late-night or pay-per-view television) has produced a large number of toys, costumes, and clothing designed specifically for young children.

Children also face messages from tobacco giants in their play. On April 25, 2001, CNN reported on the U.S. Supreme Court decision to hear a tobacco company's appeal of a Massachusetts law that bans tobacco ads from being placed within 1,000 feet of public playgrounds, parks, and schools (Bierbauer, 2001). One product demonstrates why many states, including Massachusetts, might have felt the need to put this law into effect in the first place. In a package labeled "World's Finest Candy Bats" (with a free plastic baseball included), customers actually found candy cigarettes from such prominent tobacco labels as Benson & Hedges, Pall Mall, Camel, and Kent. There were no candy "bats" at all. Corporations, seeing the potential in the up-and-coming market, sought to capture consumers at earlier and earlier ages.

The Toy Industry

Currently, two major companies dominate the toy market. Hasbro—represented by the action figure G.I. Joe—also owns Kenner, Parker Brothers, Milton Bradley, Tiger Electronics, Tonka, Playskool, Ideal, and Galoob. Mattel—represented by the ever-present Barbie—also owns Fisher Price, Hot Wheels, Matchbox Cars, Cabbage Patch Dolls, and American Girl. The creation of these toy supercompanies, as well as the dominance of superstore sellers like Walmart, Target, and Toys-R-Us, has limited the options available for toy purchasers. It has also created an industry dominated by licensed and formulaic toys. One very clear example of the dominance of industry and the adultification of children's play is embodied in Mattel's Barbie doll.

Barbie

Barbie has been, and continues to be, one of Mattel's most successful products, with annual sales grossing $1 billion worldwide (Jones, 1995). Barbie was created by one of Mattel's founders, Ruth Handler. Handler's inspiration for the ultimate doll was found in a toy marketed toward adults. Barbie (as she later became named) was modeled almost exactly after a Swiss doll named Lilli, who was based on a German comic strip character. Lilli was never meant for children. In fact, she was a provocateur and was aimed at an adult audience experienced in decoding the ever-present double entendres in the comic strip. She was sold in smoke shops and toyshops as an adult's doll. However, when the creator of Barbie saw Lilli, she immediately knew that she had found the doll on which she would base Barbie. With an ever-expanding collection of fashions and accessories sold separately from the doll, she felt that Barbie could be a commercial gold mine. She was right.

However, the fact remains that Barbie would not have been so popular if children had not desired to own her and her countless accessories. When Barbie was born over forty years ago, she was designed to appeal to girls aged eight to twelve years. For today's eight-year-old girl, Barbie has lost her allure; instead, today's young girls focus on the traditional teen interests of clothes, music, and computer games (MacPherson, 2001). Therefore, Mattel has recently made the decision to include younger children in its marketing strategy for Barbie and is now for the first time deliberately targeting preschool children (Lord, 1994). Because Barbie is no longer being consumed by the original target audience, Mattel is in effect being forced to find another consumer, a younger consumer, for her. The powerhouse Mattel corporation, when viewed through this new lens, ceases to appear powerful. They are nothing more than desperate peddlers trying anything to get children to buy their Barbie dolls. Their desperation has now reached the point that they are selling to children who can barely pronounce the word, "Barbie."

THE VICIOUS CYCLE

As the powerful toy companies cast their advertising nets over younger and younger children, children as consumers are in turn dictating what will sell and what will not. This vicious cycle is driven by desire: desire on the part of the toy companies to sell their toys to an increasingly larger and younger audience, and desire on the part of children (the consumers) to have the latest and the greatest toys.

Within this cycle, children (the consumers) simultaneously create and receive influence from the marketing of desire, as corporations are both creating and being influenced by desire. This ties in perfectly with Levy and Weingartner's (1990) notion of our nation's marketplace as ever changing and ever demanding, a "throwaway" society. Desire fuels more desire, and the vicious cycle of desire on the part of both consumer and corporation never ends (see Figure 26.1).

CONCLUSION

"The Merchants of Cool" (Dretzin, 2001) demonstrates ways in which corporations (including media and toy manufacturers) and children interact. The saddest part of this may be that toys themselves are no longer being marketed to older children (Kurnit, 2001). Older children may be in such a rush to adultify themselves that they are missing out on the opportunity to be children and to play. The United States has always prided itself on its freedom and the rights of people to make decisions for themselves and their children. Regulating the toy and media industries

Figure 26.1
Consumer/Corporation Cycle of Desire

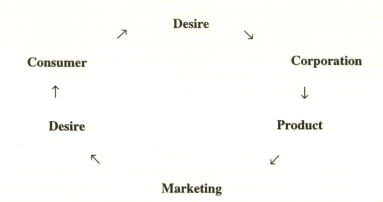

may not be a realistic solution in today's political climate, but where does that leave concerned parents and educators who are worried about the potential and real consequences of toys and media that increasingly market violence, drugs, and sex to our children?

The purpose of this chapter is not to provide answers to such questions. Instead, our objective is simply to encourage child advocates to challenge their assumptions about toys, marketing, media, and children's play. Our goal is not to encourage an activist movement that bans particular toys or the media, but rather to raise questions that may not have been present before. The next time you stroll down the aisle of a toy store deciding which toys you will allow your child to play with, take a moment to consider how the decisions made by adults adultify and influence children's play.

REFERENCES

American Academy of Pediatrics. (2001). Children, Adolescents, and Television. *Pediatrics* 107(2): 423.

Bierbauer, C. (2001, April 25). *CNN Law Report* [Television broadcast] Atlanta: CNN.

Consumer Product Safety Commission. (1985). *Guidelines for Relating Children's Ages to Toy Characteristics* (No. 85-1089). Washington, DC: Consumer Product Safety Commission.

Cross, G. (1997). *Kids' Stuff: Toys and the Changing World of American Childhood*. Cambridge: Harvard University Press.

Dretzin, R. (2001, February 27). The Merchants of Cool. *Frontline*. [Television broadcast] Boston: Public Broadcasting Service.

John, D. R. (1999). Through the Eyes of a Child: Children's Knowledge and Understanding of Advertising. In M. C. Macklin and L. Carlson (Eds.), *Advertising to Children: Concepts and Controversies* (pp. 3–26). Thousand Oaks, CA: Sage.

Jones, M. (1995). Pristine Barbie Image Revised for the '90's Buyer. *The Age*, March 23: 27–29.

Kirn, W., & W. Cole. (2001) Whatever Happened to Play? *Time* 157(17): 56–58.

Kline, S. (1993). *Out of the Garden: Toys, TV, and Children's Culture in the Age of Marketing*. London: Verso.

Kurnit, P. (2001). *Kids, Toys, Time and Money*. Paper presented at the Toy Manufacturers of America Fair, New York.

Levy, R., & R. Weingartner. (1990). *Inside Santa's Workshop*. New York: Henry Holt.

Lord, M. (1994). *Forever Barbie*. New York: Avon Books.

MacPherson, K. (2001, February 27). Younger Children Are Playing Older and Older. Retrieved from http://www.post-gazette.com/healthscience.

Pipher, M. (1994). *Reviving Ophelia: Saving the Selves of Adolescent Girls*. New York: Putnam.

Rosenberg, J. (2001). Brand Loyalty Begins Early. *Advertising Age* 72(7): 2.

Seiter, E. (1993). *Sold Separately: Children and Parents in Consumer Culture*. New Brunswick, NJ: Rutgers University Press.

Steinberg, S. R., & J. L. Kincheloe. (1998). *Kinderculture: The Corporate Construction of Childhood*. Boulder, CO: Westview Press.

TodÈ, C. (2001). Evolution of Tweens' Tastes Keeps Retailers on their Toes. *Advertising Age* 72(7): 6.

Tosa, M. (1997). *Barbie: Four Decades of Fashion, Fantasy and Fun*. New York: Harry N. Abrams.

Vandenberg, B. (1990). Toys and Intentions. *Contemporary Education* 61(4): 200–203.

27

Integration of Traditional Play and Games to Enhance Learning

Elaine M. Van Lue

This chapter explains how programs offering traditional fun and games in the curriculum assist children in becoming more physically fit, active, well coordinated, and adjusted. Physical, social, emotional, creative, and mental skills can be enhanced through a planned motor skills program. Games and play can also be a prime motivating force for a young child's self-concept, determining the way he or she feels about her- or himself and others.

MOVEMENT

Children need opportunities to move about. A child's primary means of expression and learning involves movement. The term "movement" involves many elements, including life, self-discovery, discovery of the environment, freedom, safety, communication, sheer enjoyment, sensuous pleasure, and acceptance. Body awareness is essential for physical and psychological development.

As children learn to understand and control the many ways their bodies move, they are better able to direct the actions of the body, the control of which results in increased confidence in work and play. When a child's movement patterns and skills improve, one can assume academic skills will also improve. According to research (Mandigo & Thompson, 1998; Davis, 2001; Roswell, 1999), through perceptual motor development children can lengthen attention span, increase personal rapport between teachers and peers, reduce tension, establish a "success syndrome," and enhance academic readiness and intellectual potential.

MOVEMENT THROUGH DANCE

The functioning of the brain is enhanced with repetition of specific developmental movements, fostering the whole child—body, mind, and spirit. All of the senses can be used, which include kinesthetic, feeling shapes bodies make; visual, responding to images seen or imagined; auditory, responding to sounds; and tactile, touching one another. Creative movement or dance involves communicating images (such as the wind), ideas (like taking a journey), or a feeling (such as strength) through body actions. Social skills of sharing space with others in an interactive environment in individual ways are also enhanced.

The urban environment has placed many physical limitations on children using vigorous movement to become physically agile. It is still important to offer movement experiences. Plans can be made with adaptations and variations to still provide creative dance, although somewhat limited, in any environment.

DRAMA

Dramatizing helps children understand themselves and others. Since learning comes from experiencing things, firsthand experiences can be provided through dramatization and simulation. The children can use gestures to create and communicate roles and situations, contributing to the development of future visualization and abstract thinking skills used for language, math, and reasoning abilities. Practice with pantomime enhances empathic feelings of others, considering perspectives and roles in varied situations.

Boys and girls enjoy poetry, rhymes, and finger plays equally. When acted out with the fingers or bodily movement, poetry or rhymes contribute to a child's understanding of word pronunciation, as well as development of manual and physical dexterity. Dramatizing the words involves not only the use of imagination but also learning to effectively modulate the voice.

TRADITIONAL GAMES AND TOYS

Honig (2000) confirmed that play is the passion of young children and essential for the promotion of brain growth and development. Learning through games provides a child with a sense of well-being while developing sensory-motor skills and enhancing self- and social awareness. Games help the child organize experiences in relation to time, space, sequence, number, cause, and effect. The child's abilities to focus, sustain attention, exercise self-control, and react quickly are also influenced by games.

In most countries, children make their own toys for specific games. All toys serve socializing purposes, such as the reproduction of roles, attitudes, customs, and values passed down from one generation to the next. Besides being safe, sturdy, and manipulated by the child, games and toys should provide the child with strength and variety of motor skills, drama and imitation, creative construction, development of artistic abilities, and development of the intellect. The more children are provided with formal schooling, the less time is available for traditional games to be learned in the family, streets, or fields, all of which are valuable for the child's development. Interesting toys may be created from common household items (see the appendix to this chapter).

Toys are also used by parents for bonding and for solitary play. Children enjoy the use of adult tools (e.g., Dad's wheelbarrow, tools, keys, etc.). The role of older siblings and peers is overwhelmingly important and significant in shaping gender identity. While playing, children develop their own repertoire of procedures and techniques for negotiating roles, plans, actions, and objects in play. Play allows children some control over learning (Bergen, 2000–2001).

Traditions provide approaches to play that have withstood the test of time (de la Cruz, Cage, & Lian, 2000). So what is the challenge? The challenge is to teach from a more global and multicultural perspective. Teachers play an important role in helping students to be more sensitive to and have a broader perspective with their peer group. Multicultural education perspectives need to be infused into all curriculua.

Children of the future expect to enjoy educational experiences. However, due to the fast pace of technology, expectations are often set too high for children to obtain mastery. Bergen (2000–2001) researched the cause of addiction to computer games, explaining how they combine three types of play: practice (self-directed repetition and elaboration of actions until mastery), symbolic (provides the world of "what if"), and game play (offers challenge and competition).

It should be noted, however, that many video and computer games are played in solitude. Casbergue & Kieff (1998) described many variations for the traditional games of Jacks, Marbles, and Dominoes that are played by cultures worldwide. The traditional games are inexpensive alternatives to technology-driven games. They offer children opportunities to consolidate knowledge and skills, develop logical and orderly styles of thinking, and become established within the peer group.

DIVERSITY

Sensitivity to gender and race is important in designing an effective curriculum, and appears to be a persistent problem in our society as our country becomes more diverse (Hansman, Jackson, Grant, & Spencer, 1999). Unfortunately, many school administrators are unaware of or unwilling to address racial or gender issues. Poussaint and Linn (2001) clarified how prejudicial attitudes can be harmful to children's understanding of the world. Educators need to help children show practice positive ways to interact with the diverse world in which they live. A lifestyle reflecting confidence and self-respect helps children further develop a positive identity and empathy toward others.

COMPETITION

Children should be given their play and their childhood. Which is better—children playing a street baseball game, laughing and enjoying themselves, or a Little League game with tense players shouldering the responsibility of dozens of adults, doing well for Mom and Dad, for the team, the coach, and the community? Childhood, or even an entire life, can be destroyed by the ramifications of competition. Winning isn't everything!

In mere game playing, there is comradeship, intensity of all-out effort, strong resistance to what you want to do, respect for opponents, and the desire to play a game well. However, many games and sports have become so distorted and competitive that they no longer can be classified as meaningful play. Competition often calls attention to only the gifted athletes and devastates the child who needs fitness or physical education the most. In addition, the "loser" attitude often carries over to academics.

Can society afford to have students concerned only about winning rather than their personal welfare or the welfare of others? What are some adults doing to children? Adult standards often distort the play life of children. Children cannot cope with adult-style competition. They are only capable of performing at their own developmental level, the natural competition of give and take in a child's world. Children need an adult's support rather than imposition and interference.

SUMMARY

Active play can enhance cognitive (intellectual) development by increasing a child's understanding of the concepts of size, shape, direction, distance, number, and position. Also, the way a child sees his or her body and the ability to successfully perform movement tasks influences several aspects of affective (emotional–social) development. The purpose of a planned program of physical movement activities is to insure each child's successful participation in a variety of activities that will promote maximum development.

Active play can help every child be a winner, respect one another, love physical activity, and have a positive attitude toward self and school. It is believed that a planned motor skills program assists a child in becoming a more physically fit, active, well-coordinated individual and may also enhance improvement in academic readiness and intellectual potential. Success in motor skills can also be a prime motivating force for young children in the development of a positive self-concept, which determines the way children feel about themselves and others.

APPENDIX: THE BEST TOYS IN LIFE ARE FREE

A is for acoustic tile—with colored golf tees for a peg board.

B is for bubble wrap—for stepping on in rhythm to music and innumerable other uses.

C is for clothespins—the plain old-fashioned kind without springs and splinter-free.

D is for dough—half flour, half salt, with enough water kneaded in to make dough to roll and cut, decorate, and bake.

E is for eggbeater—the lightweight dime-store kind, plus a bowl of water and soap flakes to make noise and bubbles.

F is for findings—buttons, beads, rickrack, bias tape, feathers, glitter, anything and everything safe from your sewing basket, to string, sort, arrange, or paste onto paper.

G is for gallon juice jugs—used as scoops for sand or ball catching.

H is for hats—discarded, for dress-up or for decoration.

I is for inner tubes—three to four laid flat on the lawn or in the playroom, to step in and out of, as "baskets" for a game of beanbag pitch, for making make-believe boats, or just one to roll and tug and stretch.

J is for Jell-o—children can "cook" as soon as they can stand on a stool set up near the kitchen counter. Limit your interference to providing accurately measured ingredients.

K is for keys—the mystery set left from the house you used to live in or the car you used to drive, for the preschooler to try on all doors and the "sheriff" to hang on his holster belt.

L is for ladder—a small aluminum stepladder the youngest can carry around with him, to make his inevitable climbing a bit safer and somewhat more "socially acceptable," or a long rung ladder for all the children to play on in the yard, made into a ramp, a board for a seesaw, or a horizontal jungle gym placed at the right height.

M is for macaroni—the shells, wagon-wheels, alphabet, and other fascinating shapes, for painting with, brush or dye in a bowl or vegetable coloring, then paste onto cardboard in designs.

N is for nutshells—walnut halves, especially to make a tub fleet with possible toothpick masts and paper sails.

O is for orange crate—to become a dollhouse, a two-seated boat or plane, a doghouse or zoo, if sanded smoothly.

P is for plastic bottles—to use for water, sand, and possessions. Squeeze bottles have a special fascination for babies, who like the sound they make when squeezed, or for playing store.

Q is for quilt—an old one, supplied along with a card table or big clothes basket, to make a hiding place.

R is for rubber stamps—endlessly interesting and totally stainless if offered with a blotter soaked in food coloring.

S is for spools—saved up from the sewing basket or empty film canisters. Can be decorated, strung, and hammered, or used for milk-carton trains.

T is for tools—real grown-up ones. Some garden tools, especially trowels, are excellent sand and dirt toys.

U is for utensils—from the kitchen, measuring spoons and cups of metal or plastic, plastic mixing bowls, wooden or plastic spoons, molds, cookie cutters, and pans or lids to make music.

V is for vests—always left from suits, for "dress-up."

W is for wallpaper—samples to cover boxes with, cut up, and paste, or decorate dollhouses.

X is for "Xmas" cards—saved from last year and brought out at different intervals. Also fascinating to arrange, stand up in rows, color, cut, and sort.

Y is for yours—anything that *is*, is treasured!

Z is for zippers—for dressing practice.

REFERENCES

Bergen, D. (2000–2001). Education or Edu-tainment? *Childhood Education* (Winter): 114–116.

Casbergue, R., & J. Kieff. (1998). Marbles, Anyone? Traditional Games in the Classroom. *Childhood Education* 74 (Spring): 143–147.

Davis, J. (2001). *The Music-Movement Connection in Early Childhood.* Retrieved January 21, 2001 from http://www.galstar.com/~davii/mus-move.htm.

de la Cruz, R. E., C. E. Cage, & M. J. Lian. (2000). Let's Play Mancala and Sungkka! Learning Math and Social Skills through Ancient Multicultural Games. *Teaching Exceptional Children* 32(3): 38–42.

Hansman, C., M. Jackson, D. Grant, & L. Spencer. (1999). Assessing Graduate Students' Sensitivity to Gender, Race, Equality and Diversity: Implications for Curriculum Development. *College Student Journal* 33(2): 261–268.

Honig, A. (2000). A Passion for Play. *Scholastic Early Childhood Today* 15(3): 32, 36.

Mandigo, J., & L. Thompson. (1998). Go with Their Flow Theory Can Help Practitioners to Intrinsically Motivate Children to Be Physically Active. *Physical Educator* 55(3): 145–159.

Poussaint, A., & S. Linn. (2001). Raising Our Children Free of Prejudice. *The Learning Network.* Retrieved May 3, 2001 from http://familyeducation.com/article/0,1120,3-1530,00.html.

Roswell, D. (1999). Today Child Motor Development. Retrieved May 3, 2001 from http://www.angelfire.com/on3/todayschild/motorskills.htm.

28

Creating Homemade Play Equipment

Joanne Hynes-Dusel

For children, play is as natural as breathing—and as necessary.
—Mimi Brodsky Chenfeld

Teachers and recreation specialists from all over the world often find conditions less than desirable. That is, too many children and not enough equipment. This deprives children of quality and quantity of movement experiences that allow for the development of stability, locomotor skills, and manipulative skills through games, rhythms, and gymnastic activities. The purpose of this chapter is to provide teachers and parents with innovative ideas for constructing and utilizing homemade equipment. The use of homemade equipment would enable every child to have a piece of equipment and be physically involved in the development of efficient movement patterns.

The nature of homemade equipment should be adaptable for use by all children. Changes in the size, weight, and shape of specific equipment would make it more useful for children, whether they be young or old, large or small. Commercially produced equipment is not always adaptable. Homemade equipment may also be specifically adapted for use by handicapped children. The use of homemade equipment allows each child to explore various movement patterns, as an individual or with small groups, and it is especially adaptable to movement education situations during primary grades. Children need to be encouraged in exploring the various movement qualities of space, force, time, and flow as they experience gymnastics and locomotor and manipulative activities.

When planning to create homemade equipment, it is advisable that teachers encourage children to bring various items from the home and have collection boxes to keep items sorted according to use. Construction of the various pieces of equipment can be made by the children and/or by parents or volunteer groups from the PTA. All that is needed is time, effort, and commitment on the part of children, parents, and teachers.

BALLS

The following types of balls are soft and nonthreatening. Since they are soft, children are not afraid when trying to catch the ball. These balls can be used to develop eye–hand/eye–foot coordination, fine motor coordination, and sport and game-playing skills.

It takes one to two skeins or yarn to make one *yarn ball*. Cardboard circles are needed. The larger the diameter (4"–6"+), the larger the ball. Cut a two-inch hole in the middle of each circle and put each circle together. Wrap the yarn around both circles through and around the whole circle until the two-inch hole is completely filled. Cut the yarn between the cardboard circles with a razor blade all the way around. Place a strong piece of string between the cardboard circles and tie tightly. Cut and remove both pieces of cardboard.

For a *paper ball,* crumble pieces of newspaper or magazines and use duct tape to retain a round shape. Many pieces of newspaper crumbled into one another yields a bigger ball.

For a *nylon ball*, stuff nylon hose into an old sock until desired-size ball is achieved. Stuff snuggly so that it becomes resilient. Tuck the loose end of the sock inside the ball and sew the opening.

For *doughnuts*, cut two one-inch strips from thick elastic nylon hose. Set aside for later use. Pull the thick elastic end over the elbow of one arm, letting the excess hang from your hand (some children find it easier to make doughnuts on their legs rather than their arms). Fold over the top edge of the nylon, then roll it down your arm. When the roll reaches your wrist, pull it up your arm and roll it down again. The tighter you pull and roll, the more solid the doughnut will be. When you reach the end of the nylon, roll the doughnut off your arm. Roll the doughnut until the thin end of the nylon is even all around. Take the strips you cut earlier, and cut them into four strips. Tie the strips around the nylon doughnut to keep the edge from unrolling.

Eight doughnuts are needed to create a *Geoball*. Arrange six doughnuts around a central doughnut so all of the seams are facing up. Tie the six doughnuts to the center doughnut, and then tie them to each other. Tie an eighth doughnut to one of the outer doughnuts. This is your new center doughnut. Tie each of the outer doughnuts to the new center doughnut. Place an uninflated balloon inside the Geoball and blow it up. When the ball takes shape, tie off the balloon.

A *rag ball* is created much like the yarn ball, but uses nylon hose instead of yarn.

Activities with balls can include movement exploration, rolling and fielding, throwing and catching, bouncing and dribbling, volleying, foot dribbling and kicking games, and self-testing activities.

FOXTAILS

Foxtails help develop eye–hand coordination, throwing and catching abilities, partner cooperation, and the development of creative and original games. To make a Foxtail, place a tennisball or racquetball in the toe of an old tube sock. You can tie a knot close to the ball if you want, so that the ball does not fall out. The children can decorate the foxtail as they wish. Activities for the Foxtail include tossing and catching and volleying skills. Encourage children to create their own game using the foxtail.

PUPPETS

Puppets can be made from nylon hose, clothespins, socks, and paper bags.

Nylon hose puppets are constructed just like rackets (see instructions later). Decorate the hose to look like a character from a favorite book, or the like.

Clothespin chatterboxes are constructed out of one-piece clothespins. Children can decorate their clothespins as any character they want. Use buttons for hats, felt for clothes, pipe cleaners for arms.

Sock and paper bag puppets are great, especially on a rainy day. Use any and all scraps of stuff lying around the house to create these puppets. Yarn, buttons, markers, felt, and pipe cleaners can be used.

BOUNDARIES, GOALS, AND MARKERS

Plastic bottles of all shapes and sizes, including pint, quart, half-gallon, and bleach bottles and soap dispensers can be used as boundaries, goals, and/or markers. These items can be brought from home or obtained from the school. When using bottles as boundary or goal markers, first clean them to make sure there is no residue left. Once dry, place two cups of sand or rice into each. This will prevent them from blowing over. Paint numbers, symbols, and so on, on each for different activities. Keep caps on the bottles so that the contents do not spill out.

MUSICAL INSTRUMENTS AND RHYTHMIC ACTIVITY

Tin can shakers can be made by using empty tin cans of all sizes. Throw rice, dry cereal, or sand into one can. Take another can and put paper clips, nails, pebbles, or bottle caps in it. Tape the tin cans together. Paint the outside or use streamers to decorate cans. Now shake!

Tambourines can be made from paper plates. Put rice into one plate. Place another plate on top. Secure the plates so that the contents will not fall out. Decorate using streamers or bells.

Paper bag maracas can be made by first decorating a lunch-size paper bag. Put bottle tops, beans, pebbles, marbles, or rice into the bag. Inflate the bag and tie the opening with a rubber band. A coat of shellac will make it stronger.

A *balloon babbler* is created when three or four paper clips are placed into a noninflated balloon. Inflate and tie the balloon. Shake.

To make a *bottle prattle*, use any bottle (e.g., a ketchup bottle). Put screws, bolts, nails, or the like into the bottle. Replace the cap. Use the neck of the bottle as a handle and hold the bottle upside down to shake. Use paint to decorate.

For *pop-top castanets*, use heavy cardboard tubes about six inches long. Punch tiny holes in bottle caps and similar holes at the end of the cardboard. Place a bottle cap face down over the cardboard hole. Tie a string through the cap and the cardboard to secure the cap. Decorate.

For a *bell bracelet*, string twelve bells onto colorful yarn, making a knot between each bell. Wrap the yarn around the wrist, play as is, or when using a drum or tambourine: It also makes a noise. The bracelet could also be tied around an ankle.

A *humboard kazoo* can be made from a paper tube by covering the end of the cardboard tube with an oversized piece of waxed or wrapping paper. Secure the paper with a rubber band. Punch holes in the tube. Hum into the open end.

Lummi sticks (sticks that strike against one another to create a sound) can be made by cutting the two 8"–12" sticks. Sandpaper sticks are lummi sticks with sandpaper glued to them. The sticks can then be scraped back and forth across each other.

Paper streamers can be made from crepe paper. Use the streamers to develop rhythmical qualities; explore such movements as space, time, force, and flow through discovery experiences; and develop cooperation by allowing children to work together as partners to make up creative dance routines. Streamer activities help improve a child's directionality, leaping and spinning skills, body-part awareness, and shape awareness.

SPORTING EQUIPMENT

Nylon hose rackets develop eye–hand coordination, better striking abilities, teamwork, and cooperation through partner and team activities. Bend a wire hanger at the base to give the hanger a diamond shape. Straighten out the hanger hook. Insert the hanger into the hose, making sure to push the end of the hanger snugly into the toe of the stocking. Pull the stocking tightly around the hanger. Tape the handle at the base of the diamond. For greater strength, use two hangers and two nylon hoses. Some of the activities that can be performed with rackets are volleying and balancing activities.

Bowling pins, bats, and scoops can be made from plastic bottles of all shapes and sizes, including pint, quart, half-gallon, and bleach bottles and soap dispensers that can be brought from home or obtained from the school.

For regular *bowling pins*, just set them up and then knock them down. You can weight the bottles according to the developmental level of the children (i.e., heavier bottles are harder to knock down). For people who like to bowl during the winter months, put water in clear bottles, use food coloring to color the water, and freeze. Use a plastic gallon container filled with frozen water for the ball. Put the bottles on the cap to make it easier to knock down for students who have difficulty knocking the pins down.

To make a *bat*, the bottle can be attached to the end of a broom or the like. Make sure that the bottle is well secured to the handle with duct tape to prevent injury. *Scoops* can be made by removing the bottom of any container that has a handle (gallon milk jug or bleach bottle) and then taping the edge to prevent cutting. Scoop activities include throwing, catching, and rolling.

Golf holes and *target activities* can be made from empty tin cans and can be used to develop eye–hand and eye–foot coordination and gross and fine motor coordination. Be sure to use duct tape to smooth the rough edges of empty tin cans for safety purposes. For *golf putting*, use small cans for difficult holes and larger cans for easier holes. For target activities, stack and/or have a single row of tin cans. Throwing and/or kicking skills can then be utilized.

Goals, markers, bowling pins, and *targets* can be made from milk cartons and can be used to develop eye–hand and eye–foot coordination, gross and fine motor coordination, and increased arm strength in children. They can be painted and decorated using different colors, numbers, letters, geometric patterns, pictures, and so on, for throwing, kicking, and miniature golf holes.

Bats and *hockey sticks* can be made from broom handles. Both activities are used to develop eye–hand coordination.

GAMES AND ACTIVITIES

Broom and mop handles can be used to develop balance, flexibility, agility, strength, and eye–hand and eye–foot coordination. For example, cutting a broom or mop handle so that it is 3'–4' in length makes a *wand*. Activities include balancing, jumping, catching, throwing, twirling, and gymnastic actions.

Milk cartons can be used to create a *cup and ball game*. Cut the top off the container and punch a hole in the bottom. Thread a piece of string through the hole and tie a knot in one end so that the string cannot go through. Attach a ball (e.g., a whiffle ball) on the free end. Hold the container with one hand and try to move it in such a way that the ball is thrust upward and goes into the container.

Paper tubes (i.e., from paper towels, toilet paper, wax paper, etc.) can be used to make a roll-up game. First punch a pinhole at one end of the tube. Lace a piece of string through and tie at one end so it does not slip through. Attach a ball (e.g., a small whiffle ball) to the free end of the string. Try to swing or roll the ball up around the outside to the top of the tube.

Homemade equipment is an inexpensive alternative for many schools as well as before or after school programs, ensuring that all students or participants have their own piece of equipment to learn from. These ideas and activities and other great suggestions can be found in the sources listed in the bibliography.

BIBLIOGRAPHY

Carnes, C. (1983). *Awesome Elementary School Physical Education Activities*. Carmichael, CA: Education Company.

Corbin, C. (1972). *Inexpensive Equipment for Games, Play, and Physical Activity.* Dubuque, IA: W. C. Brown.

Davison, B. (1988). *Creative Physical Activities and Equipment.* Champaign, IL: Human Kinetics.

Stillwell, J. (1980). *Making and Using Creative Play Equipment.* Champaign, IL: Human Kinetics.

Werner, P., & R. Simmons. (1990). *Homemade Play Equipment.* Reston, VA: AAHPERD.

29

Scandinavian Viking Games

Gustave T. Juhlin

Viking Kubb is a game whose origin dates back to the tenth century. The traditional game pieces are made out of woods, such as ash, pine, and oak. The Vikings made the pieces with the scraps that were left over from the building of their ships and created the game during break times or possibly when they finished at day's end. Recently, the game has been revived in Sweden and reintroduced to all age groups, from elementary school children to senior citizens. It is a simple game that can be played one on one, or with up to twelve people. It can be played indoors or outside, on grass or gravel. The game pieces consist of one king and five knights for each side, and six sticks to knock the pieces over (see Figure 29.1).

The size of the field can vary from three to five yards wide and five to nine yards long, depending on the space available and the age and skill level of the participants. The playing field is set up by spreading the knights out on one end line, and the opponents on the other, with the king in the middle. The object of the game is to knock down all the opponent's knights and then knock down the king. This is possible by throwing the swords underhanded, with the end pointing toward the target. Players throw from their own end line (see Figure 29.2).

If a player does not knock down all of the knights on the other side, the opponent's team takes the knights that were knocked down and throws back to the opposite side. They are set up where they land, and the opponent must knock down the tossed knights before knocking down the opponent's knights. This is easier when there is more than one knight to knock over. After throwing the first sword, a player can try to hit it with the second knight. If successful, the second knight goes on top of the first one. They can be stacked up to three levels high. If, when tossing a knight over, it goes out of bounds, the player gets a "re-toss." If it goes out of

Figure 29.1
Games Pieces

Ten knights (five for each side), rectangular in shape. They are 6 inches high and 2½ inches on all four sides.

Six swords, cylindrical or rectangular in shape but longer and thinner than knights. They are 12 inches high and 1½ inches on all four sides.

One king piece, which is also rectangular but thicker and taller than knights. The object is 12 inches high and 3 inches on all four sides.

Four boundary markers, just 2 inches high (could really be any shape).

Figure 29.2
Kubb Field: King in the Middle, Knights on Either End Line

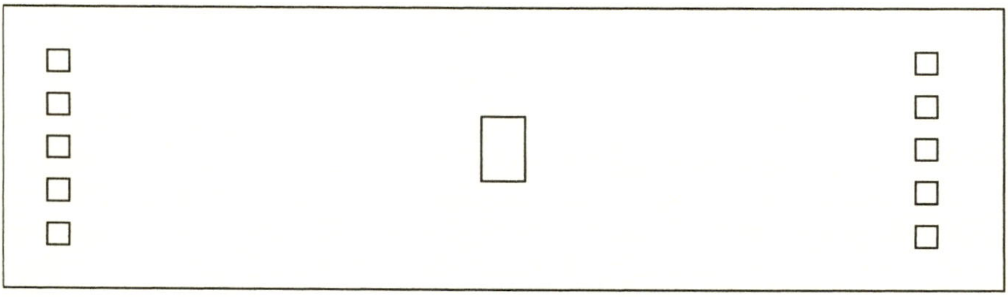

bounds two times in a row, the opponent may place the knight wherever he or she wants, except directly next to the king. It must be at least a foot away.

If players use all their swords and several knights are still standing, then a player can move up to where the furthest knight is and throw from that spot. This is repeated with the knights being knocked down and then thrown back and forth until one team knocks down all the knights on the opponent's side and successfully knocks down the king. The king must be knocked down from the end line. If, during the game, anyone knocks over the king before the end of the game, the other team automatically wins. Games can last anywhere from several minutes to over an hour.

VIKING CHESS

This is a Viking board game that was also played in the early days as a precursor to chess. The Vikings brought the game with them as they traveled throughout Europe and Asia, and artifacts have been found by archaeologists in such far-reaching places as Ireland and the Ukraine. Viking Chess is similar to traditional chess in that there are two sides, each played by one person, on a square board. One side consists of thirteen pieces (the king and twelve defenders) and the other twenty-four pieces (the attackers). The game begins with the king in the middle of the board, surrounded by defenders. The attackers are set up evenly on all four sides. The object for the player with the king piece is to move safely to one of the four castles (one at each of the four corners on the board). The object for the attackers is to capture the king piece by surrounding it on all four sides. The opponent's pieces can be taken by putting a piece on either side of the occupied square. All pieces can move the same way (like a rook in chess) along the board, as long as there are no other pieces impeding the way (see Figure 29.3).

TRAINING GAMES FOR COMBAT AND HUNTING

The Vikings used games and play to transmit a variety of cultural mores and traditions. They created games and play forms that would help the young men to assume leadership roles while developing necessary survival skills. One example of this sort of game focuses on backward jumping (how far). This game pitted the young boys against each other to see whose backward jump could cover the greatest distance. The skill of jumping backward was an important move when trying to avoid an oncoming attacker, and therefore a necessary skill for survival in the combative Viking culture. Another example of this sort of game is used to hone hunting skills. This game pitted the young men against each other for throwing accuracy. The game involved a target with a picture of an animal (most likely a reindeer) on it that the young men would be hunting for in the wild. The game was used to increase the accuracy of the future hunters and required a ball of wool to be thrown at the target. Different body parts (areas of the target) were worth different point values.

BURNBALL

This is a Scandinavian Viking children's game, similar to American baseball. There are two teams with no limit as to how many players join a side. There are no established field positions except for the "Burner." One of the differences between Burnball and baseball is that "outs" do not dictate a change of sides; a time limit dictates a change of side. For example, each team would get ten minutes at bat, which would constitute an inning. Points can be earned when at bat or in the field. A run is worth one point, and is counted in a baseball style, when a runner crosses home plate. The bases are set up in a square, as opposed to a baseball diamond configuration. Home plate and the batter's box are two separate places on the field, with the batter's box placed halfway between home plate and first base. There is a "goal line" between home and first base and the batter's box is behind that goal line. There is a "burn plate" next to the batter's box. A team can have multiple players on any base at any given time. Runners are never "forced" to run.

A home run is worth five points, but there are no "over the fence" home runs because there is no fence. Points are awarded to the fielding team with each catch of a

Figure 29.3
Viking Chess Board

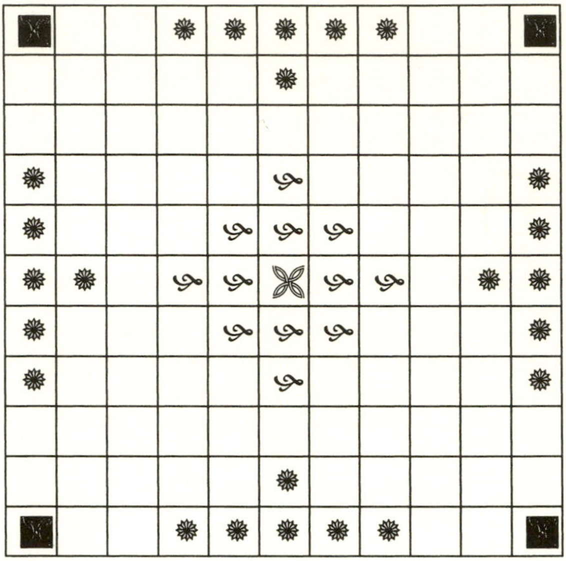

Legend:
✻—King
■—Castle
✸—Attacker
ᵥᵔ—Defender

fly ball. A two-handed catch from an outfield player equals one point, and a one-handed catch equals three points. When all the batters are on the bases and none are left to bat, then all players leave the bases and start over. This is called an "outburn" and is worth five points The other way to score a point for the fielding team is the "burn." The Burner (this position can be rotated) stands in the field with the other players, but when the ball is hit the Burner runs to the burn plate. A point is scored if the fielders get the ball back into the Burner and yell, "Burn!" The point amount corresponds to the number of players caught between bases when "Burn!" is yelled. If players are caught between bases, they must go back to first base. The Burner must stay behind the goal line until the ball is hit.

Finally, the batter gets only three swings. A miss and a ball that doesn't cross the goal line are counted as strikes. You can have self-hitting, or a pitcher who will stand to the side near enough to just throw the ball so that the batter can hit it. It can be someone from the same team (see Figure 29.4).

Figure 29.4
Burnball Field

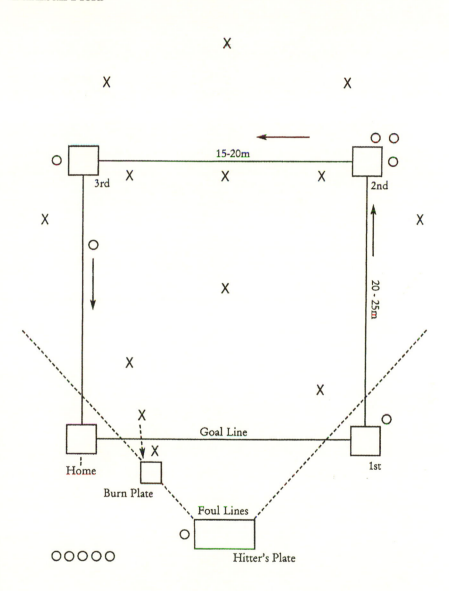

30

The Tension between
Play and Practice in Learning
a High-Skill Activity

Frederick Johnson

Imagination is more important than knowledge.
—Albert Einstein (1879–1955)

This chapter examines the elements of play and practice in teaching unicycling to middle-school-age black and Hispanic girls. Most of the observations apply to other structured recreational activities and sports that are difficult to learn and require the development of skill, such as ballet, gymnastics, ice skating, juggling, baton twirling, and perhaps competitive Double Dutch and the martial arts. Recreational activities, as defined, are designed to give the participant an introduction to the activity, a taste of the activity, whether paying for the lessons or not. Training children for high-level competition or careers in an activity is not under consideration.

Over a ten-year period, the instructor taught hundreds of girls to ride a unicycle in an after-school program located in a troubled New York City public school, where students were mostly from low-income, single-parent homes. It was started as a girls-only program because the instructor wanted to increase the physical activities offered for girls.

Riding a unicycle is difficult to learn, and it will never become as popular as the now ubiquitous scooter. In the beginning it is difficult to just sit on the unicycle without falling, even if assisted by two people. With expert instruction, a well-coordinated child practicing for one-half hour, three times a week, can learn to ride in two weeks—that is, three hours in the seat, holding on to the wall or a partner's hand to move around the gym. Time spent picking oneself up after falling (which happens a lot) and climbing back up on the unicycle does not count in that three hours. There are no lead-up skills to engage the children while practicing, and being able to ride a bicycle does not help at all. There is no fun, no play, no learning of tricks, and no showing off until the skill can be performed successfully. So why would middle-school-age girls, characteristically self-conscious and sensitive about looking klutzy in front of their peers and others, persist in learning such a difficult activity?

WHY THE GIRLS PERSIST IN LEARNING

There are three factors that account for the girls' persistence in learning. One factor is the small successes a girl achieves from the first day of working with the unicycle. When the child is wrestling with the equipment, struggling to balance, hanging on to the wall with both hands, falling and getting up again, there comes, after fifteen minutes or so, an ever-so-slight feeling of an increase in control. A second factor is evident after a few days, when the girls get to the point where they can move along the wall, touching it lightly with one hand, and as a result receive more attention. In effect, they have demonstrated a commitment. Lightly holding the girl's hand, the instructor, or one of the more experienced girls, will walk her across the gym. This might seem like a small thing, but getting away from the wall, out to the middle of the floor, is a big and welcome movement to another level. The girl feels closer to taming this treacherous contraption. If a girl does the walking exercise well, she is paired with an experienced rider. They hold hands and both ride across the gym. After doing this for a while, the same learner is paired with another learner at the same level. The two hold hands and ride across the gym. Even though neither can ride alone, they can get enough support from each other to maintain their balance. After a while they are told to ride to the middle of the gym, let go, and try to ride the rest of the way by themselves. Now they are out in the middle of the gym, in the "mix," riding with the riders, no longer the wallflowers. During these final stages the girls glow with satisfaction and pride, even more so than later, when they learn difficult tricks.

The third factor that motivates the girls is by far the most significant. Despite the falling, the slow progress, the frustrations, the embarrassments, and the instructor's initial inattention, the girls persevere, because when they see the progress others have made they focus their efforts on their own progress. On a typical day the gymnasium is filled with veteran riders on their unicycles, laughing, yelling, chasing each other, and having a great time. Some are riding in and out of the orange traffic cones lined up on the gym floor; several others are holding hands while riding in a circle; still others are holding shoulders, as in a chorus line, while riding around the gym. One girl is jumping rope by standing on the pedals, bouncing on the tire of her unicycle, and holding the seat between her knees. Another is trying to ride over a two-by-four on the floor without falling. Still another is riding a six-foot-high, chain-driven unicycle. The veteran riders that the new girls observe are their peers, their friends, classmates, and children from the neighborhood. The new girls know that there is nothing special about the veteran riders, and if those girls can do it, so can the new girls. So the new girls rush out on the gymnasium floor, to have fun and be part of the group, doing all of those neat tricks and showing off for the boys, teachers, parents, and friends.

PRACTICE VERSUS PLAY

There are no incentives provided to the girls beyond the fun and challenge of riding the unicycle. Prizes, awards, or T-shirts are not given, because competitions are just for fun, or for testing out one's skills. Attendance is voluntary and the children are free to come and go as they please.

The only exception to the "no incentives' rule is membership in the performing group, made up of eight to ten of the more skilled children, who perform a ten- to twenty-minute routine at community fairs, school assemblies, children's and senior centers, parades, and youth rallies. Each summer they were invited to an all-expenses-paid, seven-day trip to the National Unicycle Convention.

The performing group received T-shirts and performance costumes, did their tricks to music and applause, and received special privileges. At the Nationals, the group performed artistic freestyle routines, individually and in groups, and participated in races, parades, workshops, and ceremonies. They saw other parts of the country and met children (including boys) from all over the world; sometimes they even won medals. Everyone wanted to be in this performing group.

Yet the performing group was a constant struggle and eventually discontinued. Why was it a struggle? It all boiled down to the concept of practice. Practice means repeatedly doing what one already "knows how to do," and the girls did not want to do that. Performing in shows, doing the same routine over and over again, was for them practice in disguise. The distinction made is between "practice" and "working hard." Children are willing to work hard if they want to learn something. They like physical challenges. If they know that the skill is possible—and they know it is possible because they see others doing it—they are willing to persevere until they learn. No matter how arduous, frustrating, or slow the progress, they will tenaciously struggle with the unicycle until sweat drops from their brows and they are successful. After they learn to ride, they are just as tenacious and hard working in learning tricks, even difficult tricks. They do not want to do tricks in sequence; they want to jump ahead to the really difficult ones, and sometimes they learn them out of sequence. They will do this for months and months, working away without any prodding or preaching from the instructor. They thrive on the attention they receive by showing what they have learned. They squeal with delight. This is play of a high order.

The girls are not concerned with the perfect execution of the trick, or whether they are unable to replicate the trick on a regular basis. They know they have done it once, and that means that at some point they will be able to do it again. Then they want to move on to new tricks, to again experience the exhilaration of learning something new, something fun, even if it means working hard, playing hard. Practice—doing the same thing repeatedly—is not play; it is training, and they report that "it is boring."

The children all agreed that in order to perform in shows or compete at the Nationals, they had to practice a group routine, work together with considerable precision, and then do their individual tricks one after the other. They had to repeat the skills many times so that the routine was seamless and they would be confident and not thrown by showtime jitters, the small stage at the performing site, the bumpy, uneven playground surface, the different lighting, or surrounding distractions.

A skilled rider could keep up with this regimen with a minimum of two to three hours of practice a week, but she would not be learning anything new. She would just be practicing what she already knew, polishing skills, working with the group. This was no longer play. Practice also meant that each girl had to be at the gym at a specific time and stay until a specific time. She could not just drop in whenever she wanted, or leave if a friend suggested getting a pizza. Yet many girls and their parents (and a lot of adults in general) had problems with appointments, schedules, and being on time. If there were eight girls in the performing group and only five showed up—a common occurrence—what could be done? Parents sometimes sabotaged the efforts. If a daughter did not clean up her room, got a bad report card, or stayed out late, it was, "No unicycle for you, young lady!" not realizing that the other girls were being penalized, as was the eventual audience.

PLAYED OUT IN TWO YEARS

No girl maintained membership in the performing or regular group beyond two years—for some it lasted only one year. For the very skilled girls, the next level of difficult tricks was too much of a challenge, requiring too much work over too long a period of time. For most, they had learned as much as they wanted; they had fun working hard because it was play. Now it was time to try kickboxing, modern dance, cheerleading—anything to again experience the fun, the exhilaration, the challenge of learning a new skill. The pattern was the same even for the few girls whose parents had paid $100 to $170 to buy them unicycles. There was no discernible difference between the girls who came only for unicycling and the girls who participated in other after-school programs such as tutoring, counseling, sports, and dance. The older girls had a variety of distractions: high school, part-time jobs, boyfriends, new friends, more responsibilities at home, preparing meals, caring for siblings, just hanging out, or all of these. Some of the skilled veteran riders were hired as assistants, but their high school hours conflicted with the unicycling program and they had to drop out.

CONCLUSION

The two years maximum it took unicycling to play itself out may be characteristic of middle school girls, as well as characteristic of most groups—younger and older children of both sexes. It might apply to all high- and low-skill activities. If a child stays beyond two years in a recreational or sports activity, there is a parent, a coach, a special incentive, or a sports culture counteracting the child's "normal" inclination. Unfortunately, it is estimated that most girls and boys drop out of athletics and physical activities by age thirteen (Collingwood, 1997).

Resisting practicing over and over what one already knows seems characteristic of middle-school-age children. Pushing girls into performing or competing, with its practice requirements, goes against the grain of what is developmentally appropriate for middle school girls. The girls are not lazy or undisciplined; they are just normal. Yet dismissing performing and competition groups is not always so easy. Performing groups help advertise the program, aid in recruitment and fundraising, and cast the agency in a good light. More important, many coaches and teachers of high-skill activities spend many years learning the skill, and when it is no longer feasible for them to continue competing or performing, they become teachers of that specialty. Having a good performing group of "up and coming" stars reflects well on their professional esteem and sense of accomplishment and adds to the interest and excitement of the job. Teaching only the basics, the introductory course, year after year can drain any remaining passion the professional once had for the activity. Finally, with respect to performing groups, there should be an awareness of the tension between play and performing and a clarity of goals. Membership in a performing or competition group takes much time and energy that might be better spent on activities that involve more children, including the less athletic ones.

REFERENCE

Collingwood, T. R. (1997). *Helping At-Risk Youth through Physical Fitness Programming*. Champaign, IL: Human Kinetics.

31

Using Intergenerational Puppets to Convey Play and Recreational Principles

Lindsay C. Davis

Making simple rod puppets is an ideal intergenerational activity because some adult assistance is required to complete the project. By helping each other, a positive interdependence between the young and old begins to develop. The activity begins with the construction of a life-size papier-maché head placed on one end of a twelve-inch piece of dowel. When dry, acrylic paint is used for applying facial features, and wool in an appropriate color is used for styling the hair in a manner similar to its owner's. The puppet body is made from a large piece of material, the edges of which are machine stitched, and a hole is snipped in the center, allowing a dowel to be inserted up to the puppet's neck. The material is then glued in place and electrical tape is applied on the underside to secure the material to the dowel. Gloves in adult and child sizes are attached to the respective puppets. If right-handed, the left glove is stuffed and sewn in place on the material. The right glove is sewn in place, but left unstuffed to allow the puppeteer to slip on the glove. By grabbing the dowel with one hand and placing the other hand in the open glove, both child and adult are ready to play with their "just-like-me puppet" (Calvert & Schwarz, 1993).

The puppets serve two functions for the child. Together with the older adult, an intergenerational skit can be written and performed in the community, outlining the right of the child to play and the principle of older persons regarding leisure and recreation. Such an experience brings intergenerational benefits to the child, the older adult, and the community. Improved self-esteem is developed in both the child and adult as they participate in a meaningful activity together, each one becoming a resource for the other. By sharing an activity with an older person, the fear of aging, common among children, is reduced. Intergenerational puppets provide a shared physical activity that is visual and tactile, enhances listening skills, and provides an opportunity for both participants to serve others (Generations United, 1998). Making a puppet that looks like the child also provides a playmate when the real thing is not available, allowing the child to experience the joys of solitary play.

For the older adult, a further benefit is the prevention of unnatural age segregation and increased community awareness about issues that affect young and old. Loneliness and boredom are common events in the lives of many elderly people but fade away when they become actively engaged in the company of children. Opportunities to transfer culture, knowledge, skills, and values to the next generation are greatly enhanced by intergenerational projects such as this one. A deeper understanding and acceptance of today's children is also felt. From a community perspective, intergenerational puppets as teaching tools strengthen public and private agencies' ability to meet family and community needs by providing meaningful educational encounters (Generations United, 1998). Implementing an intergenerational program that provides an opportunity for both children and older adults to engage in an artistic and creative process that extends to teaching the community about their rights and principles offers exciting possibilities and unique outcomes through play.

BIBLIOGRAPHY

Calvert, J., & R. Schwarz. (1993). Look-Alikes: Go Ahead—Make a Face! *Canadian Living Magazine* 16(1): 136–137, 139.

Department of Canadian Heritage, Citizens' Participation Directorate, Minister of Supply and Services Canada. (1991). *Convention on the Rights of the Child* (as adopted by the General Assembly of the United Nations, 1989). Ottawa: Minister of Supply and Services Canada.

Douglas, R., & R. M. (1998). Macaulay. *Benefits of Intergenerational Programs*. Reprinted with permission from Intergenerational Resource Book Vancouver School Board, and Vancouver Health Department. Retrieved July 21, 1997 from http://www.intergenugo.org/About/benefits.htm.

Generations United. *Using an Intergenerational Approach to Examine Public Policies*. Retrieved July 21, 1997 from http://www.gu.org/documents/policy.htm.

Generations United. (1998). *Linking Young and Old through Intergenerational Programs*. Retrieved March 20, 1998 from http://www.gu.org/documents/program.htm.

United Nations. (1998). *International Plan of Action on Aging and United Nations Principles for Older Persons*. DPI/932/Rev.1–98-24545. New York: United Nations Department of Public Information.

32

Imaginative Play as a Component of a Multisensory Art Experience

Melissa Gemeinhardt

Developmentally Appropriate Practices for both typical and special populations in early childhood involves learning through play, using concrete experiences relevant to the lives of young children, and addressing the unique qualities of each individual child across all domains of development (Bredekamp, 2000; Bowe, 2000). Discipline Based Art Education (DBAE) emphasizes four essential principles for use with the visual arts: studio art production, art criticism, art history, and aesthetics (Zimmerman & Zimmerman, 2000). All three approaches place priority on the value of learning processes rather than products (Zimmerman & Zimmerman, 2000; Bredekamp, 2000; Bowe, 2000).

The role of the child is often visualized as an artist learning through self-initiated manipulation of material (Zimmerman and Zimmerman, 2000), or as an explorer engrossed in hands-on experiences and experimentation as play (Bredekamp, 2000; Bowe, 2000). The primary objective of both roles is for children to be the ultimate guide and director of any activity by virtue of their choices regarding involvement and their own thinking as a result of those experiences (Bredekamp, 2000). Tailoring the environment to suit children with special needs involves making adaptations that will allow their environment to remain explorable despite complications presented by such conditions as mental impairments, hearing impairments of deafness, speech or language impairments, visual impairments including blindness, emotional disturbance, orthopedic impairments, autism, traumatic brain injury, and specific learning disabilities (Bowe, 2000).

The teacher in this context provides a safe, stimulating variety of experiences suited to the needs of the children, along with unbiased encouragement and observations designed to support learning and value individual choices (Bredekamp,

2000; Bowe, 2000; Zimmerman & Zimmerman, 2000). For special populations, adaptations could include the use of sign language or print in addition to spoken direction, extra time to manipulate objects related to the lesson, care in room arrangement or equipment to accommodate children with physical differences, and a clear beginning and end to activity segments to indicate closure and provide a predictable pattern to activities (Bowe, 2000).

Multisensory instruction has been found to be especially beneficial to children with Down Syndrome and other forms of mental impairment. The combination of visual, auditory, and tactile processes provides an opportunity for the integration of information that allows learning to occur more completely. Visual input during instruction is also ideal for children with hearing aids (Bowe, 2000).

Consistent with the objective of embedding specific goals or desired experiences within the learning environment from both High Scope and Montessori (Roopnarine & Johnson, 1997) and early intervention theory (Bricker & Woods-Cripe, 1992), the segments of the Dada workshop were planned with the following possibilities for learning included: (1) an introduction, emphasizing the development of speech and social skills through opportunities for conversational dialogue, and the relation of the child as artist to other actual artists (i.e., Magritte, Duchamp); (2) an explanation of Dada art (see appendix to this chapter for historical explanation), pairing concrete objects for hands-on manipulation and experience with an abstract idea, introducing historical perspective of art through review of major styles, and encouraging playful participation in the planning and experimentation process of an artist at work, an explanation of Duchamp's sculpture (i.e., bicycle wheel mounted on kitchen stool); (3) reading *Silly Sally* by Audrey Wood (1992) to encourage cooperative dialogue, relate an abstract idea to the familiar experience of sharing a story, integrate literacy experience with art and movement, develop prediction skills, and encourage the capacity to understand rhyme; (4) singing "Shake Your Sillies In" (an adaptation of "Shake Your Sillies Out" by Raffi), for incorporating movement and music with visual arts, providing balance of active, quiet activity, and developing gross motor skills within a playful peer context; (5) drawing silly pictures to develop fine motor skills, observe for color, shape, line, pattern, or object understanding, participate in studio art experience, and make choices independently; and (6) a picture explanation/critique to develop speaking skills comfortably in a large group situation, make connections among choices and results, processes, and product, and observe for logical sequencing and descriptive forms of language.

This combination of compatible elements from DAP, Special Education, and DBAE was used successfully with several classes of eight to twenty pupils each in a large urban public school. Based on the needs of each group, segments were alternated, elaborated upon, or even eliminated when necessary to maintain an optimal level of involvement by the children. Possible topics for future workshops could include Pop Art in both 2D and 3D, portrait styles (ranging from traditional to nonrepresentational), the action painters (e.g., Jackson Pollack), and the late collage works of Matisse (to emphasize/value cutting skills and elements of random chance).

LESSON GUIDELINES

Workshop objectives are to introduce the concept of Dada Art (see appendix), reinforce with literacy and movement activities, and conclude with drawing and critique. Activities are oriented toward major drawing/painting themes of landscape, still life, portrait, pop, and illustration; the Dada Art movement; sculpture using found objects; self-evaluation and the critique process through group dialogue; and the value of art for fun and emotional expression/release.

MATERIALS

Appropriate materials would include: 11″ × 17″ copy paper, markers, *Silly Sally* by Audrey Wood, colorful dress-up outfit and hats, fruit, flowers, or other still life objects, a real pipe, bubble pipe, or picture of a pipe (taped to a poster with writing underneath, "This is not a pipe," to approximate similar painting by Rene Magritte), a bicycle wheel (optional), and a small stool (optional).

PROCEDURE

In a whole group conversation survey seeking preexperience knowledge, ask, "Why do you think we're here today?" Then, using props, briefly review art history by displaying apples and flowers to illustrate still life, putting on a dress-up hat and posing to illustrate a portrait, describing an immediate area to illustrate a landscape, and holding up any commercial material to illustrate pop art.

Describe the contrast/conflict of Dada Art. Discuss whether its main purpose was to be silly, or to have fun within the context of meaningful art experience. Display Magritte poster and ask for similar examples. Understand the interpretation of Dada in sculpture through "ready mades," the use of common objects put together in new ways. For this segment I imagined out loud with the group the decision-making process possibly utilized by Marcel Duchamp to create the stool with bicycle wheel sculpture: "Marcel wanted to make a sculpture with things from around his house. First he tried the sink . . . but it was too heavy. He tried balancing some eggs on top of a cup on top of a ball [reaching up] but what do you think happened? SPLAT! What a mess! Finally, in his neighbor Miss Tickleophelia's garage, he found [show stool and bicycle wheel]. Perfect!" Change details as needed for dramatic effect. Conclude with a reference to the children's turn to be the artist, and warm up with some silly exercises to get in the right mood.

Read *Silly Sally* slowly, with lots of pauses for group anticipation and reading. Stand up and stretch out a little and practice silly faces. Sing "Shake Your Sillies Out" by Raffi but change words to "shake your sillies in." Provide a very quiet transition to tables to draw pictures, and suggest a group discussion afterward. During drawing time, circulate to help write children's narratives of their art and make concrete references to artistic decisions being observed (e.g., I see you decided to put a lot of lines here"). After fifteen to thirty minutes of drawing time (depending on the group's interest) collect pictures for a group critique/discussion and relate to real artists' participation in this technique to get new ideas, make changes for the next time, compare methods, and so on. For all young children, the author strongly suggests limiting the critique to exploring the artists' methods and motivations ("Why or how did you do that?") and providing concrete observations rather than personal judgments.

ACTIVITY EXTENSIONS AND LINKS

A number of activities can be utilized to widen the children's exploration:

- Provide magazine or Xerox photos of animals, people, and/or objects to create a collage.
- Pair with children's books like *The Mixed Up Chameleon* by Eric Carle or *3 and 3* by Challis Walker; both are about animals with mixed-up parts.
- Use game spinners, dice, or other gamelike strategies of chance to codify artistic decisions (e.g., spinner on 7 means use green; roll 2 on die means collage a circle.)
- Allow children to bring, choose, or find objects for use in collage or sculpture.
- Create group or individual mobiles with straws or sticks, string, tape, small paper shapes, or other interesting objects.
- Create nonsense names or poetry to accompany work.
- Create Dada machine sculptures with hardware scraps and extend this with language experience stories explaining the machine.
- Link the use of found objects to Pop Art's use of everyday objects (e.g., Andy Warhol's *Campbell Soup Can*, Claes Oldenburg's *Soft Sculpture Hamburger*).
- Create a Dada "toy" from materials in the classroom and use language experience from the children to explain function.
- Combine multiple activities, and plan a Dada show with noise music, nonsense poetry, paintings, and sculpture for other classes.
- Assign objects for children to create random sentences about and attach as "real" classroom labels, or provide sentence strips and allow children to label objects independently.
- Create a class tape of environmental noises, pair with a "listening" walk through the school or around the block, inspired by the children's book *The Listening Walk* by Paul Showers.

APPENDIX A: THE DADA MOVEMENT

The Dada movement began with artists in Switzerland during the early 1900s as symbolic mockery of the art establishment of that time, and as a reaction against the social and cultural influences that these artists felt were responsible, in some part, for the suffering created by World War I. Some notable characteristics of Dada Art include the poetic use of nonsense syllables; the deliberate use of random chance in the artistic decision-making process; the use of environmental noises as music (Bruitism); playful, humorous presentation; the use of collage techniques; the use of everyday objects and machinery pieces as subject matter; mobility and found objects in sculpture; and the use of photos in collage (photomontage).

For the purpose of this early childhood workshop, the aspects most appropriate for the developmental needs of children were the playful, random quality and use of everyday objects. Older children or children in situations where social or cultural elements of conflict are present might benefit from an explanation of the Dada founding principles of mockery and rejection of accepted norms.

Artists typically associated with Dada were Jean Arp, Hugo Ball, Max Ernst, Paul Klee, Francis Picabia, Man Ray, and Kurt Schwitters. Artists featured in the workshop are Marcel Duchamp (ready-made sculptures) and Rene Magritte (the pipe).

REFERENCES

Arnason, H. H. (1770). *History of Modern Art: Painting, Sculpture and Architecture.* Englewood Cliffs, NJ: Prentice-Hall.

Bowe, F. G. (2000). *Birth to Five: Early Childhood Special Education* (2d ed.). Clifton Park, NY. Delmar Thomason Learning.

Bredekamp, S. E. (2000). Developmentally *Appropriate Practice in Early Childhood Programs Serving Children from Birth Through Age Eight.* Washington, DC: NAEYC.

Bricker, D., & J. J. Woods-Cripe. (1992). An Activity-Based Approach to Early Intervention. Baltimore: Paul H. Brooks.

Roopnarine, J. L., & J. E. Johnson (eds.). (1997). *Approaches to Early Childhood Education* (2d ed.). New York: Macmillan.

Wood, Audrey. (1992). *Silly Sally.* New York: Harcourt Trade.

Zimmerman, E., & L. Zimmerman. (2000). Art Education and Early Childhood Education: The Young Child as Creator and Meaning Maker within a Community Context. *Young Children* 55(6): 87–92.

33

Simplifying the Environment: A Look at the Effects of Open-Ended Materials on Young Minds

Gilbert M. Foley and John Castronova

This chapter describes the effects of open-ended materials on the development of school-age children with emotional disturbance attending a self-contained special education classroom. The methodology is derived from the philosophy of the City and Country School, founded by Caroline Pratt in 1916. A pioneer of the progressive education movement, Pratt recognized play as the child's natural way of learning. She designed an environment using simple, expressive materials that could be manipulated independently by the child (Pratt, 1948/1970; Pratt & Deming, 1973). The methodology was modified by Laura McDonnell and Helen Friedlander to meet the developmental and educational needs of preschoolers exposed to cocaine in utero (Lanser & McDonnell, 1991; McDonnell, 1993). It has been demonstrated at a model therapeutic nursery opened in September 1991. The program is a collaborative effort between the New York City Health and Hospitals Corporation and the New York City Board of Education.

The improvement in the preschooler's development was notable, including increased time on task, frustration tolerance, self-motivation, and coping capacities. The progress observed in this population prompted Friedlander and McDonnell to replicate the model in a self-contained special education setting serving elementary-school-age children with emotional disturbance. What follows reports the results of a formal curriculum evaluation conducted at the special education site.

The pilot study's purpose was to compare the effectiveness of a Basic Materials Augmented Curriculum to the standard special education curriculum alone to promote the acquisition of academic and coping skills and cognitive and language development in twenty-four five-, six-, and seven-year-old boys and girls classified with emotional disturbance SIEVIIA (*Educational Services*, 1991). The twenty-two boys (ten African-American and twelve Hispanic) and two girls (African-American) were matched on diagnosis, cognitive functioning, and socioeconomic status. The population was divided into four classroom groups based on standard procedures for classroom assignment. Two classrooms were designated for the treatment group (N = 12, Basic Materials Augmented Curriculum), and two classrooms for the comparison group (N = 12, Standard Curriculum).

The classes were assigned to each condition based on teacher choice. Treatment and comparison classroom personnel were matched on credentials and years of experience. A relevant training experience of comparable duration and intensity was provided to the personnel of both the treatment and comparison groups.

The Kaufman Assessment Battery for Children (cognitive processing and achievement subtests) (Kaufman & Kaufman, 1983), the Test of Language Development (Newcomer & Hammill, 1988), and the Coping Inventory (Zeitlin, 1985) were administered to the students in October by the school psychologist, guidance counselor, and classroom teachers, respectively. There were no significant pretest differences between groups based on ethnicity or age. An insufficient number of female students prevented a comparison by gender. The treatment and comparison groups received "instruction" in the respective methods from October through May.

The students in the treatment group completed an instructional day of five hours, with fifty minutes devoted to the basic materials curriculum. The basic materials period was established by reducing the time devoted to three main subject areas: mathematics, social studies, and language arts. For the remainder of the day the treatment group received instruction following the traditional special education curriculum. Students in the comparison group received a five-hour instructional day consisting of only the traditional teacher-directed special education curriculum.

The special education curriculum taught to both groups followed the New York City Board of Education guidelines developed to meet the requirements of the Part 100 Series of Regulations of the New York State Commissioner of Education regarding special education services (*Educational Services*, 1991). This curriculum provides a level of instruction that allows students to work as near to age and grade-level and as independently as possible. It is an adaptation of the general education curriculum for all subject areas, with modifications to provide for small group instruction, more intensive adult support, more opportunity to practice and generalize learned skills, and more intensive and individualized teacher-directed instruction.

The Basic Materials Methodology augmented the daily standard curriculum. An abundant and easily accessible supply of blocks, water, paint, and clay were available to the students for fifty minutes each morning. The teachers and assistants provided the daily structure within which the students played freely and independently with the materials, exploring their observable properties. The structural aspects of the environment included a set time each morning for play, a consistent and readily accessible location for the materials, a wide-open space within the room for play, and a teacher and assistant available on the periphery of the area to mediate conflicts only when absolutely necessary and to unobtrusively encourage students to interact with the materials. Otherwise, the students were allowed to freely interact with the materials and each other in a self-directed manner, predicated on the conviction that children possess the inner resources and capacity to construct knowledge from experience without the need for imposed tasks and direct instruction.

Posttesting was completed in May and group data were analyzed using a repeated measure of analysis of variance (ANOVA). There were several significant effects for the time factor alone, for all subjects. This suggests that all students progressed in these areas irrespective of curriculum. The finding, although preliminary, is noteworthy in that substituting fifty minutes of instructional time for an opportunity to play with basic materials did not harm the students' academic achievement, acquisition of coping skills, or cognitive and language development (Nourot & Van Hoorn, 1991; Scales, Almy, Nicolopoulo, & Ervin-Tripp, 1991). This is no small matter in the current curriculum climate, which has been so suspect of play that in some school districts recess has been banished from the day (Beauchamp, 1996; Hills, 1987). It is critical to note, however, that these findings are based on a population of special education students and that no valid generalization to typical students can be made.

While no statistical differences were found between groups, clinically meaningful findings in the form of large and moderate effect sizes favoring the treatment group were identified (speaking $d = 0.87$; Adaptive coping behavior composite $d = 0.89$; self active coping $d = 1.03$). These findings indicate that the children in the treatment group scored on the average 0.87 of a standard deviation unit higher in expressive language following intervention than did their peers receiving the standard curriculum alone. In the area of coping, the treatment group scored, on the average, 0.89 of a standard deviation unit greater than their peers in the comparison group on overall use of skills and behaviors to manage their world, and 1.03 standard deviation units higher in self-active coping, specifically their ability to initiate and sustain action, whether mental or physical, to meet personal needs. In addition, there were nine medium effect sizes in the language and coping domains, ranging from $d = 0.39$ to $d = 0.61$ favoring the treatment group. While these findings are preliminary at best and the study was peppered with many limitations, they are nonetheless promising.

The results of our educational experiment, combined with a growing uneasiness about the emphasis on imposed tasks, teacher-directed intervention, and educational materials as the sole means of instruction, underline the need to reexamine our accepted methodologies. The findings also support the need for further research, and add, in some small measure, to the body of knowledge that affirms play as a child's native medium of expression, as industry and learning, and a means to awaken in children the urge to complete development.

REFERENCES

Beauchamp, H. (1996). Teachers' Attitudes and Policies Regarding Play in Elementary Schools. *Psychology in the Schools* 33: 61–69.

Educational Services: For Students with Handicapping Conditions. (1991). New York: New York Board of Education.

Hills, T. (1987). Children in the Fast Lane: Implications for Early Childhood Policy and Practice. *Early Childhood Research Quarterly* 2: 265–273.

Kaufman, A. S., & N. L. Kaufman. (1983). *Kaufman Assessment Battery for Children*. Circle Pines, MN: American Guidance.

Lanser, S., & L. McDonnell. (1991). Creating Quality Curriculum Yet Not Buying Out the Store. *Young Children* 47: 4–9.

McDonnell, L. (1993, April). A New Educational Model for Cocaine-Exposed Children in a Hospital-Based Therapeutic Nursery. Paper presented at the University of Padua, Italy.

Newcomer, P. L., & D. D. Hammill. (1988). *Test of Language Development—Primary*. Austin, TX: Pro-Ed.

Nourot, P., & J. Van Hoorn. (1991). Symbolic Play in Preschool and Primary Settings. *Young Children* 46: 40–50.

Pratt, C. (1970). *I Learn from Children*. New York: Cornerstone. (Original work published 1948.)

Pratt, C., & L. Denning. (1973). The Play School. In C. B. Winsor (Ed.), *Experimental Schools Revisited* (pp. 2–18). New York: Agathon Press.

Scales, B., M. Almy, A. Nicolopoulou, & S. Ervin-Tripp. (1991). Defending Play in the Lives of Children. In B. Scales, M. Almy, A. Nicolopoulou, & S. Ervin-Tripp (Eds.), *Play and the Social Context of Development in Early Care and Education* (pp. 15–31). New York: Teachers College, Columbia University Press.

Zeitlin, S. (1985). *Coping Inventory*. Bensenville, IL: Scholastic Press.

34

Multicultural Dimensions of a Children's Play and Discovery Center in Arabia

Vicki L. Stoecklin and Randy White

The best things you can give children, next to good habits, are
good memories.

—Anonymous

One's culture can have a tremendous influence over how the world is perceived.
This chapter looks at how culture affected the development and operation of an indoor, 25,000-square-foot children's play and discovery center in the city of Dubai
in the United Arab Emirates.

Dubai is a very unusual Middle Eastern city on the east side of the Arabian
Gulf—unusual in the sense that only about 20 percent of the population is Arab,
the remainder being 55 percent Indian and about 25 percent expatriate Westerners.
These three main cultural groups live almost as parallel societies, although they
shop in the same modern stores and malls and eat in the same restaurants. A request was made to create a for-profit center where children and families of all cultures could come together in a leisure setting.

This unusual multicultural mix posed a great challenge for a design team, as
each culture has its own unique tastes and preferences. In order to understand how
society operated in this country, our firm did extensive cultural research, which included reading and studying about each of the cultures. Information was found on
the Internet, in books, and by speaking with the U.S. embassy. Many hours were
spent participating in the daily life of each of these cultures by visiting and observing families and children in museums, shopping malls, parks, *souks* (market-
places), and restaurants.

Focus-group research was conducted by interviewing children and mothers from all three cultures. This research confirmed that families of all three cultures were looking for places to play with their children in an environment that was both educational and fun. Additional preferences that were discovered as commonalties among mothers from all three cultures was a concern about cleanliness, safety, fun, and a preference for a facility where only women and children can be in the center at appointed times. Women's days are a preference in this part of the world, where many women still veil in the presence of males, except for the closest family members. By creating a women's day when no males would be present in the center, a situation was created where the Arab women might feel comfortable to unveil and really play with their children. Playing with children is a challenge when women have to be continually concerned about keeping their veils on. It would also remove the mystery of the veil and the unapproachability the veil creates for other cultures, helping to facilitate interactions and understanding between the Arab and expatriate women.

Since the play and discovery center would be used as a destination for school field trips, visits were made to both public and private schools attended by each cultural group. Appointments were also made with the Ministry of Education regarding the educational potential of the center. All of this research posed challenges, as language and interpretation of concepts are difficult in countries where some of the ideas about children's rights to play are still developing.

It was decided, after completing the research, that the center should be based on developmentally appropriate play for children under the age of ten. We chose a variety of activities to appeal to the multiple intelligences of the children. Play activities that can be enjoyed in the play and discovery center include a separate play space for children under the age of two and their caregivers; pretend fishing from a boat; a dinosaur dig in sand; blocks and other construction materials; an indoor climbing structure; a pretend house, supermarket, and pizza restaurant; do-it-yourself face painting; art studios (one for children ages two to five and one for children ages six to ten); do-it-yourself pretend mendhi or henna; and a reading room with books in many languages.

While many of these children's play events seem right out of Western culture, we incorporated cultural elements into many. For example, the pretend fishing is done from a replica of a traditional Gulf *dhow* boat, and the exterior of the pretend house was designed incorporating Arab, Indian, and Western architectural styles. The pretend dress-up features clothing and traditional jewelry from the three cultural groups, and the pretend mendhi or henna is a tradition practiced by both Arabs and Indians.

In addition, other parts of the center were adapted to meet cultural needs. We had privacy issues that had to be handled, not only in the layout of the center, but also in the central café area. The center was designed using a traditional zigzag entry, so during "ladies only" times no one can see in from the outside. In the café we put private booths with curtains that draw over the outside of the booth for Arab families with veiled women. We also designed an ablution room for Muslim women to wash before prayer, since they requested their own prayer room.

The center included many signs in both English and Arabic, explaining to parents the value of the play events for children's development. We followed the Americans with Disability Act (1990) guidelines in designing the center to make it accessible to both adults and children with disabilities. This is unheard of in their country, where there are no guidelines for designing for the disabled and the proportion of disabled is higher than the disabled population in the United States or Europe.

Research with schools and local children pointed to a theme for the center, giving it a local identity. Conservation was the theme that drew the strongest response from children and teachers. The mascot and theme chosen were based on the dugong, which is endangered in the Gulf of Arabia and a cousin of the Florida manatee. Because dugongs are matriarchal, a fictional female dugong mascot named LouLou ("pearl" in Arabic, for the "Pearl City of Dubai") Al Dugong ("of the dugongs") was created, which also provided the center's name.

Staffing the center posed another set of complex issues. A highly qualified staff is essential to the success of any center serving children and families. Positions in this center require extensive knowledge of children and how they play, and the staff must be able to interact with people from different cultures while adjusting themselves to living outside of their country in a very foreign land.

The design and consulting company was charged with interviewing and screening staff, a job that took us to India, Thailand, and Morocco. Women were chosen from these countries based on their education and experience, their tolerance for religious diversity, the role of women in their own countries, their bilingual skills, their attitudes toward play, and their understanding of the concept of hospitality (a very important concept in Arabia). The company also provided an intensive one-month training program in topics including child development, cultural diversity, play leadership, ecology, emergency management, safety, and customer service for families and children. These women were provided with a three-year work contract, housing, food, and transportation costs. Many were being paid significantly more than they could ever attain in their own countries, in addition to receiving valuable training, that could enhance their career paths later in life.

Many issues have proven to be challenges in staffing and operating such a complex center. Much of the complexity of this project was really foreign to most of the staff, who come from countries where efficiency and complexity are not known concepts. It was equally challenging to continue team-building training as cross-cultural issues among staff members arose more frequently, since they lived communally in a large villa. Also, for many of the women this was their first journey outside their own country and they were surprised by how they were treated by the local populations, especially the men in this male-dominated society. Some of the staff also struggled to understand the relationship between free play and children's healthy development.

During return visits to Dubai, countless hours of videos and observational notes were collected. A few of the positive outcomes observed in the center are as follows:

1. Women have been coming more frequently during the "ladies only" days and local women have been playing more with their children during these times.

2. Fathers have been involved in their children's play, especially Arab and Western fathers.

3. Parents have been feeling free to let their children choose play activities rather than controlling what they do—for example, letting the children paint their own faces rather than decorating their faces for them.

4. Schools in the area have been using the field trip curriculums that have been developed and are visiting the center on a regular basis.

5. Children of all ethnic backgrounds have been playing and having fun together. Local children have been exposed to written language in many formats, including Arabic, and some local families have been struggling to understand the importance of the written word, since their own culture is predominantly oral.

6. Children and families have become more aware of the need to save the local dugong from extinction, and its importance to local ecology.

7. Nannies who work for local families, many of whom were from foreign countries and had little or no interaction with women of their own cultures, have used the center as a gathering place.

8. Local schools have requested information on how to do play-based activities more frequently in their classrooms, with some schools expressing an interest in training.

LouLou Al Dugong has offered a unique view of children, their families, and a staff of many cultures learning to respect, work with, and have fun with others who are not from their own cultures. It is an ongoing learning process as each group learns more about the other. The more we are different, the more we are all the same.

REFERENCE

Americans with Disabilities Act, Accessibility Guidelines for Buildings and Facilities: Play Areas: Final Rule. (1990). 36 C.F.R. Part 1191.

35

The Collaborative Play of Parents, Children, and Teachers in Creating a Diverse Play Space

Georgianna Duarte

This chapter involves the energy, the passion, and time of many individuals who believe in play. Valued migrant parents tired from their challenging work in the fields still have the energy to be playful parents. This chapter summarizes their dreams and the vivid visions of what children want aside from Head Start Centers. This chapter clearly integrates the author's vision as a play researcher, player in life, and teacher trainer. It summarizes the belief that space for children should be a natural continuum of learning rather than fenced units of life. These play spaces are the result of the collaboration of many individuals in designing Migrant Head Start play spaces across south Texas.

Play environments are much more than the selection of complex climbers, swing sets, or appropriate space covers. The design of play environments involves an analysis of how children learn, play, and interact with their peers and the physical environment (Frost, 1992). A quality play area involves thoughtful planning, an understanding of children's play stages, different types of play, and how the play space will foster play and development. Equally important are the kinds of messages that the environment provides to the child. Is this a space that is natural, safe, and interesting, with varied plants, flowers, trees, and assorted vegetation? Is this a place where a child can climb, explore, and crawl around, over and through a natural habitat without critical risks and hazards? As many early childhood teachers already know, play spaces are much more than bare space.

Many researchers (Piaget, 1962; Van Hoorn, Nourot, Scales, & Alward, 1993) describe constructive play as a natural link between functional play and more sophisticated forms of play. In constructive play the child uses concrete objects or natural materials to create a representation of an object. Following this important type of play is dramatic play, where children are engaged in imaginary roles and situations. The construction of pretend objects is a critical component of this type of play. The play area is a space where engaging actions, interactions, and community thrive. Creative play spaces need to reflect areas that meet the various needs of children and include multiple levels of safe and challenging spaces for activity. Equally important are the types of props and materials available to the children in the outdoor spaces.

Regarding development, play areas need to be secure, inviting spaces that meet Consumer Product Safety Commission (1981) criteria for children with special needs. Educators need to ensure that in designing play areas, collaborative explorations of organizations such as the International Play Association and the National Playspace Association are sought out, for guidance and new research in how children explore their world. The play space areas need to be designed with careful attention to those age and developmental groups that plan to use them. All too frequently, large play areas are designed to meet the needs of physically large children, failing to address the needs of smaller children. For example, many programs like Migrant Head Start provide services to children and families, with children ranging from infancy to preschool levels. Consequently, the play areas need to be designed not only to provide spaces for all those age groups, but also to extend the play choices beyond the chronological years of the children. Specifically, the play spaces need to be challenging, yet not be too difficult or unsafe.

The Texas Migrant Head Start invited a group of students enrolled in a college course entitled Early Childhood Environments and their professor to design an outdoor play area for eleven centers across the state of Texas. Special attention was given not only to safety, but to issues of culture, language, and parental involvement. The design team wanted to work with parents and children to ensure that culture and language were integrated into the designs. The play areas did not need to remain static, but change over time to provide a variety of options meeting the changing needs of children.

A creative play space requires well-defined, zoned areas for optimum development. These play zones may include an active learning zone, an adventure play area, a quiet zone, a nature zone, and an animal area. The areas of development for young children include physical abilities (fine and gross motor skills), cognitive skills, social–emotional attitudes, and language skills. Areas need to be clearly and safely marked with low timber beams, or varying space cover, or equipment spaces.

The *active learning zone* is an area where children can freely exercise their large motor skills in a safe manner. An active learning area would typically contain large pieces of equipment that offer a variety of movement options. A good example would be a complex unit climber. A typical active learning zone for infants and toddlers would also include smaller size climbers, mounds, and walking areas. Tricycle paths, swing sets, crawling tubes, and platform lofts are sample features of an active zone. Active areas need clear divisions so that children can safely utilize the equipment or areas. Culturally, plazas and *palapas* would be reconfigured from small to large to encourage dramatic play.

The *adventure play areas* for infant, toddler, and preschool children will certainly look very different in size, safety, and complexity. An adventure area lends itself to equipment that can be modified and changed over time. It may include multiple-level ramps, pavilions, stages, stairs, mazes, tunnels, and walkways. It offers children a variety of options through ropes, tires, climbing materials, and pathways. Such a play zone would vary in size according to the size of the overall play space. Many parts are movable so that different pieces can be combined to provide a variety of new activities. These adventure zones would incorporate regional aspects of bird houses and river walks that are typical of the region. Jumping areas can include platforms and unusual structures such as tree stumps and ladder-like frames.

A *quiet zone* would allow for quiet reflection, observation, and time alone. These quiet zones might include small tents, small structures, park benches, picnic tables, theater benches, tree stumps, and hammocks for resting. Permanent and movable benches are excellent quiet zones. Small and large stumps serve for solitary observation and gross motor skills. Such movable items as refrigerator boxes, tents, umbrellas, beach boards with blankets, cots, or quilts for reading books serve as excellent quiet zones.

A *nature zone* is a distinct area of the play space where children can learn about the world around them. For example, a nature zone might include ramps and bridges through a forest, a long water and mud ditch, a flower garden, a garden plot of vegetables, or a water canal of activities. Natural areas of the existing terrain serve as excellent nature zones. Multiple flower or garden patches will provide variety throughout the play space. Nature zones take the form of flower paths or flower boxes. To discourage neighborhood theft, such play spaces should incorporate an area for a working garden close to the building. This area should have a tool shed or storage area nearby for tools. The garden is the learning foundation for nutrition and cultural activities. Nearby, many centers may choose to have a patio area or picnic tables, with additional benches for observation, reflection, food preparation, and eating activities.

An *animal zone* is an exciting area of any play space. This particular area may include bird houses, hamster cages, a rabbit pen complete with hutch, or a terrarium with lizards and snakes. The animal area needs very specific signs regarding the care and protection of its pets. Bird feeders and bird baths are common favorites of play spaces. However, even the temporary ownership and care of a rabbit yields tremendous benefits to the children. A single duck or visiting lizard offers numerous learning opportunities for young children. Clearly, security and care are important considerations in the selection of an animal. A science table complete with insect jars, butterfly nets, and ant farms can be a changing theme of the area. Obviously, such projects can be flowing zones throughout the total space of the play area. For example, bird feeders can be integrated across the play area in a variety of trees for a wide range of species. This was particularly significant in south Texas given the large variety of birds.

FIRST STEPS: PLAYING TOGETHER

Sixteen Texas Migrant Head Start Centers needed play areas redesigned. Teachers, children, parents, and other key staff were important contributors of ideas for the overall design of the play space. A key consideration in designing the space was to ensure that all areas were enclosed by fences and that the total space represented a community with a winding tricycle trail that flowed throughout the space. Another underlying design feature was a plaza for community gatherings of children. In south Texas and Wisconsin, migrant children were initially asked to draw pictures of their favorite spaces, their dreams, and what they liked to do in the outdoor environment. Also, an interview format was designed and data collected to determine the kinds of things children thought about for outdoor play and what they wanted and dreamed about for their play space.

PLAY IDEAS FROM CHILDREN, PARENTS, AND STAFF

To ensure the design ideas of children, parents, and staff, a number of strategies were utilized across the region. A parent, teacher, and staff survey was utilized to explore how they perceived the outdoors as a learning environment. Each person interviewed was also asked to provide additional comments and questions he or she might want to add. The ten-item survey was provided prior to the design team meetings. Sample items include the following:

1. What are your two favorite areas of the outside for children?
2. When you go outside with your children, where do you desire to play the most?
3. What toys and materials do you usually provide for outdoor play?
4. What do you not like outside that you wish were different?
5. If you could design your own play spaces, what would they look like, and what would you be sure to include in them?
6. If you could have four rules for the play space, what would they be?

As part of our collaborative design, children were interviewed through a survey format. The ten-item survey assessed how children perceived and used play areas. Sample items include the following:

1. Please describe three areas of the play space that you use most frequently and why.
2. Please identify three areas of the play space that you regard as your favorite spaces.
3. Please describe six areas of improvement or changes for your play space.
4. Please identify what toys and props that you use most frequently in the play space.
5. What specific changes or challenges have you had using your new play space?
6. Please list the most important rules that you feel are effective for your play area.

CLEAR DEVELOPMENTAL DIVISIONS

The Migrant Head Start Program serves infants, toddlers, and preschool children and is a comprehensive child and family program. To ensure quality services, the needs of children and families had to be addressed in the play designs. Distinct areas for the different age groups had to be carefully planned in the preliminary designs. For each play area, the spaces are zoned for infant, toddler, and preschool children. In a large expansive yard, it is important to carefully zone with several types of space cover. Be sure to provide grass as the preferred space cover for the younger age group. Many designers and researchers (Zeavin, 1997) critically point out the important need for separate areas for infants, toddlers, and preschoolers due to the obvious developmental differences across the three groups of children. Given that in many migrant programs siblings attend the same center for Head Start, it is even more effective for siblings to have a visual perspective of their family members in the play spaces. This is achieved through natural planning of grassy mounds, attractive shrubbery, trees, and natural flower beds that carefully zone but do not obstruct the view of teachers or the children who wish to gaze on their brothers and sisters during play.

NATURAL ENVIRONMENT: POWER OF PLAY

The results of all the surveys highlighted the important role of nature in children's dreams and play. All play spaces were spacious areas where a great deal of vegetation planning was critically required. Due to the Texas sun, the planting of trees and shade was a priority. This is an ongoing challenge in all regions due to droughts and the growth rate of trees in the region. Flower gardens, foot paths, bushes, and beautiful gardens ranging from small patches of tomatoes to larger more organized regions of vegetables began to take shape across the Rio Grande Valley. This is also a challenging project due to the seasonal schedule of these programs. Varied space cover was discussed, and as all evolving play spaces take shape, it is a learning process. Mounds of dirt, grass, sand, and wood chips were provided across the region.

Grassy mounds, trails, and larger wild-flower beds also took shape due to many community organizations like the Girl Scouts and Boy Scouts. The play space also accommodated visiting animals and butterfly exhibits, giving careful attention to supporting the natural curiosity of children and the world around them. Given the regional factors, bird houses, turtle zones, as well as bird feeders were gradually added to play spaces. For each region, unique vegetation and choices were made.

The purpose of the garden in play space is important, for it serves as a valid resource for the growing, preparation, and consumption of nutritional goods, and as a center for large and fine motor activities. The garden clearly reinforces the importance and integrity of the work of the family and community. The garden should include a variety of vegetables, be an integral part of all class activities (for all children), and be carefully maintained. Garden tools (child size) should be provided, as well as sun hats. A nearby water source is important. All facets of maintaining the garden should be delegated to the children.

Flower beds serve as an aesthetic beautification of the yard, as well as a source of learning. Care and maintenance of the flowers should involve the children, for they would appreciate the flowers' growth and change. Flower beds in the form of flower boxes can serve as safety features for decks and stairs that are unprotected.

Safety Factor

Safety is a critical factor for all play space zones. Federally funded spaces mandate safety. Thus, all Migrant Head Start Center play spaces were enclosed play areas, protected by either hurricane or privacy fences. All cement surfaces needed to be clearly indicated as walking zones, with signs or a variety of furniture to decrease the likelihood of accidents. Plastic and a variety of materials were selected rather than hot metal climbers. Consumer Product Safety Commission Guidelines and various publications of the National Playspace Association were utilized throughout the creation and analysis of safety on the sixteen play areas.

Sufficient space was allotted between zones to allow for children's free mobility and departure from pieces of equipment. For example, swing areas needed sitting benches off to one side, leaving an area clear for the use of the equipment. Small miniature signs that are representative of Department of Motor Vehicles signs (stop, yield, etc.) should be utilized in the play area, as well as portable dry eraser boards of rules and guidelines for the outdoor spaces. These items can be utilized on a movable basis and change with time. When there are clear guidelines and flexibility, there are far fewer accidents in any zoned play area.

ASSESSMENT

Once the first phase—the major placement of equipment, zoning, and landscaping—has been completed, it is vital that teachers carefully assess and document how the environment is working and consider future refinements. A play space is never truly complete, because it is a constantly evolving process of interaction and improvements. Regular inspections by children, parents, and teachers should be an integral part of the curriculum. As many teachers and staff at the Brownsville Migrant Head Start Center have pointed out, the outdoor space is as important as the indoor environment. Research has shown that more adults remember their favorite activity as being outside, rather than inside (Rivkin, 1995).

COMMUNITY PARTNERS

At the University of Texas at Brownsville, students have been involved as play partners through two undergraduate university courses. Through EDEC 4388, Play Theory and Application, they have collaborated with teachers in designing a variety of activities involving observation, record documentation, stages of play behavior, play choices, and play activities. In the EDEC 4389 course addressing early childhood indoor and outdoor design, students have been engaged in assessing how environments facilitate different kinds of behaviors and how they offer a variety of opportunities. This is an ongoing collaborative relationship each semester in that region.

CULTURAL DESIGN FEATURES

Throughout the play space, cultural aspects were integrated into all of the designs. For example, the winding tricycle trail was integrated around each play space and near small structures serving as dramatic areas. These dramatic structures evolved as *clinicas, farmacias,* and *panderias,* common in neighborhoods. Also, the theater and large mural zone emphasized the culture and arts.

Community plazas, so common throughout Mexico and Latin America, were created as meeting spaces for the children. Frequently, the *palapa* became part of a plaza. These plazas have also served as teacher and parent areas throughout the day, for gatherings and conferences. Bird houses and bird baths were later added, as the children continued providing ideas.

The functional purpose of the *palapa* is to provide quality shade for a wide variety of activities. It could not be utilized as a parking or traffic zone for large-wheel equipment or tricycles. Since the cement surface of the *palapa* does not provide a fall zone, it is critical that teachers zone this area as a quiet or learning zone. Many of the teachers from the Donna, El Couch, and Mercedes centers in Texas suggested the following usage: art activities, including easel painting, crafts, and chalk art; science activities; water activities, using a water table; literacy activities, using small chairs and tables; food activities; parent functions; block building, using a small collection of blocks clearly designated for the *palapa* area only; or dramatic activity, centered on such places as a barber shop or beauty parlor, ice cream parlor, shoe store, or fire department.

EQUIPMENT SHEDS

Teachers and staff throughout the region were critical assessors of what was needed throughout the process. The equipment shed in many regions became a reality for movable equipment, props, and materials for children of all ages. Sheds were transformed in some regions into garden sheds, garages for pull toys and tricycles, or sheds for art supplies. There were a number of requirements for equipment sheds. First, they had to be located in areas where children could independently reach and return equipment, such as tricycles. Second, the doors and location had to be assessed for safety. For security reasons, several locks had to be utilized for sheds. This storage issue decreased the possibility of accidents and the amount of dirt and so on in the center buildings.

SUMMARY

The advocacy of play should and does have a voice in every community. Clearly, play begins with children, but there must be an investment by the community that will advocate for the preservation of play in safe and creative play spaces. The collaboration, commitment, and energy of the Migrant Head Start parents, children, and staff created a resounding voice in a community, like so many others, where play is not highly valued. Every community needs a sense of creating a play community where every child can have opportunities to experience the joy and developmental benefits of play.

BIBLIOGRAPHY

Consumer Product Safety Commission. (1981). *A Handbook for Public Playground Safety*. Vol. 1: *General Guidelines for New and Existing Playgrounds*. Washington, DC: Consumer Product Safety Commission.

Davidson, J. (1996). *Emergent Literacy and Dramatic Play in Early Education*. Albany, NY: Delmar.

Frost, J. (1992). *Play and Playscapes*. Albany, NY: Delmar.

Greenman, J. (1998). *Caring Spaces, Learning Places: Children's Environments That Work*. Redmond, WA: Exchange Press.

Guddemi, M., T. Jambor, & A. Skrupskelis. (1995). *Play: An Intergenerational Experience: Proceedings of IPA/USA*. Birmingham, AL: American Affiliate of the International Association for the Child's Right to Play.

Heidemann, S., & D. Hewitt. (1992). *Pathways to Play: Developing Play Skills in Young Children*. St. Paul, MN: Redleaf Press.

Johnson, J. E., J. F. Christie, & T. D. Yawkey. (1999). *Play and Early Childhood Development*. (2d ed.). New York: HarperCollins.

Kritchevsky, S., E. Prescott, & L. Walling. (1998). *Planning Environments for Young Children: Physical Space*. Washington, DC: NAEYC.

Piaget, J. (1962). *Play, Dreams, and Imitation in Childhood*. New York: Norton.

Rivkin, M. S. (1995). *The Great Outdoors: Restoring Children's Right to Play Outside*. Washington, DC: NAEYC.

Trencher, B. A. (1991). *Child's Play*. Atlanta: Humanics Limited.

Van Hoorn, J., P. Nourot, B. Scales, & K. Alward. (1993). *Play at the Center of the Curriculum* (2d ed.). New York: Macmillan.

Zeavin, C. (1997). Toddlers at Play: Environments at Work. *Young Children* 52 (3): 72–78.

36

Designing Sensory Play Environments for Children with Special Needs

Kate Bishop

THE ROLE OF THE ENVIRONMENT

A carefully conceived play environment can provide rewarding stimulation to address the physical, intellectual, and social needs of all children, while simultaneously providing the impetus for children to play, both on their own and with their peers. An environment specifically designed to suit the needs of a particular group of children (with special needs) need not exclude other children, as most groups of children with special needs contain a diverse range of ability. By planning with special groups in mind, it ensures there is something in the play environment for children with all levels of ability.

As Allen (1980) stated, play for children with special needs may not emerge naturally and informally as it does with their peers, and therefore may need special encouragement. A child without special needs might be able to turn anything into a play object for a period of time. Children do not need to be shown the virtues of play, they know them instinctively. But for children who are sick or disabled, this instinct may be reduced or absent; therefore the challenge of encouraging these children to actively engage with the play environment is very real.

When establishing the goals for a custom-designed play environment for children with special needs, the following aims should be considered:

1. helping them discover the joy of play;
2. encouraging the children to play by presenting an environment that is attractive to them, on their levels of ability, which absorbs their interest and rewards their interaction;
3. helping intervention programs channel challenging behaviors and antisocial behaviors into more productive learning;

4. developing social skills among peers;

5. developing skills for daily living;

6. providing experiences that can be understood by both parents and children and generalized to contexts outside the play environment; and

7. providing a situation in which the best practice or recommended intervention can be observed.

A child's development is directly linked to the ability to interact with the environment. Piaget (1951) stated that children develop an understanding of themselves through their interactions with events and materials outside themselves. All environments have the ability to contribute to or retard this process. "Environment" in this instance refers to the physical environment, although a much more commanding definition comes from the Webster's dictionary, which describes it as "all conditions, circumstances and influences surrounding and affecting the development of an organism or group of organisms" (*Webster's*, 1983).

The environment, including both physical and social environments, is constantly acknowledged for its influence on learning or play for all children (Allen, 1980; Greenman, 1988; Moore & Wong, 1997; Olds, 1979; Prescott, 1987). However, statements concerning the function and value of the physical environment are typically vague and nonspecific in nature. The influence of play environments on the behavior of children with special needs has been largely overlooked. Research has focused on play behaviors or on the relationship between children with specified disabilities and play behaviors. The physical environment is frequently acknowledged as being instrumental in the success of learning, play, or intervention programs, but there have been few attempts to quantify or qualify this relationship. Gilfoyle, Grady, and Moore (1990) described four major functions of an environment that are common to all design solutions: "(a) holding function, providing bodily support; (b) a facilitating function, providing stimulation, arousal, intent and motivation to move; (c) a challenge function, helping participants reach higher levels of self potential; and (d) an interactive function, providing an interplay between the individual and the environment" (p. 19).

SENSORY QUALITY: ITS MEANING

To make an environment truly sensory, the creator of the environment must be conscious of the available tools. The textures, the colors, the smells, the sounds in the space, and the lighting qualities are all features to be considered as tools to be arranged in a variety of combinations to create a sensory-stimulating environment. A sensory environment is one that (1) interacts with and nourishes all the users' senses deliberately, (2) has sensory qualities and sensory signposts used as part of all the chief functions of a play environment and the creator has consciously and consistently supplied sensory information in this way, and (3) has made the most of its natural advantages of location and then continued to add sensory detail, conscious of what these features are adding to the overall experience within the environment.

Christopher Day (1995) talks about being conscious of the "spirit of place." He says, "The senses, all together, give a picture of a reality which is not adequately described by any *one* sense, a reality which we call spirit, the spirit of a person, event or place" (p. 19). It is the combination of sensory details—color and light and texture together—that provide the spirit of place, and none of these things ever functions alone. They provide atmosphere, sources of navigational and spatial information, sources of entertainment, magic, mystery, and surprise, and much of an environment's educational value.

It is also through the combination of these features that the "welcome, this is your space" message is written for children. Olds (1979) stressed the need for children to feel comfortable. She was referring to physical comfort, but in most cases an individual's "feeling of comfort" (p. 94) will be linked to emotional security as well as physical ease (Pagliano, 1999; Hutchinson & Kewin, 1994). Sensory features will contribute greatly to all levels of comfort or discomfort. The layout and scaling of the room have a large role to play, but children are not as conscious of these two factors as they are of such details as how the room smells and whether they like the colors that surround them.

It is important to keep in mind that for children with special needs the details of color, texture, smell, sound, and lighting might have a much greater impact, depending on their disability. These factors can therefore be a source of more intense discomfort or pleasure. This is where the intimate knowledge of the design team becomes crucial.

GETTING STARTED AND SIMPLE SOLUTIONS

In order to initiate the development of a custom-designed play environment, begin by considering low-technology, mechanically interactive solutions built from readily available materials. Aim to provide a framework in which users can add or subtract elements without requiring any special skills. If built creatively, this design can maintain interest across time without needing significant updating or incurring much ongoing cost.

In a world that promotes the latest technological advances as the solution to all problems, where do low-technology play environments fit in? The answer: in parallel. There will always be a need for mechanically interactive play equipment and environments for all children. It is not possible for sophisticated electronic solutions to compensate for all of the daily living skills required by children. They will always need to know how to unscrew lids, open latches and locks, coordinate two hands simultaneously, and balance themselves while climbing over, walking over, or running over differing surfaces. Even those children who are profoundly impaired (intellectually and physically) need to be encouraged to build upon the function they possess at all times.

WHAT SHOULD BE INCLUDED AND WHY

To begin a design workshop, start with an exercise asking participants to name their favorite recreational environment as a child. Ninety-nine percent of the time they name an outdoor environment. Then ask them to list the reasons for choosing this environment. These might well include constant variation (seasonal change), flexibility or manipulable parts, ongoing challenge and interest, all kinds of sensory richness and magical effects, and adventure, surprise, and mystery. These are all elements that should be present in any play environment. There are two levels of planning during which these elements can be included: (1) in the overall plan, by introducing a variety in the sensory quality and physical parameters within the play environment, and (2) in the variety and types of spaces, activities, and sensory detail provided within each play space.

LAYOUT

In a play environment it is necessary to strike a balance between identifying functional needs and promoting to the fullest extent the use of all abilities a child possesses, however minimal these might be. Therefore, the placement and scaling of activities is very important. It begins with the entrance into the space. There should always be an invitation to enter (Olds, 2001, p. 414). Play environments that include children with special needs should be designed to maximize the ability of children to interact easily with their surroundings by adjusting the scale, height, and weight of physical elements to the dimensions and abilities of the children, or by providing props that act as extensions of a child's limited capabilities (Olds, 1979, p. 97).

The priority should be to enable children to act for themselves wherever possible. It is important to recognize that custom designing a play environment is part of a process that has implications far beyond the immediate environment being experienced: "Each environment . . . imposes varied demands on the individual. How one perceives the demands is dependent on one's past experiences as well as a feeling of competence and control over the environment" (McEwen, 1990, p. 7).

Complexity and flexibility within a play environment are also considered essential features. Prescott (1987) defined simple, complex, and super units for describing an activity's play potential. A sandpit on its own is a simple unit. A sandpit with tools is a complex unit. A sandpit with tools and water is a super unit. She argued that an increased layering of play tools and therefore things that can be done with them holds children's interest longer and therefore has greater potential benefits.

One of the most important aspects of any environment for children is its sensory detail: "The textures, colours, and forms applied to all the surfaces of the environment are the close-at-hand qualities of the environment with which occupants come most in contact, and what they 'read' continually in experiencing a setting" (Olds, 1989, p. 10). It is these features that leave the most lasting impression of an environment on children, as these are the features that are occurring within the child's reach. For younger children in particular, nothing is irrelevant or neutral (Olds, 2001, p. 303). Olds talked about the environment's ability to provide "difference-within-sameness." She cited natural examples as the ultimate definition of this concept: a babbling brook, wafting breezes, sunlight dancing on leaves. Opportunities exist in every project to provide differences-within-sameness by varying architectural features or lighting or surface textures and through added softening materials, such as cushions, mats, and play pieces (p. 10). There is, however, a limit to the amount of detail that can be added. Overstimulating environments can work against the design goals, particularly if the child in the room has a problem processing sensory information and readily suffers from sensory overload.

SENSORY DETAIL: COLOR

Color is a marvelous design tool, and can be used to much greater purpose than just decoration and surface finish. It can be used to describe the environment, delineate areas within the room or changes in surface levels of play equipment, or as a basis for an activity in itself. Color is an excellent way of visually organizing the space or the activities (Olds, 2001, p. 274). It also plays an enormous part in the initial attraction of a play environment.

It is a misunderstanding that children prefer everything in bright primary colors. These may be the easiest to see and therefore any product using this color range may be the first to attract children's attention, but children do not necessarily *prefer* these colors. Outdoor environments are frequently stated as the preferred recreational environments for children, where there is an enormous spectrum of color to be found. Children collect subtly colored shells, autumn leaves, and pebbles if the opportunity exists, just as readily as they collect brightly colored plastic toys. The choice of colors should depend largely on the age group of children and the functions of the space.

Color and lighting in combination are particularly significant for children with visual impairments. Research conducted by the Department of Engineering at Reading University reports that children who are visually impaired do not need any particular feature highlighted. The crucial surfaces are the walls up to 1.2 meters, the floor, and principally the junctions between them. People with visual impairments scan the whole building area ahead of them rather than following one particular feature, so that the distinction between surfaces needs to be clear. Furthermore, the information needs to occur within a 2-meter radius out from their body (Hill & Wright, 1997).

The chosen color scheme should contain colors of different tonal qualities and light-reflective qualities to better define space. However, even if a good color scheme is selected, its potential can be negated by selecting the wrong materials and lighting in combination. For example, selecting shiny tiles for the floor under banks of fluorescent lights creates a very glarey surface and the color will no longer be an issue.

TEXTURE AND ITS FUNCTIONAL USE

Everything has a texture, but this is often overlooked. Children are extremely sensual beings and should be given texturally rich environments. Texture should be used as a source of interest, information, reward, and entertainment, and as a tool for education. A great variety of materials should be included, even in the most basic assembly. There are no right or wrong textures; the key is having a rich variety of textures in each situation.

Texture is useful for defining changes in areas and functions of spaces and features, right down to identifying the correct play piece. Walls of different textural interest are often beneficial features in playrooms. Different textures function as a source of entertainment in themselves, and provide variety for children to experiment with in their own time and at their own pace. This self-paced approach can be very important for children who are tactile defensive. Texture can also be used to provide spatial information. Children in wheelchairs have a much greater sense of movement if the floor surface beneath them changes as they move across the room. More subtle tactile discrimination needs to be developed by children who are visually impaired in anticipation of learning Braille, and activities in a play environment can contribute to the development of tactile discrimination.

SMELL

This is a highly influential sense in determining an impression of a space; everything has a smell, although often overlooked. Smell is one of the most potent sources of sensory information. It contributes to the welcoming atmosphere and comfort of the space and is linked to our strongest memories. It can be used to advantage in any environment. For example, if children remember a pleasant smell associated with an environment—such as the smell of biscuits baking—they may be much more willing to return to the play environment.

SOUND

The human being's sensitivity to sound is acute from birth, as is smell. It is also one of the most difficult elements in a design to control. In general, children punctuate all their activities with noise. For younger children especially, movement is synonymous with noise. Controlling the acoustics of a space can greatly effect the success of the design. Acoustics can never be treated casually, as poor design decisions here can lead to enormous discomfort. Consider children who are visually impaired, sound is their greatest source of information; yet it can also be their greatest source of distress due to poorly placed features and activities that suddenly produce loud sounds, or rooms that are always noisy. A poor selection of building materials and design decisions in combination, such as polished wooden floorboards, large panels of glass, and high ceilings, can create an acoustic nightmare. Consider children with autism: These children may experience daily changes in their vision and hearing, and uncontrollable noise levels will exacerbate their problems.

Some children with disabilities truly enjoy experimenting with sound. Auditory response in a cause-and-effect activity is simple to implement and very rewarding for these children. Activities involving sound have a greater chance of maintaining children's interest when the sound responses are more musical or have a greater range of tones than when a single noise or note is issued repeatedly from the activity. In all designs for play environments, a quiet area or a small separate space of some kind is recommended, allowing children to escape the noise of the play environment altogether. It also allows children to observe action before entering it and this can relax children who are initially intimidated by the environment.

LIGHTING

When designing a play environment, lighting should be used to help highlight activities and define the space, to create interest, or even as a source of sensory reward. Care must be taken to avoid the creation of misleading shadows and big glarey surfaces. If there are several windows in the room, be sure the layout capitalizes on the natural lighting. Greenman (1988) suggests that windows not only let in light; they also allow for a cross fertilization of environments, by letting children observe seasonal change, for example (p. 110).

A CASE STUDY

In 1995, in association with the Royal Blind Society, NSW, a design team consisting of occupational therapists, physiotherapists, and special educators created the first playroom in Australia for children with visual impairments, including total blindness. The children were up to three years of age, having a myriad of visual diagnoses; 80 percent had additional disabilities. The aim of the play environment was to provide gross motor, fine motor, musical, creative, dramatic, and sensory play for the whole age group and for the total range of abilities that might exist within it. The design also had to respond to the intervention approaches used by the many disciplines of staff, and of course had to accommodate parent needs. It was to be challenging but not intimidating, easy to negotiate, and workable within the parameters of a specified room, all with a fixed budget of $15,000 ($30,000 Australian).

This calibre of custom designing entailed research into all facets of the project, including reading widely on related subjects and interviewing blind persons considered spatially aware enough to understand (1) how they processed spatial information, (2) how they established their key information systems in negotiating space, and (3) how these were prioritized.

Everything was done to develop a greater understanding of what it is like to be without sight. One of the designers wore a blindfold around her house for a few days, undertaking all normal domestic functions. Although stressful and exhausting, it afforded a crude understanding of several things: (1) how important smell was for information and atmosphere, (2) how intrusive sound could be, and (3) how much sound there was, even in a domestic environment with no one else around. There was also an increased understanding of how crucial touch is as a source of information in all decisions for such little things as What coin is this? or Whose toothbrush is this? It was also very clear how important order and organization are for people who are blind. Preparing food was an arduous task until cupboards and the refrigerator were reorganized so that one could reasonably expect to find things where one wanted them to be.

Ninety percent of designing something well is understanding who the clients are and why they require the design at all. Both of these things are well understood by the caregivers and professionals who work with the children, although they may have no confidence in the depth of their own understanding at the outset of the project. In every instance, along with information from the caregivers, the detailed knowledge of the design team is crucial to the success of the project. Elements that were designed with only minimal reference to caregivers' knowledge were not nearly as effective as elements that were designed in close consultation with a design team. Close consultation means asking caregivers to contribute to every level of design decision: layout, the activities included, and such details of these activities as color, texture, and smell. This is important for ensuring that everybody "owns" the design and feels responsible for its success.

In the playroom, a layout was developed consisting of seven distinct areas, defined by dividers that remained fixed in their positions but not fixed to floors or walls in case the location of the room changed in time, which it did under new management in 1999. It was decided that providing a fixed geography that remained the same from visit to visit allowed the children to relax with orientation and mobility concerns and concentrate on playing with the activities they found within each section. The activities could change from visit to visit according to the children's needs. The pathways were bare of activities, and minimal color was used there. A black skirting board was used throughout the pathways to contrast the juncture between the neutral coloured floor and walls. The neutral pathways were in deliberate contrast to the activity areas, which were brightly colored and very busy.

When the playroom was redesigned and relocated in 1999, many of these features were abandoned, as they had turned out to be more of a liability than an aid, particularly the dividers. The small spaces created by the dividers were fine for the comfort of younger children but very restrictive for the older age groups. Over time the age groups using the playroom had expanded to include five-year-old children. As a result, the design did not adequately meet the spatial needs of the older age groups. The second design layout consisted principally of two areas: fine motor and gross motor zones. Within those areas we made provision for smaller activity areas for younger age groups, using the furniture to create soft barriers and organize traffic flows.

In this project, special care was taken to incorporate sensory variety and richness into both the activities and the function of the design. Sound responses, for example, provided reward and entertainment in cause-and-effect activities and musical walls, as well as a navigation system in the shape of floor mats. These were made to span the width of entrances into each section of the playroom. They would beep when children stepped on them, letting the children know they were leaving or entering an area. Being an experimental idea, as were many of the solutions in this design, they were battery operated and removable. Within the first few weeks, the floor mats were removed from the area, never to be returned. The children found jumping on the floor mats an interesting play activity in itself and this quickly became very irritating for the staff.

Such details as texture, color, lighting, and sound were major tools in facilitating the use of the space, the interest and entertainment value of all of the activities, as well as in providing orientation and navigational information systems throughout the space. Everything that was included had to be justified in terms of its educational value or practical function. Color, for example, was not allocated according to anyone's aesthetic preference. It was used consistently as a source of spatial information and orientation throughout the space. However, there always has to be some magic, mystery, surprise, and whimsy in every play environment to give it spirit of place. Interactive sensory activities such as bottle forests, musical walls, surprise boxes, textured walls, smell banks, and a light-stimulation room filled with many thrilling light effects all helped to provide these qualities.

Looking at the playroom in its completed form, it belies the careful consideration given to all its features. It does not look radically different in any way and this leads to a significant point. At the outset of this project there was no preconceived notion of what the final project would resemble. The only clear vision was that what was available was limited in its potential benefit for this group of children and needed modification. Most changes required the manipulation of basic features that could be found in any play equipment in such a way as to make the idea and function of the activity more accessible to the group of children in question. Six years from the inception of this project, none of the solutions have needed to be changed radically.

An enormous amount of the success of these design projects lies in pitching the activities at the correct levels and communicating the ideas through the sources of information that mean the most to each particular group of children.

CONCLUSION

Play environments for children with special needs can be likened to flowers. They have to have the capacity to be in full bloom, offering a plethora of rich sensory, educative, and entertaining experience. They also have to have the ability to fold away, revealing just one or two petals at a time for children who cannot cope with too much sensory stimulation. For a bud to bloom it needs the right environment: water, sun, earth. For a child to realize his or her potential to play, the right environment is also needed.

A well-conceived play environment provides clear pathways, visible boundaries, and qualitative differences in the spaces (Olds, 1979, p. 98) and activities within it. It should provide progressive challenges so that it increases all children's feelings of mastery and competence. It needs to contain elements of magic, mystery, and surprise to create a sense of place, as well as flexible and variable elements if it is to provide a continual challenge across time. Creating the "right" combinations of all of these things in each circumstance is dependent on the skill and involvement of the design team.

REFERENCES

Allen, K. E. (1980). Mainstreaming: What Have We Learned? *Young Children* 35(5): 54–63.

Day, C. (1995). *Places of the Soul*. London: Thorsons.

Greenman, J. (1988). *Caring Spaces, Learning Places: Children's Environments That Work*. Redmond, WA: Exchange Press.

Gilfoyle, E. M., A. P. Grady, & J. C. Moore. (1990). *Children Adapt*. New Jersey: SLACK.

Hill, S., & M. Wright. (1997). Lighting for Visually Impaired People in a Non-Uniformly Lit Office Environment. *Access by Design* 74: 16–18.

Hutchinson, R., & J. Kewin. (1994). *Sensations and Disabilities*. Chesterfield, UK: Rompa.

McEwen, M. (1990). The Human-Environment Interface in Occupational Therapy: a Theoretical and Philosophical Overview. In S. C. Merrill (Ed.), *Environment: Implications for Occupational Therapy Practice* (pp. 3–20). Bethesda, MD: American Occupational Therapy Association.

Moore, R. C., & H. H. Wong. (1997). *Natural Learning*. Berkeley, CA: MIG Communications.

Olds, A. R. (1979). Designing Developmentally Optimal Classrooms for Children with Special Needs. In S. J. Meisels (Ed.), *Special Education and Development* (pp. 91–138). Baltimore, MD: University Park Press.

————. (1987). Designing Settings for Infants and Toddlers. In C. S. Weinstein & T. G. David (Eds.), *Spaces for Children: The Built Environment and Child Development* (pp. 117–138). New York: Plenum.

————. (1989). Psychological and Physiological Harmony in Child Care Centre Design. *Children's Environments Quarterly* 6(4).

————. (2001). *Childcare Design Guide*. New York: McGraw-Hill.

Pagliano, P. J. (1999). *Multisensory Environments*. London: David Fulton.

Piaget, J. (1962). *Play, Dreams and Imitation in Childhood*. New York: Norton.

————. (1960). *The Child's Conception of the World*. London: Routledge.

Prescott, E. (1987). The Environment as Organiser of Intent in Child-Care Settings. In C. S. Weinstein & T. G. David (Eds.), *Spaces for Children: The Built Environment and Child Development* (pp 73–78). New York: Plenum.

Webster's New World Dictionary. (1983). New York: Simon and Schuster.

37

Community Mural:
A Visual History of Field's Corner
in Dorchester, Massachusetts

Lois A. Berggren

Once again men and women of ripe old age will sit in the streets of Jerusalem, each with cane in hand because of his age. The city streets will be filled with boys and girls playing there.
—Zechariah 8:4

The following describes the process of creating a large (9' × 17') clay mural celebrating the 100th anniversary of the Dorchester House Multi-Service Center (founded in 1887), a community collaboration in 1987 between Dorchester House and the Dorchester Historical Society, led by Lois A. Berggren. The mural located the commemorative event in its historical, cultural, institutional, and community context. It was created during an eight-week summer camp program through the efforts of more than 250 persons of all ages and abilities living in an inner-city community that is ethnically, racially, and culturally diverse. During this artful, playful adventure the participants were engaged in an experientially based process of guided inquiry. This involved exposure to evocative, historical, verbal, and visual imagery; participation in creative movement; viewing archival photos; studying Victorian architecture; reading books; embarking on neighborhood sketching expeditions; and trading intergenerational memories. All residual impressions from this communal pilgrimage through time and space were transformed into a permanent monument celebrating a moment in local history and sharing the magical, imaginative vision of children's conceptual art-making.

Dorchester House, now a multiservice agency, was established in 1887 as part Boston's extensive network of "settlement houses." Boston, with its reputation for wealth, culture, and academic and intellectual excellence, has always been a "gateway city." From early on it served as a major entry point for groups of immigrants comprising much of our nation's population. Born of nineteenth-century xenophobia, mixed with a rising social and moral consciousness, the settlement house movement focused on meeting the needs of our nation's future laborers. Settlement houses sought to "solve the problem" of the newly arrived. They imposed order on and gained control over the lives of many needy immigrants, many of whom did not even speak English. Schools and day-care centers, lessons in English as a second language, literacy programs, skill-based training for the trades industries (i.e., sewing, cooking, shoemaking, hat making, model building, typesetting, drafting, and carpentry), provision for housing and health care (overseen by visiting nurses and social workers), creative arts and drama classes, and social clubs for adults, youth, the "aged," "infirm," and "handicapped" were among the services spawned and nurtured by the early settlement house movement. The agencies, in effect, built communities around themselves. The old traditions, now codified and more precisely defined and financed, live today through the Dorchester House Multi-Service Center, as well as other similar community service agencies in large cities throughout Boston and the United States.

The Children's Expressive Arts Program at Dorchester House serves youth from the ages of five through fourteen in a school-age setting (September through June). Occasional art-based activities have been offered to preschool children (three- to five-year-olds) during mornings. During the summers Dorchester House provides a day camp for school-age children, including teenage and college-age counselors, as well as adult teachers. The summer day camp includes sports, swimming, art activities, city trips, and other excursions, together with large cultural events. At the time of the anniversary, parental participation in any and all aspects of the classes and events was frequent and always welcome. The art area was enormous, consisting of two huge contiguous rooms, plus a back door alley. There was ample storage space, two ceramic kilns, and every possible kind of art material suitable for the ages served, including recycled goods supplied by local businesses.

A separate afternoon program for adolescent students with special needs was also held at Dorchester House. These children were integrated into the ongoing after-school ceramics classes. Several of the younger children with disabilities of an emotional, behavioral, or physical nature were fully included in all aspects of the Recreation Department Program. This was done in such a way that their "special needs" were known only to the teachers and administrative staff.

The following section affords insight into the practical, historical, and cultural context of the mural. An open-ended approach to art education was imperative. Creating an atmosphere in which tolerance, understanding, respect and cooperation could flourish was most important, as was a multicultural appreciation and antiracist awareness within the community. Art-making animates the traditions residing at the core of any culture, ethnicity, or civilization. It is essential that art education for children be process oriented, and that students be directly involved in experimenting with materials, connecting them to their own creative art adventure. The goal is for children to gain an understanding of art-making as a collective, cross-cultural, and universal event. This goal requires an awareness of how various art forms have come into being. Using this approach, children are able to bring their own emotional and expressive ideas into a much larger historical and cultural arena. Creativity is enhanced by carrying literature, storytelling, sociodramatic and imaginative play, music, history, science, festivals, and seasonal celebrations into the art room. Children's art-making is a truly sacred process in which young people explore and explain their world to themselves and others. A painting, drawing, or other artistic product that a child creates may, in fact, represent the only area of total freedom and privacy in that child's life. Children's art-making, in its expanded dimensions, is an elaborate form of play. It involves exploration, experimentation, risk taking, and rule making, as well as mastery and critical problem solving. It unfolds developmentally and is skill based, creative, expressive, and often collective. It is a combination of process, product, and artifact. Art, like play, is one of the most basic forms of communication open to children. From birth (and perhaps even before) children need to be nourished by art (music, poetry, drama, play, movement, painting, and architecture included) on a self-demand schedule.

A variety of activities were initiated in the art room preceding the undertaking of mural creation. Everything that happened there was framed in the larger context of service to Dorchester's expanding community and, specifically, the Field's Corner neighborhood. In a larger context, the following factors impressed their needs, challenges, and gifts upon the expressive arts program: the changing seasons; the celebration of holidays and special events; the rhythms of the after-school program and summer day camp activities; classes for adolescents with Down's Syndrome; the demands and expectations of parents, administrators, members of the community, and coworkers; and the ethnic, racial, and socioeconomic diversity of the student population. Beside these factors, the art room was shared with two other groups: a morning group of senior citizens who worked with clay and an evening class of women who learned how to paint preformed, poured, hollow clay pieces, which were then fired and glazed.

The children's groups sang songs, learned dances, and played "Instant Orchestra" with real and homemade percussive instruments, bells, clappers, drums, and so on. Audio cassette tapes were produced and the group indulged in dramatic play by constructing a "bank" from refrigerator cartons. ("Bank robberies" occurred weekly, for a time.) Then there was an ever-popular refrigerator carton "pizza hut" for the fabrication and "sale" of unfired clay "pizzas." When parents came to collect their children, they often found "changelings" who spoke only a pseudo-Italian dialect and refused to recognize or understand the parental injunctive to "Leave Now" spoken in plain, unbroken, loud English!

The children's art program offered many diverse projects using a variety of media, including music, drama, and all kinds of artifacts, which children were absorbed with: 2D paper art, drawings, collages, painting (tempera, both wet and dry brush, watercolor), accordion books, monoprints, and collographs, at times using an antique washing-machine ringer. Engraving and intaglio printing with styrofoam trays were popular, as well as scraffito. For 3D forms, natural materials were often used, such as diverse species of seeds used as beads in jewelry making. Telephone-wire ornaments and sculptures were inspired by Alexander Calder's *Circus*.

The clay program was the most popular of all. It was approached from a process-oriented angle. Children were permitted to grate dried (but not fired) clay. This was soaked in water for a week or more, and then dried on plaster bats. The children aided this drying process by manipulating the clay in a "finger dance." The next part of the process was wedging the clay. The children cherished this part, as they were encouraged to throw and slap, and punch the clay on the table. This turned into a percussive, rhythmic musical event. We tested for air bubbles. This test passed, the children progressed, learning how to make draped forms, often embossed with plant blossoms or leaves, lace, clay stamps, and so on. Some students fashioned tubular vases and others constructed square boxes. Pieces were bisqued and painted with colored engobes, then refired and finally covered with a clear shiny glaze and fired once again. Many young children achieved a level of sophistication in building pieces by hand, amazing parents. The children really loved the clay classes, and even stressed-out parents participated from time to time, enjoying the (mostly) quiet and relaxing atmosphere of the art room.

Given this background, the mural was a surprise but welcome addition. Since Dorchester House was celebrating its 100th anniversary, the mural took on a special and important position in the community. Help was enlisted from the Dorchester Historical Society, which came up with marvelous photos of the Field's Corner area of 100 years ago. There were many conversations with the children about how things in the past were different from the way they were in 1987. When antique photographs were shown to the children, lively discussions ensued. As the art room had a senior aide, she would be asked about her grandmother, and she would gladly share stories. The children had extended access to the original photos of the Field's Corner area because they were displayed on the main bulletin board in Dorchester House.

In the meantime, Victorian architecture was researched at the Boston Public Library. One area close to the Dorchester House contained an enclave of beautifully restored "Painted Ladies," as the old houses were locally termed. This historic neighborhood had just completed a much-advertised block tour and had fortuitously published a one-page flier, designating by name and schema the elements of Victorian architecture. Armed with copies of this flier, neighborhood house walks were initiated, looking at and naming Victorian architectural elements of the many surrounding structures. On subsequent walks, children were armed with pencils, paper, and clipboards. Each child in the eight-to-twelve age range was to "adopt" a house and draw it. This was a wonderful process in which each participant had to select a favorite house and translate it in an original way onto paper. From time to time the owners of these magnificent homes would come out and proudly tell the houses' history!

The children's drawings were transferred to clay by placing the pictures on unfired clay slabs and incising the lines into the soft surface. The drawings, alas, were lost in the process. These slabs were bisqued, painted with engobes, refired, and glazed by the young children. The pieces were arranged and secured to plywood boards by the art teachers. The grouting was done by using epoxy bathroom grout in three colors: deep blue for the sea, light blue for the sky, and reddish brown for the earth. Teenaged staff members helped in this part of the process. The "cameo" portraits of the original Dorchester House (yellow in the mural) and the then new Dorchester House (1987) were commissioned to talented teens by the Recreation Department Director. Since then there is a new incarnation of this wonderful building. The existing structure has been expanded by surrounding the original walls on all sides with new walls. The old previously external walls were dismantled. The health-care part of the building has been expanded, and the mural has been temporarily and very carefully covered until the construction process is complete; then it will be restored to its original place of honor as the featured art work in the large multipurpose room.

The younger children (under eight years of age) participated in the mural-making in the most wonderful and imaginative way. The very youngest children (four- to five-year-olds) created the sky art pieces based on fantasy movement improvisation sessions through which children discovered and remembered what lives in the sky. Their extraordinary imagination populated the sky with the most splendid beings: animal, human, atmospheric, celestial, and supernatural. The process also involved reading and discussing marvelous picture-story books.

For the sea, created by six- to seven-year-olds, the book *Swimmy*, by Leo Lionni, was selected for preliminary discussions. From Dorchester House the presence of the Boston Harbor was evident in the fresh sea air, the abundance of good fish restaurants, and the boats moored at the Dorchester Yacht Club. The children created marvelous beings: fish, sea monsters, boats, seaweed, waves, water, sharks, and whales. The most remarkable creation of all was a secret place filled with sand worms, small sea turtles, minnows, and tiny pebbles, all concealed beneath piles of "seaweed" (made with a garlic press), the objects beneath nevermore to be seen with the naked eye of the viewer.

Over 250 persons, adults, teens, the staff, and children contributed to this communal work of art, which will hopefully remain in place for another 100 years. It is a commemorative historical document and a visual reminder of the constant, durable, universal, and playful art-making process of children.

Startling changes have been made at Dorchester House since 1987. Half of the former art space has been taken over by a computer laboratory. The clay program is extinct. Dorchester House as it was in 1987 seems to have been absorbed by the ever-expanding Health Care Center. When the new renovations are complete, the large multipurpose room will be restored (and the mural uncovered). It is hard to visualize what the final result of all the changes will be. Dorchester House provides an island of safety, a healthy and caring place in which children can play, grow, and learn. The multiservice portion of Dorchester House now provides health care and family services in English, Spanish, Kmer, Vietnamese, and Cambodian.

REFERENCES

Architectural Resources

Baker, J. M. (1994). *American House Styles: A Concise Guide.* New York: W. W. Norton.

Carley, R. (1994). *The Visual Dictionary of American Domestic Architecture.* New York: Henry Holt.

Crosbie, M. J., & S. Rosenthal. (1993). *Shapes.* New York: John Wiley and Sons.

Lorenz, A., & J. Schleh. (1992). *Metropolis: 10 cities, 10 centuries.* London: Dorlling Kindersley.

Mitchell, E. (comp.). (1979). *American Victoriana: Floor Plans and Renderings from the Gilded Age: Being a Gallery of Color Plates with Descriptive Text and Black and White Facsimile Pages from the Scientific American Architects and Builders' Edition, 1882 through 1905.* San Francisco, CA: Chronicle Books.

Sammarco, A. (1995). *Images of America: Dorchester.* Vols. 1 and 2. Dover, NH: Arcadia.

Wilson, F. (1988). *What It Feels Like to Be a Building.* Washington, DC: Preservation Press.

———. (1993). *Bridges Go from Here to There.* Washington, DC: Preservation Press.

Arts Education, Creative Drama, and Play Arts Resources

Anderson, F. E. (1978). *Art for All the Children: A Creative Sourcebook for the Impaired Child.* Chicago, IL: Charles C. Thomas.

D'Amico, V. E., & A. Buchman. (1954). *Assemblage: A Dimension in Creative Teaching.* New York: Museum of Modern Art.

Robertson, S. M. (1982). *Rosegarden and Labyrinth: A Study in Art Education.* Dallas: Spring.

Rogovin, M. (1975). *Mural Manual: How to Paint Murals for the Classroom, Community Center, and Street Corner* (2d ed.). Boston: Beacon Press.

Silberstein-Storfer, M. (1982). *Doing Art Together: The Remarkable Parent–Child Workshop of the Metropolitan Museum of Art.* New York: Simon and Schuster.

Spaggiari, S. (ed.). (1998). *The One Hundred Languages of Children.* Reggio Emilia, Italy: City Press.

Ceramics Resources

Berensohn, P. F. (1972). *Finding One's Way with Clay: Creating Pinched Pottery and the Color of Clay.* New York: Simon and Schuster.

Hofsted, J. (1967). *Step-by-Step Ceramics: A Complete Introduction to the Craft of Ceramics, Including Photographs in Full Color.* New York: Golden Press.

Leach, B. (1946). *A Potter's Book.* London: Transatlantic Art.

Pucci, C. (n.d.). *Pottery, a Basic Manual.* Boston: Little, Brown.

Contemporary Children's Literature Resources

Dooley, N. (1996). *Everybody Bakes Bread.* Minneapolis: Carolrhoda Books.

Leoni, L. (1994). *Swimmy.* New York: Alfred A. Knopf.

Siberell, A. (1982). *Whale in the Sky.* New York: E. P. Dutton.

Oral History and Social Studies Resources

Pearlstein, S., & J. Bliss. (1998). *Generating Community: Intergenerational Partnerships through the Expressive Arts.* Brooklyn, NY: Elders Share the Arts.

PART IV

PLAYFUL THINKING AND
THE BRAIN

Part IV emphasizes the importance that play has in the cognitive and social development of children and adults. It begins with Audrey Skrupskelis acquainting the
reader with the thoughts of several early philosophers living in the nineteenth and
early twentieth centuries who believed that play was essential to refreshing one's
mind for effective writing and creativity. It uses literature taken from personal letters and shared conversations that were documented to reinforce the need for
lengthy vacations, retreats, and holidays in order to not overtax the nervous system
of the brain. Joyce A. Wilkinson describes the work of contemporary researcher
Elizabeth Rike, whose guided dramatic play system has been used to correct language and communication deficits. Rike's system makes use of carefully designed
questions, drama elements, and language structures to show how symbolic dramatic play is a precursor of language development. The chapter further states that
the absence of dramatic play can result in language deficiencies due to insufficient
sensory–brain connections. Rike's system helps the child analyze and use the elements of drama to acquire language structures in the brain. Elizabeth Rike extends
on her own research findings concerning her dramatic play system in the next
chapter and sheds some light on the complex relationship between guided dramatic play and the brain. This is demonstrated though an in-depth interview with
neuroscientist Karl Pribram. Pribram addresses the relationship though a discussion of brain functions. The chapter is written in first person and includes many of
Rike's sample guided imaginative play activities.

Gordon M. Burghardt synthesizes findings to show how play in other species is
on a continuum with that in our own species. Based on that premise, he speculates
on some of the factors that influence the nature and extent of human play, imagina-

tion, and creativity. The chapter also outlines the major tenets of the Surplus Resource Theory (SRT) and discusses how different forms of play can ultimately awaken the individual's creativity. Neil Greenberg follows the theme of play and creativity and looks at traditional definitions of creativity as well as offering a new definition of creativity that corresponds with the belief that creativity can be explored in the world of biology. This neuroethology and neurophysiology perspective on play and creativity is described according to functions of the brain. The chapter closes with Greenberg advancing the theory that novelty, familiarity, strangeness, and stress greatly influence the human's creative behavior.

Mark Cotter's ontological perspective of play can greatly expand the reader's appreciation of playfulness and learning in both animal and human species. To do so, he cites elements of sociodramatic play, including several thoughts of Lev Vygotsky and Piaget, the role of adults as mediators, and the nature of dialogue and collaborative learning. This comprehensive overview also includes a logical connection between the brain, knowledge as an activity, and social interaction. The socialization process is continued in Connie Steele's summary of Joe Frost's belief that one cause of juvenile violence in young adults is the lack of healthy play experiences. Frost argues that the importance of play for brain growth should not be overlooked given the research that shows convicted murderers had either an absence of childhood play or engaged in abnormal play. The chapter also offers fifteen of Frost's dictums that stem from brain research and have practical application for parents and educators caring for children.

Betty J. Wagner conveys the positive effect of drama and dramatic experiences on a child's reading, language, and writing ability. Attention is given to the constructivist approach to learning, the role of improvisational drama, and a child's symbolic and iconic ability to create mental images. Practical examples are included. Patricia Sternberg defends the use of dramatic play as a critical form of therapy. Basic human emotions such as anger are used to enrich the reader's understanding of how drama therapy serves as a rehearsal for life. The chapter also includes a valuable list of definitions to differentiate between drama therapy, psychodrama, sociodrama, and creative drama. E. Paul Torrance contributes yet another powerful tool to his more than 500 articles and research studies on the topic of creativity, as he includes true/false items to identify characteristics related to improvisation, role playing, sociodrama, and other action methods of teaching, learning, and thinking. Torrance's introduction supports the need for the previously mentioned learning techniques, which he refers to as "action methods."

Part IV ends with Howard R. Pollio and Marilyn R. Pollio's exciting thematic analysis of humor and play. This analysis is extremely appropriate, since no book concerning play would be complete without an in-depth look at the power of humor and play. Theories related to laughter, joke telling, and the experiential meaning of play enlighten the reader's understanding of what it means to be a child, an adult, and, most important, alive with a keen spirit.

38

Early Playful Intellectuals

Audrey Skrupskelis

Modern technology and sophisticated instrumentation have made it possible for researchers to uncover much information about the functioning of the brain and its role in human development. At the same time, it is interesting to look back in history and learn from some of the intellectuals of the nineteenth and early twentieth centuries how they used their knowledge of the brain in their conception of human development and which conception they often applied to themselves. Often their beliefs of how the brain worked seem primitive to us; but in spite of their shortcomings in theory, they often showed good sense in applying their limited knowledge of the brain to their own human development and intellectual growth. After examining how some of the influential intellectuals of earlier times lived and played, one can propose the hypothesis that the integration of intellectual activities and amusements formed the nucleus of their creative contributions to the growing original intellectual bodies of work that were being produced in the United States.

The idea of nervous exhaustion appears in early advice books about maintaining good health. Alcott (1840) emphasized throughout his writing that any kind of fatigue, excitement, "intelligence which alarms or rejoices us" (p. 197) has a detrimental effect on the constitution; that is, exhaustion of the nervous system occurs. Until the nerves are restored, the whole body will suffer. The nervous system, as a messenger and carrier of impulses to and from the brain, had to be kept healthy and rested. After periods of any kind of extensive work of mind or body, sufficient rest (in addition to change in diet and more exercise) was critical to maintaining a feeling of well-being and productivity. This view was a predominant one in the thinking of many intellectuals and they took seriously the need for diversions and long periods of rest between heavy bouts of work; for rest, they did not take twenty-minute power naps. For rest, they took months of vacation, which was spent in activities that were not directly related to work; but ultimately led to greater productivity and the restoration of nervous energy. In *Hygiene of the Brain*, Holbrook (1879) stated that the brain and nervous system are just as susceptible to exhaustion as physical activity and that mental exhaustion can lead to nervous disorders, which he classified as a disease of the nervous system. He concluded,

In our age nervous exhaustion is in the ascendent. . . . Our hothouse education promotes it, by cultivating the mind at the expense of the body. Our sedentary ways of living promote it. . . . It is time for us to consider this matter in the light of science and common-sense, and see if something cannot be done to relieve our generation from the curse of nervous exhaustion and show people how to conduct their lives so that peace and serenity shall take place of haste, excitement, and all their attending evils. (p. 52)

The remainder of his book offered many suggestions for relieving the brain from exhaustion, and many of these suggestions centered around play and amusement for sustained periods of time. Open-air activities were considered by him as brain-nurturing activities, as were such amusements as singing, playing instruments, playing with children, storytelling, and doing anything that caused laughter. Maybe the scientific understanding of the physiology and functioning of the brain was not exactly correct in light of modern-day brain research, but certainly the suggestions offered for preserving the vitality of the brain and some causes of loss of this vitality are just as true today, if not more so, as they were more than a hundred years ago.

Louisa May Alcott (1832–1888), a writer whose works have endeared her to multitudes of readers throughout the decades, was obsessed with theater—she attended once or twice a week. Because her life was unusual in many ways and filled with a variety of hardships and poverty, she seemed to have found relief in theatrical diversions, which let her creative mind and passion for writing to blossom. Her father Bronson Alcott applied his innovative pedagogical ideas to his four daughters. This pedagogy "stressed 'unfoldment' through self-expression, encouraged conversation and discussion often on sensitive subjects, resorted to allegories and parables, and endorsed keeping of journals" (Myerson, Shealy, & Stern, 1987, pp. xvii–xix). Louisa May Alcott's physical exhaustion found relief in journal writing and theatrical drama. Her keen observation of life led to her writing stories and later books based on her own experiences. She participated in masquerades and evening plays, which were common forms of evening amusements. In a letter dated April 6, 1862, Sophy wrote to Alfred Whitman that "May was the Goddess of Dancing & looked lovely in crimson sandals, white & gold dress & curly head a la Greek" (p. 73). In another letter dated April 1866, Louisa wrote to Ellen Conway, "As I am not 'written all over with money, talent or beauty' I may not be able to get at any English hearts, but they cant shut me out of their parks, ruins, castles & streets so I shall get something, & enjoy larks if I cant see the poets, & babies & buttercups at Wimbleton if the Queen wont let me in at Windsor" (p. 112). Given the hardships with which Louisa May Alcott dealt most of her life, it seems that journal writing and simple diversions provided her not only relief from everyday worries, but fed her fertile imagination, which resulted in numerous important literary contributions, many of which are as loved today as they were in her lifetime.

Among the great American thinkers of the nineteenth century, a leader in the intellectual life at that time was the philosopher and "father of pragmatism," William James (1842–1910). He believed, as did many of his contemporaries, that nervous force was a fixed quantity and it was expected that this force would be exhausted and depleted by overtaxation of the nervous system or the brain. In modern times, brain exhaustion is viewed more as a metaphor, and the "condition" can be "cured" by short periods of rest and relief from work. In an essay titled "Vacation" (1873; Burkhardt & Bowers, 1987), James wrote about the importance of the trend for people getting at least a fortnight of vacation, which he considered not nearly enough, but at least on the right path:

For however civilized and far-plotting we have become, to dwell in the open air, with no plans or cares beyond tomorrow, has been the lot of our ancestors, brute or human, for receding centuries of generations. And for us to dip into it again awakens half-extinguished feelings of delight, washes away the cobwebs and smoothes out the wrinkles from the care-worn mind, as surely as sleep makes the weary body fresh again. (p. 6.)

In this essay he suggested that it would be a profoundly beneficial "charity" idea to donate money to a special fund that would enable people who otherwise would not have an opportunity to enjoy a month of idleness in a year, which would remove them "far from the scene of their cares. Help them heal their nervous exhaustion so that they could function again in their circumstances" (p. 7).

Most Americans have no more than two weeks of vacation time per year. This, according to James, is not enough. In American society the dichotomy between work and play is very big, and work is considered more important. In fact, even young children's nervous systems are being taxed to the limit, with very little time left for them to play. For James, the interrelationship between work and play allowed a person to become more productive and creative. His own life exemplified this belief, and he took long vacations every year, traveled, walked, and enjoyed the company of friends for months at a time. Yet his "work" output was tremendous and made important and lasting contributions to American intellectual thinking. Actually, James was very interested in brain physiology, and in 1890 was appointed professor of psychology at Harvard University. In his graduate seminar he taught brain anatomy (Burkhardt & Bowers, 1987).

In the early 1870s a group of friends, among them William James, Dr. Charles Putnam, James Jackson Putnam, and Henry Pickering Bowditch, went on a walking trip in the Adirondacks. The beauty of Keene Valley enchanted them and later they purchased a farmhouse, which became known as Putnam's Shanty. They, along with Annie and Lizzie Putnam (sisters of the Putnam brothers) and numerous friends and cousins, spent many summers at Putnam's Shanty relaxing, socializing, and generally curing their exhausted nervous forces by occupying themselves in walking, carpentry, conversations, playing such games as charades, writing and performing evening plays, and even organizing parades. For others, photography provided much needed relaxation, and a darkroom was established. Henry Bowditch, the physiologist from Harvard Medical School whose principal interest was the study of the localizations of functions of the brain, took charge of this operation. He rigged up a combination of telescope and camera, long before photo attachments became available. Elizabeth Putnam McIver (1941) wrote, "The general principle at the Shanty was that if you wanted something, you made it: and such was the spirit of the place that you felt that you *could* make almost anything" (p. 9). Throughout the years of its existence, many eminent people spent time in play at the Shanty, including Ralph Waldo Emerson (essayist and poet), Robert Browning and Elizabeth Barrett Browning (poets), and Sir James Bryce (the English ambassador).

The socialization of the children of the founders of the Shanty was an important function during these long periods of relaxation. Adult play with the children was important in the transmission of social knowledge and values. Indeed, Miss Lizzie Putnam played a role as "matchmaker" for the children as they grew older. McIver (1941) wrote,

A leader in all such festivities,—who not only enjoyed them but *believed* in them,—was Mr. Richard Hodgson, an Englishman from Australia who came to America as Secretary to the American Branch of the Society for Physical Research. . . . We were utterly devoted to him and he to us. We counted the minutes till he arrived to play with us; and I don't believe it ever crossed our minds that he was, after all, a grownup. . . . He taught each child a song of his own to sing at the campfire,—and saw that he had a chance to sing it. . . . He took complete charge of our mountain-climbing,—saw that we did not attempt anything beyond our strength. . . . And all our gains were his triumphs as much as ours. (pp. 11–12)

Dr. James Putnam, a neurologist who introduced Freud and psychoanalysis to America and one of the founders of this place of refuge, wrote, "There reserve and formality could be laid aside, and free play allowed the instincts of hospitality, sociability and the playfulness of boyhood at its best." (McIver, 1941, p. 17). About William James, James Putnam's mother wrote, "He was delightful with the children and sometimes joined in their escapades" (p. 20). McIver concluded her reminiscences of times spent at the Putnam Shanty as follows:

I have asked a number of people most of whom had spent their childhood at the Shanty. . . . One and all they have said: "Freedom,—we could go anywhere and do everything." To me, that last seemed literally true . . . we put on wings, which carried us lightly over ordinary limitations and disabilities and brought us to a world where all lay open to our touch. Whether the grown people quite knew this magic transformation I do not know; but sure it is that their spirits expanded to the simplicity, the fun and the friendships so readily attained in these surroundings. (pp. 27–28)

The benefits of spending time in Keene Valley appear in William James's letters to his brother Henry James. In a letter dated September 1, 1887, William wrote, "After spending 9 days in the imperishable beauty of Keene Valley, and getting as great an amount of refreshment as I ever got in the same space of time, I came back via Albany and New York. . . . I go back to Cambridge next week, ready to address the multitude (I have about 100 men in one of my courses) on the 29th" (Skrupskelis & Berkeley, 1993, pp. 66–67). References to the benefits of going to Keene Valley were regularly made in the correspondence between William and Henry. Henry wrote to William on October 17, 1907,

> I may deem things well with you when I see you so mobile & so mobilazible (so emanci-pated & unchained for being so, as well as so fecund and so still overflowing. Your annual go at Keene Valley (wh: I'm never to have so much as beheld) & the nature of your refer-ences to it—as this one tonight—fill me with pangs & yearnings, I mean the bitterness, al-most, of envy: there is so little of the Keene Valley side of things in my life. But I went up to Scotland a month ago . . . & there, in absolutely exquisite weather, had a brief but deep draught of the glory of moor & mountain as that air, & ten-mile trudges through the heather & by the braeside (to lunch with the shooters,) delightfully give it. (Skrupskelis & Berkeley, 1994, p. 347)

Henry never visited the Shanty. But he did like to take time off. Occasionally he would tour the English countryside with Edith Wharton, who had a chauffeur. He also enjoyed puttering in a garden as a way of relaxation and taking a brain rest.

The conversations that took place between those who came to Putnam Shanty for extended visits were, no doubt, carried on in a playful, congenial atmosphere and certainly led to the development of ideas that later appeared in the writing of these individuals. One may argue that it was the extended time spent in these play-ful conversations that allowed the ideas to ferment and grow into important bodies of intellectual writing. In other words, the brain was not exhausted, but rather in a "recuperative" state and there was no pressure or deadlines for finished products. What is also important to consider is that the children were, from an early age, in-cluded in the playfulness of the adults. In fact, intergenerational play, whether it consisted of just hiking in the mountains or putting on elaborate plays, was not only an important tool for the socialization of children into adult society; it also taught children that adults rested and played for extended periods of time, restor-ing the brain's potential for productive work.

G. Stanley Hall (1846–1924), a psychologist, a person of incredible energy and productivity, the "father of the questionnaire," and the founder of Child Studies and the American Journal of Psychology, took time off, as did his contemporaries. His biographer, D. Ross (1972), described Hall as an active child who was always looking for ways to feed his imagination:

> Though he took advantage of the ordinary opportunities for amusement the community of-fered, he was also an exceptionally imaginative child. . . . He spent much of his time alone, collecting species of whatnot, carrying out imaginary adventures, and conjuring upon the farmland the people and settings of the books and stories he knew. . . . As Hall entered his teens . . . he started an autobiography, kept a daily journal, and wrote poems, stories, and adventures by the dozen. Flushed by his local oratorical success, he imagined himself speak-ing before huge and admiring audiences. (pp. 12–13)

His insatiable thirst for knowledge led to prolific writing on many different topics, especially psychology. He investigated children, adolescents, and senescence throughout his life. He believed in play as "an expressive function of childhood" and "that much of children's play was a reversionary expression of earlier activities of the race; thus the free expression of these impulses was necessary to the later emergence of a more civilized activity" (p. 299–300). His interest in scientific observation of children resulted in collections of thousands of children's games, which he studied and categorized, hoping that this would help teachers in the use of these games for educational purposes. He echoed the James' idea of the direct interrelationship between work and play. He wanted work to be "infused with the interest and zest characteristic of play." (p. 300). Dewey's idea that play needed to be directed toward work was unacceptable to Hall. His own life altered between periods of incredible activity and intense work and periods of inactivity and doing nothing. But even during his summer vacations, his keen observations and journal recordings of children at play in a sand pile ended in an important study of the educational benefits of play that was allowed to develop naturally without adult interference.

In his recollections of his childhood, Nathaniel Southgate Shaler (1909), who later became a professor of geology at Harvard University, talked about growing up in Kentucky. He had been a sickly lad, and because of his frail condition literally had had no schooling and could barely read and write at twelve. His earliest memories were those of playfulness, especially enjoying parades and bands, horseback riding with his father, and generally having the freedom to roam around the countryside. From hearing his mother read about the activities of soldiers in the Mexican War, his imagination had been fueled and he had fashioned himself the necessary materials to reenact his "imaginary war." At the same time, he had developed keen sense of observation by watching various birds performing their tasks of nest building, and the like. Obviously, the early time he had spent in acquiring an informal education through the playful, imaginative activities he devised for himself did not in any way detract from his academic achievements in adult life. In fact, one could probably make the argument that the imaginative play in which he had engaged during the time when his peers were being formally drilled at schools could have contributed much more to the development of his brain power than if he had been schooled formally. As an adult he spent many of his summers on Cape Cod in the company of friends and colleagues. He was known for his wit and was considered a most interesting companion. During these vacations he regaled his companions with stories and engaged them in fascinating, playful conversations.

While one should not romanticize or make broad generalizations that all intellectuals living in the time period under discussion spent months at a time in playful activities, there seems to be a pattern in the lives of many of them that does not distinguish playfulness from the drudgery of "brain" work. Rather, it is the combination of play and work that seemed to contribute to their vast output of important writings in a variety of fields. Many voiced concerns similar to those of today about the lack of playfulness in schools, the necessity for relief from brainwork, and the importance of engaging in imaginative activities that allow students to expand their viewpoints and look at subject matter from different perspectives based not only on individual experiences, but on collective experiences as well. Boyer (1899), in writing about the methodology of teaching iteration, stressed that overtaxation of the brain by the continual repetition of various drills puts students in danger of "shunting the functions used in his efforts, and may become a total dwarf" (p. 67). He, too, emphasized the importance of the use of imagination and developing the powers of imagination in lessons through observing nature, looking at things that are beautiful, such as art, and making associations of imagination and thought. He wrote, "The importance of cultivating imagination until it becomes what it ought to be in quantity, propensity, and quality, is too often forgotten by teachers" (p. 83).

Boyer (1899) described one of the phases of imagination as the "mental emancipation from perception-limits of space and time, and from the normal correlations of parts, epochs, etc." (p. 14). In the imaginative play of children and adults, possibilities could open up that would not be possible if all were work and no play. In modern-day schools there seems to be a fear of allowing students to exercise their imaginations because then they will not learn what "needs to be learned." In other words, and despite what both anecdotal and experimental research is telling us about how the brain works and the importance of making as many dendrite connections as possible, we still refuse to give up the myth that imaginative play and work are not natural companions. Again, to quote Boyer, "Inasmuch as play is the manifestation of aptitudes, it becomes the educational key to the child's talent and destiny" (p. 35). In these brief sketches of some of our important intellectual figures, obviously, imagination and playfulness did not stunt their intellectual growth, but rather seemed to trigger it.

In the present day, according to statistics, many children spend about twenty-eight hours on average "engaged" in watching television (Levin, 1998). Television viewing puts the brain "on hold" in terms of imagination because others have already decided all the imaginative stuff on television. While certainly some television shows evolve into thematic play with children, this thematic play seems to rely on what was already seen and interpreted for children. In comparing the kinds of play in which the people mentioned in this chapter were involved, much of it centered on originality, imagination, playful conversations, and congeniality.

A delightful book, *What Shall We Do To Night?* (Mayne, 1873) listed hundreds of activities for evening amusements. Many of these activities were geared for using originality, ingenuity, and cleverness. Dressing up, puppet shows, original plays, complicated guessing games, and witty play with words formed the cores of these games. Participants all were involved in the merriment and enjoyed the outcomes. Much thinking went into devising scripts, costumes, and props. Now, much of this is already done and requires not too much brain power to implement. The activities listed in this book both work and relax the brain simultaneously, giving more credence to the idea that play and work together are much more powerful than work by itself.

It appears that many ideas conceived through playful social interaction were later translated into serious works. As society moves more and more deeply into the traps and lures of technology and, consequently, a greater increase in solitary interactions with machines, it should become more critical to revive conviviality in the classroom and return to the idea of playful conversations as springboards for the freshness of connections and originality of ideas. The increasing solitary nature of education, even at the college level, denies the brain much needed food that can easily be fed through social interaction and imaginative play. Aficionados of the technological world claim that the growing numbers of virtual communities in cyberspace provide a fertile ground for playful development of ideas. Somehow I find it hard to believe those conversations between William James and Emerson or Hodgson or any other of his numerous friends and colleagues, had they been conducted in cyberspace, would have resulted in the same fertility of ideas. Somehow the actual human contact seemed to be the spark that set off such magnificent and impressive intellectual growth.

Actually, it is interesting to note that even in James's time there was some concern already being expressed for the decline in the art of conversation. In a letter to James dated March 20, 1901, Frances Rollins Morse, a social worker, wrote,

She and some friends belong to a discussion club at one meeting of which they were discussing the decline in the art of conversation. One reason is "cheap postage which allows fragments of conversations, questions, ejaculations, to go flying about the world on bits of paper." Another reason is the rise of scientific education after Darwin. Scientific education has "fitted people to think more closely, & to seek truth more earnestly, but provides them with a smaller stock of opinions—preferences—appreciations & cc, as playthings. (Morse, 1901)

If one can "accuse" cheap postage of leading to the decline in playful conversation, what can one say about the quickness and brevity of e-mail "conversations?" Or telephone talk? Some of the art of intellectual playfulness does continue at annual conferences of various learned societies, but here again, these conversations usually revolve around specialized shop talk and are not too interdisciplinary in nature, and after the conferences the threads of potentially new creative ideas are broken off and not given more nurturing to develop to full fruition through continued playfulness and conversation. At the higher education level, with busy schedules and expectations to churn out publications, teach full loads, and do service to the university and the community, precious little time is left for playfulness. Sabbaticals are far and few between, and there is the economic necessity of teaching summer school sessions. All contribute to a lack of playfulness and to brain exhaustion, in some cases not only exhaustion but also the demoralization that one simply cannot have the time to play with ideas in the company of congenial colleagues. The trend toward total quality management and the complete lack of understanding of how the brain functions and the time it needs to play around and "imagine if" have done much to bring about a decline in serious academic production. Elementary and high schools, similarly, ignore what many of our famous forefathers preached, what they practiced, and what current brain research is telling us about the nature and importance of developing "dendrites, dendrites, dendrites" in the growth of human cognition.

Carl E. Seashore (1866–1949), in his 1910 presidential address to the Western Division of the American Philosophical Association, beautifully summarized both the definition of play and the role of play in the development of the mind, as understood and practiced by his contemporaries. His definition of play as the "self-expression for the pleasure of expression" (p. 324) seems to fit the categories of both brain development and playful activities, and tie them together into an inseparable category. Within his definition of play he contended that all senses develop through the activity of play and develop from simple to complex concepts as the human being develops and matures. According to him, what in an infant is simple hearing and playing with random sounds either from the environment or of his or her own choosing eventually are refined into an appreciation of the intricacies of music—"higher order" sounds. Similarly, genius artists develop from simple manipulations of materials to refinement, resulting in artful masterpieces. Again, the building and taking apart of various constructions in childhood can lead to development of keen powers of observation needed by scientists. In general, playing with the senses that occurs naturally in childhood when given the opportunity progresses to the development of higher levels of mental powers. Seashore rated play with imagination as the most influential facet in developing brainpower. According to Seashore, play is both a preparation for life and the chief realization of life (p. 327), and far more development occurs through play than through work:

The moments of highest realization and appreciation of life come from those activities which are most conspicuously characterized by play attitudes; either from play, pure and simple, or from work in which play motives dominate. What is it that the child is interested in, all satisfied with—most effective and at home in? It is play or playful work. Witness the lives of developed men and women who have felt the thrill of satisfaction from life. These are the persons whose minds have been full of play; whose attitudes have been a spontaneous and natural expression. (p. 328)

In fact, ideally one engages in playful work throughout one's lifetime and Seashore (1910/1999) pities adults who have lost the power to play: "The greater part of life is neither play nor work pure and simple, but a blending of the two" (p. 335). The remainder of his address skillfully weaves this playful attitude into the development of spirituality through religion. In our work-driven society, with the work ethic that seems to be drilled into younger and younger children as they begin their formal schooling, it may benefit them much more if school "work" were infused with much more playfulness, conversation, and other amusements. In other words, it may eliminate many so-called problems of low achievement if education were approached with a playful attitude and the distinction between work and play became more blurred. Why not try some of the playful practices of those who achieved greatness academically? After all, a rested brain certainly functions better!

One of the most famous philosophers of them all, Immanuel Kant (1797/1974) said it better than anyone about the importance of levity in every person's life:

Dining alone (solipsismus convictorii) is unhealthy for any scholar who *philosophizes*; instead of restoring his powers it exhausts him . . . ; it is fatiguing work, not a stimulating play of thought. . . . At a well laid table . . . the conversation usually goes through three stages: 1) *narration*, 2) reasoning, 3) joking. . . . But reasoning is always a form of work and an effort, and after we have engaged in it . . . it eventually becomes onerous. So the conversation naturally descends into a mere play of wit. . . . No matter how insignificant these laws of refined humanity may seem . . . anything that promotes sociability, even if it consists only in pleasing maxims or manners is a garment that dresses virtue to advantage. (pp. 145–147)

James Bissett Pratt (1915), an American philosopher traveling in India at the beginning of the twentieth century, came upon a group of Indians who, as part of a traditional religious ceremony, had taken one of their gods for a ride in the country. He wrote,

I once met one of the gods returning in his car from a week in the country where he had gone to enjoy the bath in a sacred tank. It was evening and a long procession preceded and followed the chariot. . . . There was a great deal of shouting and laughing and merrymaking and obviously everyone was having a good time—the priests particularly. Nearly everyone seemed to regard it as a kind of lark; a kind of lark, it should be added, in which religion becomes a grownup way of playing dolls. (p. 22)

If even the gods needed an "airing-out," then who are we, mere mortals, to question the importance of periods of playful levity to relieve our exhausted nervous and brain energy?

REFERENCES

Alcott, W. A. (1840). *The Library of Health and Teacher on the Human Condition.* Vol. 4. Boston: George W. Light.

Boyer, C. C. (1899). *Principles and Methods of Teaching.* Philadelphia: J. B. Lippincott.

Burkhardt, F., & F. Bowers (eds.). (1987). *The Works of William James.* Cambridge: Harvard University Press.

Holbrook, M. L. (1879). *Hygiene of the Brain.* New York: M. L. Holbrook.

Kant, I. (1974). *Anthropology from a Pragmatic Point of View.* The Hague: Martinus Nijhoff. (Original work published 1797.)

Levin, D. E. (1998). *Remote Control Childhood: Combatting the Hazards of Media Culture.* Washington, DC: NAEYC.

Mayne, L. D. (1873). *What Shall We Do To Night?* New York: Dick and Fitzgerald.

McIver, E. P. (1941). *Early Days at Putnam Camp.* Paper read at the Annual Meeting of the Keene Valley Historical Society, September.

Morse, F. R. (1901). Unpublished letter to William James, 20 March. Houghton Library, Harvard University.

Myerson, J., D. Shealy, & M. Stern. (1987). *The Selected Letters of Louisa May Alcott.* Boston: Little, Brown.

Pratt, J. B. (1915). *India and Its Faiths.* Boston: Houghton Mifflin.

Ross, D. (1972). *G. Stanley Hall.* Chicago: University of Chicago Press.

Seashore, C. E. (1999). The Play Impulse and Attitude in Religion. In R. T. Hull (Ed.), *Presidential Addresses of the American Philosophical Association 1901–1910* (1999). Boston: Kluwer Academic. (Original work published 1910.)

Shaler, N. S. (1909). *The Autobiography of Nathaniel Southgate Shaler.* Boston: Houghton
        Mifflin.
Skrupskelis, I. K, & E. M. Berkeley (eds.). (1993). *The Correspondence of William James*,
        vol. 2. Charlottesville: University of Virginia Press.
————— . (1994). *The Correspondence of William James.* Vol. 3. Charlottesville: University
        of Virginia Press.

39

Rike's Guided Dramatic Play System, the Brain, and Language

Joyce A. Wilkinson

Don't force the child to learn, create a desire in him to want to learn.
—Jean-Jacques Rousseau (1712–1778)

Illiteracy remains a pervasive problem in North America despite countless, costly, contemporary literacy initiatives. Remedial English classes in university and college, business, and community settings endeavour to repattern students' brains to master narrative functions of language, including sequential writing and improved grammar, paragraphing, and syntax. Within programs at all levels, little attention has been accorded the effects of dramatic play, the "language" art form, on embedding neuronal pathways during language acquisition. From its inception, however, creative drama theoretical literature (Slade, 1954; Way, 1967) has cited verbal and nonverbal behavior as central to the dramatic process, but integrating drama into language arts (Wilkinson, 1970) based on the premise of the integral role of drama in language development became a controversial notion to some language authorities despite Smilansky's (1968) empirical finding that rapid language growth accompanied sociodramatic play. While considerable subsequent research in educational drama (Kardash & Wright, 1987; Vitz, 1983; Wagner, 1988, 1998; Wilkinson, 1988) has explored the impact of drama on language, few studies have examined how guided dramatic play links higher-order thinking skills like imagination and creativity with language skills while structuring the brain and establishing the roots of literacy (Wilkinson & Rike, 1993).

An exception to this status quo is the career research of Elizabeth Kerr Rike. Beginning in the 1970s and subsequently replicated within multiple contexts and age groups, Rike's action research has evolved into the creation of a new system of dramatic play, language, and literacy cognizant of how the brain functions. Guidance by a dramatic play/language specialist skilled in the deliberate manipulation of the drama elements in order to embed literacy patterns in the brain represents the innovation of Rike's work. Within this system, guided dramatic play may be defined as the enactment of a role within a fictional context in which an adult occasionally enters into the playing as a tutor assuming responsibility for guiding or leading the player(s), through questioning and conscious use of the drama elements, into discovery, acquisition, and use of language structures. This process may function as initial learning for prespeech or language-delayed children, remediation for the language deficient, or reinforcement for the emergent literate. This cumulative system progresses from the dramatic play of the infant toddler through to the sophisticated functions of the playwright. According to Rike's system, language/writing deficits evident in adults originate when they are toddlers learning oral language, and could be reversed if a trained adult entered into their dramatic play to help them pattern the interconnected processes of narrative structure in the brain. Such is the innate content of dramatic play.

Within the domain of dramatic play, the state of the art of research examining Rike's guided dramatic play system is in its infancy. A few studies provide empirical analysis, while an impressive amount of testimonial or anecdotal evidence from educators at all levels and in all contexts leaves no doubt of its efficacy to those facing language challenges. In defense of such evidence, Thomas Ryan (Ryan & Rike, 1986), English and drama professor emeritus at the University of Tennessee, claims no before-and-after tests are necessary when a clearly observable lack of specific skills is replaced by mastery after even one guided dramatic play session. Howard Russell (1990), professor emeritus at the Ontario Institute for Studies in Education of the University of Toronto, suggests large sample studies are unnecessary if one can show that after treatment a single subject demonstrates behavior absent prior to intervention. Considerable data meeting Ryan and/or Russell's evidence criteria exist in relation to Rike's system.

For example, to validate the construct of the dramatic play–language–creativity connection, Rike (1984), more than a decade after refining and implementing its components in practice and while a graduate student at the University of Tennessee, designed an instrument to assess the simultaneous emergence of language, imagination, and play skills during guided dramatic play. The Rike Guided Dramatic Play Observation Measure documents cumulative development at three-month intervals between ages two and three in traits such as attending, repeating, imitating pantomime, imitating pantomime with words, holophrastic speech, swapping roles, speech expression, problem solving, verbal and ideational fluency, and speech complexity. An independent, expert panel, including a kindergarten teacher and parent of a two-year-old, a school supervisor of parent involvement, a child and family studies university student and mother of a two-year-old, and a director of a university pediatric language clinic, evaluated the reliability of the instrument. A creative drama specialist verified its face validity. These early childhood educators analyzed audio recordings of two kinds of guided dramatic play tasks performed by the same boy at intervals between two and three years of age: Form A, responses to modeled play that became ritual through repetition to assess the child's increasing language competence, and Form B, use of objects in spontaneous play to determine the child's self-generation of creative ideas.

Interrater reliability ranged from 80- to 100-percent agreement on Form A: Ritualized Themes. Analysis of the few discrepancies revealed rater error as the cause of differences. Adjusted scores after clarifying discussions showed 100 percent agreement on both language and imaginative play dimensions of the measure. Evaluation of Form B: Symbolic Understanding/Use of Objects resulted in "100% agreement in every one of the levels for both play skills and language skills except for one tape" (Rike, 1984, p. 44). In this one exception among twenty-one discrete assessments in the total score of each evaluator, one evaluator had assigned the highest level of verbal fluency in sentence construction while others selected one level below. Rike interpreted this as distinguishing between the more fluent and complex language of the tasks requiring spontaneous conversation and dialogue and those tasks in Form A demonstrating the gradual progression from two-word sentences to filling in the complete sentences exactly as modeled (Rike, 1984, p. 44). Even with this marginal scoring difference, Rike concluded that intensive training in guided dramatic play techniques for language tutoring was crucial for all raters.

Rike (1984) also conceded the possibility of refining the instrument to include increasing variety in the use of objects and in divergent thinking, because the fluency of creative ideas could exceed the capacity of the instrument when used for assessing language/drama skills beyond three years of age. For instance, in his time-machine adventure, five-year-old Stephen wanted to land at Easter but found someone had taken it off the map, so he landed instead at Thanksgiving and later went on to Christmas. This response required expansion of the scale to accommodate such heightened creativity and abstract thought not acknowledged by the original instrument. Rike perceived that the creative thinking evident in language used while developing play skills and ideational fluency (Torrance, 1974) demonstrated the "imagining" uses of language that Tough (1977) found missing by three years of age in disadvantaged children.

Generalization of the efficacy of Rike's one-to-one guided symbolic dramatic play to groups of children had already occurred through practice in many contexts. Empirical validation was established through the pre- and posttesting of two disadvantaged kindergarten classes that participated in dramatic play sessions twice weekly and two control classes in two different schools that did not (Rike, 1974). Rike, as a specialist trained in the methods of stimulating and guiding children in developing the skills essential to engaging in dramatic play, taught the sessions. In both fall and spring, classroom teachers administered a county-created diagnostic test (Sams, 1973) to assess skill levels of the preschool children in the four equal-size groups. Pretest results revealed one control group with few failures to be an advantaged class, while the other control group scored as many failures as the two dramatic play groups. The results of the posttest, administered only to children who had failed the pretest, were analyzed in relation to specific skills inherent in the dramatic play sessions experienced by the two treatment groups.

Rike (1974) selected four key pretest language skills for comparative analysis with the posttest results. The first skill, following directions, revealed failures in two schools on the pretest: nine students failed in one dramatic play class while five failed in the equally disadvantaged control class. The posttest indicated no failures in the dramatic play group, while the control group remained at five failures. Significantly, children rated by their teachers as having short attention spans and/or not following directions on the social skills scale of the diagnostic test were in the same dramatic play group. In drama lessons, they repeatedly listened and followed directions during sessions that progressively increased from twenty to forty-five minutes in length. Rike concluded that this gradual lengthening of the experience and use of repetition contributed to their improvement in following directions. The 100-percent improvement in the dramatic play group and lack of improvement in the control group, may also be due to the intrinsic motivation (Moffett & Wagner, 1983) children experience in symbolic dramatic play guided by a trained specialist. Intense enjoyment, the desire to play, and emotional payoffs (Salisbury, 1982) lead to greater depth in dramatic engagement. Players focus, listen, and follow directions in order to transfer the teacher's words into action; otherwise, children playing elves cannot obey a magician's commands.

In the second area examined, perceptual motor skills, the children had to repeat two different sentences correctly, as well as complete items testing rhythm and word repetition (Rike, 1974). All groups improved in the latter two tasks, but significant differences were evident regarding sentence repetition. The disadvantaged control group increased its failures from nine to ten, while the two disadvantaged dramatic play groups reduced their failures from eleven to two and two to one. Proportionately, the superior control group's failure reduction from six to four was substantially less than that of either disadvantaged treatment group.

Rike (1974) interpreted this 50 percent to 80 percent improvement in the dramatic play classes, compared to 0 percent to 30 percent in the control groups, as due to the sensory experiences repeated during concentration activities in auditory discrimination. The language skill of sentence repetition, requiring both listening and speaking to repeat a sentence verbatim, had been reinforced by such specific dramatic play tasks as making sounds, imitating speech patterns, and repeating characters' exact sentences in dramatized stories. Repeated practice in dramatic play sessions allowed children to speak, to dialogue with others, to listen in order to be good players, and to receive positive peer approval when helping to keep the creation flowing.

The third skill area, animal naming (Rike, 1974), required children to name at least six animals in one minute or less. The superior control group improved from six to zero failures in this task on the posttest. The two dramatic play groups improved from seven and eight failures each to zero failures, while the disadvantaged control group reduced its failures from six to three. An integral factor in interpreting these results is John's (1990) observation that disadvantaged children tend to be physically oriented and to learn kinesthetically. Visual, aural, and/or tactile strategies had been used for animal study in the control group kindergartens. Use of dramatic play in the treatment groups had added the elements of movement and creative thinking, allowing the children to move as animals, imagine being the animal, or make strong emotional connections through playing animals in story situations. By playing big and little creatures, farm animals, pets, and zoo and circus animals, children used classification, the skill Vygotsky (1962) claims as second in importance to word meaning, to help them with recall. After the treatment groups visited a real circus, they played circus in drama sessions. Recall and retention were enhanced because they remembered what they enjoyed doing more than what they had seen or heard. It appears as if the multisensory impact of the imaginative physical movement, language, and sound on the cells of the body helped embed new neuronal patterns, enabling memory and recall more readily than methods having lesser sensory impact.

The fourth area, body awareness, used draw-a-man pictures completed in September compared with repeated drawings at year's end (Rike, 1974). Using educational connoisseurship (Eisner, 1985), the Knox County art supervisor verified the improvement shown by the dramatic play groups. Repeated sensory-awareness tasks, creative movement, connecting and shaping body parts, facial expressions, and drawing experiences after guided dramatic play sessions may have influenced this change by imprinting both perception and retrieval cues in the children's brains.

Because dramatic play involves the whole body and the whole brain (Wilkinson, 1989, 1993), it engages all of the multiple intelligences (Gardner, 1985) and matches the learning styles (Kolb, 1983) of all children. This resulting increase in self-confidence (Wright, 1972) in turn increases verbal fluency. Rike (1974) noted the development of positive self-image in both dramatic play groups whose pretests had indicated negative social skills.

In another study, Rike (1985) succeeded in adapting her guided dramatic play system to teach fifth grade grammar, specifically parts of speech, to a ten-year-old grandson. Different forms of pre- and posttests indicated dramatic improvement after only one session of less than three hours. A pre-test score of twelve out of thirty correct doubled four days later to twenty-four correct. Errors included parts of speech that had already been taught for several years but had not yet been experienced through dramatic play. Replicated with another boy and recorded on videotape (Rike, 1987), this mastery of grammar in a brief time through dramatic play has since been successfully repeated in numerous classrooms in America, Canada, and China.

The power of Rike's guided dramatic play as a tool of natural grammar acquisition is most evident in this excerpt (Rike, 1993, p. 39) from an audiotaped play session with her youngest grandson at age two years, eleven months:

Rike: Michael, let's pretend we are your daddy going to work (drive to office and go in). What does your daddy do at work?

Michael: He just sits (sitting).

Rike: Now what does he do next?

Michael: He don't do nothing.

Rike: He doesn't do anything?

Michael: Nope. He just sits there. (Father is a lawyer.)

As play tutor, Rike made no mention of the double negative; she did not correct it, but did model the accurate form within the play situation. Michael seemed not to notice the mismatch. The next day, as they played going to work again in the same sequence up to "Now what does he do?," Michael said, "He didn't do n—," stopped himself, paused, and then said "anything." The pattern in his brain had been restructured as he self-corrected his own grammar twice within the same play experience. In contrast to this child-linguist transformation is an example in which a mother parrots correct form to a child while the child persists in repeating the double negative only to add, after eight repetitions, verb-agreement errors as well (Clark & Eve, 1977). As language tutors using Rike's guided dramatic play system, trained adults help the child experience language structures throughout the whole physical system.

Having validated an instrument and having successfully generalized results to individuals and groups of various ages, Rike undertook replication of her system by training others in its precepts through workshops and/or courses. Highly positive results, too numerous to recount in full, have accumulated in nine databanks of evidence. In one case, writing portfolios begun in September with a severely disadvantaged, rural eighth-grade African-American Elementary Secondary Education Act class show initial stories of one or two sentences or fragments with no paragraph development, implying little to no motivation or understanding of how to start a story or of story structure. Those who did write competently copied their ideas from television shows. After an October teachers' workshop with Rike, the teacher involved these students in Rike's 7W guided play system, which focuses on identifying not only "Who, what, where, and why?" but also asks "What can happen to cause a problem?" and "What can be done to solve the problem?" April samples of writing by these youngsters demonstrated mastery of structure, originality, and increased motivation to write. Their principal evaluated this outcome as "their greatest creative writing of all eight years of school," while their teacher verified that "their reading scores improved dramatically . . . their reading improved greater than any time in their prior history" (Rike, 1996, p. 55). Although some stories were two or three pages in length, the following, barring its "invented" mechanics, demonstrated the mastery of story grammar gained through involvement in Rike's guided dramatic play:

On August 5, 1962, a man stole the president's car. The president call the polies. They chase the man and catch him and took him prisoner they took him to jail three days later they had his count [court]. In the count the mam [man] asked for mercy. The president tole the judge to sent him to prisone for a year. They put him in prisone. There was a jail brate [break] and he was killed.

In an urban setting, a fifth-grade teacher introduced Rike's system to children with Attention Deficit Disorder to help them create and solve math problems. During this process, the children improved not only their problem-solving skills but also their story writing. Their teacher attributed Rike's 7W system as the reason for "their progression from the multi-sensory approach, starting with the physical (the movement), the body being involved, and then eventually moving to the abstract. These elementary children especially need to go through these steps before they are given the abstract or paper and pencil, and told to do something they really don't understand" (Rike, 1996, p. 54). After using the 7W system in mathematics, children who one year earlier had not been able to finish a story wrote complex story grammars, while improving their math ability, as Lisa illustrated in her self-typed story:

TO THE MALL
ON MONDAY, LISA WENT TO EAST TOWN MALL BECAUSE SHE HAD $100.00 TO SPEND. SHE DID CHORES FOR HER MOM TO EARN THIS MONEY. SHE BOUGHT A CAKE FOR $10.00 AND A DOLL FOR $70.00. LATER IN THE DAY SHE BOUGHT TWO PIECES OF CANDY FOR $1.00, SOME MARKERS FOR $8.00 AND A USED BIKE FOR $10.00. HOW MUCH MONEY DID SHE SPEND AT THE MALL? DID SHE HAVE ANY MONEY LEFT? IF SO, HOW MUCH MONEY WAS LEFT AFTER HER TRIP TO THE MALL?

Replications of Rike's system also occurred through a drama teacher literacy project following a course for elementary teachers and theatre graduates taught by Rike at the University of Tennessee. The writer interviewed all participants at the conclusion of the course to assess their understanding of the convergence of the elements and structure of drama and story and the use of the 7W building blocks to create and/or write stories integrating the basic skills of the language arts curriculum. Follow-up interviews (Wilkinson, 1992a) with these teacher-participants one year later revealed that both successful and enthusiastic implementation had been achieved in all grade levels. One teacher claimed that the drama course "not only teaches the basic skills mandated by our State language arts curriculum, but offers every child the experience of feasting on the bounty of his own imagination and creativity" (Rike, 1996, p. 54).

In addition to Rike's success in replicating her system and that of others she has taught, educators further afield have experienced similar results. A grade-two teacher who attended a workshop taught by a drama specialist teacher who had learned Rike's system in one of my undergraduate classes shares being "thrilled to have finally found such a 'user friendly' way to teach story writing. This tremendous method is wonderfully motivating" (Rike, 1996, p. 54). Advantages of this method cited by this teacher included "each child is writing and completing their stories. The top students are free to create and the low students are having excellent success by just finishing" (Rike, 1996, p. 54). Regardless of ability differences, these students consistently demonstrate their grasp of the 5W beginning sentences of "Who, what, where, and why?" and their sense of story structure in their writing:

GOING ON A FIELD TRIP
by Melissa

Our grade 2 class was going on a field trip to the Dinosaur Museum at 9 o'clock on a rainy morning because we wanted to have fun. The bus broke down. The driver fixed it.

FIELDTRIP TROUBLE
by Deanna

Our class was going on a field trip to Kinsman Park for an excuse to get away from school. When we got there we heard a click. The bus driver went to Tim Horton's to get a coffee. She accidently locked the door behind her. I took my cell phone out of my bag and phoned the Edmonton Eskimo's football team to break down the door. They came and did it and we all had fun.

PUPPETS IN THE BAG
by Daniel

I was performing a puppet play in an old chip bag in the evening because it was president ant's birthday. Robber ant jumped out of the curtain and stole one of the puppets. So we called the ant police and they caught him in action.

In another action research context (Wilkinson, in press), a grade-four music teacher demonstrated Rike's system with two Canadian classes of grade-four boys who had not previously experienced guided dramatic play. Approximately one half of the thirty-six students ranged in ability from average to bright, while the other half demonstrated lower linguistic ability. In writing completed within five minutes of enacting individually created 7W stories, all of these boys demonstrated a grasp of story structure and the basic literary/drama elements. Most wrote original, realistic fiction, while 40 percent created believable fantasy using an average of five to six sentences, accompanied in some instances by dialogue, onomatopoeia, or complex structure. Four children who communicated only in sentence fragments also conveyed a sense of story grammar. Prevalent omission among the group of where and why aspects in their scenarios was more a condition of limited time-on-task and the teacher's hastily acquired expertise in this system than of deficiencies with the method. None of these boys wrote in the same way, on the same topic, or without story structure, but each exercised his own free-will creative choices with imaginative results, as shown by these examples:

> There was 5 seconds left in the game.
> I pulled up for a three pointer.
> I knew I only kneeded 2 points to win the finals.
> To be on the safe side I went up closer.
> Thoughts of winning the basketball cup
> were only 3 seconds away.
> Oh no my ankle was now starting to hurt.
> I went on, 3, 2, and the shot. Beep . . .
> It was GOOD! the championships were ours!
> over the Knicks.
> —Michel Jordan

Uh Oh!
Oh no! i'm under attack on this
unknown planet!"
exclaimed Spok. "Beam me up scotty!"
vzzt. Spok was onboard but
there was no captan on the ship. He started
flying when all of a sudden the steering wheel
fell off. "Uh oh" he thought, "better screw
it back on. ah here is the screwdriver. think its fixed.
now to find the captan."

My name is Romeo.
I was purposing to my lover Juilet.
I'm afraid she doesn't love me because
I killed her cousin. now I'm standing in
the rain waiting for her to kiss me back
She though about it and now we love each other.

Rather than dismissing the Rike system as formulaic or mechanistic, teachers
aware of its strategies when confronted with language-challenged students repeatedly observe success after only one session, where other methods have failed for
eight years or more to deliver satisfactory change.

The significance of using guided dramatic play to facilitate language and literacy development is enhanced by early childhood brain research (McCain & Mustard, 1999), confirming that

the early experiences and stimulating, positive interactions with adults and other children are far more important for brain development than previously realized . . . The
early years, from conception to age six, have the most important influence of any time
in the life cycle on brain development and subsequent learning, behaviour and health.
The effects of early experience, particularly during the first three years, on the wiring
and sculpting of the brain's billions of neurons, last a lifetime. A young child's brain
develops through stimulation of the sensing pathways (e.g., seeing, hearing, touching,
smelling, tasting) from early experiences. . . . A child who misses positive stimulation
in the first years of life may have difficulty overcoming a bad early start. Learning in
the early years must be based on quality, developmentally-attuned interactions with
primary caregivers and opportunities for play-based problem-solving with other children that stimulates brain development. (p. 7)

These conclusions about early brain development from such disciplinary fields
as epidemiology, anthropology, sociology, developmental psychology, and pediatrics redouble the import of my earlier hypothesis (Wilkinson, 1978): Symbolic
dramatic play is a precursor of language, an essential component of it as well as of
cumulative language development culminating in literacy. Its absence results in
language deficiencies. Integral to this assumption is the notion of symbiosis: The
elements of drama, learned by many children during the make-believe play of
early childhood, are fused together with the literary elements that are the infrastructure of literacy. Unlike Mustard, who suggests that unless sufficient sen-

sory–brain connections are established in the first three years of life they can never be acquired, I argue that guided dramatic play may be the tool whereby such losses can be regained, perhaps in their entirety, given scientific evidence of the ability of a deeply felt experience to override previous patterns in the brain (Bower, 1981).

Results from a longitudinal study (Wilkinson, 1998) of influences on student achievement and behavior, during professionally guided expressive arts experiences support such an argument. The holistic engagement of the arts creates the whole brain/whole body state integral to improving interpersonal and intellectual achievement. Furthermore, such growth or healing is a precursor to learning for many if not all children. Intensely felt, three-dimensional arts participation immerses the whole body in empowering experiences that physically override prior knowledge embedded in every cell of the body. This, in turn, physically restructures neuronal pathways in the brain, allowing the repatterning of ingrained thinking habits that reappear as transformations in values, attitudes, and behaviors, as new neural networks. One intensive experience in the arts, synthesizing several intelligences, simultaneously prompts instantaneous change and thus places the arts at the core of learning in postmodern society (pp. 122–123).

Other mutually exclusive evidence lends additional credence to the drama/language/literacy connection evident in Rike's work. The 1997 Scholastic Aptitude Test (SAT) scores (College Board, 1997) indicate that students who took drama courses for four or more years outscored the mean, while those with no drama courses scored lower than the average SAT score. Students taking courses in Acting/Play Production scored 68 points higher on the verbal SAT test and 40 points higher on the SAT math test than students with no courses or experience in the arts. SAT scores for those with general courses in drama study or appreciation were 57 points higher on the verbal test and 29 points higher on the math test than those with no drama study. Students with Acting/Play Production scored 40 points above the mean SAT score on the verbal test and 21 points above the math mean. This pattern has been manifesting consistently since at least 1987.

Such independent school exit results reinforce the trend established by the school entry gains made by Rike's disadvantaged kindergarten groups (Rike, 1974). The highest verbal SAT scores achieved by students who studied Acting and/or Play Production or Drama Study and Appreciation are also reminiscent of the high self-monitoring (the regulating of verbal and nonverbal behavior) (Snyder, 1972) scores achieved by the highly involved drama students, as measured by the Developmental Drama Scale (Wilkinson, 1983). It seems that dramatic play, with its spontaneity, creativity, and laughter, engages the whole brain through whole-body immersion in a holographic paradigm of learning. The 5W patterning of guided dramatic play creates pathways in the brain that structure sentences, make meaning of word concepts, and embed basic drama elements. The 7Ws of story creation structure the dramatic form or story grammar and develop paths of empathy and point of view essential to reading, writing, and storytelling. Guided dramatic play as imaginative creation thus becomes an essential building block of thinking (Greenberg, 1999) as Rike's system helps the learner analyze and use the elements of drama to acquire language structures in the brain.

Drama, including dramatic play, is a hologram, as is the brain (Pribram, 1982, 1986, 1999); the part is in the whole, the whole in the part. As a three-dimensional metaphor of life itself, drama imprints narrative structures on this holographic brain. Within the heightened awareness of the dramatic play context, it is as if the body itself becomes a brain, a massive multisensory scanner receiving strong emotional stimuli that imprint deep neuronal pathways among the dendrites so that when the child returns to play he or she can either repeat the story or, as demonstrated many times in various settings, create an original one based on personal experience. Contrary to the myth that adults must not intervene in or model a child's play, dramatic play audiotapes recorded during this action research program (Rike, 1984) repeatedly confirm that the children spontaneously invent responses based on their own life experiences.

Dramatic play skills, which emerge in children around the same time as language skills (Piaget, 1973), cannot function without the creative thinking or imagination and communication skills essential to learning language. The unique nature of group creation within dramatic play and the specially trained leader's strategies and knowledge of questioning help motivate children to listen, think, imagine, create, and express feelings independently. Guided dramatic play structures thinking through visualizing, organizing, and sequencing the language of the participants. It assists the acquisition of metalinguistic knowledge of language at the discourse level (McGhee & Charlesworth, 1982), through developing word meaning or concepts together with encoding of structure, and sequential understanding through repeated patterning of sentences, grammar, and story schema. The elements of drama pivotal to Rike's guided dramatic play system bring the elements of literacy to conscious awareness. Communication skills and creative thinking skills, language and imagination, converge in guided dramatic play.

As considerable research shows, when play skills improve, verbal skills increase; if play is not encouraged or allowed, both language and imagination stagnate (Wilkinson & Rike, 1993). With language, imaging, creativity, and dramatic play symbiotically linked, guided dramatic play becomes a missing link to literacy. Rike's system unlocks the code that reveals how this drama– literacy linkage works under the tutelage of a skilled coplayer.

BIBLIOGRAPHY

Bower, G. H. (1981). Mood and Memory. *American Psychologist* 36: 129–148.

Clark, H. H., & V. Eve. (1977). *Psychology and Language*. New York: Harcourt Brace Jovanovich.

Clements, R. (1999). President's Message. *IPA Newsletter USA* 57: 4–5.

College Board (1997). *Profile of SAT Program Test Takers for 1996 and 1997*. New York: College Entrance Examination Board.

Eisner, E. W. (1985). *The Art of Educational Evaluation*. Philadelphia: Falmer Press.

Gardner, H. (1983, 1985). *Frames of Mind: The Theory of Multiple Intelligences*. New York: Basic Books.

Greenberg, K. H. (1999). *The Cognet Education Model: A Mediated Learning Approach to Family–School Partnerships for Teaching Children How to Learn*. Presentation to the Imaginative Play and Brain Research Summit Meeting, University of Tennessee, Knoxville.

Hensel, N. H. (1977). *Evaluating Children's Development in Creativity and Creative Drama*. San Francisco: R & E Research Associates.

John, K. (1990). *Able Insights #13*. Dallas, TX: Centre for Slow Learners.

Kardash, C.A.M., & L. Wright. (1987). Does Creative Drama Benefit Elementary School Students? A Meta-Analysis. *Youth Theatre Journal* 1(3): 11–18.

Kolb, D. A. (1983). *Experiential Learning: Experience as the Source of Learning and Development*. New York: Prentice-Hall.

McCain, M. N., & J. F. Mustard. (1999). *Early Years Study: Reversing the Real Brain Drain*. Toronto, Ontario: Children's Secretariat.

McGhee, L., & R. Charlesworth. (1982). Metalinguistic Knowledge: Another Look at Beginning Reading. *Journal of Childhood Education* (November/December): 123–127.

Moffett, J., & B. J. Wagner. (1983). *Student-Centered Language Arts and Reading K–13*. Boston: Houghton Mifflin.

Piaget, J. (1973). *Play, Dreams and Imitation in Childhood*. New York: Academic Press.

Pribram, K. (1982). What the Fuss Is All About. In K. Wilber (Ed.), *The Holographic Paradigm and Other Paradoxes: Exploring the Leading Edge of Science* (pp. 27–34). Boston: New Science Library.

———. (1986). *Brain and Meaning*. Paper presented to the Children's Theatre Foundation Drama as a Meaning Maker Symposium, Rutgers University, New Jersey.

———. (1999). *Play and the Brain*. Presentation to the Imaginative Play and Brain Research Summit Meeting, University of Tennessee, Knoxville.

Rike, E. (1974). *Curriculum Objectives for Creative Drama in Kindergarten and First Grade: A Comparative Analysis of the Skills Needed to Engage in the Process of Guided Dramatic Play and Those Skills Necessary to Reading Readiness, as Defined in Knox County Schools' Developmental Learning Program*. Unpublished manuscript. Knox County Schools, Knoxville, TN.

———. (1984). *Project TIPS: Teaching Imaginative Play Skills Instrument Research*. Unpublished paper, University of Tennessee, Knoxville.

———. (1985). *Grammar by Gramma and Stephen: Creative Grammatics One-to-One Play*. Knoxville, TN: 3 R't's Press.

———. (prod./dir.). (1987). *Grammar by Gramma* [Videotape]. Knoxville, TN: The Play Studio.

———. (1993). Guided Symbolic Dramatic Play as the Missing Link to Literacy. In J. Wilkinson (Ed.), *The Symbolic Dramatic Play–Literacy Connection: Whole Brain, Whole Body, Whole Learning* (pp. 25–42). Needham Heights, MA: Ginn Press.

———. (1996). *Workshops That Work*. Knoxville, TN: The Play Studio.

Russell, H. (1990). *Research with a Sample of One: Presentation to Research and Inquiry in Arts Education Seminar*. Toronto: Ontario Institute for Studies in Education.

Ryan, T. K. (prod.), & E. Rike (dir.). (1986). *Motivating and Developing the Communication Skills* [Videotape]. Knoxville, TN: The Play Studio.

Salisbury, B.T. (1982). *A Descriptive Analysis of the Teaching/Learning Behaviors in Creative Drama in an Elementary Classroom Taught by a Drama Specialist*. Unpublished doctoral dissertation, University of Washington.

Sams, R. (1973). *KIDS Test*. Knoxville, TN: Knox County Schools.

Slade, P. (1954). *Child Drama*. London: University of London Press.

Smilansky, S. (1968). *The Effects of Sociodramatic Play on Disadvantaged Preschool Children.* New York: John Wiley and Sons.

Snyder, M. (1972). *Individual Differences and Self-Control of Expressive Behavior.* Unpublished doctoral dissertation, Stanford University.

Torrance, E. P. (1974). *Norms-Technical Manual: Torrance Tests of Creative Thinking.* Lexington, MA: Ginn.

Tough, J. (1977). *The Development of Meaning.* New York: John Wiley and Sons.

Vitz, K. (1983). A Review of Empirical Research in Drama and Language. *Children's Theatre Review* 32(4): 17–25.

Vygotsky, L. (1962). *Thought and Language.* Cambridge: MIT Press.

Wagner, B. H. (1988). Research Currents: Does Classroom Drama Affect the Arts of Language? *Language Arts* 65(1): 46–55.

———. (1998). *Educational Drama and Language Arts: What Research Shows.* Portsmouth, NH: Heinemann.

Way, B. (1967). *Development through Drama.* London: Longmans.

Wilkinson, J. A. (1970). *A Time for Joy: Integrating Drama in Language Arts.* Brandon, Manitoba: Brandon University Press.

———. (1978). *Drama: The Missing Link.* Unpublished manuscript, University of Minnesota Department of Education, Minneapolis.

———. (1983). On Evaluation of Involvement in Developmental Drama and Its Relationship to Self-Monitoring and Hemisphericity. *Children's Theatre Review: Research Issue* 32(2): 15–19.

———. (1988). On the Integration of Drama in Language Arts. *Youth Theatre Journal* 3(1): 10–14.

———. (1989). Drama, Brain and Meaning. In J. Kase-Polisini (ed.), *Drama as a Meaning Maker* (pp. 21–33). Lanham, MD: University Press of America.

———. (1990). Forging the Future: Issues and Trends. *Youth Theatre Journal* 4(4): 10–13.

———. (interviewer). (1992a). *Interviews with Teacher Participants of Elizabeth Rike's Summer Institute* [Cassette Recording]. Available from author.

———. (1992b). Student Voices: Self-Assessment for Drama and Theater Education. *Drama/Theatre Teacher* 4(3): 24–26.

———. (ed.). (1993). *The Symbolic Dramatic Play–Literacy Connection: Whole Brain, Whole Body, Whole Learning.* Needham Heights, MA: Ginn Press.

———. (1998). *Transmission, Transformation and Transcendence: The Year III Assessment of "Learning through the Arts."* Toronto: Ontario Institute for Studies in Education of the University of Toronto.

———. (1999a). *Creating a Community of Learners: Year IV Assessment of "Learning through the Arts" 1998–1999.* Toronto: Ontario Institute for Studies in Education of the University of Toronto.

———. (1999b). Stories of Transmission through the Arts. *Artspaper* 9(4): 1, 3.

———. (ed.). (In press). *Drama and Second Language Education.* Toronto, Ontario: China–Canada Drama Education Exchange Consortium.

Wilkinson, J. A., & E. K. Rike. (1993). Guided Symbolic Dramatic Play as the Missing Link to Literacy. In J. A. Wilkinson (Ed.), *The Symbolic Dramatic Play–Literacy Connection: Whole Brain, Whole Body, Whole Learning* (pp. 9–24). Needham Heights, MA: Ginn Press.

Wright, L. (1972). *The Effects of Creative Drama on Person Perception.* Unpublished doctoral dissertation, University of Minnesota.

40

Imaginative Play and the Neurology of Creative Growth in Infants through Adults: Exchanges between Elizabeth Rike and Karl Pribram

Elizabeth Rike

INTRODUCTION TO KARL PRIBRAM

Globally, our adult play leaders champion the child's right to play at all ages and bemoan the diminishing opportunities or the absence of play. They desire adults to join in the play for the sheer joy of playing, and place less emphasis on studying what skills are involved concerning the brain. However, unless someone can convert adults in charge of education, play will be considered something you can just grow out of, not essential to the classroom. "Don't play in here little boy . . . sit still, and forget recess." Also, few drama play specialists will ever be trained to help teachers, to prevent work from boring the brains to extinction, as boredom shrinks teen brains in the loss of dendrite trees. The ability to imagine is an endangered species for all ages! If we are to communicate the value or necessity of imaginative play, someone needs to learn a common language between brain terminology and play.

What neuroscientist Karl Pribram studies is important for our understanding of learning and play. There are skills involved like "perceptual" skills or "motor" skills that are significant to our ability to play and learn. We need to ask the following:

- How can we engage in play without our bodies' muscles, eyes, ears, nose, mouth—our receptors? (Perception)
- How can we invent a new game without using all of the above, for "sense" memory without the creative imagination?
- How can we store the memory in our brain? Where does each sense memory go? Is it in one location or distributed all over? (Distributive Memory)

- How can our playmate's input of a word (or pantomime action) retrieve the memory and the sequence of play so that we can play the game again tomorrow and tell new players how to play?
- How are words in any language stored and retrieved?
- How can we write the word symbols down for others to read? What process enables us to interpret books describing games or wars or personal autobiographies of episodes about the who, what, where from past, present, or future—or make-believe fiction?
- How do we apply our understanding of these processes to aid not only toddlers and teens, but also the elderly, in our work?

Many of these questions can be addressed in the world of neuroscience.

LEARNING, MEMORY, AND, INCIDENTALLY, PERCEPTION

The following is a condensed version of Karl Pribram's informal thoughts, in which he describes his journey to understand the holographic-like distributive functions of the brain as they relate to perception, memory storage and retrieval, and language. Pribram takes us on a journey of discovery of the brain which, for the sake of brevity, we must highlight.

MEMORY AND THE HOLOGRAM

The hologram can be an excellent metaphor for understanding learning. It is a mathematical invention made by Dennis Gabor in 1948. Almost no one understood what the hologram was until Leith was able to implement the mathematics in an optical device in 1964. In my experience, the way the holographic metaphor came about was that Jack Hilgard was revising his introductory psychology textbook. He and I were walking on campus at Yale and Jack said to me, "What can I say about perception?" At the time, I found his question difficult to answer. Hubel and Wiesel had just discovered that cells in the brain are sensitive to changes in the orientation and location of lines. I had shown that these cells were also sensitive to the number of lines, the velocity, and the direction of motion. But these findings were unable to explain how we see images and objects.

Because many of the cells were needed to define even the simplest design, I suggested that the coding of visual form is much like what you see if I ask, "Everyone wearing glasses, please raise your hands high." That is a pattern of hands, right? Now I ask, "Everyone who is partially bald, raise your hands." Now the pattern is completely different. In short, coding of visual form must be in terms of patterns, not lines per se. Storing patterns in this fashion would mean that the geometry of brain cell response should geometrically resemble the pattern of the visual input. However, experiments that I had completed a few years earlier showed that this was not so.

So Jack Hilgard's question about perception stimulated me to wonder whether perhaps the patterns of brain responses might look like wave fronts. Karl Lashley suggested that such wave fronts might produce interference effects, but neither he nor I could figure out what sort of wave fronts were being created and how interference effects might explain anything at all.

Shortly afterward, a colleague came in with a book written by John Eccles, who received the 1963 Nobel prize for Physiology or Medicine, in which he pointed out that, although he had studied synapses (the junctions between neurons in the brain) all his life, he had only been able to study them one at a time. He noted that this is not the way things happen. Every axon splits into branches before it synapses, so there are many more or less identical synaptic events occurring simultaneously. Eccles suggested that these simultaneous synaptic events make up a wave front. I felt like kicking myself, because it was such an obvious way of thinking. Brilliant. It meant that there could be interference patterns in the brain. Lashley had been on the right track. Given the interference pattern of the brain—so what? I made the next discovery by reading an article in *Scientific American* on holograms. The article was written by Emmett Leith, who had developed an optical system that demonstrated Gabor's mathematics. Gabor's mathematical proposal was that if you stored interference patterns on a photographic film, with a simple maneuver, you could get a picture that was much clearer than a picture taken as an ordinary photograph; meanwhile, you could store much more information on that film. Within a week, we had a metaphor not only for how the brain might organize perception, but also how the brain might be using *distributed storage* for memory—which is why Lashley could not find an engram that looked like a photographic image.

There are those of us who have no understanding of terms such as "interference pattern." If we review what Restak (1979) wrote about Pribram's work, the terms will become clearer, and it will be more exciting to read his own explanation of the hologram:

Karl Pribram has suggested a model for brain function based on holography, a special type of photographic record in which parts of the picture are used, like the pieces of our hypothetical jigsaw puzzle, to reconstruct the whole paragraph. It depends on its effectiveness on the use of light containing a single wavelength. Ordinary light—sunlight or the light from an incandescent bulb—is the most concentrated at its source and [scatters] as it travels through space. . . . It's made up of electromagnetic waves, which oscillate at varying frequencies along the electromagnetic spectrum. (When white light is broken up by a prism, the resulting colors correspond to some of these different frequencies.) Light that oscillates at only one frequency . . . [makes up] the coherent light of a laser beam.

Scientists take advantage of a laser light's single frequency (its coherency) in the construction of holograms. An object, whose hologram is to be obtained, is first illuminated with the laser beam. The laser light strikes the object and impinges on a photographic plate at the same time as a reference beam—light from the same laser (but reflected from a mirror) arrives at the film. Since the two waves have the same frequency but strike the plate at different angles, their interaction forms an interference pattern, which is recorded on the plate. When looking at the resulting "photograph," the viewer sees only a smudge of rings and stripes corresponding to the "interference pattern" made by the two coherent waves.

The word "hologram" is coined from the word "holos," meaning "whole," and it was chosen by its inventor, Dennis Gabor, to stress the fact that a hologram contains complete information about a wave. To this extent, holography is the science of light waves and their interference patterns.

In order to "see" the hologram, the photographic plate is placed in its original position and the reference beam from the laser is switched on. At this moment, looking through the hologram is like looking through a window. The viewer can see the object at its previous position exactly as if the object were still present. In fact, if the hologram is a good one, the viewer can't tell the projected image from its original!

THE BRAIN

If one removes only the lens of a slide projector, leaving the slide in place, what do you see on the screen? What you see is nothing. No thing. But that does not mean it is empty. The information on that slide is all there, but it is distributed all over the place, and any little part of that light cone contains all the information needed to recreate the picture of the brain. That's a hologram. I could show this by taking my reading glasses and holding them within the light cone. Everywhere I put the glasses you would again see the image on the slide appear on the screen. If I move both of the lenses on my glasses into the light cone, you see two images of the slide on the screen. This means that the information within the light cone has been distributed all over it. Therefore, what we need to look for in the brain is something that looks like an interference pattern, not an image; in other words, I look at your face and I would not find a face in the brain, only the electrochemical activity arranged as interfering wave fronts, just as Eccles suggested.

Now why would the brain want to encode things in this way? For the same reason that image construction in hospitals—such as CAT scans and fMRIs—are produced this way. Furthermore, those of you who have taken psychology and statistics have used FFTs (fast Fourier transforms) whenever you want to do correlations. (Gabor functions, such as the mathematical functions in a holographic image, are constrained Fourier transforms.) Technically the data set from any perspective is together in such a way as to correlate it. That's why our brain uses this technique. We can correlate, correlate, correlate. It's a snap. But to try to find causality, that's a much more difficult problem: We mistake causality where there is no evidence for it and attribute a causal effect when there isn't any. But at correlating, we are superb.

PERCEPTION: SENSORY SYSTEM
(SOUND)—PIANO METAPHOR

The way to think about this is in terms of another metaphor: Think of it as if your sensory system is like a piano. The keyboard is the input source (the receptor surface). The input source is anatomically strictly connected with the strings in the sounding board (the cortex of the brain). The high notes are generated over here, and the low notes are generated over there. But the music you make depends on the *vibrations* of the strings, which form interacting wave fronts similar to those that make up the hologram. When the vibrations (the oscillations of brain electrical potentials) resonate to the input, musical images are made possible.

MEMORY RETRIEVAL OF DISTRIBUTIVE STORE
AND LOCALIZED STORE

One important thing that remains to be explained is how one retrieves ordinary experienced images from the holographic-like memory store. An easy way to think about this is that when you have a distributive store and have to retrieve it, you need something more localized, very much like in a computer, a program that retrieves what's stored in the hard drive. I call such programs the surface structure of memory. One can't just talk in terms of memory storage versus retrieval, because the retrieval process must also be learned (coded) and stored. Thus, there are two kinds of memory: a distributed store and a localized store. How does the localized store work?

APPLICATION OF LANGUAGE TO
MEMORY STORAGE

When you use language other than English, don't you think in that language? You don't translate it. Parlez-vous francais? Let's see—I'll translate. That means, "Do you speak French?" You see, I'm not doing so well. It takes too long. Basically, we *thought* in the language rather than translated it. For example, what if there's a chair. Something in my brain says "chair," which I can address in any of the languages. The concept that we store everything in every language that we know is almost impossible to imagine! The alternative is that there is a deep store that is addressed by all of the languages we know.

So if you had this distributed deep store, you could address it just the way it stored itself on a hard disk and then address it with whatever program (language) you are putting in—and that makes it relatively easy. The same memory is addressed by a variety of word processing systems. So you've got the distributed, holographic store, and then you've got a much more localized focal set of programs (operating and word processing systems).

One more fact: While a current computer system is location addressable, as in the postal system, holographic systems are content addressable, as in telecommunication, radio, and television. Retrieval is tuned to (resonates) locating the memory wherever (which is everywhere) the memory is. Your television or radio works in any location within the radius of the broadcast.

DENDRITES, DENDRITES, DENDRITES

The key to the holographic metaphor lay in the synapse. Simultaneous firing of synapses makes up wave fronts. Interference patterns—much as exist in a hologram—resulting from wave fronts would support distributed brain storage and retrieval. I have believed for some time that we would benefit by continued study of the dendrites, dendrites, dendrites—where most synapses in the brain occur.

RESPONSE TO PRIBRAM: A GROUP
DEMONSTRATION OF GUIDED IMAGINATIVE PLAY

Modern imaging techniques have enabled scientists to study the brain in ways once unimaginable, providing an understanding of the chemical processes that make memories. With positron emission tomography and functional magnetic resonance imaging, for example, neuroscientists can pinpoint brain activity during different memory tasks. At the National Institute of Mental Health (NIMH), Alex Martin, chief of the section on cognitive neuropsychology, and colleagues have used these techniques to explore how the brain stores information. According to Martin and his colleagues (1995), we are able to see the whole cascade that is going on in milliseconds within the brain." The findings have revealed a brain organized around the processes of learning, finding dwellings not on each stored object, but on the way each object is used. The image of a hammer, for instance, is stored in an area that involves motion, while the image of a cat is placed in a part of the brain that contains other visual shapes. A ball, like the hammer, would be stored in an area that involves motion—body motion!

(Rike picks up a real ball.) "Would you stand and catch this please? (Throws to someone and has him or her throw it back.) That was easy, wasn't it? Is there anyone in this room who has never thrown a ball? Then that will save a lot of time, won't it? We don't have to have the ball. I have brought some invisible balls here. Watch! I'm going to throw you different size balls. (A magic ball! You can all catch them at the same time.) Watch my hands and decide which size (how big it is) and catch the same size as I throw! Tell me what kind of ball . . . throw it back to me. (The teacher pantomimes throwing to the whole group; they catch, guess that it is a basketball, and throw it back to the teacher, who catches it.) Good! You caught my big ball. What was it? (Repeat a second time) Now, look again! (Cups hands like baseball, throws.) Throw it back! What was it? It is fun for the teacher to miss and have to look for the ball on the floor.

You were so good! Why is it so easy? How did you know how to throw those balls when you didn't have a real one? (Guesses.) Because you have thrown a ball. So your muscle has a memory. Do you know that everything you have ever done is stored in your head? Think how smart you are! My goodness, you've been moving, doing things since you were born! Think of how many memories you've stored up inside you! And because you have an imagination, too, you can do anything I say! I'll prove it! Try this: Everybody hammer (all pantomime hammering). See, I told you!

Pribram's and my efforts meet together. He said that the word "chair," in any language, would have to be stored in the same spot. An Asian investigator believed that every language is stored in a different place in the brain. Pribram says that is impossible, and I agree. Any language can be taught quickly through my game of Throw Ball! In a Tokyo playground there was a ball in the sandbox where a little five-year-old boy was playing as his mother watched on the bench. No common words were spoken between us. I picked up a real ball and said "ball." Then I said, "throw ball," matching the verb word to my action. I threw it to him and he caught it. I told him to "throw ball," motioning him to throw it back. We repeated this, saying "throw ball," and playing real ball for a few times. Then I put the ball down, made the same sized ball with my hands, and said, "throw ball." He repeatedly caught my invisible ball, as I matched my words to the imaginary play action. We laughed together. Suddenly, his little mother stood up and said, "Ahhh, throw ball!" Her excitement was immense, for she had learned two English words for the first time. What was significant to my research was that I was in Tokyo to show thirty nationalities that guided symbolic dramatic play is the child's tool for acquiring language! I asked these people to act as cave men, without any language, asked how they would communicate a dream. I asked them to dream they were "rocking a baby in the crook of their arm," and show their partner, without words, what they were doing. All pantomimed the same action (dramatic play?). When I asked them to say what they were doing in their own language, all babbled: Same action, different word sounds. Dr. Pribram and I were on the same wavelength! As he had said about the English word "chair," "throw ball" could be programmed into a spot in the brain, to be retrieved by the same action in any other language—just a different word sound. The deep meaning was the same, the surface structures were different.

The Hammer

This time, watch me and hold up your hand if you can guess what it is that I am doing. (Pantomime hammering a nail and mashing your thumb. Frown, shake the hand, and put the thumb in the mouth to show pain.) Yes, I was hammering and hit my finger. And did it make me feel happy? No. (Laughter.) It hurt. How could you tell? By the expression on my face and the way I wrung my hands. I didn't even say "ouch" and you knew, without words. Well, how did you know that I was hammering? Did you see a hammer in my hands? Where is it? You said that I was hammering! It looked as though I held a hammer in my hand, and moved my arm as if I were hammering. Yes. What I was doing we call *pantomime*. (Spell the word on the board.) Who can think how to say what pantomime is then? (It is "acting like" making believe, as if we are doing something without words—without an object in our hand. It is showing how we feel inside on the outside, by our facial expressions and our body movements.)

To make you believe required concentration. I pretended so hard that I forgot you were there. I pictured the hammer in my mind's eye, and my body remembered how it felt to move that hammer, and to mash my finger (my body memory). It made me frown and move as if it really hurt! Sense of pain is stored too.

Now what does science say about my hammering lesson? Dr. Martin and his colleagues (1995) theorize that to identify an object we instantly retrieve information by the features that define it. What does it look like? What color is it? How does it move or how do we manipulate it, if it's a tool? For example, the studies found that verbs are stored in areas of the brain just in front of regions involved in the perception of motion. Colors of objects—the memory of a bright yellow hue of a pencil, for example—are stored next to the perception of color. A hammer is stored three ways in the brain: once for its form, once for its use or motion, and once for the memory of the motor skill needed to use it. We store these bits of information about objects near their feature and it's all very logical. According to Martin (1995), it seems that how we store information follows a plan, and the plan is organized the same way our sensory and motor systems are organized. Color goes with color, form goes with form, motor information with motor information.

That is exactly what Pribram had discovered about the brain, and exactly the action I had used in teaching the drama play skill of pantomime to make people aware of the "muscle memory" concept: how we store and retrieve memories using five senses, visualize how an object looks and feels in movement. To treat that which is unreal calls for practicing sense awareness, sense image and recall, and sense reaction to memory. The vividness with which we can pretend depends upon the vividness with which we perceive the real world. Or, to summarize Pribram,'s thoughts (1986), the retrieval process must be learned (coded) and stored—that is, you have to learn a thing (a memory) before you can retrieve it.

FUN, LONG-TERM MEMORY, AND THE DENDRITES

In drama/play workshops I begin by playing sports and games in pantomime inside the classroom. Let's stand! Let's play ball! Most kids play real sports or watch sports games, so what we can do for fun—alerting our amygdala and exercising the imagination dendrites—is exciting and inexpensive. We can play without any equipment! We can do this right now, ourselves, and then watch videos of children of all ages loving the same imagination pantomime. After introducing throwing the ball, we can give each group of students a sport to do to let the class guess what they are doing. We can whisper twirl an imaginary jumprope, and anyone who can guess what they are doing may join in. Eager volunteers line up, pause to catch the rhythm, and jump in. The leader can say "hot pepper" and some do a complicated way of jumping two ropes at a time. Laughter! Oxygen to the blood, brain, and cardiovascular system, action-giving relief to boys' legs and boredom! In lieu of Ritalin it is exciting to use their own energy and learn (Breggin, 1994).

We can pantomime a baseball game secretly planned by a group: I am up to bat, and the umpire will pantomime each strike with a finger gesture: strike 1, 2, 3! I did not try to hit that second pitch, was angry with the umpire (because anyone could see that the second ball was a ball, and he called it a strike), and threw my bat down! After these beginning demos, the class can be divided into groups, each choosing a sport to pantomime for the other groups to guess. When they speak of it in words (what they saw happening), it becomes a story.

What is happening to the imagination dendrites? The neural pathway goes through the limbic system to the motor cortex and back to the cerebellum for long-term memory storage! This is called muscle memory (procedural memory). We have many classroom examples of the powerful effects that movement (pantomime movement) has on the long-term memory of any subject given the use of the strongest synapse in play/action, and the dendrite branches get thicker through using the body movement, imagination, and excitement of play power.

STORAGE OF MEMORIES: DISTRIBUTED AND LOCALIZED STORAGE AND PERCEPTION

Blank TV Screen

My metaphor is the TV screen in your mind and I make the students aware of the five senses and movement as channels to select and get instant replay of the memory. Our TV is blank until I select one channel to turn on. Let's try a sound (close your eyes; I play the tape-recorded sound of a merry-go-round). What is that sound? Where do you see it? At the fairgrounds. That one sense was retrieved from its own localized spot but it orchestrated all the other senses and retrieved the whole TV screen of the mind; like an instant replay. We could turn our whole playing space now into a fairground and retrieve the memory of all the smells and tastes and picture the different food booths. We divided into different groups, with each group deciding what they were selling. Deciding who was making the food, who the sellers and buyers were, and pantomiming for others to guess what they were eating or drinking as they left the booth.

Recalling what they remembered seeing and doing at the midway, some may pantomime shooting the little artificial ducks, some being the rows of mechanical ducks. We auditioned strong men, fire eaters, sword swallowers, tightrope walkers. Then, adding speech, there were barkers trying to get people into their show. I have had the fun of leading a huge group of all ages, with the elderly making canned goods, pies, and crafts for the prize exhibits. In the school setting it is tied in with the drama lessons in beginning skills of pantomime, sense awareness, sense recall, sense reaction, and the language arts program; they loved it! The hearing impaired can participate in the pantomime and learn language.

Every nationality playing "the fair" can guess the pantomime of each group improvisation, but they are also participating themselves in doing the imagined action—doing and saying words in the situation's context—speaking the word order pattern of an English sentence and learning that it can be written down. With all the fun that they were having, children were unaware that they had covered a chapter on writing about session memories at the fair.

This is clearly a "procedural" (muscle) memory of an event, and simultaneously a "semantic" memory, because a word meaning is learned and stored in the left side of the brain through action, first as words, then structured into a sentence, and then a story. The fair's narrative or story is told by answering the open-ended questions of the leader known as the 5Ws: Who are you? What are you doing? Where? When? and Why? When we talk or write our stories, the words evoke "episodic" memory (a personal story); at the same time, the syntax–word order (in writing) says, "I am a vendor selling and eating hot dogs at the fair one afternoon." It could be the beginning of a story, but it would have no plot. The leader can instigate the sixth W question: What can happen to cause a problem? (creative choice: a sudden storm, a lost child, a thief), and the group spontaneously galvanizes into action, improvising the play-as-we-go story, and could even add a seventh W question: What could you do to solve it? (Or, How could you solve the problem?)

LINKING MEMORY TO THE EXPERIENCE, EMOTION, AND MOTION

We can also learn by doing. The following can be used as a "warm-up" activity for whole groups to do prior to analyzing the motion/emotion storage retrieved connection.

Warm-Up: Walk as If

Walk as if sequenced for the whole group: "We are going to walk. Walk about the room and be in your own world. Just mill about without looking at anyone—no eye contact. *Freeze!*

* Walk as if you were enjoying a beautiful time of day. *Freeze!*
* Walk as if you wanted to annoy the people below you for keeping you awake partying. *Freeze!*
* Walk as if you were waiting anxiously outside the operating room door. Oh, it's been an hour! What's taking so long? *Freeze!*
* Walk as if you thought you were the greatest—nobody is your equal! *Freeze!*
* Walk as if one of your shoes is too little. *Freeze!*

Hold up the words on a card as each question is asked. When we say the word after we have performed the action and then see the word, visual learning makes this practice holistic in the brain.

	WHY	BECAUSE
Walk "as if":	WALK	Inside feeling
1. Just a nice day	STROLL	Happy
2. Want to get even with people downstairs for keeping you awake	STOMP	Angry
3. Outside the operating room	PACE	Anxious
4. You're the greatest	STRUT	Conceit
5. Your shoe is tight	LIMP	Foot hurts

When you were walking, I didn't tell you to stomp but everybody STOMPED. When did you stomp? Why? (When you wanted to get even for keeping you awake.) Why did you stomp? Because you were angry! I didn't tell you to PACE, but you were pacing. When? Where? Outside the hospital? Why? Because you were anxious, worried. I didn't tell you to STRUT, but you all strutted. When? Why? Because of your inner attitude—conceited, stuck up!

So you see your inside feelings showed on the outside with your body movement/face. That was an acting exercise! I didn't have to tell you how to walk! Your whole body remembers how you act in situations—your original feelings. Walk is an action verb, and it has synonyms. You don't just walk! There was a song,

"There's a certain walk you walk when you are feeling happy; there's a certain walk you walk when you're feeling sad." In short, emotions are the driving force behind any human movement or behavior. When you experience a real situation, your senses and muscles store a memory in your brain. Remember the brain–body connection; when you throw a real ball, muscle stores a memory; when we pretend afterward, we use imagination and our muscle memory enables us to act as if we were throwing a real ball when it's no longer present! Likewise, when you experienced a real situation, that evoked anger. That original feeling and physical reaction went through the body, through the limbic center of our brain where feelings are, and made a strong imprint that is stored in memory banks. Sensory stimulation of a similar situation triggers the memory. The imaginary situations suggested by my words as you walked caused you to retrieve the memory similarly and your entire sensory motor (muscle emotions) memory enabled you to automatically "walk as if" you were reliving the actual situation. I call your response "intuitive" acting. The words for your emotion did not even have to be spoken. In fact, the wrong way to teach acting would be to tell the child to "act mad" or make a sad face without giving a situation to trigger sense and emotion memory retrieval. We can make the student aware of the word for the emotion he or she showed and felt. Humans need to use words to express feelings; it is as important to a child's mental health (particularly in traumatized children who are motivated by play to talk and be healed) as it is to a playwright's or actor's word power.

The early training exercises of Jerry Grotowski (Carney, 1980) demand that the mind, body, and emotions be used simultaneously. Grotowski conducted research into the body–mind continuum and concluded that remembering is not a symbolic mental process but rather an experiential feeling and sensing process. For example, think back to the times you have caught yourself holding your breath when afraid. Or remember driving through the woods at night and glimpsing an animal frozen with fear in the glare of your headlights. Freezing, holding the breath, "butterflies in the stomach," and "pains in the neck" are all ways in which we come to recognize the feeling states in our lives. Just as we feel our feelings in our bodies as we experience our life, so it seems our bodies retain the feelings; that is, the memories of other times that rush in when once again the breath is held, the body freezes, or the queasy stomach returns. Grotowski believed that all of the senses, images, and feelings of our lives live on in the muscular holding.

Medical doctors also remind us that our mental states, our minds, can make our bodies sick. Some illnesses can be "psychosomatic." We also know now that putting on a "happy face" and walking "as if" you feel great releases good serotonin chemicals. Conversely, when you walk "as if" you feel terrible you talk with your mouth down and you actually feel worse. Your thoughts can control your actions. Russian neuroscientists were the first to study Stanislovsky, who invented the term "psychoneuroimmunology" (Moore, 1960).

In teaching the actor to study human behavior and "act as if" his character were happy-go-lucky, the actor has to "act as if" he were in the mood of the person, even if the actor had just suffered the loss of a sweetheart or a loved one. You cannot really change your feeling, but you can change your thoughts, which can change the way you walk, the pace of your actions. We move as if we were happy or angry—we think *as if.* It will actually help your immune system to fool the chemicals in your brain, by acting and talking happily. Our chemistry does not need a "pepper up" (medicine)! When we improvise it is fun! Laughter releases the feeling of being high. Nowhere is laughter and stirring up good sense memories more sorely needed than in the classroom. So, in response to Pribram's work, we need to experience something to show the holistic nature of guided imaginative play and the hologram—light waves and interference in the brain.

TEACHING IMAGINATIVE PLAY SKILLS

My adult workshops usually begin by having the participants understand the holistic nature of the domain of drama. I proceed to help adults rediscover their dramatic imagination and them teach how to teach parents the imaginative play skills. But before analyzing what skills are involved in this multipurpose tool of drama, adults stand to show that one cannot do drama without involving the whole person.

Warm-Up

(Pantomime to recorded jazz pianist: "Let's play like we're playing a piano.") First we are going to do something and then analyze what was happening. I want you to get in touch with your imagination and your body. What I want you to do is stand in a close circle. Make sure you are in touching distance to the person on the right and to the person on the left. How many of you have ever played the piano? How many have seen someone play? You might have had a secret ambition all of your life to have been a great piano player. So now here is your chance! There is a piano in front of you. (Turn tape recorder on.) Alright, begin playing the piano with me. You are playing beautifully! Now play it high in the air . . . play it low to the ground . . . turn to your right and play it on your neighbor's back . . . down his arms . . . play on his head . . . now turn to your left and play on his back . . . it feels so good between your shoulders . . . play down his arm . . . on his head . . . now turn to the front and play your piano. That activity get your cardiovascular circulation going? Did your blood give your brain oxygen to catch your breath.

Hot Potato

Now, let's try another game called "Pass It On." I am going to pass something to you and you pass it on to the next person. Copy what I do and say. (Pass quickly to person on the right.) Each person says, "Hot Potato" . . . hotter and hotter and hotter around until you have completed the circle. When it returns to the leader, don't take it back. Pretend to look at the dropped potato on the ground and in surprise say, "I told you it was hot!" Now sit down and analyze what happened.

I have the prepared word cards ready to place on the prepared poster. It is better to do, analyze, and play a card on this chart as you go. But my overhead transparency will do if you cannot prepare charts and cards as a kit for presentations to different groups. Also, I have ready the transparency sketch of the brain to analyze hemispheres (see Figure 40.1).

Adult Guides Symbolic Dramatic Play

Well, you didn't have a piano to play, or a real potato. What did you have to use? (All say "imagination.")

I was hoping you would say that. (Teacher places the word "imagination" on the right under "creative thinking skills.")

And did you know what we call it when you pretend to do something without an object and without words? (Most say "pantomime.")

Yes, "pantomime, body movement." (Place in the center spot.) But was there any language? Yes, as you were "playing" piano. I was speaking words and you were listening, concentrating, translating my words into movement! We were communicating through language. (Place "language" word on left [receptive language], under "communication skills.")

When we did our Hot Potato Game, we were using our whole brain–body connection. If we could look at brain scan (picture of what is going on inside the brain), it would show action going on in every area of the brain—neural synapses firing off all over triggered by my words and our interaction. Since we were also enjoying the laughter, your brain picture should be crackling, sparking all over like fireworks!

The Tree

Close your eyes and think of a tree. When I clap my hands, turn into a *tree*! (Clap.) You are all different—What kind of a tree are you? When I asked the children to grow from a tiny seed—taller and taller, and then asked each one what kind of a tree each one answered with: pine tree, boxwood, weeping willow, or an "orange juice tree." See the branches? You had to use your outside self-body action to make those trees. This is how you looked. To show the memory of a tree you see inside your mind's eye. You can show on the outside, but when you imagine your brain uses these inside-your-brain trees—called dendrites! You have a tree growing inside your head! But when I look at all of your trees together, you look like a forest and you have more than one dendrite tree inside your brain. Let's look! You could be a dendrite tree! But actually inside your brain is a whole forest of dendrites, excited, connected with each other—the more you use your imagination the branches get thicker and thicker in the forest of trees in your mind—the right side of your head is imagination and they get thinner and thinner if they are not nourished by imagination exercises.

Not training adults to exercise those neural pathways is keeping the brains of many in darkness. Whole forests of dendrites are dying out from lack of use. Only the branches traveled on are nourished and flourish. I see the right side of the brain of the "imagination dendrites" unfed. That whole inner world of the brain—the arts and sciences, communication skills—is processed first from right brain body actions (panto-

Figure 40.1
Dendrite Tree

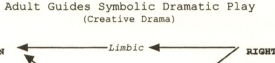

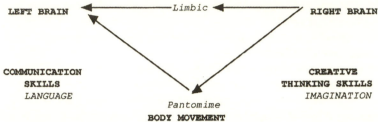

mime pretending) to cross the middle brain bridge to achieve the left brain verbal. This is the Royal Path to learning all "intelligences" (not just I.Q.): verbal, creative, rational, emotional, moral, social. The dramatic education is holistic.

Immediately, when my brain tells your brain to turn into trees, I see a whole forest of trees in action in your bodies! You receive my words through your ears and visualize trees (sense memory, recall), then it immediately triggers the amygdala and sends words almost simultaneously to travel through your motor cortex and you move all muscles. Likewise, Pribram chose the metaphor of a piano to explain what was going on in the brain when the input causes the vibrations of strings—the wave oscillations. I chose the piano as an exercise in the imagination to analyze what was gong on inside the mind and asked the group to "play like" (pantomime as if) they were playing a piano to the sound of a tape-recorded real piano.

It is interesting now to analyze what the scientist said was going on in the brain when my objective was to analyze what was going on in the mind simultaneously in this imagination exercise. My objective was to have the participants do the experiencing, to analyze the holistic effect in the interaction of my words and their whole body—brain—mind—the sensory motor effect of the input of the sound of my words and the sound of a piano (that was not present). The motor cortex involved in the right brain imagination exercises in pantomime, sending words and body movement to the left hemisphere of language. As Pribram explains this pathway in the brain, in describing brain I showed how the input of a teacher of "let's play like" (make believe drama) involves the motor cortex in the brain's right and left hemispheres through midbrain (limbic system to frontal lobe and back).

IMPORTANCE OF THIS SEQUENCE

We can summarize a few points. Begin by reminding the students that they were using skills of imagination and communication: nonverbal/verbal in the way they shake hands with a warm grip. Eye contact is important. (Poor self-concept people can't.) But for any student groups, laughter is what I'm after.

Did you see how much laughter and enjoyment there was in our interaction with each other? This is a key element, in all my creative play exercises, this wonderful gift we call laughter! Victor Borge said, "Laughter is the shortest distance between two people." When we can laugh together, we know there is a healing power of laughter. Norman Cousins (1981) found that laughter helps the body produce endorphins, a substance two hundred times more powerful than morphine; when they are released into your brain, these chemicals can even deaden pain, and elevate moods. He theorizes that laughter joggles the internal skeleton muscles, but whether or not it does that, my point is that we are born with the inner capacity to play. Unfortunately, adults do not do this kind of play. For this reason, I think it is good to get in touch with the child in us and have fun.

These sample dramatic activities foster laughter because of the creativity that comes out of you, and laughter comes when we interact and share with each other. The skills involved are basic to learning and play is learning and healing, too. You could be a recreational drama therapist. But you can also be a teacher of communication skills and language in drama.

When you pantomime without words—or say the word as you do the action—like Hot Potato, any non-English-speaking student could understand that something is hot. We can teach ESL through our use of pantomime as a skill for the child (actor) to develop. Pantomime is God's gift to mankind, man's first step in communicating universal feelings. That may be why Charlie Chaplin's silent movies are used with many immigrants (Robinson, 1985). In this relaxed atmosphere we can reawaken in ourselves something that is neglected in schools and society. Our dramatic imagination in action is fun and develops basic communication and social skills for group living, bonding or "theatre ensemble" when we begin group improvisations. The whole person learns and retains the memory.

In Pribram's (1986) presentation on distributive memory and perception, he talked of statistics that are made. We showed how we developed the teaching practices to teach awareness of sensory motor and communication skills needed in the domain of drama for imaginative play in the genetically programmed brain (Wilkinson, 1993). But when we examine education statistics on learning and retaining through the senses we find that they only note statistics on the five senses, leaving out the kinesthetic sense (movement) and omitting both motion memory and motion. They do show that we retain 90 percent of the things we say as we do, which also means pretend play (muscle memory). By omitting the guided imaginative play skills, we are failing to teach the way that the brain learns. With the joy of play, we reflect, "Tell me and I'll forget. Show me, and I may not remember. Involve me, and I'll understand." What adults forget is the play power of the imagination in action—which we omit—perhaps because we don't classify it as one of the senses—but a creative thinking skill "as if"—the dendrites that shrivel without use.

BIBLIOGRAPHY

Anderson, Dale L. (1995). *Act Now! Successful Acting Techniques You Can Use Every Day to Dramatically Improve Health, Wealth, and Relationships*. Minneapolis: Chronimed.

AP Wire Service. (2000, January 3). Memory and Brain Discoveries. *Post Courier* (Charleston, SC), p. 10.

Breggin, P. (1994). *Toxic Psychiatry*. New York: St. Martin's Press.

Carney, K. (1980). *Grotowsky Method*. New York: American Theater Association Convention.

Cousins, N. (1981). *Human Options: An Autobiographical Notebook*. New York: Norton.

Eccles, J. (1989). *Evolution of the Brain: Creation of the Self*. London: Routledge.

Gehring, W. D. (1983). *Charlie Chaplin: A Bio-Bibliography*. Westport, CT: Greenwood Press.

Leith, E., & Upatnieks, J. (1965). Photography by Lazu. *Scientific American* 212: 24–35.

Martin, A., J. V. Haxby, F. M. Lalonde, & L. G. Ungerleider. (1995). Discrete Cortical Regions Associated with Knowledge of Color and Knowledge of Action. *Science* 270: 102–105.

Moore, S. (1960). *The Stanislovski System*. New York: Viking Press.

Pribram, K. (1986). Brain and Meaning. Paper presented at the Drama as Meaning Maker, Children's Theatre Symposium, Rutgers University, New Brunswick, NJ.

Restak, R. (1979). *The Brain*. New York: Warner Books.

Robinson, D. (1985). *Chaplin: His Life and Art*. New York: McGraw-Hill.

Weidman, N. M. (1999). *Constructing Scientific Psychology: Karl Lashley's Mind–Brain Debates*. Melbourne, Australia: Cambridge University Press.

Wilkinson, J. A., & E. Rike. (1993). *The Symbolic Dramatic Play–Literacy Connection: Whole Brain, Whole Body, Holistic Learning*. Needham Heights, MA: Ginn Press.

41

Play and the Brain in Comparative Perspective

Gordon M. Burghardt

Play is an important aspect of neurobehavioral development, but we do not really know why. Play is related to brain activity, but we do not really know how. Play is commonly observed in many species in addition to *Homo sapiens*, but we do not know how many and which ones. To make matters worse, there is even disagreement on what play is and the relationships of motoric or behavioral play with mental play (fantasy, imagination, cognitive rehearsal). In actuality, our ignorance about the causation, ontogeny, evolution, and function of play is great, and a true science of play will strive to gain answers to all these issues and more. From an ethological or naturalistic perspective, the tendency to ignore the biological and evolutionary roots of play in most recent texts on play in children is as constraining as the tendency for those studying play in nonhuman animals to ignore the rich literature on child play. Therefore, the following presents criteria for reorganizing play that lessens the ambiguities in earlier definitions and attempts to cover accepted examples of play in human and nonhuman species.

WHAT IS PLAY?

Although this may seem obvious when applied to children, it is not a trivial question. Parents, teachers, and day-care workers often confuse play with the "real thing," as in the common plaint of children that "I was only playing." This can apply to both rough and tumble wrestling or sociodramatic play with politically suspect props (toy gun) or words. The following criteria are not meant to solve all the problems in recognizing play, as play raises issues of intentionally and even theory of mind, but was initially directed to trying to incorporate all the major kinds of *be-havioral* play seen in diverse species, from fish and lizards to birds and mammals.

In the approach suggested here, all of the following five criteria must be met in at least one respect before the play label is appropriate. These criteria are based on the literature from both human and nonhuman species. The goal was to provide criteria for play that could accommodate those approaching behavioral phenomena from different methodological and conceptual orientations (physiological, cognitive, sociological, developmental, ethological, etc.).

The first criterion for recognizing play is that the performance of the behavior is not fully functional in the form or context in which it is expressed; that is, it includes elements, or is directed toward stimuli, that do not contribute to current survival. The critical term is "not completely functional," instead of "purposeless," nonadaptive, or having a "delayed benefit." This recognizes that play may have an important current utility while not being focused directly on survival, such as eating or fighting.

The second criterion for recognizing play is that the behavior is spontaneous, voluntary, intentional, pleasurable, rewarding, or autotelic ("done for its own sake"). Here only one term of these often overlapping concepts need apply. Note that this criterion also accommodates any subjective or emotional concomitants of play (having fun, enjoyable), but does not make this essential for recognizing play.

The third criterion for recognizing play is that it differs from the "serious" performance of ethotypic behavior in at least one respect: incompletion (generally through inhibited or dropped final elements), exaggeration, awkwardness, preciousness, or involvement with signals, role reversals, or other behavior patterns with modified form, sequencing, or targeting. This criterion acknowledges, but does not require, that play may be found only in juveniles. The common element to these items is that there is a structural or temporal difference from the serious version.

The fourth criterion for recognizing play is that it be repeatedly observed during at least a portion of an animal's life. This criterion might seem a bit counterintuitive, since that apparent freedom, flexibility, and versatility of play have been so often noted, especially in discussions of play in children. However, repetition is found in all play and games in both human and nonhuman animals. This criterion also distinguishes transient responses to novel stimuli or environments from the play actions that may follow such initial exploratory behavior.

The fifth criterion for recognizing play is that it is initiated only when an animal is adequately fed, healthy, and free from stress (e.g., predator threat, harsh microclimate, crowding, social instability), or intense competing motivations (e.g., feeding, mating, resource competition, nest building): In other words, the animal or child is in a "relaxed field" or feels psychologically "safe." This contextual criterion appears essential for the occurrence of play, as play is one of the first types of behavior to drop out when animals, including children, are hungry, threatened, mistreated, or exposed to nasty weather.

While these criteria do not provide a crisp, one-line definition, they do seem to cover every accepted behavioral example of play and to exclude, with consistent reasoning, much that is problematic and controversial. Play is not limited to social behavior, or juvenile behavior, or behavior that involves special signals. It excludes stereotyped, abnormal behavior as well as exploration (some authors include play as a form of exploration, but then they have to subdivide exploration, creating terminological confusion). Although most behavior called play is vigorous and energetic from a human perspective, this also is not required. Certainly, much child play can be quiet and slow paced. In applying the individual criteria, the apparent fuzziness of the boundaries in some cases reflects the fact that various features of play and nonplay lie on a continuum. Nonetheless, if all of these criteria are met, the behavior deserves to be called play for the purpose of subsequent analysis. Note that the five criteria make no assumptions about the function of play. Incorporating a function or aim of play in criteria for recognizing play makes play hostage to often empirically unproven, even unprovable, evidence. Note also that social interactions may be playful from one participant's perspective but not the other, as in teasing.

Keeping in mind the nuances underlying each word, a one-sentence definition could then read as follows: Play is repeated incompletely functional behavior differing from more functional versions structurally, contextually, or ontogenetically, and initiated voluntarily when the animal is in a relaxed or unstressed setting. All child play should fit these criteria. Note that if a child is forced to play, then for that child the activity is no play. This might be important to keep in mind, as highly structured activities increasingly replace the "messiness" of free play in so many settings.

Obviously, certain kinds of play will possess many more attributes than these, but these criteria are meant to include incipient playfulness as well as well-developed games, pretend play, and so on. Play also can be partitioned into *primary process play*, which may not be functional but is the outcome of, for example, excess energy or boredom (fidgeting), and *secondary process play*, which is more organized and may have some derived function, such as acquisition of social knowledge or cognitive or physiological development (Burghardt, 1998b, 2001). This helps to explain the paradoxical nature of play, in which some critics dismiss play as a distraction or waste of time while others see play as essential for social and cognitive development. Nonetheless, to assume that play has certain benefits on the basis of theory centered more on hope than on evidence has for too long permeated the literature on play in both child development and ethology. Sutton-Smith (1997) has pointed out that the progressivist view of play is only one of several rhetorics of play found in the social sciences and humanities.

SURPLUS RESOURCE THEORY

Surplus resource theory is focused on the origins of primary process play as well as the conditions in which secondary process play will flourish. The original impetus for studying play was to try to understand why many mammals, but virtually no nonavian (ectothermic) reptiles, are considered playful. Four main factors are involved: (1) Metabolic energy (both energy stores and the capacity for sustained vigorous activity), (2) buffering from serious stress and food shortages (as when young animals are well cared for by parents), (3) the need for enhanced stimulation for an "optimal" level of arousal or stimulation for physiological functioning (susceptibility to boredom), and (4) a lifestyle that involves diverse and unpredictable environmental and/or social resources (generalist species should play more than those with more rigid specialized behavioral repertoires). Play in all species, then, including children, will be most prevalent when there are excess resources along with appropriate evolved motivational, physiological, and ecological systems. Child and adult human play are most prevalent and developed when children or (some) adults have the time to expend in less than essential activities (e.g., those needed for immediate survival). The most creative societies appear to have been those with sufficient resources to offer at least a subset of the population with free time.

SRT combines elements of the surplus energy theory popularized by Spencer (1872) and the recapitulation theory of play popularized by G. Stanley Hall (1904). These theories dealt with primary processes in play, along with the derived (secondary) functions of play that most researchers contend are the major reasons for play. In brief, the surplus energy theory held that play occurred when well-fed "higher" animals had an excess of energy and needed to "blow it off" through vigorous activity. The recapitulation view held that juvenile play, which resembled adult "serious" behavior, was a necessary biological developmental process that animals, including people, went through, recapitulating behavior patterns once necessary for survival in earlier times. The practice theory, most vigorously popularized by Groos (1898, 1901), held that play was important solely as a means to perfect adult behavior in species with long periods of immaturity and extensive parental care. The more common view today that play is essential for enhanced cognitive and social abilities and flexibility derives from the practice view.

The tendency of most early and even some current writers on play to confuse proximate mechanisms and adaptive value led to much needless controversy, especially to a neglect of the former (Burghardt, 1984). Play can thus be viewed as both a product and cause of evolutionary change; that is, playful activities may be a source of enhanced behavioral and mental functioning, as well as a by-product or remnant or prior evolutionary events. According to SRT it is a common but very serious error to think that play originally evolved in order to provide such advantages, and this mistake may have hindered a more accurate and scientifically supported analysis of play. It is not mere coincidence, perhaps, that the major tenets of SRT were laid down a century ago and that more recent psychoanalytic, behavioristic, cognitive, and developmental (e.g., Piagetian) approaches largely ignore the crucial issue of origins of play.

A major premise of SRT, then, is that the initial advantages of incipient playlike behavior did not involve any particular functions, such as perfecting later behavior, increasing endurance, or facilitating behavioral flexibility. Play is paradoxical in that it can indeed, as Puritans and educational traditionalists argue, be wasteful, dangerous, inefficient, and even morally suspect (gambling, ballroom dancing). A balanced perspective on play is necessary before it can be effectively used for socially and cognitively positive ends. From an evolutionary perspective, play can evolve independently whenever physiological (including neural), life history, metabolic, ecological, and psychological conditions, in conjunction with a species' behavioral repertoire, reach a threshold level. Play then appears, and its fate depends on its consequences in the lives of animals. In mammals, however, play may have been both a cause and consequence of the evolving disparity between periods of juvenile dependence and adult responsibilities. More specifically, according to the model advanced here, the advent of parental care led to the deterioration of some neonatal response systems ("instincts") through less precise functional motor patterns, the lowering of stimulus thresholds, and the broadening of effective stimuli. In this way, new response patterns could arise that would themselves be retained by natural selection if they had an advantage over animals with different modes of response. Such reorganized developmental processes involving incipient play may well have had to be exploited by mammals for continued survival by replacing lost, suppressed, or maturationally delayed response systems. For example, if natural selection is continually honing predatory skills so that less successful juvenile predators starve or are otherwise less fit compared to more skilled predators, then, once selection is removed, the mechanisms for capturing prey should become less precise. This removal of selection on the original role of such behaviors provided an opportunity for selection on different aspects of behavioral phenotypes. These ideas can be applied to various childhood play types, from construction play to language games to chase games to games of skill and chance.

Today we know that the phenotypic expression of behavior patterns is a complex epigenetic outcome of interactions and feedback occurring at many levels, from gene allele to protein synthesis (gene expression) to behavioral practice to social experience. Selection can operate on all of these levels and more, at least indirectly. If so, play may have a subtle, yet profound, role in behavioral ontogeny and phylogeny that we are only beginning to appreciate.

One influential approach to the developmental emergence of play is Piagetian and neo-Piagetian developmental research in children and nonhuman primates (Parker & McKinney, 1999), where much though not all research finds that four periods of cognitive development (sensorimotor, preoperations, concrete operations, and formal operations) build on one another sequentially, as do several stages within each period. Play, as characterized earlier, is an integral important component in cognitive development (Piaget, 1962). For example, the sensorimotor intelligence series involves a sequence of stages, including circular and secondary circular reactions. The latter include repeated actions on the environment, such as repeatedly striking a mobile or shaking a rattle. These are found in many species. In this approach, pretend play does not occur until the symbolic preoperations subperiod. Work on other primates, including monkeys and apes, shows that they go through a similar set of stages, although humans go through them more quickly relative to ontogenetic maturation and reach higher levels. This model is overtly recapitulationist (Parker & McKinney, 1999) and thus recalls the views of Hall from a century before.

THE COMPARATIVE DIVERSITY OF PLAY

Nonhuman animal play is usually divided into the categories of object play, solitary locomotor play, and social play. These are not always distinct; nonetheless, some animals, such as cats, engage in one kind of play more than another. Also, as in cats, the trajectory of play can vary such that one type of play appears at one age and others at different ages. This is, of course, also found in human play (e.g., Johnston, Christie, & Yawkey, 1999). The most current thorough review comparing nonhuman play and child play using a common framework is that of Power (2000).

Traditionally, animal play has been considered limited to mammals, being especially prominent in primates and carnivores, and a few birds, such as crows and parrots. Fagen (1981) provides a comprehensive review reflecting this position. Though open to considering play in other groups, he found little convincing evidence. In revisiting the topic (Burghardt, in press) we find that, utilizing the play criteria here, there is convincing evidence of play in turtles, lizards, diverse fishes, octopi, and even some arthropods (Burghardt, 1999, 2001). Where play is found, the conditions that SRT suggest would facilitate play are often present, such as generalist or carnivorous food habits, highly active lifestyle, complex social behavior, and relatively large body size. In any event, the comparative data show that playfulness did not arise late in verytebrate evolution, but has repeatedly evolved throughout animal evolution dating back to the invertebrate–vertebrate split and before, perhaps over a billion years! Thus, play must be looked at in an evolutionary context to fully understand its dynamics and functional significance.

PLAY AND THE BRAIN

Play may be very important in brain and cognitive/social development. If so, this is almost certainly a highly derived process. There are many studies and reviews of the roles of various brain parts and neurochemicals in play. Since play is a protean concept, it is certain that play can involve many neural systems; any claims to find the "real" neural seat or neural function of play should be viewed with skepticism. Furthermore, most research on the role of the brain in play is based on play fighting in rats, a narrow slice of play, and species diversity. Nonetheless, many tentative statements can be made with some support.

With the limitations of such taxonomic and play-type bias acknowledged, as well as interpretive problems in localizing brain function, it is possible to begin to answer some of the questions about the neural substrates of play. Most of the evidence implicates the forebrain, particularly the telencephlan. In the diencephalon, some hypothalamic lesions that disrupt sexual and aggressive behavior (e.g., medial preoptic) did not affect play at all, whereas other hypothalamic areas (e.g., ventromedial) decreased play initiation and maintenance, perhaps due to increased aggression (Panksepp, Siviy, & Normansell, 1984; Vanderschuren, Niesink, & Van Ree, 1997). Thalamic lesions interfacing with somatosensory transmission disrupt play bouts (e.g., reducing pinning) but not play initiation. Immediately it is seen that even in the play fighting of a single species, neural control may be complex and stage (initiation, engagement) specific.

Various neural (brain and neurochemical) substrates and their possible neural connections to play lead to predictions that can be tested with lesion, stimulation, and brain-imaging studies. However, the larger message might be that many parts of the nervous system are involved, varying across play types and among aspects of a given type of play. For example, the motor systems underlying play may be more fixed than the perceptual and contextual aspects of play. While the motor patterns used in play may become refined, the integration of sensory and motor systems may be more heavily affected due to the unpredictable consequences of interacting with objects, social partners, and even one's own body (Spinka, Newberry, & Bekoff, 2001). These aspects of play are shared with other behavioral systems, of course, but play may exaggerate, push, or refine other developmental systems.

The basal ganglia or striatopallidal complex is composed of the dorsal and ventral striatum and pallidum and include such structures as the caudate nucleus, putamen, globus pallidus, nucleus accumbens, olfactory tubercle, and substantia innominata. Basil ganglia lesions interfere with motor patterning, including play fighting in rats, where the nucleus accumbens and caudate putamen seem particularly involved in social play. Exploratory and appetitive "seeking" behavior are also influenced by the basal ganglia. While exploration is not itself play when applying all five criteria, it shares some similarities with play, especially early in ontogeny, and could well be an essential precursor of play. In humans, brain-imaging studies have shown that the ventral striatum responds to novel information, such as subtle visual sequence changes, and that this process occurs without awareness. Changes in neuronal firing in the sensorimotor (caudal) striatum can occur during learning and habit information. Dysfunctions of basal ganglia systems are indicated when organisms have difficulty either initiating or stopping actions, or in switching from one behavioral sequence to another.

The limbic system is composed of the hippocampus, dentate gyrus, subicular and entorhinal cortices, cingulate gyrus, amygdala, and septum, but is also involved with the striatum and diencephalon (thalamus and hypothalamus). The limbic system is associated with emotional responses more positive than the rage and fear associated with the striatopallidal complex and may modulate the latter. In fact, the limbic system seems involved with addictions, and it would be important to find out if play addictions (e.g., gambling) have neural correlates similar to chemical dependencies. Social play seems to depend on the limbic system in that affiliation is required for the physical contact and "bonding" seen among play partners. This affiliation depends on the amygdala and cingulate gyrus in both rodents and primates (Pellis & Pellis, 1998a).

Play is marked by sequences of behavior derived from the normal behavioral repertoire of the species. Graybiel (1995) concluded that the basal ganglia and limbic system act as a goal-attainment system, with the former responsible for the establishment and execution of motor patterns and the latter with the recognition of goals and evaluation of behavioral outcomes. This may be the basis for the linkage of cognitive systems with motoric play systems, as discussed later. In short, the basal ganglia and limbic system are tightly interconnected in mammals, and thus tie the motivation and emotion regions of the brain with both effector systems and more cognitive neocortical (e.g., prefrontal cortex) processing.

Learning that takes place through locomotor and object play might be consolidated in the hippocampus, as there is increasing evidence that the hippocampus is involved in spatial learning as well as affective responses. In fact, mice raised in enriched environments with many objects with which to interact had 15 percent more neurons in the dentate gyrus than controls and showed better spatial learning in a water maze (Kempermann, Kuhn, & Gage, 1997). In rats, enriched environments lead to similar improvements on the same task as well as greater levels of nerve growth factor (involved in dendrite formation) in the hippocampus (Pham, Söderström, Winblad, & Mohammed, 1999). Thus, a derived process for object and locomotor play may be increased neuron growth, which can then be deployed for enhanced learning in other settings that may not involve play at all. This may help explain why the search for direct functions of play has proven so difficult.

Similar convergences in the neural substrates of play systems almost certainly exist. For example, the prefrontal cortex might be particularly important in the motor performance of voluntary activity generated in the basal ganglia and limbic system, as well as involved in spatial working memory (Beiser & Houk, 1998; Halgren & Marinkovic, 1995). Activity in the prefrontal cortex may also be inhibited by stress.

The most complex neural expressions of behavioral and cognitive plasticity is found in the neocortex, but even here motor and perceptual processes are heavily represented. In mammals the dorsal pallium becomes expanded and becomes the most voluminous part of the brain in many species. Kolb and Whishaw (1998) provide a comprehensive review of brain plasticity and document that living in enriched environments may lead to significant gains in both brain weight and number of neurons and synapses. Taken all together, the evidence makes a strong case for a relationship between brain plasticity and behavioral change. Can play be responsible for much of this change?

Interestingly, play fighting in rats is not dependent on having a cortex, as studies of decorticate rodents have repeatedly shown complex play fighting in these animals. This shows that the elements of social play have ancient roots in the forebrain; interestingly, sexual, feeding, and aggressive behavior patterns are also shown by decorticate rats. However, decorticate rats do show abnormal sexual behavior as adults, and these deficiencies are similar to those found in rats raised in isolation as juveniles and thus deprived of opportunities for social play. These findings suggest that social play as juveniles may refine adult behavior, although it does not shape it. A social play bout has both offensive and defensive moves and feints that are frequently very quick (Pellis & Pellis, 1998b). As noted in the preceding section, experiences involving object play can significantly increase neuron density in areas other than the neocortex.

Although most research has involved the role of the forebrain in play, the cerebellum, forming the roof of the hindbrain, may also be an important region. Recent research has expanded its traditional role in balance and orientation to being a major vertebrate brain site for the control of motor learning and accurate precise movements, including the tracking of both external moving objects and the animal's own movements (Bell, Cordo, & Harnad, 1996; Paulin, 1993). The cerebellar cortex is well suited for the task of incorporating patterned behavioral organization into motor and learning systems in the brain (Houk, Buckingham, & Barto, 1996).

The role of the cerebellum in play ontogeny has been a subject of recent theory. In a review of the functions of play, especially the exercise or "getting in shape" theories, Byers and Walker (1995) point out that none of sixteen different physiological exercise effects posited for play, such as increased oxygen-carrying capacity in the blood, increased blood volume, and increased endurance, have permanent effects. Once a long-distance runner shifts to the couch, one can't keep the fitness accrued by prior exercise in the bank, let alone amass interest! By looking at the ages when play peaks in three domestic species (mice, rats, and cats), Byers and Walker found that these play peaks coincided closely with the ages that apparently permanent experience-dependent synaptic development occurred in the cerebellum. Although this correlation is based on a small sample size, the idea that play is associated with a sensitive period for neural integration is an important one (Byers, 1998). It might underlie the drive to engage in play even by socially isolated animals. A recent study with limited social play deprivation in rats found a decrement in amount of social interaction in adulthood when rats were not able to play during a period comparable to the period that Byers and Walker (1995) argue is the critical period for cerebellar synapse formation (van den Berg et al., 1999). Certainly the cerebellum is involved in play activities and may also be involved in the refining of movements performed in play. Nonetheless, although the relationship of play with degree of cerebellar development is intriguing, there are some questions. One is that different kinds of play (social, object, locomotor) wax and wane at different times. Second, changes in many other parts of the brain may also be taking place at the same time rapid cerebellar changes are occurring, and it is most likely that play, being such a diverse phenomenon, may be involved in brain development over many parts of the nervous system. The evidence reviewed here on extensive cortical development due to enrichment suggests that rather permanent changes in synapse connections might be occurring in other brain areas.

In conclusion, the neural circuits specifically involved in any type of play are still little known and there is no definitive evidence for neural circuits limited to play (Panskepp, 1998). There is now need for brain-imaging studies to localize patterns of brain activity accompanying play and related phenomena, although doing so without immobilization is not yet possible.

We can conclude that the basal ganglia, ventral tegmental area, prefrontal cortex, and dopamine systems seem especially involved in reward, anticipation, memory, and goal orientation observed in the often fast-paced, contextually sensitive, and anticipatory responses (Pellis & Pellis, 1998) of locomotor, object, and social play. However, these systems are also involved in many nonplay activities, suggesting that the pathways involved may overlap, converge, or reinforce a variety of behavior systems, including addictions and repetitive compulsive behavior. The hypothesis that play originated in the initiation and execution of instinctive behavior sequences in which motor performance was itself rewarding and through which repeated performance could enhance performance through practice in changing contexts and experience-based modifications of sequences is plausible. The difficulty in isolating specific long-term benefits through play may be due to the fact that play may be only one of several ways to enhance behavioral and cognitive performance; a facilitator not essential in every case. Play may be the preferred method if animals are in good conditions characterizing the "relaxed field" criterion, but relying just on this easily inhibited activity would not be adaptive: Play as a more incremental system to enhance behavior might be more readily evolved. Nevertheless, although the exact neural systems involved in behavior and learning are still only imperfectly understood, play as characterized here may be a key concept in integrating the often narrowly focused neuroscience research with the development and evolution of behavior and the landmarks of higher mental performance.

FROM PLAYFUL ACTION TO IMAGINATION

In people, including children, play fighting and rough and tumble play are little studied. With the exception of organized sports, this is actually true of physical activity play in general (Pellegrini & Smith, 1998). Outside of the movements (e.g., circular reactions) of infants, the literature on human play generally focuses on sociodramatic play, pretend play, imaginary play, verbal play, creativity, and fantasy (Burghardt, 1999), which may all be summarized as mental play. The putative importance of these kinds of play for cognitive and social–emotional development is emphasized by postulating internal processes that are indirectly measured through behavioral output such as artistic production, building block structures, role playing, ability at board games, and so on. These types of play are favored and encouraged because they are thought to enhance cognitive ability and social–emotional skills (Johnston et al., 1999). The neglect of physical "free" play as valuable for children is shown by the reduction in recess time in elementary schools in the United States.

If evolutionary origins and ontogenetic precursors of "mental play" are in active motor play, then the neglect of active motor play in preschool through elementary grades might actually impair some areas of cognitive and social performance of children and adults. Pellegrini and Smith (1998) argue for a continuity of physical play from the rhythmic stereotypes of infants (aids in control of specific movements) to exercise play (which may have some incidental cognitive benefits) to rough and tumble play (learning of social dominance roles). These are immediate rather than deferred benefits.

It has been difficult to show with animals that the skills or enhanced physical condition derived through motor play can only be accomplished by physical activity in play (Burghardt, 1984). Play, as a product of surplus resources, may be, in terms of physical conditions and prowess, only one of several means to this end. As shown, the endogenous motivational and emotional concomitants of play (criterion 2) might serve as mechanisms to stimulate activity in animals, including humans. Perhaps much motoric play is more important for cognitive and emotional development than it is for motor development; if so, we need to examine the relationship between physical and mental play by searching for neurological connections between the two processes.

Play involves activity with the self, objects, other species of animals, and especially conspecifics. Prominent features of vigorous play activities include feints, exaggerated movements, and other actions critical to predicting and anticipating actions of objects or other organisms. Visual–motor integration may be heavily involved, although, of course, other sensory systems may be at play as well. Can these aspects of play be linked in any way to imagination?

A body of work is accumulating on the relations among motoric acts, mental imagery, and the brain. Circuits in the basal ganglia are involved in both motor learning and cognitive behavior, suggesting that the links between motor performance and cognitive processes are either very ancient or slight modifications from ancestral vertebrate systems (Katz & Harris-Warrick, 1999). Striatal projection neurons depend on afferent and loop circuits in both neocortex, especially premotor, parietal, and prefrontal cortex, and the thalamus.

Particularly intriguing are a series of papers from an Italian research group in Parma, Italy, that suggest a mechanism whereby a more direct cognitive link may be made. Initially, this research group showed that neurons in area F5 of the premotor cortex (near the arcuate sulcus) fired when monkeys (*Macaca nemestrina*) performed a goal-directed action, such as reaching for and grasping a piece of food. However, they also showed that some of these same neurons fired when the monkeys just *observed* the experimenter doing the same thing (Gallese, Fadiga, Fogassi, & Rizzolatti, 1996). The authors termed these neurons "mirror neurons" because they mirrored what the animal itself could perform. They found several types of the neurons. Some of the neurons were specific to single actions by the monkey or the observed experimenter, such as grasping, holding, manipulating, and placing. Other mirror neurons were specific to two or three actions combined, such as grasping and placing, placing and holding, or grasping, placing, and holding. It is interesting to note that this area of the premotor cortex has been considered homologous with Broca's area in the human brain. The authors argue that such mirror neuronal systems in humans could be involved in the recognition of both actions and sounds. Further experiments showed that the mirror neurons did not fire when the observed experimenter reached for food that was not present or if he was in darkness and could not have been seen. Suggestive evidence has been gained from people also (Fadiga, Fogassi, Pavesi, & Rizzolatti, 1995). Mirror neurons might underlie imitation, and some evidence suggests that play in animals facilitates imitation of novel behavior (Miklosi, 1999).

These and other studies suggest that mental imagery, physical movements, and perception can be linked in areas of the brain even down to involvement of the same neuron (Jeannerod, 1994). Thus, "imagery is a bridge between perception and motor control" (Kosslyn & Sussman, 1995, p. 1040). This may be a common phenomenon. With accumulating evidence on the great dendritic (synaptic) changes that can rapidly occur in the brain, practice and repetition of similar but not identical behavior during play may subserve a role in the shifting mental states involved in anticipating, predicting, and controlling one's own behavior in relation to external stimuli.

These studies model how we could move from play as a motoric, active response to stimuli to active play involving pretense and make believe and eventually behavior largely divorced from physical actions, such as imagination, fantasy, creativity, and complex social assessments. These phenomena may be more closely linked than our theories suggest. Many people need to draw, sound out, or act out their ideas to "test them." Talking to oneself is commonplace; doing it soundlessly may be the essence of "thinking," which is often the rehearsal of different actions and possible outcomes. Is there any evidence for merely thinking affecting motor behavior?

Motor imagery is the process of imagining behavioral actions. When people are asked to imagine movements, the neurophysiological responses in various brain regions resemble those made when such movements are actually executed (Kosslyn & Sussman, 1995; Yágüez, Canavan, Lange, & Hömberg, 1999). This also happened with mental rotation tasks in people and in monkeys when preparing to move an arm in a specific way (Kosslyn & Sussman, 1995). When people were asked to imagine writing a letter and then actually wrote the letter, the same areas in the cerebellum, prefrontal cortex, and supplementary motor cortex were activated (Kosslyn & Sussman, 1995). Is it possible that there is a functional link between mental imagery and physical performance in that the former enhances the latter? Intriguing support is provided by the experiments of Smith, Collins, Holmes, & Layland (1998), which demonstrated that merely imagining exercise had beneficial effects on subsequent physical ability. Groups of subjects engaged in mental (imaginary) or actual physical practice of strength training of a finger, along with a no-practice control. All three groups were tested afterward on changes in the strength of their fingers. The control group did not change and the physical-practice group showed an improvement of 33 percent. What is remarkable is that the mental-practice-only group showed a significant improvement of 16 percent. We know that exercise, including that gained through play, might have at least short-term benefits physiologically. This study actually posits a physical benefit from just thinking about a specific action.

If merely imagining activity is functional and thus evolutionary adaptive, the next step is to mentally rehearse different actions. What might lead to such rehearsal? Some demand or problem facing an individual could certainly lead to the adaptive consequence of making a choice among alternative actions before making a behavioral commitment. Linking these mental rehearsals with possible outcomes is a hallmark of creativity, innovation, and social adeptness. Those organisms producing more of these mental options should then have, through natural selection, an advantage in producing more of the innovations that "take." Play can thus be involved in creativity and behavioral innovation, not just by the selecting of different behavioral options, but by selection for animals that can create such options via internal processes. Note that a criterion for play is that it be initiated when the animal is not under serious stress. Yet we know that in our own species, at least, play can itself become stressful as the social competition or difficulty of the game becomes frustrating.

Thus, we can view play and stress as fostering creativity by rewarding novel ways of accomplishing some end. It is well-known in motivational psychology that extreme arousal or stress interferes with complex problem solving as compared to rote tasks. In fact, play used as an "escape" may become not only repetitive, but obsessively so. Thus, such behavior not only ceases to be play, but is definitely not destined to be creative! Play performed under appropriate levels of arousal and complexity may facilitate a mental rehearsal mode that could be a means of fostering creativity. On the other hand, because of the diverse origins of play, much play may be repetitive and not novel for the species.

If these ideas have some merit we would expect to be able to trace the operation of brain mechanisms in a comparative fashion. Although this has not yet been done, initial studies in human adults and children seem promising (Frith & Frith, 1999). Functional magnetic resonance imaging and positron emission tomography both indicated that the medial prefrontal cortex and superior temporal sulcus are involved in interpreting the mental states (intentionality) of characters in stories or cartoons. These authors, in trying to explain the origin of such mental imagination, suggest that they arise from the following four "preexisting abilities that are relevant to mentalizing," all of which have a demonstrated neural basis (p. 1693): (1) distinguishing animate from inanimate entities, (2) following the gaze of another individual, (3) representing goal-directed actions, and (4) distinguishing actions of self from those of others.

There might indeed be similar neural involvement in motor representations and the highest cognitive abilities attributed to imagination, role-playing, fantasy, and other types of "mental" play. Moreover, dopamine may be the link among them all. Brain size is not necessarily related to play (Iwaniuk, Nelson, & Pellis, 2001). Rather, play may have secondarily provided expanded opportunities for behavioral flexibility, plasticity, and cognitive decision making through the operation of natural selection on behavior, and thus the nervous system, instigated by the evolution of parental care, endothermy, and increased metabolic rates.

The ultimate transmutation of motor activity to imaginary events may lie in dreaming. Panksepp (1998) has argued for the similarity of the play and dream systems neurologically. Interestingly, young birds may actually rehearse, refine, and learn aspects of their songs while they sleep (Dave & Margoliash, 2000; Dave, Yu, & Margoliash, 1998). Apparently, during sleep neurons in two brain areas important to song learning responded to the songs, while only one of the areas did so in birds that were awake. Much more needs to be done in this area, but this pioneering study does suggest a playlike role for the ultimate relaxed field.

CONCLUSIONS

The view of play and its origins outlined here suggests the episodic development throughout vertebrate evolution of playlike behavior under suitable ecological and physiological conditions. Using the five criteria for play, there is compelling evidence that play evolved independently in several lines of fishes, turtles, squamate reptiles, crocidilians, birds, and marsupials, as well as virtually all families of placental mammals (Burghardt, in press). Nonetheless, play is clearly most common in mammals and birds, groups with high metabolic rates, endothermy, parental care, and relatively large brains, although the specific relationships among these variables is not yet well established.

Play is derived from instinctive behavior patterns whose patterning and motivation are controlled by the basal ganglia of the telencephalon and structures in the diencephalon. The rapid rate of evolutionary changes in endothermic animals, especially mammals, in genome size, brain size, and behavioral complexity are remarkable and still misunderstood. Play may have been a major engine in this rapid cascade of evolutionary change that led to increased cognitive complexity. Such changes may occur by moving initially playful responses to more serious endeavors and functions; in this way once playful behavior has been transformed and "fixed" so that it has been transformed to being outside the realm of play using the criteria developed here. The thesis here is that after a period of evolutionary reorganization in behavioral ontogeny, accentuated by the lengthening of parental care (Burghardt, 1988), play can facilitate rapid behavioral and mental development by providing altered phenotypes for natural selection to prune and shape. Play, when combined with the need to solve a problem, may lead to novel or creative behavior. Guided imaginative play, as pioneered in the work of Elizabeth Rike, may be an especially valuable means of fostering creativity in children. This method involves the substitution of imagined objects, social partners, and contexts for the "real" ones, while still involving overt behavior. Thus, her approach formally applies ideas independently derived here from comparative and biological considerations. Nonetheless, play can also reflect deteriorated or developmentally stalled behavior, such as found in some domesticated species, such as dogs that retain juvenile behavior indefinitely (Burghardt, 1984; 1999). We need to vigorously apply our imaginations and scientific skills to understanding the connections between play and imagination.

REFERENCES

Beiser, D. G., & J. C. Houk. (1998). Model of Cortical–Basal Ganglionic Processing: Encoding the Serial Order of Sensory Events. *Journal of Neurophysiology* 79: 3168–3188.

Bell, C., P. Cordo, & S. Harnad. (1996.) Controversies in Neuroscience IV: Motor Learning and Synaptric Plasticity in the Cerebellum. *Behavioral and Brain Sciences* 19: 339–527.

Burghardt, G. M. (1984). On the Origins of Play. In P. K. Smith (Ed.), *Play in Animals and Humans* (pp. 5–41). Oxford: Basil Blackwell.

———. (1988). Precocity, Play, and the Ectotherm-Endotherm Transition: Superficial Adaptation or Profound Reorganization? In E. M. Blass (Ed.), *Handbook of Behavioral Neurobiology* (pp. 107–148). Vol. 9. New York: Plenum.

———. (1998a). The Evolutionary Origins of Play Revisited: Lessons from Turtles. In M. Beckoff & J. A. Byers (Eds.), *Animal Play: Evolutionary, Comparative, and Ecological Perspectives* (pp. 1–26). Cambridge: Cambridge University Press.

————. (1998b). Play. In G. Greenberg & M. Haraway (Eds.), *Comparative Psychology: A Handbook* (pp. 757–767). New York: Garland.

————. (1999). Conceptions of Play and the Evolution of Animal Minds. *Evolution and Cognition* 5(2): 115–123.

————. (2001). Play: Attributes and Neural Substrates. In E. M. Blass (Ed.), *Handbook of Behavioral Neurobiology*, vol. 13: *Developmental Psychobiology, Developmental Neurobiology and Behavioral Ecology: Mechanisms and Early Principles* (pp. 757–767). New York: Plenum.

————. (In press). *The Genesis of Animal Play: Testing the Limits.* Cambridge: MIT Press.

Byers, J. A. (1998). Biological Effects of Locomotor Play: Getting into Shape, or Something More Specific? In M. Berkoff & J. A. Byers (Eds.), *Animal Play: Evolutionary, Comparative, and Ecological Perspectives* (pp. 205–220). Cambridge: Cambridge University Press.

Byers, J. A., & C. Walker. (1995). Refining the Motor Training Hypothesis for the Evolution of Play. *American Naturalist* 146: 25–40.

Dave, A. S., & D. Margoliash. (2000). Song Replay during Sleep and Computational Rules for Sensorimotor Vocal Learning. *Science* 290: 812–816.

Dave, A. S., A. C. Yu, & D. Margoliash. (1998). Behavioral State Modulation of Auditory Activity in a Vocal Motor System. *Science* 282: 2250–2254.

Fadiga, L., L. Fogassi, G. Pavesi, & G. Rizzolatti. (1995). Motor Facilitation during Action Observation: A Magnetic Stimulation Study. *Journal of Neurophysiology* 73: 2608–2611.

Fagen, R. (1981). *Animal Play Behavior.* New York: Oxford University Press.

Frith, C. D., & U. Frith. (1999). Interacting Minds—A Biological Basis. *Science* 286: 1692–1695.

Gallese, V., L. Fadiga, L. Fogassi, & G. Rizzolatti. (1996). Action Recognition in the Premotor Cortex. *Brain* 119: 593–609.

Graybiel, A. M. (1995). Building Action Repertoires: Memory and Learning Functions of the Basal Ganglia. *Current Opinion in Neurobiology* 5: 711–733.

Groos, K. (1898). *The Play of Animals* (E. L. Baldwin, Trans.). New York: D. Appelton.

————. (1901). *The Play of Man* (E. L. Baldwin, Trans.). New York: D. Appleton.

Halgren, E., & K. Marinkovic. (1995). Neurophysiological Networks Integrating Human Emotions. In M. S. Gazzaniga (Ed.), *The Cognitive Neurosciences* (pp. 1137–1151). Cambridge: MIT Press.

Hall, G. S. (1904). *Adolescence: Its Psychology and Its Relations to Physiology, Anthropology, Sociology, Sex, Crime, Religion, and Education.* New York: D. Appelton.

Houk, J. C., J. T. Buckingham, & A. G. Barto. (1996). Models of the Cerebellum and Motor Learning. *Behavioral and Brain Sciences* 19: 368–383.

Iwaniuk, A. N, J. E. Nelson, & S. M. Pellis. (2001). Do Big-Brained Animals Play More? Comparative Analyses of Play and Relative Brain Size in Mammals. *Journal of Comparative Psychology* 115: 29–41.

Jeannerod, M. (1994). The Representing Brain: Neural Correlates of Motor Intention and Imagery. *Behavioral and Brain Sciences* 17: 187–245.

Johnson, J. E., J. F. Christie, & T. D. Yawkey. (1999). *Play and Early Childhood Development.* 2d ed. New York: Addison-Wesley.

Katz, P. S., & R. M. Harris-Warrick. (1999). The Evolution of Neuonal Circuits underlying Species-Specific Behavior. *Current Opinion in Neurobiology* 9: 628–633.

Kempermann, G., H. Kuhn, & F. H. Gage. (1997). More Hippocampal Neurons in Adult Mice Living in an Enriched Environment. *Nature* 386: 493–495.

Kolb, B., & I. Q. Whishaw. (1998). Brain Plasticity and Behavior. *Annual Review of Psychology* 49: 43–64.

Kosslyn, S. M., & A. L. Sussman. (1995). Role of Imagery in Perception: Or, There Is No Such Thing as Immaculate Perception. In M. S. Gazzaniga (Ed.), *The Cognitive Neurosciences* (pp. 1035–1042). Cambridge: MIT Press.

Miklosi, A. (1999). The Ethological Analysis of Imitation. *Biological Review* 74: 347–374.

Panksepp, J. (1998). *Affective Neuroscience.* New York: Oxford University Press.

Panksepp, J., S. Siviy, & L. Normansell. (1984). The Psychobiology of Play: Theoretical and Methodological Perspectives. *Neuroscience and Biobehavior Reviews* 8: 465–492.

Parker, S. T., & M. L. McKinney. (1999). *Origins of Intelligence: The Evolution of Cognitive Development in Monkeys, Apes, and Humans.* Baltimore, MD: Johns Hopkins University Press.

Paulin, M. G. (1993). The Role of the Cerebellum in Motor Control and Perception. *Brain, Behavior and Evolution* 41: 39–50.

Pellegrini, A. D., & P. K. Smith. (1998). Physical Activity Play: The Nature and Function of a Neglected Aspect of Play. *Child Development* 69: 577–598.

Pellis, S. M., & V. C. Pellis. (1998a). Play Fighting of Rats in Comparative Perspective: A Schema for Neurobehavioral Analysis. *Neuroscience and Biobehavioral Reviews* 23: 87–101.

———. (1998b). Structure–Function Interface in the Analysis of Play Fighting. In M. Bekoff & J. A. Byers (Eds.), *Animal Play: Evolutionary, Comparative, and Ecological Perspectives* (pp. 115–140). Cambridge: Cambridge University Press.

Pham, T. M., S. Söderström, B. Winblad, & A. H. Mohammed. (1999). Effects of Environmental Enrichment on Cognitive Function and Hippocampal NGF in the Non-handled Rats. *Behavioural Brain Research* 103: 63–70.

Piaget, J. (1962). *Play, Dreams and Imitation in Childhood.* New York: Norton.

Power, T. G. (2000). *Play and Exploration in Children and Animals.* Mahwah, NJ: Lawrence Erlbaum Associates.

Smith, D., D. Collins, P. Holmes, & K. Layland. (1998). The Effect of Mental Practice on Strength Performance and EMG Activity. Proceedings of the *British Psychological Society.*

Spencer, H. (1872). *Principles of Psychology* 2d ed., Vol. 2. New York: D. Appleton.

Spinka, M., R. C. Newberry, & M. Bekoff. (2001). Mammalian Play: Training for the Unexpected. *Quarterly Review of Biology* 76: 141–168.

Sutton-Smith, B. (1997). *The Ambiguity of Play.* Cambridge: Harvard University Press.

van den Berg, C. L., T. Hol, J. M. Van Ree, B. M. Spruijt, H. Everts, & J. M. Koolhaas. (1999). Play Is Indispensable for an Adequate Development of Coping with Social Challenges in the Rat. *Developmental Psychobiology* 34: 129–138.

Vanderschuren, L.J.M.J., R.J.M. Niesink, & J. M. Van Ree. (1997). The Neurobiology of Social Play Behavior in Rats. *Neuroscience and Biobehavioral Reviews* 21: 309–326.

Yágüez, L., A.G.M. Canavan, H. W. Lange, & V. Hömberg. (1999). Motor Learning by Imagery Is Differentially Affected in Parkinson's and Huntington's Diseases. *Behavioural Brain Research* 102: 115.

42

The Beast at Play: The Neuroethology of Creativity

Neil Greenberg

Creativity is the supreme behavioral adaptation of our species. An ethological approach to the causes and consequences of creativity necessarily involves several domains of biological inquiry. However, the concept has not yet enjoyed the scrutiny of ethologists, partly because an accessible definition is not available. As a first approach to this problem, creativity is defined here, which makes the phenomenon more accessible to biologists. Using this approach, creativity can be viewed as a biological trait that has likely evolved from fundamental but much less dramatic precursors, such as associative learning. Play and art represent developmental and expressive dimensions of creativity in our species and also often their fullest expression, but creative behavior is not limited to these behavioral patterns to our species.

A consideration of the role of the brain in the adaptive expression of creativity calls unexpected attention to the corpus striatum of the basal forebrain. This area is also identified by clinicians as the basal ganglia and by some neuroanatomists as the r-complex ("r" is for "reptilian"), playfully nicknamed the "beast in the brain." The structures of this area are traditionally associated with motor functions and relatively primitive stereotyped behavioral patterns. But the emerging view that the basal ganglia are also an interface among cognitive, affective, and motivational functions is calling attention to its significance to cognitive behavior and creativity. Further consideration of the origins and control of behavior patterns calls attention to the importance of the physiological responses of the organism to real or perceived stressors in its environment.

The philosopher, Eric Hoffer (1951) once said, "It is the child in man that is the source of his uniqueness and creativeness, and the playground is the optimal milieu for the unfolding of his capacities and talents." The ideal university, like the research laboratory and the artist's studio, should have much in common with the playground.

Our understanding of the development and expression of creativity will profit from the critical scrutiny of biology. Creativity can be viewed as a fundamental behavioral trait that is grounded in the basic biology of the brain. Further, it has likely evolved under the influence of the physiological stress response, originally designed to help organisms cope with challenges to their stability. As such, the capacity to recognize and deal with novelty and change are driving forces. Art can be construed as an extreme example of creativity capable of engendering insight in one's self and others. Depending on *who* those others might be, we may speak of artists with varying measures of skill, specific constituencies, or even very limited audiences—the "artist's artist." As such, art is a form of communication or a bridge linking the painter's mind with the viewer" (E. Delacroix, 1798–1863). But like all communications, it may also constitute an important bridge between different parts of an artist's mind (C. D. Lewis, 1946, wrote, "We do not write in order to be understood; we write in order to understand"). Thus, while one's creative gifts are known by the breadth or depth of their capacity to communicate, effective communications can also feed back into one's personal development. Indeed, this may be a key to the therapeutic and self-actualizing dimension of art and creative experience. In his seminal *Psychoanalytic Explorations in Art*, Ernst Kris (1952) outlined how the dual processes of primary and secondary processes of mind are put in the service of creativity and art. As communications, he noted, art serves in two ways: one in which the id communicates with the ego and one in which its processes are submitted to others (p. 61).

Creativity is central to a full understanding of both play and art. This apparently innocent assertion implies a deep continuity between these activities as well as the position that creativity is present by degrees in all humans and not a characteristic of unusual individuals with rare conjugations of highly developed abilities. The intent to view these behavioral patterns from the ethological perspective reveals a conviction that they are also present by degrees in related species. Creative activities have come to possess their present form by the kinds of processes that have guided the emergence of other adaptive traits from unexpected beginnings in their evolutionary ancestors.

CREATIVITY DEFINED

"A definition," Samuel Butler once said, "is the enclosing a wilderness of ideas within a wall of words," but as Joseph Campbell (1968) cautioned, "The best things can't be told." To bring order to the chaotic wilderness of ideas about creativity is in itself a major creative undertaking. The formidable Council of Scholars of the Library of Congress assembled when Daniel Boorstin was librarian sought to "rescue" the term "creativity," "for use in the world of ideas and culture" (Hutson, 1981). While they agreed that "innovation" was at its core, they also argued that for innovation to be creative it must be "important." The twenty-eight scholars sought to reclaim "creativity" from trivial applications, such as "preschoolers' finger painting." I am also seeking a central essence for creativity and seeking to reclaim this behavioral pattern as a suitable subject for ethology, that unique multidisciplinary field in which biology and comparative psychology collaborate in seeking to understand the causes and consequences of behavior. Creativity is a trait of living organisms and must be made amenable to the development of predictive, testable hypotheses about its underlying biological causation and control if it is to be understood.

Traditional Definitions of Creativity

Etymology can be instructive. The *Random House Dictionary of the English Language* (1987) and the *Merriam-Webster's Dictionary Online* (n.d.) identify "create" as a verb rooted in Middle English, from Latin *creatus*, past participle of *creare*, akin to Latin *crescere* to grow, also, to originate or invent, from at least the fourteenth century. In its transitive senses it means first "to cause to come into being, as something unique that would not naturally evolve or that is not made by ordinary processes"—to bring into existence, as in "God created the heaven and the earth" (Gen 1:1). It is also the cause or occasion of a phenomenon, as in "famine creates high food prices." A later definition deals with the sense most familiar to scholars: "to produce through imaginative skill," as in "create a painting; that is "to evolve from one's own thought or imagination, as a work of art or an invention," or "to cause to happen; bring about; arrange, as by intention or design"—or to design, as to "create dresses" or to create a revolution or an opportunity to, for example, ask for a raise. In its intransitive senses, it means to make or bring into existence something new. Creativity used to be regarded less as an intrinsic human capacity than as theophany, a "manifestation of a transcendent deity who inspired the work and whose glory was expressed within it" (Novitz, 1987). The influence of that perspective lingers.

Evolution: Needs and Coping, Adaptation and Fitness

To make the idea of creativity more accessible to biology, I must argue that it is an adaptive biological trait. As an adjective, "adaptative" refers to a demonstrable contribution to fitness. The great virtue of defining creativity as an evolved biological phenomenon is that the insights and methods of biology can be brought to bear in ways that can better illuminate its causes and consequences for the organisms expressing it. "Adaptationism" harnesses the common (and commonly misguided) assumption that extant traits in organisms have come about because they necessarily enhance the fitness of the organism that manifests them. It is true that enhanced fitness describes the central dimension in the selection process that results in one organism or group of organisms prevailing over another in evolutionary time, but the path by which the present condition is attained is not usually obvious and may require an understanding of environmental selective forces that no longer exist. In this sense, an adaptationist explanation is an hypothesis, a plausible rationale awaiting confirmation. The contribution of creative behavior to fitness is not necessarily obvious in many of its most extreme expressions, but extreme positions generally represent the tail end of a continuum that is manifest in a relatively small part of a population while natural selection generally occurs mainly in the larger population manifesting less extreme expressions. Unusual members of the population typically prevail in unusual times.

Creativity is a potent biological adaptation in that it catalyzes or facilitates a regulatory or advantageous change in response to a real or perceived stress by an individual or group of individuals. Characteristic of adaptive traits is their tendency to compensate for or to allow the organism to compensate for change, to preserve stability, the status quo. This fundamental conservatism of organisms was termed "Romer's Rule" by the anthropologists Hockett and Ascher (1964): "The initial survival value of a favorable innovation is conservative, in that it renders possible the maintenance of a traditional way of life in the face of changed circumstance" (p. 137). Fitness involves contributions to future generations in terms of one's own offspring (direct fitness) or those of nondescendent kin (such as siblings; indirect fitness). "Inclusive" fitness is the combination of these two kinds of contributions to the future (Hamilton, 1964). Usually the contribution is conceptualized in genetic terms, but the relentless logic of evolution requires only that information is reliably transmitted across generations, thus opening the way to conceptualize evolution in cultural terms also. In the spirit of investigating creativity as an adaptive trait, we can define it thus:

Creativity involves both the process and product of unprecedented or novel perception, thoughts, or actions by which an organism or group of organisms copes with present or potential changes in the composition and structure of its environment. In particular, it manifests an enhanced intensity of perception, cognition, and expression that occurs either spontaneously or is elicited by specific stimuli to relate and integrate variables not ordinarily associated with each other. (adapted from Greenberg, 1998)

This definition effectively incorporates and enlarges Poincaré's (1913) famous definition: "To create consists of making new combinations of associative elements which are useful" (p. 286). Creative perceptions, thoughts, or actions within individuals will associate familiar or novel stimuli in varying combinations to help that individual meet its needs, which may be of varying urgency (Maslow, 1954). Intrinsic reward systems operate to maintain this valuable activity. When these perceptions, thoughts, or actions are communicated by setting an example (modeling) or by pedagogy (teaching) to serve social needs, the creative individual is identified and acknowledged.

A key corollary of a biological approach informed by modern evolutionary theory is that many traits have come to have their adaptive function by being transformed in the evolutionary process from something else. Advantageous modifications of morphology or physiology, however slight between generations, can, when subject to natural selection, eventually lead to organs or systems so transformed as to be barely recognizable. Here evolutionary biology points out the various kinds of changes in size, shape, timing, or control of a trait that converging internal (genetic) and external (environmental) stimuli might have on its expression. We can be confident that evolutionary change has occurred when a thread of descent can be demonstrated by comparing related species. The path from a mouse's forelimb to the wing of a bat, or from the thermoregulatory feather fluffing of a sparrow to the spreading of a courting peacock's tail can be viewed as homologous—fundamentally similar even if dissimilar in function. To apply this corollary to creativity as an evolved behavioral pattern we would have to look at what it has in common with traits observed in related species that are likely precursors to the organism we are studying. When several lines of evidence converge on defending the hypothesis that a specific trait we are studying is much like one in a related species, we can be confident that evolution has occurred.

Treating creativity as a rare trait, as Martindale (1999) does in his essay "Biological Bases of Creativity," makes it more difficult to study by obscuring related traits with which it may form an evolutionary continuum. Although constructed of several common traits, the necessary conjunction of all of them in the same person is, in Martindale's view, rare. But he also employs Poincaré's famous definition of creativity, mentioned earlier, including his observation that new combinations can "reveal to us unsuspected kinships between other facts well known but wrongly believed to be strangers to one another" (Poincaré, 1913, cited by Martindale, 1999, p. 37). But the discovery or invention of new combinations is not rare, it is the essence of education. It appears to be a spontaneous process to a point, but is facilitated by the mediation of a "more knowledgeable other." Such a person, or the internalized voice of that person, leads the learner or creator to the brink of insight, no matter how modest, but only the person can actually make the connection. Many connections involve quite complex constellations of ideas that no amount of mediation can facilitate: Here is where further communications fail. As mentioned, "The best things cannot be told, the second best are misunderstood. After that comes civilized conversation" (Campbell, 1968).

Art Itself

Works of art are conspicuous expressions of creativity that are particularly effective at communicating. What is commonly called art is often more clearly identified as a "work of art," the artifact of the creative process and the principle way in which it is known. As Coomaraswamy (1956) famously put it, "The words *artifact* and *artificial* imply . . . the thing made is a work of art, made by art, but not itself art; the art remains in the artist and is the knowledge by which things are made" (1956, p. 18). Art is recognized by its capacity to communicate and thereby evoke an enlarged consciousness of some potentially relevant aspect of one's self, one's relationship to others, or one's environment. It is aesthetic because it does this by means of the senses and can also evoke more or less intense experiences of growth and change, the most extreme of which are epiphanous aesthetic experiences, transformative personal insights that can serve one's needs and perhaps enhance one's fitness.

Play and Art

Play and art, while often perceived as functionally related to each other, are also often seen as a luxury, apparently irrelevant to the urgent needs of everyday survival. In Konrad Lorenz's (1981) term, *autotelic*, meaning that they exist only for themselves, they are "self-justifying." Lorenz also saw play as a source of deep aesthetic value attributable to its economy of energy and harmony of impulses. As Gordon Burghardt (1999) points out, apparent purposelessness was long part of the most accepted definition of play. Artists who sense that complete freedom of expression is central to true creativity frequently demand respect for art for its own sake. Many view true freedom as necessarily detached from function, or at least current utility. Certainly, not all functions are obvious, or even extant—we can only speculate about the original function of many contemporary traits that were forged in an ancestral environment.

Play is generally assumed to be pleasurable. As Winner (1982) points out, Sigmund Freud believed that pleasures are never abandoned, they are replaced by other pleasures. In normal adults, Freud believed, daydreams replaced play, but in artists, apparently, play was replaced by artistic creativity. Winner (1982) identifies here the thread here that weaves from play through daydreaming and productive work, with passes through neurosis and dreaming along the way. These are all energized, said Freud, by unsatisfied desires, unfulfilled wishes.

Ellen Dissanayake (1992) explored the relationship of art to play in *Homo Aesthetics*, where she commented on "Play theories of art" associated with Friedrich Schiller, Herbert Spencer, Sigmund Freud, and Johan Huizinga (1949). Desmond Morris (1962), in *The Biology of Arts*, suggested that art has been derived from play and exploration; Richard Alexander (1989) derived the human psyche (including art) from "scenario building" that evolved from play. Dissanayake (1992) emphasized "making special" as a litmus test of art (p. 95), a quality of a stimulus that can evoke a different and more intrinsically rewarding constellation of neurological activations than can the mundane. The most complete evaluation of the comparative approach to play is Gordon Burghardt's (2001) review in which play or playlike behavior is identified in many species. This helps establish the idea of evolutionary continuity but also underscores its adaptive significance by relating it to ecological and physiological variables.

Art is arguably derived from play, and certainly science is also. Our candidate for an archetypal player might be Sir Isaac Newton, who characterized himself in the midst of his search for the truths of science as "a boy playing on the sea-shore" who diverted himself from time to time with a smoother pebble or a prettier shell.

In Mark Twain's (1903) novel, Tom Sawyer's view that "Work consists of whatever a body is obliged to do, and play consists of whatever a body is not obliged to do," (p. 33) is consistent with a traditional view of play as somehow "irrelevant" to the survival of an animal, but this is not likely. Although the association of play with creative art and science has been made since research on play began, insight must await advances in the biology of cognition, breakthroughs that may emerge from studies of animal play (Fagen, 1981). When play is defined, as by Klopfer (1970), as a kind of exploratory activity "by which the organism 'tests' different proprioceptive patterns for their goodness of fit" (p. 420), we can accept his thesis that even thought and abstraction is play: "Perhaps certain patterns of cortical activity do produce behavior of selective value . . . behavior that is harmonious with the . . . features of the universe in which we share. Abstractions may be the play through which we learn how to think well" (p. 403).

Play Is Serious

As Freud pointed out in "Creative Writers and Day-Dreaming" (1959), the opposite of play is not the serious but the real. Might we approach reality more closely in the most perfectly polarized play of pure imagination?

Generically, all the discoveries and innovations of pure science and fine art—those intellectual and aesthetic pursuits which are carried on without reference to technology or utility—may be credited to functioning of the human play impulses. . . . They rest on the play impulse, which is connected with growth but is dissociated from preservation, comfort, or utility, and which in science and art is translated into the realm of imagination, abstraction, relations, and sensuous form. (Kroeber, 1948)

Play was associated with education by Plato (for example, Krentz, 1998) and with the discharge of emotions (catharsis) by Aristotle (1962). In *Eros and Civilization,* Marcuse (1955) outlined Schiller's view that the play impulse mediates the conflict between intuition/sensuousness and cognition/reason. The play impulse allows man to reconcile feelings and affections with the laws of reason (Chap. 9). It is also the source of creativity insofar as "new forms of realization and of discovering the world" will be attained (p. 204). The truths of sensuousness are the content of aesthetics and its function is *the perfection of sensitive cognition*. "Here the step is made that transforms aesthetics, the science of sensuousness, into the science of *art*." Art which "challenges the prevailing principle of reason: in representing the order of sensuousness, it invokes a tabooed logic—the logic of gratification as against that of repression" (Marcuse, 1955, p. 204).

The "perfection of sensitive cognition" must surely involve what have been termed the primary and secondary processes of cognition. The revelation of "unsuspected kinships" between ideas recalls the primary process cognition of dreaming, reverie, and psychosis and the secondary process cognition involving the "abstract, logical, reality-oriented thought of waking consciousness" (Fromm, 1978, cited by Martindale, 1999, p. 138). There is an assortment of support for the idea that creative individuals can more easily shift gears from primary process, unfocused attention (associated with low levels of cortical arousal), to a more focused secondary process (higher levels of cortical arousal) for the expression or implementation of creative insights. This "dual processing" viewpoint evokes Ernst Kris's (1952) idea of "regression in service to the ego." The reservoir of free associations of the primary processes are utilized but reigned in by the secondary.

THE NEUROETHOLOGY OF CREATIVITY

Our working definition of creativity is packed with ideas that invite the neuroethologist's scrutiny, processes that enlarge sensory capacities, accelerate thinking, and specify actions that can help an organism or population cope with real, perceived, or anticipated changes in the physical or psychological environment. Even dissonance can activate the mechanisms of stress and emotion that have among their consequences an enhanced intensity of perception, cognition, and expression (Greenberg, in press).

Any of these processes—perception, cognition, or expression—can be the initial focus of the neuroethologist's perspective on creativity and art. How do specific kinds or configurations of stimuli affect the brain? What qualities of stimuli can evoke memory and energize cognitive processing? How do stimuli, perceptions, memories, and cognition interact to cause a specific action or emotional response? Among the several starting points for an inquiry, I will emphasize the basal ganglia of the forebrain as an important coordinating and integrative center for the motor and cognitive functions that converge in creativity and thus in art and play. I will also propose that elements of the physiological stress response are critical to energizing the creative processes.

Semir Zeki, a cognitive neurologist at University College, London, viewed the function of art as an extension of the visual function of the brain. His concern was with the perceptive aspects of art, specifically a "search for constancies with the aim of obtaining knowledge about the world" (Zeki, 1999a, p. 79). Taking the biologist's approach, he was able to obtain important information about the manner in which the brain extracts information from visual stimuli. In this he claimed that the artists themselves are also "studying the brain [but] with techniques that are unique to them" (Zeki, 1999b, p. 10).

In "Brain and the Creative Act," Karl Pribram (1999) presents his view that the hippocampal system, critical to memory and learning, may also play a key role in creativity. In particular, it appears to be important to the process Arthur Koestler (1964) famously termed "bisociation." Koestler coined this term to distinguish between routine thinking on a single plane and creative thinking, which in his view always involves more than one plane. Pribram describes this phenomenon as "recombinant processing of experience." Experience involves memory, although one may not necessarily be conscious of certain kinds of memories. In Pribram's (1991) *Brain and Perception*, he develops the neurobiological underpinnings of his ideas about creativity, including the fact that it often appears to depend on unique stimuli or common stimuli uniquely construed as a catalyst. Pribram pointed out that familiar stimuli can be perceived as novel (with an attending change in their salience) due to internally generated change, such as a change in motivation. When the ensemble of internal and external contexts confront little more than recurrent regularities, the system is relatively stable, but when stability is reduced, Pribram tells us, there is fertile ground for creative innovation. When the "comprehensive contexts that map individual strategies become perturbed," hippocampal activity is desynchronized, indicating that "the critical vectors that specify each context are no longer aligned within the map but come to point along many independent directions," leading to the possible discovery of new paths (Pribram, 1991, Appendix F).

THE BASAL GANGLIA: FUNCTIONS OF THE CORPUS STRIATUM

The corpus striatum of the basal forebrain is also identified by clinicians as the basal ganglia. This constellation of structures is represented in Paul D. MacLean's (1990) famous triune brain model as the "R (for 'reptilian') complex," sometimes playfully nicknamed "The Beast in the Brain." MacLean analyzed the anatomy and functions of this area in detail in his magisterial *The Triune Brain in Evolution*, where he also points out the naïve but persistent view of the basal ganglia as principally regulating motor functions and relatively primitive stereotyped behavioral patterns. The view that MacLean foresaw and that is now emerging is that the basal ganglia are also involved in many cognitive functions.

In many respects the study of basal ganglia functions presents an exemplar of the "logic of the lamppost." Employing this seductive mode of reasoning, traditionally treated by analogy with looking for lost keys in a dark parking lot where we can search only under the illumination of a solitary lamppost, we tend to forget that the keys may yet be discovered someplace in the darkness. Our illumination until quite recently has been the more easily discerned clinical evidence of motor dysfunction as a consequence of striatal damage. The dramatic motor problems (e.g., Parkinson's Disease) attributable to impaired basal ganglia have dominated perceptions of its function for generations, but among the symptoms of the "Shaking Palsy" described early in 1817 by James Parkinson was an impairment of intellectual and cognitive processes ("bradyphrenia") with an associated depression sometimes preceding the more overt neurological symptoms. Autonomic dysfunctions are also present and physical or psychological stress can alter the clinical profile in one of two ways: "freezing," an exacerbation or precipitation of neurological deficits, or "paradoxical kinesia," a transient remission of bradykinesia when confronted with a life-threatening emergency (Brown & Marsden, 1998).

The presumed dependence on dopaminergic function believed to be at the heart of certain movement disorders was, however, being shadowed by other interesting observations. Synapses utilizing dopamine (DA) as a neurotransmitter have been of interest since the 1960s, when some antischizophrenic drugs were found to have their principal effect by binding to and blocking D_2 receptors. This complemented the finding that DA agonists (such as amphetamine) cause schizophrenic-like behavior. Dopamine, then, is implicated in cognitive as well as motor functions of the basal ganglia (Roffler-Tarlov & Graybiel, 1984). Even basic personality traits are associated with dopamine. More recently, slight variations (attributable to genetic polymorphisms) in specific dopamine receptors were found to be associated with specific personality types, such as "novelty seekers" or "reward-dependent" (Ebstein et al., 1996, 1997).

The basal ganglia can, in fact, constitute a series of interfaces between cognitive, affective, and motivational functions that may be relevant to our consideration of neural influences on creativity (Greenberg, in press). Among the functions identified with the basal ganglia are acquisition, retention, and expression of cognitive patterns (Graybiel, 1997), activation related to expectancies (Schultz, 1998; Cotterill, 2001), selective attention (Parent, 1986, p. 247), as well as "focused and sustained attention in concert with flexibility of thought . . . planning and regulation of adaptive and goal directed behavior . . . [utilizing] working memory" (Peigneux et al., 2000).

Novelty Is Important

Novelty is a critical element of creativity. Of course, all growth and change deals with novelty and what is novel to a student may be routine to a teacher. All forms of memory are demanding processes, but only novel stimuli or configurations need mobilize the brain's machinery. The organism thus possesses a fundamental need to identify novelty and its possible salience. Many organisms, particularly at appropriate developmental stages, are eager seekers after novelty. In a stable environment the cost of seeking novelty may in time exceed its benefit, but there are always other environments. The intrinsically motivating quality of novelty can evoke the sense of pleasure centered in the basal ganglia, one of the brain's most powerful mechanisms for energizing the process that can lead to consolidation of memory. The caudate nucleus has recently been found to integrate visual inputs with motivational values in the control of specific motor patterns (Kawagoe et al., 1998). With respect to the importance of novelty, the activity of the neurons in the basal ganglia are controlled by the neurotransmitter dopamine produced lower in the neural axis in the substantia nigra and ventral tegmental area. Although rewarding stimuli activate these structures, the activation is more intense when the reward is unexpected (Hollerman & Schultz, 1998). The nucleus accumbens is a ventral striatal site regarded as essential to reward and thus learning (as well as addiction), but its activation by dopamine may depend more on novelty or the expectation or reward than on reward per se (Garris et al., 1999). The path by which emotion (affect) enters the picture involves what is sometimes called the "extended amygdala," a series of structures connecting the amygdaloid nuclei, long known to be critical to the expression of emotions, with the nucleus accumbens. Its "downstream" connections, then, affecting the hypothalamus and brainstem, constitutes what may be called an "emotional-motor" interface (Alheid and Heimer, 1996).

Input, Integration, and Output

All behavior is controlled by various proportions of internal and external stimuli. When external information is compared to or integrated with internal information, an appropriate response can be selected. Many responses are reflexive, highly programmed, or especially easily acquired, possibly in the context of play and other forms of practice that integrate the input (sensory), integrative, and motor functions of the nervous system into automatized sequences. The frontal cortex complements and extends this process by the conscious use of mental models to help us pick an appropriate action—it is our organ of planning and prediction, of imagination.

Behavior is the outcome of the interaction of external and internal factors. The readiness to perform any specific response is profoundly affected by its real (or perceived) biological relevance. Specific responses are provided with more or less highly automatized programs of control depending upon the relative urgency of the biological function they serve—they can be conceived as more or less motivated. Thus, the most fundamental biological needs (such as maintaining the stability of the physiological environment; homeostasis) or self-preservation (Maslow, 1954) has highly automatized programs of control. Motivation therefore reflects real or perceived biological urgency and is profoundly affected by the real or perceived environment.

Familiarity and Strangeness

Relative novelty of a stimulus is a dimension of experience that can profoundly affect an organism's relation to its environment. It cannot be simple because organisms have a need for stimulation in order to maintain tone that will maintain readiness for future likely responses. If stimulation is sufficiently deficient, organisms are stressed in ways that evoke compensating mechanisms, often resulting in anomalous and/or dysfunctional experiences ranging from pathological boredom through hallucination. MacLean (1990) regarded familiarity and strangeness as "indeterminate affects" (emotions) partly because their subjective agreeableness or disagreeableness is context dependent. He noted that these episodes of emotion affects may alternate during the aura preceding a psychomotor seizure, suggesting "a reciprocal innervation of affects that compares to the reciprocal innervation of muscles" (p. 450).

What sorts of effects might novelty have on the brain? For example, what brain areas might be affected as novel versus familiar pictures are being studied. Tulving et al. (1996) visualized brains in volunteers as they were doing just that, and were able to determine that "familiarity activations, signaling aspects of retrieval, were observed in the left and right frontal areas, and posterior regions bilaterally." Goldberg (2001) has pointed out that *unfamiliar* experience is processed predominantly with the right hemisphere, but *familiar* experiences get proportionally more attention from the left hemisphere, although this changes as learning occurs—what the author describes as the "novelty–routinization distinction."

Cotterill (2001) identified processes described by Carpenter that may articulate with the process of creativity: the "race-to-threshold" mechanism (see Carpenter & Williams, 1995) and the randomization of behavior (Carpenter, 1999). The creative dimension emerges from unexpected correlations that may constitute novelty. When these correlations are "captured" by such areas as the ventral striatum, which will be activated when stimuli appear in an unanticipated context, the potential for creative associations will be enhanced by their feedback, serving a wider spread than feed-forward counterparts (Zeki & Shipp, 1988).

If this scenario proves to be reliable, it would indicate that the neural connectedness between areas is a vital ingredient in creativity. But while rich connections might be something that one is born with, experience, particularly during an infant's first two years, can contribute significantly to further enrichment. The study of how connections between neurons are created and dissolved and how their fields of influence expand and contract has an enticing parallelism with ideas about how creativity itself works. Indeed, the connectionist model of neural function has been a powerful source of insight and provocative hypotheses for neurobehavioral scientists to examine (see, for example, Boden, 1990). The connectionist model involves both ephemeral and permanent changes in the nervous system from the synaptic level through the interactions of specific anatomically or cytochemically definable neural structures. The foundations of the approach are relatively recent, having found much recent support in the views of Gerald Edelman, who deals in detail with the dynamic nature of brain function in his book, *Neural Darwinism* (1987).

HOW STRESS AFFECTS CREATIVITY

Stressors are stimuli that organisms perceive as challenges to their ability to meet their needs. They typically evoke a stereotyped ensemble of physiological coping responses that can vary depending on the perceived urgency of the need. In most vertebrates, depending on the intensity and timing of the stressor, the response is constrained by a threshold for detection of the stimulus, by attention based on apparent relevance, and by capacity to respond. While related, each of these can vary independently. Unfortunately, the popular view of stress is dominated by a model deeply informed by medical concerns about its harmful effects when experienced in excess. Our modern view of stress and its potential for harm was forged by the incredibly productive Hans Selye. Selye identified a "General Adaptation Syndrome" in which the initial response to an emergency (the sympathetic nervous system harnessed to the adrenal medulla which produced epinephrine and norepinephrine) was supplanted by a response in which the hypothalamic part of the brain initiated responses involving the anterior pituitary gland (producing ACTH) and the adrenal cortex (producing corticosteroid hormones). These responses were mobilized when the organism was confronted with an acute, repeated, or sustained stressor (Selye, 1936, 1956). The process reallocates resources to cope, but sustained stress can lead to potentially deadly "diseases of adaptation." Years later Seymour Levine (1971) reported that effective behavior depended upon some optimal level of stress, and now we know that stress is involved at many levels, all unified by the organism's desire to cope. For example, as Goldstein (1990) observed, even modest dissonances that might occur when expectations are not met or when there is a mismatch between internal understanding and external experience can evoke the neural pathways and physiological machinery of the stress response.

The behavioral patterns evoked by the stress response are typically very effective in coping with the stressor, but they can also overcompensate or exacerbate behavioral dysfunction (Antelman & Caggiula, 1980).

Stress as a Basis for Adaptive Behavior

Many behavioral patterns originated as responses to acute stressors but have subsequently been transformed and incorporated into the behavioral repertoire when it is adaptive to do so. The neurophysiological input, integration, and action paths of the stress response may be utilized to cope with certain predictable events in an organism's life history. For example, when appropriately stimulated the stress axis can evoke changes in activity levels or motivation to eat in preparation for seasonal lifestyle changes such as migration or hibernation (Lee & McDonald, 1985; Silverin, 1997, Wingfield et al., 1997, Raminofsky, 1990; other references in Greenberg et al., 2003). More famously, many signals exchanged by social species can be seen to have built upon functions originally designed to conserve metabolic resources when stressed, such as changing circulation of blood or thermoregulation. Desmond Morris's (1956) observation that many social signals in birds utilize feathers, the primary function of which is thermoregulation, led to his review of the concept of ritualization, the evolutionary changes in reflexes or fragments of a motor pattern that lead to a social signal. Autonomic reflexes are a key element of the stress response, and the neural and endocrine support for thermoregulatory feather fluffing that Morris observed is much like that utilized in courtship feather fluffing or even the male peacock's spectacular tail display. Relevant for our interests, another consequence of stress involves neural changes that can enhance cognition, evoke affect, and energize motivation.

Two related dimensions affect the profile of endocrine response and neural activity: the positive or negative affect associated with the stressor and the sense of controllability over the stressor. The emotions identified with one's experience of stress can be positive or negative, but all involve the activation of the same key neural and neuroendocrine pathways and always demand resources. Thus, the physiological demands of positive stress can contribute as much as negative stress to the exhaustion of resources. There is, however, an important element of the perception of positive versus negative stress that cannot be overestimated. When considering psychological variables, it is the perception of stress that is relevant. In the absence of trauma or tissue damage, the body mobilizes resources as though in anticipation of an impaired ability to meet its biological needs. But the pattern of stress responses depends to a large measure on the perception of the utility of a specific tactical response; that is, for example, the decision to attack or flee depends on an estimate of the prospects for success. Costs and benefits of specific responses are assessed at several potential levels of response (including cognition), and the most efficient of alternative behavioral patterns are energized. In other words, alternative strategies are apparently evoked by this perception of controllability. When there is a perception of lack of control or a sense of helplessness, organisms tend to intensify their conservation of resources (Seligman, 1975). This is a significant contribution to "diseases of adaptation" involving depressed behavior as well as impaired functions of digestive, reproductive, or immune systems.

The intensity of the stress response is important to the evocation of specific compensating mechanisms, including behavior. A well-known example of this is the tendency of mild stress to energize activity and intense stress to paralyze it

(Leshner, 1978). Another apparent shift in response programs apparently dependent upon the intensity of the stress response is manifest in the suppression of prefrontal cortical (cognitive, planning) activity. The frontal cortex evolved in part to liberate the animal from proximate environmental control by the environment. This adaptive innovation is frivolous next to basic biological survival needs, and stress appears to take the prefrontal cortex "off-line" to allow more habitual responses mediated by posterior cortical and subcortical structures to regulate behavior (Arnsten, 1997). Another comparable pattern may be the impairment of hippocampal activity with commensurate facilitation of the amygdala that suggests, as LeDoux (1996) put it, "the possibility that stress shifts us into a mode of operation in which we react to danger rather than just think about it" (p. 247). The threshold for switching between more or less executive and automatic control of behavior likely changes with development. For example, children may be particularly sensitive to stressful or traumatic experiences (Mayes, 2000), which may cause enduring changes in the brain.

Stress and Cognition

With respect to its influence on cognition, de Kloet et al. (1999) observed that while cell damage in specific parts of the brain can be caused by extreme stress (for example, post-traumatic stress disorder), the hormones responsible more normally protect the brain and are necessary for cognition. Part of this apparent paradox is resolved by the fact that there are two kinds of adrenal cortical steroid hormones, which affect the brain in different ways. While activation of corticosteroid receptors in the brain usually favor adaptive coping behavior involving changes in attention and selection of appropriate responses, if the two corticosteroid-receptor types are imbalanced for a prolonged period of time, maladaptive responses can be evoked. Further, the stage of ongoing information processing (acquisition, consolidation, retention) affects the manner in which the brain responds to the hormones.

CONCLUSIONS

Defining creativity in biological terms broadens the scholarly and applied contexts in which it can be investigated and in which insights gained might be applied. By reconfiguring our perception of creativity in terms of the ethologist's collaborative developmental, ecological, evolutionary, and physiological approaches, our understanding of the biology of stress and the functional neurophysiology of the basal ganglia can be put in the service of understanding the causes and consequences of creative behavior and its key beneficiaries, art and science, and its key corollaries, play and learning.

Neurophysiology helps us appreciate the extent to which creativity involves the confluence of cognition, affect, and motivation in the basal ganglia of the forebrain. Stress biology helps us understand the importance of dissonance and the ways in which the creative process can be energized or stultified by the autonomic neural and endocrine systems. Ethology helps us view creativity as an evolutionary extension of the more mundane processes involving the accommodation and assimilation of novel experiences as we learn. Informed by connectionist ideas of cognitive neuroscience and inspired by the well-known evolutionary process of ritualization, we can truly view creativity as "the peacock's tail of learning," the fullest expression of our disposition to connect the diverse elements of our world with each other and with ourselves.

BIBLIOGRAPHY

Alexander, R. (1989). The Evolution of the Human Psyche. In P. Mellars and C. Stringer (Eds.), *The Human Revolution: Behavioral and Biological Perspectives on the Origins of Modern Humans* (pp. 455–513). Princeton, NJ: Princeton University Press.

Alheid, G. F., & L. Heimer. (1996). Theories of Basal Forebrain Organization and the "Emotional Motor System." *Progress in Brain Research* 107: 461–484.

Andre, B. (1955). *Les manifestes du surrealisme.* Paris: Editions du Sagittaire.

Antelman, S. M., & C. A. Caggiulla. (1980). Stress-Induced Behavior: Chemotherapy Without Drugs. In J. M. Davidson & R. J. Davidson (Eds.), *The Psychobiology of Consciousness* (pp. 65–104). New York: Plenum Press.

Aristotle. (1962). *The Politics* (E. Barker, Trans.). New York: Oxford University Press.

Arnsten, A. F. (1997). Catecholamine Regulation of the Prefrontal Cortex. *Journal of Psychopharmacology* 11(2): 151–162.

Bardo, M. T., R. L. Donohew, & N. G. Harrington. (1996). Psychobiology of Novelty Seeking and Drug Seeking Behavior. *Behavioral Brain Research* 77(1–2): 23–43.

Berns, G. S., S. M. McClure, G. Pagnoni, & P. R. Montague. (2001). Predictability Modulates Human Brain Response to Reward. *Journal of Neuroscience* 21(8): 2793–2798.

Boden, M. (1990). *The Creative Mind.* New York: Basic Books.

Bowers, W. J., R. M. Zacharko, & H. Anisman. (1987). Evaluation of Stressor Effects on Intracranial Self-Stimulation from the Nucleus Accumbens and the Substantia Nigra in a Current Intensity Paradigm. *Behavioral Brain Research* 23: 85–93.

Breuer, J., & S. Freud. (1937/1957). *Studies on Hysteria* (James Strachey, Ed. and Trans., in collaboration with Anna Freud, assisted by Alix Strachey & Alan Tyson). New York: Basic Books.

Brown, P., & C. D. Marsden. (1998). What Do the Basal Ganglia Do? *Lancet* 351: 1801–1804.

Burghardt, G. M. (1999). Conceptions of Play and the Evolution of Animal Minds. *Evolution and Cognition,* 5(2): 115–123.

———. (2001). Play: Attributes and Neural Substrates. In E. M. Blass (Ed.), *Handbook of Behavioral Neurobiology* (pp. 317–356). New York: Plenum Press.

Bussey, T. (1999). Novelty in the Brain. *Trends in Cognitive Sciences* 3(4): 126.

Butler, S. (1912). *Notebooks.* Retrieved November 21, 2002 from http://ibiblio.org/gutenberg/etext04/nbsb10.txt.

Cabib, S., & S. Puglisi-Allegra. (1996). Stress, Depression and the Mesolimbic Dopamine System. *Psychopharmacology* (Berl) 128(4): 331–342.

Campbell, J. (1968). *The Masks of God: Creative Mythology.* New York: Viking Press.

Cardinal, R. N., D. R. Pennicott, C. L. Sugathapala, T. W. Robbins, & B. J. Everitt. (2001). Impulsive Choice Induced in Rats by Lesions of the Nucleus Accumbens Core. *Sci-*

ence (May 24). Retrieved May 24, 2001 from Science Express Reports, http://www.scienceexpress.org.

Carpenter, R.H.S. (1999). A Neural Mechanism that Randomizes Behavior. *Journal of Consciousness Studies* 6: 13–22.

Carpenter, R.H.S., & M.L.L. Williams. (1995). Neural Computation of Log Likelihood in the Control of Saccadic Eye Movements. *Nature* 377: 59–62.

Chapman, L. F., R. D. Walter, C. H. Markham, R. W. Rand, & P. H. Crandall. (1967). Memory Changes Induced by Stimulation of Hippocampus or Amygdala in Epilepsy Patients with Implanted Electrodes. *Trans. American Neurological Association* 92: 50–56.

Coomaraswamy, A. K. (1956). *Christian and Oriental Philosophy of Art*. New York: Dover.

Cotterill, R.M.J. (2001). Cooperation of the Basal Ganglia, Cerebellum, Sensory Cerebrum and Hippocampus: Possible Implications for Cognition, Consciousness, Intelligence and Creativity. *Progress in Neurobiology* 64: 1–33.

Crawford, C. (1998). Environments and Adaptations: Then and Now. In C. Crawford & D. L. Krebs (Eds.), *Handbook of Evolutionary Psychology* (pp. 275–302). Mahwah, NJ: Earlbaum.

de Kloet, E. R., M. S. Oitzl, & M. Joëls. (1999). Stress and Cognition: Are Corticosteroids Good or Bad Guys? *Trends in Neurosciences* 22(10): 422–426.

Dellu, F., P. V. Piazza, W. Mayo, M. Le Moal, & H. Simon. (1996). Novelty-Seeking in Rats—Biobehavioral Characteristics and Possible Relationship with the Sensation-Seeking Trait in Man. *Neuropsychobiology* 34(3): 136–145.

Dewey, J. (1934). *Art as Experience*. London: George Allen & Unwin.

Dissanayake, E. (1992). *Homo Aesthetics: Where Art Comes From and Why*. New York: Free New York Press/Macmillan.

Ebstein, R. P., O. Novick, R. Umansky, B. Priel, Y. Osher, D. Blain, E. R. Bennett, L. Nemanov, M. Katz, & R. H. Belmaker. (1996). Dopamine D4 Receptor (D4DR) Exon III Polymorphism Associated with the Human Personality Trait of Novelty Seeking. *Nature Genetics* 12(1): 78–80.

Ebstein, R. P., R. Segman, J. Benjamin, Y. Osher, L. Nemanov, & R. H. Belmaker. (1997). 5-HT2C (HTR2C) Serotonin Receptor Gene Polymorphism Associated with the Human Personality Trait of Reward Dependence: Interaction with Dopamine D4 Receptor (D4DR) and Dopamine D3 Receptor (D3DR) Polymorphisms. *American Journal of Medical Genetics* 74(1): 65–72.

Edelman, G. M. (1987). *Neural Darwinism: The Theory of Neuronal Group Selection*. New York: Basic Books.

Fagen, R. (1981). *Animal Play Behavior*. New York: Oxford University Press.

Freud, S. (1959). Creative Writers and Day-Dreaming. In J. Strachey (Ed.), The Standard Edition. Vol. 9. London: Hogarth Press.

Fromm, E. (1978). Primary and Secondary Process in Waking and in Altered States of Consciousness. *Journal of Altered States of Consciousness* 4: 115–128.

Furlow, Bryant. (2001). Play's the Thing. *New Scientist* (June 9). Retrieved May 3, 2001 from http://www.newscientist.com/features/features.jsp?id=ns229412.

Garris, P. A., M. Kilpatrick, M. A. Bunin, D. Michael, Q. D. Walker, & R. M. Wrightman. (1999). Dissociation of Dopamine Release in the Nucleus Accumbens from Intracranial Self-Stimulation. *Nature* 398: 67–69.

Goldberg, , E. (2001). *The Executive Brain: Frontal Lobes and the Civilized Mind*. New York: Oxford University Press.

Goldstein, D. S. (1990). Neurotransmitters and Stress. *Biofeedback and Self-Regulation* 15(3): 243–272.

Graybiel, A. M. (1997). The Basal Ganglia and Cognitive Pattern Generators. *Schizophrenia Bulletin* 23(3): 459–469.

Greenberg, N. (1998, July 12–13). The Evolutionary Physiology of Creativity Lecture for the Human Behavior and Evolution Society, Tenth Annual Meeting, University of California, Davis.

———. (2002). Adaptive Functions of the Corpus Striatum: The Past and Future of the R-Complex. In G. Cory & R. Gardner (Eds.), *Neuroethology: Frontiers and Convergences* (pp. 45–81). Westport, CT: Praeger.

———. (2003). Sociality, Stress, and the Corpus Striatum of the Green Anolis Lizard. *Physiology and Behavior* 79(3): 429–440.

Greenberg, N., C. A. Carr, & C. H. Summers. (2001). Ethological Causes and Consequences of the Stress Response. *Journal of Integrative and Comparative Biology* 42(3): 508–516.

Hamilton, W. D. (1964). The Genetical Evolution of Social Behaviour, vols. I, II. *Journal of Theoretical Biology* 7: 1–52.

Herve, D., G. Blanc, J. Glowinski, & J. P. Tassin. (1982). Reduction of Dopamine Utilization in the Prefrontal Cortex but Not in the Nucleus Accumbens after Selective Destruction of Noradrenergic Fibers Innervating the Ventral Tegmental Area in the Rat. *Brain Research* 237: 510–516.

Hockett, C. F., & R. Ascher. (1964). The Human Revolution. *Current Anthropology* 5(3): 135–168.

Hoffer, E. (1951). *The True Believer*. New York: Harper and Row.

Hollerman, J. R., & W. Schultz. (1998). Dopamine Neurons Report an Error in the Temporal Prediction of Reward during Learning. *Nature Neuroscience* 1(4): 304–309.

Huether G. (1996). The Central Adaptation Syndrome: Psychosocial Stress as a Trigger for Adaptive Modifications of Brain Structure and Brain Function. *Progress in Neurobiology* 48(6): 569–612.

Hutson, J.H. (1981). *Creativity: A Continuing Inventory of Knowledge*. Washington, DC: Library of Congress.

Huizinga, J. (1949). *Homo Ludens: A Study of the Play Element in Culture* (R.F.C. Hull, Trans.). London: Routledge and Kegan Paul.

Kawagoe, R., Y. Takakawa, & O. Hikosaka. (1998). Expectation of Reward Modulates Cognitive Signals in the Basal Ganglia. *Nature Neuroscience* 1(5): 411–416.

Kihlstrom, J. F. (1987). The Cognitive Unconscious. *Science* 237: 1445–1452.

Klopfer, P. H. (1970). Sensory Physiology and Esthetics. *American Scientist* 58: 399–403.

Knight R. T., & T. Nakada. (1998). Cortico-Limbic Circuits and Novelty: A Review of EEG and Blood Flow Data. *Neuroscience Review* 9: 1, 57–70.

Koestler, A. (1964). *The Act of Creation*. New York: Macmillan.

Krentz, A. A. (1998, August 10–15). Play and Education in Plato's *Republic*. Paper presented at the Twentieth World Congress of Philosophy, Boston. Retrieved June 2001 Paideia Project Online, Boston University, http://www.bu.edu/wcp/Papers/Educ/EducKren.htm.

Kris, E. (1952). *Psychoanalytic Explorations in Art*. New York: International Universities Press.

Kroeber, A. L. (1948). *Anthropology*. Rev. Ed. New York: Harcourt Brace.

LeDoux, J. (1996). *The Emotional Brain*. New York: Simon and Schuster.

Lee, A.J.K., & I. R. McDonald. (1985). Stress and Population Regulation in Small Mammals. In J. R. Clarke (Ed.), *Oxford Reviews of Reproductive Biology* (pp. 261–304). Oxford: Clarendon Press.

Leshner, A. (1978). *An Introduction to Behavioral Endocrinology*. New York: Oxford University Press.

Levine, S. (1971). Stress and Behavior. *Scientific American* 224(1): 26–31.

Lewis, C. D. (1946). *The Poetic Image*. New York: Oxford University Press.

Lorenz, K. Z. (1981). *The Foundations of Ethology*. New York: Simon and Schuster.

MacLean, P. D. (1990). *The Triune Brain in Evolution*. New York: Plenum Press.

Marcuse, H. (1955). *Eros and Civilization: A Philosophical Investigation into Freud*. Boston: Beacon Press.

Martindale, C. (1999). Biological Bases of Creativity. In R. Sternberg (Ed.), *Handbook of Creativity* (pp. 137–152). Cambridge: Cambridge University Press.

Maslow, A. (1954). *Motivation and Personality*. New York: Harper.

Mayes, L. C. (2000). A Developmental Perspective on the Regulation of Arousal States. *Semin. Perinatol* 24(4): 267–279.

Merriam-Webster's Dictionary Online. (n.d.) Available at http://www.m-w.com/cgi-bin/netdict.

Mook, D. G. (1996). *Motivation: The Organization of Action*. New York: W. W. Norton.

Morris, D. (1956). The Feather Postures of Birds and the Problem of the Origin of Social Signals. *Behavior* 9: 75–113.

———— . (1962). *The Biology of Art*. New York: Knopf.

Nesse, N. C., & K. C. Berridge. (1997). Psychoactive Drug Use in Evolutionary Perspective. *Science* 278: 63–66.

Novitz, D. (1987). *Knowledge, Fiction and Imagination*. Philadelphia: Temple University Press.

Paradiso S., D. L. Johnson, N. C. Andreasen, D. S. O'Leary, G. L. Watkins, L.L.B. Ponto, & R. D. Hichwa. (1999). Cerebral Blood Flow Changes Associated with Attribution of Emotional Valence to Pleasant, Unpleasant, and Neutral Visual Stimuli in a PET Study of Normal Subjects. *American Journal of Psychiatry* 156(10): 1618–1629.

Parent, A. (1986). *Comparative Neurobiology of the Basal Ganglia*. New York: Wiley.

Parker A., E. Wilding, & C. Akerman. (1998). The von Restorff Effect in Visual Object Recognition Memory in Humans and Monkeys: The Role of Frontal/Perirhinal Interaction. *Journal of Cognitive Neuroscience* 10: 691–703.

Peigneux P., P. Maquet, T. Meulemans, A. Destrebecqz, S. Laureys, C. Degueldre, G. Delfiore, J. Aerts, A. Luxen, G. Franck, M. Van der Linden, & A. Cleeremans. (2000). Striatum Forever, Despite Sequence Learning Variability: A Random Effect Analysis of PET Data. *Human Brain Mapping* 10(4): 179–194.

Poincaré, H. (1913). *The Foundations of Science*. Lancaster, PA: Science Press.

Pribram, K. (1991). *Brain and Perception*. Hillsdale: NJ: Lawrence Erlbaum.

———— . (1998). On Brain and Value: Utility, Preference, Play and Creativity. In Karl H. Pribram et al. (Eds.) *Brain and Values: Is a Biological Science of Values Possible?* (pp. 43–54). Mahwah, NJ: Lawrence Erlbaum.

———— . (1999). Brain and the Creative Act. In *Encyclopedia of Creativity* (pp. 213–217). New York: Academic Press.

Pribram, K.H., & D. McGuinness. (1975). Arousal, Activation and Effort in the Control of Attention. *Psychological Reviews* 82(2): 116–149.

Ramachandran, V. S. (1998). The Neurology and Evolution of Humor, Laughter, and Smiling: The False Alarm Theory. *Medical Hypotheses* 51(4): 351–354.

————. (2000). Concerning "The Science of Art": Response from V. S. Ramachandran. *Journal of Consciousness Studies* 7(8–9): 17–20.

Ramachandran, V. S., & W. Hirstein. (1999). The Science of Art: A Neurological Theory of Aesthetic Experience. *Journal of Consciousness Studies* 6(6–7): 15–51.

Ramenofsky, M. (1990). Fat Storage and Fat Metabolism in Relation to Migration. In E. Gwinner (Ed.), *Bird Migration: Physiology and Ecophysiology* (pp. 214–231). Berlin: Springer-Verlag.

Random House Dictionary of the English Language (2d ed.). (1987). New York: Random House.

Rizzolatti, G., & M. Arbib. (1998). Language within Our Grasp. *Trends in Neurosciences* 21: 188–194.

Roffler-Tarlov, S., & A. M. Graybiel. (1984). Weaver Mutation Has Differential Effects on the Dopamine-Containing Innervation of the Limbic and Nonlimbic Striatum. *Nature* 307: 62–66.

Rozin, P. (1976). The Evolution of Intelligence and Access to the Cognitive Unconscious. *Progress in Psychobiology and Physiological Psychology* 6: 245–280.

Schultz, W. (1998). Predictive Reward Signal of Dopamine Neurons. *Journal of Neurophysiology* 80(1): 1–27.

Seligman, M. (1975). *Helplessness*. San Francisco: Freeman.

Seligman, M., R. Rosellini, & M. Kozak. (1975). Learned Helplessness in the Rat. *Journal of Comparative Physioliology & Psychology* 88: 542–547.

Selye, H. (1936). A Syndrome Produced by Diverse Nocuous Agents. *Nature* 138: 32.

————. (1956). *The Stress of Life*. New York: McGraw-Hill.

Silverin, B. (1997). The Stress Response and Autumn Dispersal Behavior in Willow Tits. *Animal Behaviour* 53: 541–549.

Taylor, J. A. (1999). Koans of Silence: The Teaching Not Taught. *Parabola* 24(2): 6–11.

Tulving, E., H. J. Markowitsch, F. E. Craik, R. Habib, & S. Houle. (1996). Novelty and Familiarity Activations in PET Studies of Memory Encoding and Retrieval. *Cerebral Cortex* 6: 171–179.

Twain, M. (1903). *The Adventures of Tom Sawyer*. New York: Harper Brothers.

Wingfield, J. C., C. Breuner, & J. Jacobs. (1997). Corticosterone and Behavioral Responses to Unpredictable Events. In S. Harvey & R. J. Etches (Eds.), *Perspectives in Avian Endocrinology* (pp. 267–278). Bristol: Journal of Endocrinology.

Winner, E. (1982). *Invented Worlds: The Psychology of the Arts*. Cambridge: Harvard University Press.

Wise, R. A., & M. A. Bozarth. (1984). Brain Reward Circuitry: Four Circuit Elements "Wired" in Apparent Series. *Brain Research Bulletin* 12: 203–208.

Zeki, S. (1999a). Art and the Brain. *Journal of Consciousness Studies* 6: 76–95.

————. (1999b). *Inner Vision: An Exploration of Art and the Brain*. New York: Oxford University Press.

Zeki, S., & S. Shipp. (1988). The Functional Logic of Cortical Connections. *Nature* 335: 311–317.

43

A Closer Look at the
Ontological Role of Play

Mark Cotter

Streams of molten lava had forced the villagers to small dots of higher ground. As one spot of safe ground became swallowed up by the advancing flow, acts of ingenuity and courage combined to rescue the hapless. As one adventurous young man climbed to a high spot and poised to leap to another, the voice of an elder rang out, "Not from that top bunk you don't. You'll break your neck." Such is the nature of sociodramatic play.

The preceding drama, which unfolded in the bunkhouse at a rainy church retreat, typifies the enigmatic nature of play. What is going on when children play? On the surface, it seems to make no sense. There seems to be no salient biological need for play or an evolutionary benefit from it—in fact, as the lava story exemplifies, play can be downright dangerous and detrimental to the survival of the organism (Fagen, 1981; Byers, 1998). One important defining factor of play is that the activity of the player has no discernible outcome or payoff (Bekoff & Byers, 1981; Biben, 1979). Despite this absence of functional consequences, almost all social animals engage in play. In response to this apparent enigma, researchers have shifted their focus to look past the immediate to the delayed benefits of play, those that exhibit some enhanced ability in adult behavior (Smith, 1995; Martin & Caro, 1985).

PLAY IN THE EVOLUTIONARY SCHEME

Play is common to almost all animals. The logic in examining commonalities and differences in play in lower animals and play in humans is to discern which elements of play are attributable to the organism as automaton and as "free agent." There is, admittedly, an arguably dubious assumption in claiming that lower species lack the intentionality and mental activity we usually ascribe to humans alone; however, since there is evidence of play in such a variety of species, I will continue on the strength of the argument that play is organic in its origins, and that there is continuity between ourselves and other animals (Shotter, 1993). The first task is to define play. Martin and Caro (1985) reviewed a number of authors to compile a list of features of play:

- Play involves exaggeration and repetition of motor acts and the reordering of behavioral sequences.
- Play is initiated by play signals.
- Play occurs when basic needs are met and the animal is in a relaxed state.
- Sequences of motor acts are incomplete and fragmented.
- Role reversing and self-handicapping occurs.
- Play is fun.

They conclude, however, that no one feature of play is sufficient to define play: In their words, play is "polythetically defined" or "playful behavior" (p. 62). The approach to the investigation of play assumes the stance that there is a continuity of these and other features of play through several species, including the human species. As in other species, human play peaks during certain periods of juvenile development, then drops off (Byers, 1998); however, some species, such as the human, exhibit playful behavior (though in other forms) through adulthood.

Our survivability as a species may depend on our ability to reconfigure our behaviors according to the context of the environment, to take on whatever functional paradigm for which the occasion demands. Humans have populated the most diverse environments and produced artifacts and communication modes in varieties far more complex than that of any other animal. Adaptability has relied on a capability for developmental flexibility in which the social or physical environment is the most unpredictable and unstable (Thompson, 1998).

With the advent of parental care, natural selection for the maintenance of these [instinctive behaviors] was relaxed as the performance of such behavior patterns became less necessary and even maladaptive. Conceivably therefore, in the absence of strong selection, the degree of hard-wired proficiency in the behaviors decreased while other, more experientially-based, supports increased. This can, simplistically, be viewed as a shift from closed to open genetic programs. (Burghardt, 1984, p. 34)

Although humans share aspects of play with other animals, "no obvious parallels exist between the linguistic, fantasy, and sociodramatic play of children and play in other species" (Martin & Caro, 1985, p. 75). Sociodramatic play is defined by the use of language and imagination along with sensory processes, characterization, improvisation, and dramatization (McIntyre, 1974). Dramatization defines the parameters of the playful situation. The players spontaneously develop a script detailing who the characters are to be, what action they are to play, where and when this is happening, and why it is happening, what Rike (1993) terms as the "five Ws." Central to the activity, the lure that draws the players into the activity, is a problem facing the players, and the resolution to this problem (Rike, 1993). Sociodramatic play involve composite characters working together to solve problems that are existentialist in nature—themes and metaphors for the struggles all humans face (Sternberg & Garcia, 1989). The uniqueness of the human animal is reflected in the nature of our play.

Given the premise that behavior patterns in mammals are more experientially based, it is plausible that humans, who exhibit the most complex repertoire of behaviors, must consequently have been exposed to a very complex environment. The sensory information available to humans is not, however, so different from the other species around us (such as household pets and apes raised alongside human families for language training) to explain the discrepancy in behaviors. The human brain has evolved into a more complex organ than its animal counterpart. Sensory information is processed via integration of different areas of the brain working in concert.

Humans differ from most other animals in that our brain has prolonged cell division and diversification along with delays in synaptic trimming through the juvenile period. It would seem that during this period of organization and refinement of dendrite connections, children are able to construct experiences that are not dependent on the immediate environment. If neural differenttiation is dependent on the experiences of the organism, the possibilities for volitional development of the brain take on a greater significance, shifting the focus to the interpersonal and cultural realms. In effect, we have to some extent become the master of our own evolution.

VYGOTSKY

Lev Vygotsky, very much influenced by his contemporary Jean Piaget, examined the period of childhood when both play and language develop to make the child unique from other members of the animal kingdom. During this period, roughly between the ages of two and five, the development of thought and speech coincide and intermingle to initiate a new form of behavior (Vygotsky, 1962). Vygotsky examined what he called "inner speech," which he saw as not functionally different from overt speech. He noted that overt speech precedes inner speech in that the child "masters the syntax of speech before syntax of thought" (p. 46).

Several of Vygotsky's notions about language resonate in his thought about play. The origins of play arise as a coping mechanism for fulfilling the child's developing but unrealizable desires as he or she moves from toddlerhood to preschool. Vygotsky averred that the child is able to achieve anything in his or her imagination-in-action. This active playing is the precursor of the more covert imagination in the older child and adult, who Vygotsky saw as still needing to deal with unrealizable desires. Although Vygotsky sees imagination as the sole domain of humans, the basic function of play as serving to establish delayed gratification of needs is not entirely unlike the findings that play in animals has an affect on the ability of adults to cope with unrealizable desires to dominate. In concert with this is the adherence to rules, an essential ingredient in play. Participants must obey the rules of behavior: If the player is going to be a villager escaping lava flows, he or she must act like a villager and play within the parameters of the heat and movement of real lava. The acquisition of rules, since they are self-imposed, leads to traits essential to autonomy, self-restraint, and self-determination. Vygotsky also observed that the rule-guided behavior and cooperation required in play may serve to instill the virtue of delayed self-gratification.

The age of children during this peak time of play fits the stage of development Piaget defined as the preoperational period (Piaget, 1976; Flavell, 1963), when children begin to use symbols. As Vygotsky saw it, the child is able to accomplish this because play acts as a separator of fields of vision and meaning. As Vygotsky states, the child has "thought that is totally free of real situations" (Vygotsky, 1933, p. 67). By severing thought from object, the child is able to act independently of what he or she sees, guided by meaning. Whereas Piaget looked at play as an assimilation, where the child negotiates the world to fit developing organizational skills, Vygotsky noted features of play more attuned to accommodation. This accommodation would most likely take place within the symbolic interaction, a complex multilevel integration into the world-space of another that results in deep understanding or "meaning." This accommodation, to Vygotsky, takes the form of what he calls the "zone of proximal development": "In play a child is always above his average age, above his daily behavior; in play it is as though he were a head taller than himself. As in the focus of a magnifying glass, play contains all the developmental tendencies in a condensed form; in play it is as though the child were trying to jump above the level of his normal behavior" (p. 70).

As in other animals, a degree of challenge serves to keep play going. Although skill building may be evident, the process of persisting may be the more enduring outcome. The adult–child play noted by Vygotsky and Piaget centers on the role of the adult placing the child into the zone of proximal development and the parent handicapping himself or herself just enough for the child to persist in the activity (Vygotsky, 1933; Piaget, 1976). This natural relationship evolves into a more formal process as the child matures and the parent makes the conscious decision to mold the child into a functioning member of society.

MEDIATORS

The role of the adult in providing the rules for behavior fades in importance as the child progresses through play in determining his or her own rules (Vygotsky, 1933). This is an emancipation for the child from the mediation that takes place when the adult inserts himself or herself between the child and the stimulus and gives meaning to the otherwise meaningless behavior (Vygotsky, 1962). "In other words, cultural transmission through adult transactions usually involves relating cultural values and norms in a manner which transcends the immediate needs of the given circumstances and thus constitutes mediated learning" (Greenberg, 1991, p. 244).

Reuven Feuerstein formalizes the mediated learning experience (MLE) through his work with "culturally deprived" individuals. He defines the culturally deprived individual as "one who, either not having been exposed or not having been able to benefit from his exposure to mediated learning experience, is devoid of learning tools, habits, dispositions, and propensities to learn" (Feuerstein, Klein, & Tannenbaum, 1991, p. 5). These individuals included those who had to "learn to learn" (p. 5) through formal mediation "because they were not exposed to their own culture" (p. 5), and therefore had an inability to "benefit from direct exposure to stimuli" (p. 5). The necessary conditions for MLE—intentionality and reciprocity, mediation of transcendence, and mediation of meaning (Feuerstein, Klein, & Tannenbaum, 1991)—formalize the conditions of play. The effort of the mediator is to "transform the mental, emotional, and motivational state of the mediatee" (p. 18). The mediation of transcendence serves, somewhat metaphorically, to establish ways of solving problems that go beyond the immediate goals to broader themes and struggles. The who, what, when, and where of the two previous conditions for MLE are given import by the mediation of meaning, the "energetic dimension of the interaction; it answers the questions of why, what for" (p. 24).

Kenneth Gergen (1982, 1997) cites Lev Vygotsky for the increased interest in learning as a social process: "Thus the emphasis of pedagogical practices shifts toward forms of dialogue ('interanimation') and group problem solving, patterns of teacher student interdependency, the role of the teacher in carrying social norms, and the potential of students as teachers" (Gergen, 1997, p. 199).

Feuerstein struggles with the ethics of this possibly propagandist role served by MLE, but justifies his position by setting a priority on the efficiency of functioning within society over freedom of choice. The mediation of others calls stimuli into consciousness and integrates them into functional paradigms important to the culture. Similarly, Paulo Freire and Miles Horton, advocates of popular schools and proponents of the emancipatory goals of education, assert that the teacher must also serve a political role, but one that is tempered by a dialogical relationship that places a high value on jointly derived rules for knowing (Peters & Armstrong, 1998; Freire, 1970). Both educators emphasize a change that must come about in the mediator as well as the mediatee. After all, "being exposed to stimuli even once produces changes in the mental condition of the organism" (Feurstein, Klein, & Tannenbaum, 1991, p. 8).

THE DIALOGISTS

The choice between mediation serving as oppression versus liberation frames the dialogue among those who concentrate on the act of dialogue itself (Brown, 1995; Isaacs, 1993; Bohm, Factor, & Garrett, 1997). Like Feuerstein, Horton, and Freire, they envision higher goals and ideals for dialogue. These goals are reflected in what children do in sociodramatic play. "Successful pretend play rests on effective communication, and very heavily so. It takes cooperative efforts, and role enactment requires role taking of a fairly high order" (Garvey, 1977, p. 115).

Judy Brown (1995) describes dialogue as the "good conversation" found in most preindustrial countries. She describes dialogue akin to something left behind in childhood, "that which we have forgotten to remember" (p. 154). Reminiscent of Socratic dialogue, Brown's mechanics of dialogue call for moments of reflective silence. Brown does have a list of parameters conducive to dialogue: listening for understanding, asking questions from a place of genuine not knowing (similar to Merleau-Ponty's 1962 comments about being open to the world), and granting others the respect of being an authority over their own thoughts and feelings.

Within the dialogue of colleagues we have established rules for dialogue that are common to the writing of various authors on the subject. These are the same rules thta are common to play (that is, to playing "nice"):

- Dialogue takes place in an environment of trust.
- Dialogue involves taking turns.
- Everyone is invited to dialogue.
- Understand what is acceptable.
- Be mindful of others.
- Respect the ideas of others.
- Let others have their way sometimes.

Dialogue is "a discipline of collective thinking and inquiry, a process for transforming the quality of conversation and, in particular, the thinking that lies beneath it" (Isaacs, 1993, p. 25). William Isaacs (1993) points out that "dialogue" is derived from the Greek *dia* and *logos*, suggesting "flowing through." In genuine dialogue, the intent is "to establish a field of genuine meeting and inquiry" (p. 25) in contrast to debate and consensus. Dialogue is a tool to uncover the ways in which we perceive reality. It acknowledges that "our perceptions and thoughts can literally create our worlds" (p. 29). To Isaacs, dialogue leads to "an attempt to perceive the world with new eyes" (p. 30). Dialogue has no agenda, leader, or task, but is reflective in nature, calling on the participants to stand above the act of dialogue to observe and mediate each other. It is people purposefully coming together to create shared meaning.

The physicist David Bohm views dialogue as a medium for bringing to the surface and altering the tacit infrastructure of thought. Dialogue is a metacognitive ("collective proprioception") technique with idealistic goals such as increased harmony, fellowship, and creativity. Once blocks are overcome, dialogue achieves a state where the participants "relax and bask in the 'high' that accompanies the experience" (Bohm, Factor, & Garrett, 1997). Dialogue is not a discussion, a debate, or a "salon" (to entertain, gossip, or exchange friendship). It is critical in Bohm's vision of dialogue to suspend thoughts, impulses, and judgements.

The imperative of mediation brings to bear one of the often undiscussed natures of play: It is often cruel. As most parents can attest, unsupervised play can take an ugly turn toward bullying and other types of destructive and violent themes. The same can be said to be true of dialogue. The social construction of a reality does not necessarily mean the creation of a fair and just reality. The life space of the bigot, anarchist, and terrorist is possibly as "valid" a reality for them as the more placid reality is to the mainstream of the "civilized" culture. The students of dialogue seldom mention the playful contact and questioning of authority that can come with Socratic dialogue. Their guidelines seem geared to avoid the decay of dialogue into the Minippean carnival of mockery (Cheyne & Tarulli, 1999) that is perhaps best exemplified by the derisive and bullying tactics of some of our more popular media pundits. The rules for dialogue that could create a greater good require the same mediating supervision that is required in the play of younger children.

PLAY AS FLOW

Mihaly Csikszentmihayli (1979) looks at adult play as what he terms "flow," evolving out of ludic behavior. Csikszentmihayli examines the experience of playfulness in which he has found merging of action and awareness, a focused concentration where irrelevant stimuli is filtered out. In this state, time is warped or suspended, goals are clear, and there is an immediate feedback and feeling of control. "Paradoxically, this feeling of control goes hand in hand with the loss of ego. . . . Some people describe it as a transcendence, as a merging with the environment, as a union with the activity or purpose" (p. 261).

Gadamer (1976) similarly describes "a peculiar freedom and buoyancy that determines the consciousness of the player" (p. 53) in game playing. Gadamer, however, emphasizes the back-and-forth relationship between the players as a "unified form of movement as a whole that unifies the fluid activity of both" (p. 54), and he relates this to the act of dialogue: "The common agreement that takes place in speaking with others is itself a game" (p. 56), and in this game of dialogue, the players lose self-consciousness. Play would, in effect, serve to place some stimuli in the background of experience to the benefit of the stimuli, which requires complete concentration, the kind of concentration you would want from your surgeon. In children and adults with Attention Deficit Hyperactivity Disorder (ADHD), this uncoupling seems to be a critical factor. Students with ADHD report an inability to filter out irrelevant stimuli (Wender, 1997; Bellock and Marsh, 1997). As children have less time to play both in and out of school, it is perhaps no coincidence that the use of Ritalin in the classroom becomes more commonplace.

Gadamer (1976) describes a kind of dialogue we might term "pure dialogue." He uses games as a metaphor for dialogue where thought is suspended and self-consciousness is lost to conversation. Like play, there is the mediation of the rules and a drifting in and out of self-consciousness into the concentration on, or absorption in, the act of dialogue. This state of dialogue is pleasurable. Pure dialogue is a more phenomenological realm—it is the act itself—and what Bohm, Isaacs, Brown, and Tarule have practiced is the more paradigm-based choosing of what *should* stand out from the background of a world created in pure dialogue. The disorder of raw experience gives way to order via the joint action of the dialogical relationship (Shotter, 1993). This mediated, transformative experience stands out as metaphorical. Stephen Brookfield (1990) suggests the use of critical reflection to examine critical incidents that are the catalysts for change. His process involves steps toward "recognition and analysis of assumptions" (p. 177) and eventual reconstituting of these assumptions. Mezirow (1990) also asserts that "more inclusive, discriminating, permeable, and integrative perspectives are superior perspectives that adults choose if they can because they are motivated to better understand the meaning of their experience" (p. 14). The act of play begins with playfulness, a kind of disorder that becomes order through the narrative structure and mediation of rules.

CONSTRUCTIONISTS

Heidegger (1996), Husserl (1982), and Merleau-Ponty (1962) extend the concept of the Gestalt within the framework of intentionality, or our "being-in-the-world." In play, the child chooses an orientation to the world and engages the world in unreflected action. This is the flexibility that allows the child to live within the naive experience, free for the moment from the constraints of cultural heritage.

The act of an utterance in dialogue calls out a response of some kind and acts similarly to the invitational stance seen in play. "In responding and reacting to each other, we create shared momentary 'dialogical spaces' between us" (Shotter, 1999). The origin and primitive form of a language game is a certain reaction occurring in "spontaneous, unreflected ways" (p. 9). John Shotter (1998) sums up Wittgenstein's approach to language by stating that language is not simply a computational code—its power lies in how it is embedded into the fabric of the rest of our activities.

In play, synaptic connections are made based on stimuli that are not readily available to the senses—that is to say, a *reality* is created based on symbols. Similarly, there exists in philosophical circles the notion of dialogical realities. Within the realm of pure dialogue, where direct sensorial stimuli assume the background to the field, dialogue is now the source of new dendrite connections. This is social construction—when neural development is concerned, it is quite literally construction-based on social interaction. Like play, dialogue bounces back and forth from rule-guided negotiation to the flowlike state. Social construction is tempered by the limits of the "world as it is," by biological imperatives, and by historical cultural constraints.

The limits to the knowledge of which we are capable, if there can be any, would be the limits of social interaction. Knowledge is not a static thing. It exists in the moment and then is something else, something new and different. In a phenomenological approach to both play and dialogue, where the ludic is entertained, the language game serves as an iconoclastic device shattering the participants' otherwise stagnant view of the world. Knowledge is an activity, a social action, and can therefore have no boundaries.

COLLABORATIVE LEARNING

When children come together to play, the only common goal is to play. The outcome of play depends on the objects at their disposal (a blanket, a stick, a cardboard box) and the disposition of the players. A player with an artifact as a pivot and an openness to the other players (even if those players are in the sole participant's imagination) will create something that previously never existed and could never be predicted. I see the same forces at work (or should I say "at play"?) in the construction of knowing that is defined as collaborative learning.

Adults often come together for no other purpose than just to talk. What happens in this talk depends on the topics that stand out in the field of experience of the participants and the relationships within the group. The interaction generally has no agenda, and when it does the group can easily use the agenda as the seed of interacting. The group constructs a knowledge that did not exist within any one individual and does not reside inside the head of any one individual (Shotter, 1993; Peters & Armstrong, 1998). The contribution of any individual comes about through the positioning of that individual toward the others (Davies & Harre, 1999) and the addressivity (Shotter, 1999), or the invitational stance, of that individual to dialogue with another. The knowledge is something that moves from person to person, from person to group, and back from group to person (Peters & Armstrong, 1998). It has meaning mainly to the group—its deep understanding is relational and cannot be reconstructed. As Bakhtin proposed, knowledge reflects a multiplicity of voices (polyphony) that, once experienced, forever alters the subject (Holquist, 1990). The change in the participants occurs at a perceptual level such that the reflection on the dialogue is done by a participant who now perceives differently because of the experience. The same can be said of the reader of text, who upon a second or third reading, finds the text to be something quite different from previous readings. The written words have not changed, but the reader has changed for having read them.

As dialogue progresses, self-consciousness gives way to group consciousness. Members talk into the group and from the group (Peters & Armstrong, 1998). The shift in the focus moves to the naive experience of dialogue. Words flow spontaneously without regard to defending a point of view. Members begin to trust and respect other members and to expose their genuine openness to learn—this is no easy task, especially when there are often impediments of power differentials when dialogue includes different ranks within an organization or, as is often the case, members who bring an interpersonal agenda to the dialogue. (In such situations it is good to remember the lessons of self-handicapping and role reversal developed in play.)

In playing out the role of another, we have developed the process for the Gestalt shift of perception and sharing the life world of the other. Understanding comes not from the world itself—we could not possibly be expected to take in all of the world presented to us at once—but from our approach to the world. The naïve experience of the life world of the other does not necessarily change our long-held assumptions. It is what we take from the experience in reflection that is transformational. A change in our assumptions, or the shift in our perception, is evidenced by the reaction to the return to the regular milieu. Brookfield (1994) discusses some of the dangers inherent in critical reflection: He had found themes of cultural suicide, impostership, and lost innocence in individuals who have practiced reflection and discovered a different view of their taken-for-granted world.

DISCUSSION

Play has evolved in its function from serving the biological imperatives of animals to laying the groundwork for co-constituted realities of diverse communities. The implication is that language and the social interaction that predicates it serve a major if not critical role in what we can term the construction of knowledge. It also suggests a certain selectivity in the processing of information. Features of information that are not conducive to temporal or hierarchical organization would tend to fade into the background or the perceptual field. This occurs as the knowledge constituted between people moves to the individual (Vygotsky, 1967). The efficiency of attending to only relevant input may seem advantageous; it can also be viewed as limiting, performing somewhat like the capacity of a computer modem. We find ourselves totally immersed in the world when we are in the state of flow, but lose (for the moment) some details of the experience when we make sense of this according to the culturally determined rules of organization. In an evolutionary sense, we can consider ourselves to be far more knowledgeable than any other species—maybe. Consider the way a snake perceives the world: A snake "sees" by sensing the very fine variations in temperature. We can only imagine what knowledge we are missing by this disability in our species. Snakes articulate the world through heat and, in this sense, have a very different reality from humans. Francois Jacob (1998) poses the following:

We might wonder whether there isn't some limit to the power of the resolution of the human brain or the human sensory system. For the moment, we can't really imagine what might restrict our analytical power this way. But you never know. The human brain might be incapable of understanding the human brain. (p. B5)

Knowledge is far more than analytical power. "Whatever account we give of the world or self finds its origins within relationships (Gergen and Gergen, 2000). Language is given meaning through social interaction, and "phenomena are made available to people, picked out from the 'hurly burly' of life [as Wittgenstein put it] by perceptual skills that are in part made what they are by the learning of language" (Harre, 2000). But suppose that a more advanced brain (as Jacob views the brain) were to evolve? Would a new form of knowledge be possible? Because we are unable to articulate any new form of mental activity, we are inclined to believe this is not possible. I would speculate that this phenomenon of advanced evolution has already occurred, and probably occurred often. Where are these advanced beings then? My guess—probably my hope—is that they are caught up in a fantastic story about villagers escaping hot lava or perhaps chatting away amiably in some café. It is a bit like having a 56K modem on a 28K line though. Mental activity can only progress as far as our artifacts allow us to share our worlds.

REFERENCES

Bekoff, M., & J. A. Byers. (1981). A Critical Reanalysis of the Ontogeny and Phylogeny of Mammalian Social and Locomotor Play: An Ethological Hornet's Nest. In K.

Immelmann, G. W. Barlow, L. Petrinovich, & M. Main (Eds.), *Behavioral Development* (pp. 296–337). London: Cambridge University Press.

Bellock, L., & H. Marsh. (1997). The Use of Ego Function Assessment for the Study of ADHD in Adults. *Psychiatric Annals* 27(8): 563–571.

Biben, M. (1979). Predation and Predatory Play Behavior of Domestic Cats. *Animal Behavior* 27: 81–94.

——— . (1998). Squirrel Monkeys Playfighting: Making the Case for a Cognitive Training Function for Play. In M. Bekoff & J. A. Byers (Eds.), *Animal Play: Evolutionary, Comparative, and Ecological Perspectives* (pp. 161–182). Cambridge: Cambridge University Press.

Bohm, D., D. Factor, & P. Garrett. (1997). Dialogue: A Proposal [On-line serial]. Retrieved May 3, 2001 from http://www.world.std.com/~lo/bohm/0000.html & ~lo/bohm/0001.html.

Brookfield, S. (1990). Using Critical Incidents to Explore Learners' Assumptions. In J. Mezirow & Associates (Eds.), *Fostering Critical Reflection in Adulthood: A Guide to Transformational Learning and Emancipatory Learning* (pp. 177–193). San Francisco: Jossey-Bass.

——— . (1994). Tales from the Darkside: A Phenomenology of Adult Critical Reflection. *International Journal of Lifelong Education* 13(3): 204–216.

Brown, J. (1995). Dialogue: Capacities and Stories. In S. Chawla & J. Renesch (Eds.), *Learning Organizations: Developing Cultures for Tomorrow's Workplace* (pp. 153–164). Portland, OR: Productivity Press.

Burghardt, G. M. (1984). On the Origins of Play. In P. K. Smith (Ed.), *Play in Animals and Humans* (pp. 5–41). Oxford: Basil Blackwell.

Byers, J. A. (1998). Biological Effects of Locomotor Play: Getting into Shape, or Something more Specific? In M. Bekoff & J. A. Byers (Eds.), *Animal Play: Evolutionary, Comparative, and Ecological Perspectives* (pp. 1161–1167). Cambridge: Cambridge University Press.

Cheyne, J. A., & D. Tarulli. (1999). Dialogue, Difference, and the "Third Voice" in the Zone of Proximal Development [On-line serial]. Retrieved December 3, 2001 from http://www.watarts.uwaterloo.ca/~acheyne/ZPD.html.

Csikszentmihalyi, M. (1979). The Concept of Flow. In B. Sutton-Smith (Ed.), Play and Learning. New York: Gardner.

Davies, B., & R. Hare. (1999). Positioning: The Discursive Production of Selves. Retrieved October 1999 from ftp:hostname: massey.ac.nz Directory ~alock/position/htm.

Fagen, R. (1981). *Animal Play Behavior*. New York: Oxford University Press.

Feuerstein, R., P. S. Klein, & A. J. Tannenbaum. (1991). *Mediated Learning Experience (MLE): Theoretical, Psychosocial, and Learning Implications*. London: Freund.

Flavell, J. H. (1963). *The Developmental Psychology of Jean Piaget*. New York: Van Nostrand.

Freire, P. (1970). *Pedagogy of the Oppressed* (M.B. Ramos, Trans.). New York: Seabury Press.

Gadamer, H. (1976). *Philosophical Hermeneutics*. Berkeley and Los Angeles: University of California Press.

Garvey, C. (1977). *Play*. Cambridge: Harvard University Press.

Gergen, K. J. (1982). Toward Transformation in Social Knowledge. New York: Springer-Verlag.

——— . (1997). Constructing Constructionists. *Issues in education* 3(2): 195–201.

————. (1999). Constructionist Dialogues and the Vicissitudes of the Political. Draft copy for volume edited by I. Velody for Sage, London [On-line serial]. Available at http://www.swarthmore.edu/SocSci/kgergen/text7.html (May).

Gergen, K. J., and M. M. Gergen. (2000). Toward a Cultural Constructionist Psychology [On-line serial]. Retrieved April 2001 from http://www.swarthmore.edu/SocSci/kgergen1/tccp.html.

Greenberg, K. H. (1991). A Model for Providing Intensive Mediated Learning Experiences in Preschool Settings. In R. Feuerstein, P. S. Klein, & A. J. Tannenbaum (Eds.), *Mediated Learning Experience (MLE): Theoretical, Psychosocial, and Learning Implications*. London: Freund.

Harre, R. (2000). Social Construction and Consciousness [On-line serial]. Retrieved January 5, 2001 from http://www.massey.ac.nz/Alock/virtual/max.htm.

Heidegger, M. (1996). *Being and Time: A Translation of Sein und Zeit* (J. Stambaugh, Trans.). Albany: State University of New York Press.

Holquist, M. (1990). *Dialogism—Bakhtin and His World*. London & New York: Routledge.

Howes, C. (1992). Mastery of the Communication of Meaning in Social Pretend Play. In C. Howes (Ed.), *The Collaborative Construction of Pretend*. Albany: State University of New York Press.

Husserl, E. (1982). *General Introduction to a Pure Phenomenology* (F. Kersten, Trans.). Boston: M. Nijhoff.

Hutt, C. (1979). Exploration and Play. In B. Sutton-Smith (Ed.), *Play and Learning* (pp. 175–194). New York: Gardner Press.

Isaacs, W. (1993). Taking Flight: Dialogue, Collective Thinking, and Organizational Learning. *Organizational dynamics* 22(2): 24–39.

Jacob, F. (1998). Nucleic Acids and Memory: Imagining the Limits of Scientific Research. *Chronicle of Higher Education*, December 11, (pp. B4–B5.

Kardash, C.A.M., & L. Wright. (1987). Does Creative Drama Benefit Elementary School Students: A Meta-Analysis. *Youth-Theatre Journal* 1(3): 11–18.

Martin, P., & T. M. Caro. (1985). On the Functions of Play and Its Role in Behavioral Development. *Advances in the Study of Behavior* 15: 59–103.

McIntyre, B. M. (1974). *Creative Drama in the Elementary School*. Itaska, IL: F. E. Peacock.

Merleau-Ponty, M. (1962). *The Phenomenology of Perception* (C. Smith, Trans.). London: Routledge and Kegan Paul.

Mezirow, J. (1990). How Critical Reflection Triggers Transformative Learning. In J. Mezirow & Associates (Eds.), *Fostering Critical Reflection in Adulthood* (pp. 1–20). San Francisco: Jossey-Bass.

Pellis, S. G. (1996). Sex and the Evolution of Play Fighting: A Review and Model Based on the Behavior of Muroid Rodents. *Play Theory & Research* 1(1): 55–75.

Peters, J. M., & J. L. Armstrong. (1998). Collaborative Learning: People Learning Together to Construct Knowledge. *New Directions for Adult & Continuing Education* 79(Fall): 75–85.

Piaget, J. (1976). Symbolic Play. In J. S. Bruner, A. Jolly, & K. Silva (Eds.), *Play—Its Role in Development and Evolution* (pp. 555–569). New York: Basic Books.

Pollio, H. R., T. B. Henley, & C. J. Thompson. (1997). *The Phenomenology of Everyday Life*. Cambridge: Cambridge University Press.

Rike, E. (1992). *Workshops that Work: Dramatic Structure/Language Arts Skills*. Knoxville: Play Studio.

————. (1993). Guided Symbolic Dramatic Play as the Missing Link to Literacy. In J. A. Wilkinson (Ed.), *The Symbolic Dramatic Play–Literacy Connection: Whole Brain, Whole Body, Whole Learning* (pp. 118–129). Needham Heights, MA: Ginn Press.

Shotter, J. (1993). *The Cultural Politics of Everyday Life*. Toronto: University of Toronto Press.

————. (1999). *Life Inside the Dialogically Structured Mind: Bakhtin's and Volosinov's Account of Mind as Out in the World between Us*. Retrieved December 2001 from http://www.massey.ac.nz/Alock/virtual/rowan.htm.

Smith, P. K. (1995). Play, Ethology, and Education: A Personal Account. In A. D. Pellegrini (Ed.), *The Future of Play Theory: A Multidisciplinary Inquiry into the Contributions of Brian Sutton-Smith* (pp. 3–21). Albany: State University of New York Press.

Sternberg, P., & A. Garcia. (1989). *Sociodrama: Who's in Your Shoes?* New York: Praeger.

Suomi, S. J., & H. F. Harlow. (1976). Monkeys without Play. In J. S. Bruner, A. Jolly, & K. Silva (Eds.), *Play—Its Role in Development and Evolution* (pp. 490–495). New York: Basic Books.

Sutton-Smith, B. (1979). *Play and Learning*. New York: Gardner Press.

Tarule, J. M. (1992). Dialogue and Adult Learning. *Liberal Education* 78(4): 12–19.

Thompson, K. V. (1998). Self-Assessment in Juvenile Play. In M. Bekoff & J. A. Byers (Eds.), *Animal Play: Evolutionary, Comparative, and Ecological Perspectives* (pp. 183–204). Cambridge: Cambridge University Press.

Vygotsky, L. S. (1967). Play and Its Role in the Mental Development of the Child. *Soviet Psychology* 12: 62–76.

————. (1962). *Thought and Language* (E. Hanfmann & G. Vaker, Eds. & Trans.). Cambridge: MIT Press.

Wender, D. (1997). Attention Deficit Hyperactivity Disorder in Adults: A Wide View of a Widespread Condition. *Psychiatric Annals* 27(8): 556.

44

Play Deprivation and Juvenile Violence: Neuroscience, Play, and Child Development

Joe Frost,
as summarized by Connie Steele

Joe Frost, well-known author and playground design specialist, suggested that deprivation of the opportunities to play freely for the infant and young child may lead to juvenile violence (Frost & Jacobs, 1996). He provided a convincing rationale for his position, for children have been committing a rapidly growing number of violent crimes. These criminals are getting younger and the crimes more violent. The rise in juvenile violence is a cry for security and belonging. Children need to spend a great deal of time with adults who hold positive values—cooperative, friendly, unselfish, caring, giving, sharing, loyal, supportive adults. Yet children are bombarded with a never-ending array of violent, sexually explicit television programs, movies, and video games that shape values and behavior and deprive children of traditional play and games. One consequence of such play deprivation is juvenile violence.

Play is commonly characterized as pleasurable, self-motivated, non-goal-directed, spontaneous, and free of adult-imposed rules. Play is evident in the random, expressive movements of the infant, in the free-wheeling exploration of toddlers, in the pretended, imaginative, and constructive activities of the preschoolers, and in the chases games, rough and tumble and organized, cooperative/competitive games of the school-age child; these are all creative expressions of play. Creative free play has therapeutic powers. The child's make-believe play gives children a sense of control over traumatic life experiences.

However, children no longer have the freedom to play when and where they choose. They have hectic schedules with very little time for free play. Most public park, public school, and child-care-center playgrounds are hazardous and ill-equipped. Schools have shortened or eliminated recess altogether under the pressure for academic excellence. Once upon a time, children could roam with relative safety through their neighborhoods, play with their friends, and interact with the adults they met. Now they must deal with the paranoia of staying inside, keeping the doors locked, not talking to strangers, and managing the loneliness. When children go to the park with parents, their activities are often restricted by the scarcity of other children to play with, the lack of toys, and unsafe or age-inappropriate playground equipment.

Frost proposed that creative play is a viable alternative and antidote for violence, as violence for many children is a cry for attention and help, for power and control. Children who commit violent acts desperately need to be heard, to know someone is listening and that someone cares. They do not simply wake up one day violent and decide to go kill someone. From an early age, children need caring, considerate adults to help them develop positive values; they need adults who will respect their feelings and provide many rich opportunities and environments for social interaction and creative expression. But many contemporary children rarely or never experience the wonders of the farm, the wilderness, or even a creative, challenging playground to stimulate the imagination, sharpen skills, and create a sense of awe and wonder.

In 1998, Frost addressed the International Play Association (IPA) Triennial National Conference with renewed hope in his recommendations that children be given many opportunities for creative play. He said that play, still considered by some as frivolous, unimportant behavior with no apparent purpose, has currently earned new respect as biologists, neuroscientists, psychologists, and others see that play is indeed serious business and is perhaps equally as important as other basic drives of sleep, rest, and food. In fact, Frost stated: "The importance of play for brain growth and child development will influence families, schools and other social and corporate institutions to rearrange their attitudes and priorities about play, recess, physical education, music, games, art, and rich personal interactions between caregivers and children."

In Frost's (1998) IPA presentation, entitled "Neuroscience, Play, and Child Development," he examined the attention to brain development in the last fifty years. In the 1960s a number of professionals concluded from both animal and human studies that infancy and early childhood were optimum periods for development and that the brain is most plastic during these periods and highly influenced by environmental stimulation. He recalled J. McVicker Hunt's (1961) classic work that garnered extensive evidence to conclude that the concept of fixed intelligence was no longer tenable. Frost also referred to the insights of Jean Piaget, who analyzed how the stimulation of a child in varied play environments during infancy and early childhood would lead to intellectual development. After describing the human brain's electrochemical transmissions and the number of synapses that increase during the first three years of a child's life, Frost concluded,

The early experiences of children play a critical role in determining the wiring of the brain, and the range and quality of the child's intellectual abilities. . . . The pathways that are repeatedly activated or used are protected and retained into adulthood. . . . Brain development is truly a "use or lose it" process. Early experiences determine which neurons are to be used and which are to die, and, consequently, whether the child will be brilliant or dull, confident or fearful, articulate or tongue-tied.

Frost (1998) continued, "Much of the violence in the United States may be related to the lack of appropriate attachments of young children to adults." Stroufe's (in prerss) long-term research confirmed the link between attachment and violence. What we know is that neglect by parents, social deprivation, stressful living conditions, and lack of appropriate stimulation jeopardize early brain development and may result in immature social and emotional behavior, impulsivity, violence, and dramatic reduction in capacity for later learning.

Frost documented the linkages between brain development and play during the early childhood years:

1. All healthy young mammals play; therefore, parents of human infants must both initiate and give structure and direction to play. That structure acts as a scaffolding for development.

2. The range and complexity of play quickly increase as neurons start hard-wiring connections at a remarkable rate. Play programs neural structure and resulting, increasingly complex neural structures influence ever more complex play.

3. The early games and frivolity of animals and humans equip them for the skills they will need in later life. They learn flexibility, inventiveness, and versatility. They practice motor, language, and negotiation skills. They engage in socially and culturally mediated task analysis and problem solving during their play.

4. Play is essential for healthy development. Early childhood experiences exert a dramatic, precise impact on the wiring of the neural circuits. During the first years it is playful activity, not direct instruction, seclusion, deprivation, or abuse, that makes a positive difference in brain development and subsequent human functioning. Children who don't play much or are rarely touched develop brains 20 to 30 percent smaller than normal for their age.

5. Play deprivation results, then, in aberrant behavior. Frost cited the research of Stuart Brown, a physician, psychiatrist, and play researcher, who in one study found that twenty-six convicted Texas murderers had either an absence of childhood play or engaged in such abnormal play as bullying, sadism, cruelty to animals, or extreme teasing.

What neuroscientists are doing with their physical evidence in brain scans is revealing the relative consequences of environmental stimulation or neglect. The endless games that the very young play are in reality storehouses for programming the brain for language, art, music, math, science, kinesthetic, and interpersonal abilities and intelligence. Children's imaginative or make-believe play is a powerful medium for allowing them to make complex and frightening events manageable and comprehensible. Adults must provide experiences that program the neural structures for the skills to be achieved, and they must do so in a caring, supportive context.

Frost (1998) offers fifteen dictums for parents and educators that come from brain research, as it has practical applications in how to care for our children:

1. Start early—at conception, involving two healthy adults.

2. Spend lots of time playing with the child—for secure attachment and bonding.

3. Be positive, playful, warm, and nurturing—support healthy brain development.

4. Pay attention to the child's moral development—taking turns, sharing, listening.

5. Challenge the child, but not beyond his or her range of abilities—make play doable.

6. Hug the infant—touch, caress, pat, cuddle, and gently rock back and forth.

7. Talk to the child—respond to his or her cooing and babbling, use "parentese."

8. Introduce music and art early—play soft, soothing, classical music.

9. Substitute play, art, music, and family outings for television.

10. Make home drug free—model drug-free behavior for the children.

11. Provide blocks, beads, sand, water, simple tools, pots and pans, dress-up clothes, and other simple raw materials at age-appropriate times.

12. Protect the child from stress and trauma, including scolding.

13. Don't overstimulate the child with too many toys, too much meaningless talk.

14. Read to the child, sing with the child, and play simple games every day.

15. Don't accept the growing pattern of deleting recess, physical education, and art and music.

In closing, of particular relevance is Frost's quotation from Begley's (1996) study: "Zap: neurons in the brain's amygdala send pulses of electricity through the circuits that control emotion. You hold him on your lap and talk . . . and neurons from his ears start hard-wiring connections to the auditory cortex. And you thought you were just playing with your kid" (p. 55).

REFERENCES

Begley, S. (1996). Your Child's Brain. *Newsweek* (February 29): 55–58.

Brown, S. L. (1994). Animals at Play. *National Geographic* 186(6): 2–35.

Frost, J. L. (1998). Neuroscience, Play, and Child Development. Paper presented at the IPA/USA Triennial National Conference, Longmont, CO, June.

Frost, J. L., & P. J. Jacobs. (1995). Play Deprivation and Juvenile Violence. *Dimensions* 23(3): 13–20, 39.

Frost, J. L., S. Wortham, & S. Reifel. (2001). Neuroscience, Play Deprivation, and Pay-for-Play. In *Play and Child Development* (pp. 77–115). Columbus: Merrill Prentice-Hall.

Hunt, J. M. (1961). *Intelligence and Experience*. New York: Ronald Press.

Piaget, J. (1962). *Play, Dreams and Imitation in Childhood*. New York: Norton.

Stroufe, L. A. (in press). *Psychotherapy as Development*.

45

Educational Drama and Learning

Betty J. Wagner

> Play is practice for more serious behaviors. Children do not play be-
> cause they are young; they have their youth because they must play.
> —Karl Groos (1861–1946)

Educational or improvisational drama affects the ways students think and learn.
When children engage in improvisational drama, they are behaving symbolically.
They are saying, for example, that for the purposes of imaginative play a certain
chair is a pilot's cockpit. This ability to say that this stands for that is critical to
thought. Unless children can respond to and create symbols, they cannot learn to
read, write, or engage in mathematical thinking. Why do any of us want to converse, read, write, and reason? We engage in these processes in order to perceive,
to expand our perspective on, and to more deeply understand and enter into our
world. As we do this we use symbols. Young children spontaneously engage in
imaginative play for the same three reasons: to understand, to gain a larger perspective on, and to interact more profoundly with their world. In drama (just as in
thinking, reading, and writing) students make meaning by connecting their prior
experience to the challenge of the moment, be it to come up with an apt image and
response as a player in an improvisation or an apt image and response as a reader or
writer of a text.

THE EFFECT OF DRAMA ON COGNITION, ORAL LANGUAGE, READING, AND WRITING

Many educators believe that drama develops thinking, oral language, reading, and writing. They also believe that drama improves students' cognitive growth as reflected in language skills, problem-solving ability, and I.Q. Moreover, the changes are lasting (Wagner, 1998). Several studies show that drama also improves role taking (Wagner, 1998), which is comprehending and correctly inferring attributes of another person. These inferences, which include another's thinking, attitudes, and emotions, are a function of cognitive perception. In Piaget's (1926) terms, to engage in role taking is to "decenter" or move away from a predominantly egocentric stage of development. Growth in cognition is dependent on growth in role taking. Not surprisingly, drama improves oral language as well as thinking. I looked at thirty-two quasi-experimental or correlational studies of the effects of drama on oral language development found in the literature, and found that twenty-five of these show that drama improves or correlates with improvement of oral language (Wagner, 1998). What is the effect of drama on reading? Five literature reviews concluded that drama seems to be effective in promoting literacy (Wagner, 1998). Eighteen out of twenty-nine quasi-experimental studies that I found in the literature show that drama improves story recall, comprehension, and/or vocabulary (Wagner, 1998). To illustrate, let's look at the stunning results of the Whirlwind Program in Chicago.

Whirlwind has developed a Reading Comprehension through Drama program that is currently conducting a series of twenty drama lessons in many Chicago public schools. Their widely respected statistical study (Parks & Rose, 1997) of fourth graders showed that the students who participated in the Whirlwind program improved three months more than the control-group students in their Iowa Test of Basic Skills reading scores. The Whirlwind students improved by 12.1 months, and those without Whirlwind 9.1 months.

In the reading comprehension program, a group of Whirlwind actors read short stories to the children in grades K–8 and then work together with them to act out the stories, draw pictures of them, and create three-dimensional miniversions of them. In the process, they form more detailed images in their heads as they read; these images are what help them to remember and understand the facts and inferences of the story. The program's results have recently come to the attention of the Chicago public schools. If Whirlwind had chosen to measure only the effect of the program on the drama skills of children, which did improve significantly, by the way, the impact might not have been noticed. But when reading skills improved, it was front-page news in the *Chicago Tribune* (Beeler, 1999). This is why it is politically important for those of us who advocate drama to share results like these with policy makers.

Drama has a positive effect on writing as well. Emergent literacy studies show that children give their early writing a multimodality associated with gesture and graphics (Wagner, 1998). Drama serves as an effective prewriting strategy, clarifying for children concepts they might want to explore through writing. Recent observational studies report remarkable maturity in student writing that emerges from drama (Wagner, 1998). Significant shifts in audience awareness occur before, during, and after drama. The writing produced in role shows more attention to sensory imagery, addressing the reader, insight into characters' feelings and empathy, and the need to clarify information and disclose it selectively. Seven statistical studies, including one that I conducted, show that drama improves the quality of writing. It is significantly correlated with early word-writing fluency as well as the quality of writing. Preschoolers who engage in symbolic play and drawing are more likely to read and write early. Some of the best writing my own students have produced over the years has come when they are writing in role. At this stage in my career I cannot imagine teaching any content at any level, including the graduate level (as my doctoral students will tell you), without drama. It is a powerful stimulus for thinking and writing.

THEORETICAL UNDERPINNINGS

What is the theory that explains the efficacy of improvisational or educational drama as a foundation for thinking, reading, and writing? Both educational drama and literacy are rooted in the same assumptions about learning. Two of the most generative learning theories to explain the role of improvisational drama are those of Lev Vygotsky (1966, 1978) and Jerome Bruner (1983, 1986, 1990). Both were instrumental in ushering in the constructivist theory of learning and both provide a solid foundation for using drama in the classroom as a way to deepen and enlarge understanding of any subject matter. In addition, several other major theorists have asserted that imaginative role playing is central to the development of thinking: Barnes (1968), Britton (1970), and Moffett (Moffett & Wagner, 1992). Nor should we overlook the guiding educational philosopher of the early decades of this century, John Dewey (1959), nor Jean Piaget (1962), who, like Vygotsky (1966), showed how pretend play, especially the use of objects in a nonliteral fashion, parallels cognitive development. Piaget asserted that conceptual thinking develops through activity, spontaneous play, manipulation of objects, and social collaboration. He showed how participation in drama leads to improved listening, comprehension, and sequential understanding, and the integration of thought, action, and language.

CONSTRUCTIVIST THEORY OF LEARNING

Our understanding of the learning process has undergone a sea change in the last three decades, and thanks to the brain research quantum that scientists are currently conducting, we may be on the verge of another sea change. Simplistic behaviorist models of learning are now largely discredited, except to account for mastering the simplest of mechanical skills. Back in the 1950s, Karl Pribram and others were breaking new ground in understanding the neurobiology of the brain, and Jerome Bruner and other cognitive psychologists in New York were discovering the brilliant Russian psychologist, Lev Vygotsky. They were not just tinkering with or reforming behaviorism, they were replacing it by putting the significance of meaning and values back into the center of human psychology. They began a quest to discover and describe formally how human beings create meaning. In so doing, they climbed into bed with thinkers who had been banished from psychology's house for most of this century: philosophers, historians, anthropologists, linguists, novelists, poets, and dramatists.

The result has been the positing of the now widely held "constructivist theory of learning." Children are no longer described as Dickens's schoolmaster Gradgrind in the novel *Hard Times* saw them: "little vessels . . . ready to have imperial gallons of facts poured into them until they were full to the brim" (p. 1). Now there is a widespread recognition that knowledge is not poured into students' passive little heads, but instead is constructed by each learner. As children actively engage in experiencing the world, they are just as actively constructing models in their minds to account for what they are undergoing. The way they think is literally transformed by their experience and by their attempts to make sense of it, and especially by those experiences that call for responses that are just beyond what they can generate on their own. Except for those psychologists who in the last quarter century have shifted from the *construction* of meaning to the *processing* of information, likening the brain to a computer, major learning theorists keep the making of meaning at the center of their understanding of how the mind works (Bruner, 1990, p. 4).

Constructivist theory posits that human beings actively create their own models or hypotheses as to how the world works, not just with the mental stuff of their biological brains, but in dialogue with the culture in which they are immersed. As Bruner (1986) suggested, humans construct meaning in the presence of three worlds: (1) the world they are born with, their innate human propensity to make sense of the world and their capacity to acquire language; (2) the objective reality of the real world; and (3) the culture in which they are immersed.

According to Bruner (1983), all theory in science and all narrative and interpretive knowing in the humanities is dependent on the human capacity to create, to imagine a world. This is the amazing capacity that markedly sets us off from other members of the animal kingdom. As Susanne Langer (1957) put it, "Imagination is the primary talent of the human mind, the activity in whose service language was evolved" (cited in Berthoff, 1984, p. 2)

Children are active meaning makers in both their play and their work. They imagine how things work and they test out those imaginings. In other words, learners are active, goal-oriented, hypothesis-generating symbol manipulators. Learners express the understandings they have constructed in symbols—in gestures first, then in spoken words and drawings, and finally in written language. As they are pressured to find answers on their own, they are actively learning. Each drama creates a problem for students before they have been taught how to respond. They act first and then reflect on their actions. Perhaps this accounts for drama's power in effecting learning.

Another characteristic of drama is its emotional component. Because of the immediacy of the dramatic present and the pressure to respond aptly in role in a social setting, participants are vividly alive to the moment and alert to what is expected of them. As they get caught up in the emotion of the dramatic activity, they are often able to express themselves in a more mature manner and language than they could otherwise.

ZONE OF PROXIMAL DEVELOPMENT

Both dramatic improvisation and dialogue with a teacher or more knowledge-able peer can provide the lure to learn in what Vygotsky (1978, p. 86) calls the "zone of proximal development," the level just beyond the level at which they can function on their own. Watch children in their spontaneous play. They typically take on adult roles. Perhaps because they are little and powerless, they want to be the captain of the rocket ship, the most powerful ninja, or the bossy mother who knows what everyone needs and should be doing.

As children engage in spontaneous symbolic play or classroom drama directed by a teacher, they assume not only the language, but also the personas of significant adults. In the process they are catapulted into a developmental level that is above their actual one. As they improvise, they are pressured to behave and use language in new and previously untried ways.

For example, Lee Galda and Anthony Pellegrini (1990) report on a three-year-old and a four-year-old girl who are playing doctor together. As they take off the doll's imaginary diaper, one reprimands the other for using the word "poo poo" when in role as the doctor (p. 94). The act of taking on a new persona demands a word choice beyond the language of her everyday life. The experiences the child has had in the society of adults is brought to bear on the task at hand, and the pull is toward internalizing a diction that had not ever before been part of the child's own repertoire.

How is an improvisational drama different from a story the child hears or reads? Drama is done with the body and gesture as well as with words, and it can be engaged in long before the child is ready to read and write. Therefore, Vygotsky (1967) sees it as the powerful prelude to and appropriate extension of literacy. Although young children often role play alone, accompanying their actions with a flood of egocentric speech, when they start dramatic play with other children they are engaging in a profoundly challenging social event. They must negotiate a single vision of what the drama is about, what the setting looks like, who takes which roles, and so on.

Often in improvisational drama we find children "scaffolding," to use Jerome Bruner's (1983) term. They provide a framework on which other children can stand as they are pressured into Vygotsky's zone of proximal development. Holly Giffin (1984) presented an example of this in an observation of a child in the role as queen who is playing with a boy who is not quite yet able to imagine himself in his role. She orders him to bring her a vial of poison, and he comes back with a paper cup with real water. He grins sheepishly and smiles, "It's only water." Without for a moment stepping out of role, the queen takes it, sniffs it, and decides, "You're right! Go get me the other vial." The next time her page comes in, he is firmly in role. "Here is the poison, your Majesty." Drama can challenge children to use language and gesture they have never needed before.

THE ROLE OF GESTURE

Our first experiences both before and after birth were centered in our bodies. As newborns, we knew when we were hungry, dry, comfortable, held in strong and loving arms. As infants, every part of our bodies were engaged in making sense of our world, in constructing meaning. Before we could talk, we used gestures to communicate. Vygotsky sees these as the earliest symbolic behavior. We reached toward and pointed at what we wanted. We waved "bye, bye" before we had a word to go with the gesture. Thus, movement and gesture, even before vocalization, are the beginning of communication. Gesture starts as random movement and ends as precise symbol. Random vocalization grows into speech; gesture develops into drawing and, later, writing. Writing begins with a baby's gestures in the air; these are signs and symbols, just as our later pictures and writings on paper are also signs and symbols.

Watch a child turn a block into an airplane or rocket. The gesture becomes the thing, and the child who is making this happen knows perfectly well this is a game of pretend. Because of the way he is moving the object, it has become for the moment a symbol for something else. If you ask him if this is a real rocket, he will look at you as if you were stupid. Of course it is not. But please, lets keep the game going; don't stop the pretending to ask dumb questions like that.

Gesture—because it is done with the hand—also leads to drawing. The first drawings children do are not representational; rather, they are metaphorical symbols. This circle stands for a face. Most young children go through the familiar stage of drawing tadpole people. These simple drawings are not representations of the real people they see. Instead they are simply shorthand symbols. Arms and legs are just sticks attached to the circle. Gardner (1980) stated that such early pictures "stand for the entire class or represent an ideal type, instead of depicting particulars that can be identified and then paired up with their realization in the real world" (p. 65). Vygotsky (1978) sees both drawing and drama developing from gesture. From the symbolizing in drawing and drama, it is just a short step to writing.

ENACTIVE, ICONIC, AND SYMBOLIC REPRESENTATIONS OF THE WORLD

Now let us consider the theory of the second major constructivist, Jerome Bruner. He sees gesture as enactive representation.

Enactive Representation

Enactive is with the hand, iconic with the eye, and symbolic with the brain. In enactive knowing we learn "by doing," by experiencing with our bodies. Iconic knowing is knowing through an image, either in the mind, in drawing, or in gesture. Symbolic knowing encompasses translation into language, the symbol system par excellence. However, all three kinds of knowing are actually symbolic.

We can easily see that drama involves all three kinds of representation. Role players use their bodies, create images in their minds and with their gestures, and use language to symbolize experience. Often in educational drama, participants stop to create drawings to help them visualize their common experience. Participants in drama engage them in enactive, iconic, and symbolic representation.

Before concluding that only drama uses all three modes of representation, however, reading and writing with these three lenses should be considered. Even these two primarily verbal processes resonate enactively and iconically. Reading at first sight seems the opposite of enactivity. It is a quiet engagement with written symbols. I was led to rethink this perception about reading recently when comprehending Deborah G. Jacque's (1993) teacher research. She read *The Judge* five times to her kindergarten students, and videotaped the first and last sessions. What she discovered was that during the first reading, when the children had difficulty understanding the story, they sat very quietly. Their excitement and questions increased with each reading, and, interestingly, by the final reading there was a marked increase in body movements, conveying the story's meaning. "For example, [two children] acted out 'closer day by day' together, children acted out the meaning of scoundrel with killing hand motions, and [one boy] physically hid his body from the horrible thing as it appeared behind the judge."

> Its eyes are scary,
> Its tail is hairy,
> Its paws have claws,
> It snaps its jaws.
> I tell you judge we all better pray!

In Bruner's terms, they were learning enactively.

In Chicago, in addition to the reading comprehension program described earlier, the Whirlwind artists showed first graders how to make letters with their bodies—enactively learning to connect shapes with sounds, essential for early reading development. A statistical study (Rose, 1999) showed that after twenty sessions the children who physically represented sounds by making shapes with their bodies improved significantly more than control students in their ability to recognize both consonant and vowel sounds and to separate spoken words into their phonemes. Enactive learning is very effective with young children.

Iconic Representation

Now let us look at iconic representation—knowing through images. Like role playing, drawing stems from gesture. It is gesture crystallized. But not only drawing or drama creates images. Without imaging in our minds we cannot read or write either. Like enactive representation, iconic knowing is not unique to drama.

The growth of representational or symbolic thought is largely dependent on the ability to create mental images. Image begins as fleeting sensate happening, neural firings, and sensorimotor rehearsal. With the onset of the stage of development that Piaget (1962) has termed "object permanence," the child can hold the image and recall it when the object is absent. This gives way to symbolic thought and dramatic play. Giving children a good environment that encourages them to imitate and symbolically play with experience will enhance imagery skills and cognitive development. Studies have shown that the ability to fantasize freely is a cognitive skill related to concentration, fluency, and the ability to organize and integrate diverse stimuli. Drama influences imagery toward increased discrimination and vividness, and enhances the students' ability to control their images.

Readers engage in iconic knowing, translating words into pictures in their minds. Read this line by the cowboy poet Tim Henderson: "When the live oaks make witch fingers on a red Comanche moon." Can you see the image? Words lead to iconic knowing. Not only do we see the night sky, but the witch fingers tell us the time of year. Live oaks only become witches when the leaves have fallen. We also have in that line a sense of place. The Comanches once roamed the great southwestern plains of the United States. "When the live oaks make witch fingers on a red Comanche moon." Writing, like reading, is dependent on iconic representation. The challenge, especially for the fiction writer and poet, is in large part to create pictures with words.

Symbolic Representation

As noted earlier, both dramatic play and drawing are ways children enter imaginatively into their worlds. In both they are engaging in symbolism. Because dramatic play and drawing are ways of saying this stands for that, Vygotsky (1978) sees both as a precursor to writing. Like gestures, all three—dramatic play, drawing, and writing—are symbolic acts. It is just a step from drawing and drama to using letters symbolically, because writing is simply another way of symbolizing, and like drama and drawing it has its roots in gesture. It is done with the hand, not the voice. It is putting onto a page something that stands for something else. A letter of the alphabet is simply a symbol for a speech sound.

Like drawing and writing, in improvisational drama one thing stands for another. The only difference is that the setting for drama must be a social one. Even here, however, there is an overlap with reading and writing. Literacy events for young children tend to be highly social occasions as well, as Anne Haas Dyson (1990) has so richly documented.

THE FIRST SCREAM

The chapter will close with a final illustration of the power of drama and the other arts in helping students learn enactively and iconically. In this illustration, focusing on the concrete led to the children's understanding of a much larger and more abstract issue: the need for safety regulations in factories.

This is an account of an eight-year-old's response to a well-developed week-long unit of study incorporating drama as well as other arts in Bradford, England. Christopher Ford conducted this history lesson for a group of seven- to nine-year-olds. He used a true story about an event in the history of the school as the theme for the first week of the school year. The event was a tragic one, set in 1869, when the boiler had exploded in a bobbin mill that had stood next door to the school the students attended. The safety valve of this steam boiler had been blowing off frequently in the weeks leading up to the tragedy. Local shopkeepers had complained. The manager of the mill told the boiler-keeper to do something to stop the complaints. He did. He put weights on top of the safety valve and tied them down with heavy rope.

At 10:25 on a Wednesday morning, just after the primary children had gone out into the playground next to the mill for recess, the boiler exploded. It demolished the mill, killing many workers inside, including the manager's son. The wall collapsed onto the playground, killing eight children and injuring many more. The bodies of two five-year-old boys were discovered with the hobbyhorse on which they were playing. The heavy safety valve from the boiler was found over a quarter of a mile away in a railway goods yard. The country was outraged. New laws about factory safety were passed as a result.

The class of children explored this story through drama, reading, and writing for the entire week. Mr. Ford led them through enactive, iconic, and symbolic representations of the event. The children looked at Victorian photographs and found out about Victorian schools. They read the local newspapers of the day and paid special attention to the *London Times* of 1869 to see what the children or their parents might have talked about at the breakfast table on the day of the tragedy. They looked for news items that children of that day might have noticed. Then they used the enactive symbolization of dance to explore a theme of force and power against the fragility of people. They explored though drama the actions of town persons who heard about the tragedy and the reactions of relatives and friends of those who were killed or injured. They took on the roles of those who were near rather than actually in the explosion.

One source of information puzzled them. It was the original school logbook, which the school still keeps. There they read the headmaster's comments of that day. It merely said, "Was obliged to send the children home today owing to the boiler explosion, eight of the children having been killed and many injured." Nothing more. The next entry was for three weeks later and read, "Commenced school today with a very fair attendance."

After a few days of absorbing information about this event, the children focused on the first scream. Here the work became iconic, to use Bruner's (1983) term. The children used art materials to create an image of the first scream. Lydia's clay piece was a stark profile of a face with a wide-open mouth. Then they dramatized that first scream, moving to enactive representation. Then they froze the action to capture a moment in time. They shared with each other their split-second pictures created with their bodies. The teacher asked them to think about a piece of writing that could capture a split second of the whole event, but that would somehow tell people everything they needed to know about what happened. Lydia's poem shows the way her iconic and enactive learning fed into her use of words:

The First Scream

One day.
An ordinary school day.
Wednesday 9th July 1869, an eight-year-old screamed in the
National School on Park Road.
Children in the school were as still
And silent as mice and stared across the room

To where Emily Grey was standing.
Now, Emily Grey was a nice girl. She had blond curly hair, blue
Eyes, rosy red cheeks, and pinky-red smooth lips.
But now she had wide, peeled eyes, pale face and a dry sore
Throat.
Emily Grey was petrified.
She had her eyes fixed outside. All kinds of thoughts were
Jumbled in her mind.
Astonished, puzzled, confused, hurt.
In the playground below, bricks piled high.
Heavy, jagged, sharp, rough.
And underneath a face,
Soft, gentle, delicate, smooth.
Blond hair, blue eyes, rosy cheeks.
Her sister.
   By Lydia, aged 8

This young child was able to capture the ordinariness of the scene and the sense that this little girl did not deserve this fate—she was "nice." The poem builds from the sound of the scream that riveted the attention of the class to Emily Grey's face, then to what she saw outside, and finally to the denouement of the last two words. The juxtaposition of adjectives painted the picture graphically: "heavy, jagged, sharp, rough" versus "soft, gentle, delicate, smooth." Economy of language, sensory imagery, dramatic juxtaposition, and the shock of the last line—all lead to the powerful impact of this profound response to a real but at first distant historical event.

Soon after the school held one of many open houses for children to share their work with their parents. The teacher explained to Lydia's mother that it had taken a whole week to write those few lines, and that no other writing had been done during that week. He asked her how she felt about that. Did she mind that her daughter wrote only a few lines in a whole week? She replied that she had spent all of her life never writing lines like that, so her daughter taking only a few days to do it was a wonder, not a worry.

In conclusion, drama aids thinking because it has the same goal as the goal of all cognition: to understand, to gain a larger perspective, and to engage more profoundly with the world.

REFERENCES

Barnes, D. (1968). *Drama in the English Classroom*. Urbana, IL: National Council of Teachers of English.

Beeler, A. (1999). Whirlwind Program Puts New Spin on Reading Class. *Chicago Tribune*, July 18, pp. 1, 3.

Berthoff, A. E. (ed.). (1984). *Reclaiming the Imagination: Philosophical Perspectives for Writing and Teachers of Writing*. Upper Montclair, NJ: Boynton/Cook.

Britton, J. (1970). *Language and Learning*. Baltimore: Penguin.

Bruner, J. S. (1983). *Child's Talk: Learning to Use Language*. New York: W. W. Norton.

———. (1986). Play, Thought, and Language. *Prospects* 16: 77–83.

————. (1990). *Acts of Meaning*. Cambridge: Harvard University Press.

Christie, J. F. (ed.). (1991). *Play and Early Literacy Development*. Albany: State University of New York Press.

Dewey, J. (1959). *Art as Experience*. New York: G. P. Putnam's Sons.

Dickens, C. (1993). *Hard Times*. New York: W. W. Norton.

Dyson, A. H. (1990). Talking Up a Writing Community: The Role of Talk in Learning to Write. In S. Hynds & D. L. Rubin (Eds.), *Perspectives on Thought and Learning* (pp. 99–114). Urbana, IL: National Council of Teachers of English.

Eisner, E. W. (1990). Implications of Artistic Intelligences for Education. In W. J. Moody (Ed.), *Artistic Intelligences: Implications for Education* (pp. 31–42). New York: Teachers College Press.

Flynn, R. M., & G. A. Carr. (1994). Exploring Classroom Literature through Drama: A Specialist and a Teacher Collaborate. *Language Arts* 71: 38–43.

Galda, L., & A. D. Pellegrini. (1990). Play Talk, School Talk, and Emergent Literacy. In S. Hynds & D. L. Rubin (Eds.), *Perspectives on Thought and Learning* (pp. 91–97). Urbana, IL: National Council of Teachers of English.

Gardner, H. (1980). *Artful Scribbles*. New York: Basic Books.

Giffin, H. (1984). Coordination of Meaning in Shared Make Believe. In I. Bretherton (Ed.), *Symbolic Play: The Development of Social Understanding* (pp. 73–100). New York: Academic Press.

Greene, M. (1995). *Releasing the Imagination*. San Francisco: Jossey-Bass.

Heath, S. B. (1993). Inner City Life through Drama: Imagining the Language Classroom. *TESOL Quarterly* 27(2): 177–192.

Heathcote, D., & G. Bolton. (1995). *Drama for Learning: Dorothy Heathcote's Mantle of the Expert Approach to Education*. Portsmouth, NH: Heinemann.

Jacque, D. G. (1993). The Judge Comes to Kindergarten. In K. E. Holland, R. A. Hungerford, & S. B. Ernst (Eds.), *Journeying: Children Responding to Literature* (pp. 43–52). Portsmouth, NH: Heinimann.

Langer, S. L. (1957). *Philosophy in a New Key*. Cambridge: Harvard University Press.

Miller, C., & J. Saxton (eds.). (1999). *International Conversations*. Victoria, BC: International Drama in Education Research Institute.

Moffett, J., & B. J. Wagner. (1992). *Student-Centered Language Arts and Reading, K–12*. Portsmouth, NH: Boynton/Cook Heinemann.

O'Neill, C. (1995). *Drama Worlds: A Framework for Process Drama*. Portsmouth, NH: Heinemann.

Paley, V. G. (1978). The Use of Dramatics in Kindergarten. *Elementary School Journal* 78: 319–323.

————. (1990). *The Boy Who Would Be a Helicopter*. Cambridge: Harvard University Press.

Parks, M., & D. Rose. (1997). *The Impact of Whirlwind's Reading Comprehension Through Drama Program on 4th Grade Students' Reading Skills and Standardized Test Scores*. San Francisco: 3-D Group.

Pellegrini, A. D., L. Galda, J. Dresden, & S. Cox. (1991). A Longitudinal Study of the Predictive Relations among Symbolic Play, Linguistic Verbs, and Early Literacy. *Research in the Teaching of English* 25: 219–235.

Piaget, J. (1926). *The Language and Thought of the Child*. London: Routledge and Kegan Paul.

————. (1962). *Play, Dreams, and Imitation in Childhood*. New York: Norton.

Pribram, K. H. (1999). Brain and the Creative Act. In M. Runco & S. Pritzker (Eds.), *Encyclopedia of Creativity* (pp. 213–217). New York: Academic Press.

Rogers, T., & C. O'Neill. (1992). Creating Multiple Worlds: Drama and Literary Response. In G. Newell & R. Durst (Eds.), *Exploring Texts: The Role of Discussion and Writing in the Teaching and Learning of Literature* (pp. 69–89). Norwood, MA: Christopher Gordon.

Rose, D. (1999). *The Impact of Whirlwind's Basic Reading through Dance Program on First Grade Students' Basic Reading Skills: Study II.* San Francisco: 3-D Group.

Rosen, R. S., & S. M. Koziol, Jr. (1990). The Relationship of Oral Reading, Dramatic Activities, and Theatrical Production to Student Communication Skills, Knowledge, Comprehension, and Attitudes. *Youth Theatre Journal* 4(3): 7–10.

Saldaña, J. (1998). Ethical Issues in an Ethnographic Performance Text: The "Dramatic Impact" of "Juicy Stuff." *Research in Drama Education* 3(2): 181–196.

Saxton, J., & C. Miller (eds.). (1998). *The Research of Practice: The Practice of Research.* Victoria, BC: IDEA Publications.

Somers, J. (ed.). (1996). *Drama and Theatre in Education: Contemporary Research.* North York, Ontario: Captus University Publications.

Taylor, P. (ed.). (1996). *Researching Drama and Arts Education: Paradigms and Possibilities.* London: Falmer.

————. (1998). *Redcoats and Patriots: Reflective Practice in Drama and Social Studies.* Portsmouth, NH: Heinemann.

Taylor, P., & C. Hoepper (eds.). (1995). *Selected Readings in Drama and Theatre Education: The IDEA '95 Papers.* Brisbane, Queensland, Australia: NADIE.

Vygotsky, L. S. (1967). Play and Its Role in the Mental Development of the Child. *Soviet Psychology* 12: 62–76.

————. (1978). *Mind in Society: The Development of Higher Psychological Processes.* Cambridge: Harvard University Press.

Wagner, B. J. (1990). Dramatic Improvisation in the Classroom. In D. L. Rubin & S. Hynds (Eds.), *Perspectives on Talk and Learning* (pp. 195–211). Urbana, IL: National Council of Teachers of English.

————. (1994). Drama and Writing. In Alan C. Purvis (Ed.), *The Encyclopedia of English Studies and Language Arts.* Vol. 1 (pp. 403–405). New York: National Council of Teachers of English and Scholastic.

————. (1997). *Books at Play.* Worthington, OH: SRA/McGraw-Hill.

————. (1998). *Educational Drama and Language Arts: What Research Shows.* Portsmouth, NH: Heinemann.

————. (ed.). (1999). *Building Moral Communities through Educational Drama.* Greenwich, CT: Ablex.

————. (1999). *Dorothy Heathcote: Drama as a Learning Medium.* Portland, ME: Calendar Islands.

————. (2000). Imaginative Expression. In J. Flood, J. M. Jensen, D. Lapp, & J. R. Squire (Eds.), *Handbook of Research on Teaching the English Language Arts* (sponsored by the International Reading Association and the National Council of Teachers of English) (pp. 787–804). New York: Macmillan.

Wilhelm, J. D., & B. Edmiston. (1997). *Imagining to Learn: Inquiry, Ethics, and Integration through Drama.* Portsmouth, NH: Heinemann.

46

Dramatic Play for Healing

Patricia Sternberg

Indeed, the single best childhood predictor of adult adaptation is not I.Q., not school grades, and not classroom behavior, but rather the adequacy with which the child gets along with other children.
—Willard Hartup

DRAMATIC PLAY

Play is the foundation upon which all drama is based, whether it is called dramatic play, role play, or drama therapy. The very nature of all drama is play in a variety of forms. Drama offers a world of imagination in which physically and mentally challenged children can still participate. A natural outgrowth of playing and pretending is trying on new roles in life. A young child becomes a fireman or policeman, and when he is a little older he is an astronaut. Teenagers like to play the role of their favorite rock star by dressing, talking, and acting like that person. Along with playing new roles, participants in drama learn to identify problems in these roles and to simulate new behaviors for their characters and for themselves. This gives those involved in dramatic play the opportunity to discover alternatives in their problem solving and to come up with more than one solution to a problem.

ROLE PLAY

Dramatic play is usually defined as the unstructured play of young children. When structure is added to that dramatic play, it becomes role play. Role play can occur in a formal theater production or in an informal problem-solving exercise.

Wherever it is practiced, role play offers practice for living, helps participants discover their own inner resources, and affords insight into the character being played. Playing a role different from one's self is very liberating. It offers the opportunity to comment as the outsider on the role played. This in turn promotes the ability to identify and verbalize feelings from within the role and to comment on those feelings as the person outside the role. It helps the players to enhance their sensory awareness and learn to use the imagination as a problem-solving tool.

Role play allows clients to play a role different from themselves or to play themselves with a new set of behaviors. For example, many people, especially young ones, have difficulty saying "No" to others. A role play scene is set up in which the person must maintain the character who will not give in, who will say "No." In effect, he or she is in a rehearsal for life. He or she practices in role what he wishes to do in reality. The more rehearsal, the smoother the performance and/or the behavior.

All of the arts, including drama, have a therapeutic effect. How many times have we heard, "Music soothes the savage beast." On the other hand, people have been drawn to drama because it allows them to play the savage beast. Both modalities serve their unique purpose. The human need to play and create art in some form is probably as old as humanity itself. Many of us have seen reproductions of cave paintings on the walls of prehistoric sites. Those paintings probably came from recalling the drama when the cave man arrived home from the hunt and acted out his daring adventure for the assembled group. The artist was tempted to draw it, the musician to play it, and the dramatist to recreate it by acting it out.

Formal theater came much later, when politicians and religious leaders realized the power they could wield to provide moral and ethical lessons for the people of the times, as well as comedies to entertain and lighten their burdens. Religious leaders further recognized the power of drama as a method of teaching their beliefs to the people, of adding elements to their rituals. Theater practitioners and drama leaders have always been aware of the therapeutic value of drama. When did the crossover occur from therapeutic to therapy?

DRAMA AS THERAPY

Drama therapy takes dramatic play and role play a step further. Drama therapy adds the drama/theater process that combines those techniques with psychotherapy in an action-based method to help people find solutions for social and emotional problems. In its most well-known form, drama therapy uses role play to help participants learn healthier behavior patterns. This creative arts therapy is also used to promote and maintain mental and emotional growth. It offers a method of enriching the patient's sense of self-worth through the discovery of his or her own inner resources and of learning how to interact with others and function in a group. It offers methods of simple problem solving to the most difficult dilemmas of human relations.

This modality helps people get in touch with their feelings and understand how those feelings affect their bodies. Take a look at anger. During anger, the body can become a tightly coiled spring that can erupt into violence. By becoming aware of personal triggers to anger and violence, both physically and emotionally, the client is forearmed when an incident occurs. His or her red flag goes up and hopefully he or she has learned a new behavior rather than the one that would usually cause a violent outburst. Through the exploration and practice of dealing with such situations, the individual is better able to handle anger when it erupts in real life. He or she has had a rehearsal on how to successfully handle life situations that can cause harm to oneself and to others. By identifying and verbalizing feelings, young people learn that they are not alone in those feelings. They are validated by the leader of the group and their peers. One has to wonder if recent school tragedies could have been averted if some of those young people had the opportunity to talk about their feelings and have those feelings validated by others.

Like all of the creative arts therapies, drama therapy is rooted in the concept that the creative act can be a healing act. Drama calls upon the brain, the senses, the imagination, the act of play, and even the spirit of adventure. The effort required to create and order a dramatic world is precisely the same effort required to order and to reintegrate oneself into the "real" world.

Drama therapy offers a vision of something outside the self and beyond one's narrow view of the world to expand one's universe and understanding of that universe. Drama therapy is a rehearsal for life that offers the opportunity for new performances in our everyday world. Drama therapists use such techniques as improvisation, role play, theater games, concentration exercises, mime, masks, and puppetry, as well as scripted dramatizations and open-ended scripts. These techniques of process drama further emotional growth and psychological integration. Drama therapists provide evaluation and treatment; they coordinate their efforts with psychiatrists, psychologists, nurses, social workers, and other personnel as part of a team treatment approach. In addition, some therapists use their theater skills to create full-fledged theater performances, either for the benefit of their clients in role or for stimulating the audience into asking questions about the problem presented, and sometimes for offering alternative play endings. Drama therapists do their work in a variety of ways and a variety of milieus that can sometimes create confusion as to what drama therapy is. Most often drama therapy is practiced in groups, but it can be engaged in one-on-one with the client.

DEFINITIONS

Most people outside the field of therapy, recreation, or drama/theatre have little or no idea what drama therapy is all about. In fact the field is still so new that some of them are not familiar with the modality. I am often asked the question, What is drama therapy anyway? When the question comes from a colleague or other professional, he or she usually wants specific information and/or an explanation of how drama therapy differs from psychodrama, sociodrama, and creative drama. In fact, this question comes up so frequently that I keep a printed sheet in my briefcase that offers brief definitions put forth by various professional organizations. The first is the definition of drama therapy as defined by the National Association for Drama Therapy (NADT).

Drama therapy has its roots in psychology, drama, and theater and is defined by the NADT (1999–2000) as the "systematic and intentional use of drama/theatre process and products to achieve the therapeutic goals of symptom relief, emotional and physical integration and personal growth. Drama therapy is an active experiential approach that facilitates the client's ability to tell his/her story, solve problems, set goals, express feelings appropriately, achieve catharsis, extend the depth and breadth of inner experience, improver interpersonal skills and relationships, and strengthen the ability to perform personal life roles while increasing flexibility between roles" (NADT, 2001–2002).

The next two definitions are from the American Society for Group Psychodrama and Psychotherapy (ASGPP, 1942):

Psychodrama "focuses on private role aspects and on the individual's personal problems. It aims to discover 'truth' through the spontaneous enacting of a situation. The focus is directly on role play. It is a form of cathartic therapy in which a patient acts out spontaneous improvisational situations related to his problem, with the aid of auxiliaries who represent others as part of or the cause of his problem" (Sternberg & Garcia, 2000, p. 6).

Sociodrama "is an outgrowth of psychodrama but concerns itself with the group problem, central concern or common issue (not a personal one). It is a group action method in which participants act out agreed-upon social situations spontaneously and discover alternative ways of dealing with that problem. It concerns itself with those aspects of roles that we share with others and helps people to express their thoughts and feelings, solve problems, and clarify their values" (Sternberg & Garcia, 2000, p. 4).

Creative drama, which I consider a foundation for all of the earlier definitions, focuses on the creativity in every person, "the individuality of the individual," and is created by the players themselves. The former Children's Theatre Association of America, now named American Alliance for Theatre and Education, defines it this way: "Creative drama is an improvisational, nonexhibitional, process centered form of drama in which the participants are guided by a leader to imagine, enact, and reflect upon the human experience. Although creative drama has been thought of in relation to children and young people, it is appropriate to all ages" (McCaslin, 1990, p. 8).

It is evident that drama therapy differs from the other three, yet it encompasses elements from all. Most children are ready and willing to participate in dramatic play, with little need for coaxing. The word "therapy" does not have to come up. Drama is play acting. A few hats, costume pieces, or props are usually all that are needed to take on a new role or enact a story, theirs or someone else's. Children can pretend anything they want, pretend to be anyone they like, and pretend to go anywhere in the universe. They can use puppets to deal with all kinds of problems.

Adolescents usually ask such questions as, "You gonna make me a star?" or "Do you think I could be on television?" My answer to such questions is usually something like, "Who knows!" If it is one of my substance abuse clients who asks the question, he or she usually adds, "I ain't no actor you know. I can't do that stupid stuff." To that I usually answer, "Drama therapy isn't acting, it's just human behavior, and everybody does that."

When I begin a session, I usually explain drama therapy with this simple statement. "Drama therapy is an exploration of our strengths. I work with the five senses, learning how to use our sensory awareness to the fullest. I use imagination as a problem-solving device, and we do role play scenes dealing with issues you would like to work on." My little speech usually includes this disclaimer as well: "I won't ask people to do anything they don't want to do." That seems to dispel some of their apprehensions. I always add another line to the speech also: "And last but not least . . . we usually have some fun too." From there I start "getting to know you" activities. The highest accolade from a substance abuse group comes at the end of a session when one of them says, "I never knew I could have so much fun without being high!"

ORIGINS OF DRAMA THERAPY

Most people are familiar with art therapy, music therapy, or dance or movement therapy simply because these modalities have been around longer as recognized and licensed therapies. Indeed, we have many things in common with all of them. Drama therapy was developed separately (but along parallel paths) by psychotherapists, drama practitioners and theater artists, and educators who drew on a variety of sources to find a way allowing them to help clients when traditional verbal therapies proved too inflexible to allow the client to express and work with his or her individual material. Since drama therapy utilizes equally strong nonverbal components, any clients who otherwise would be untouched by therapy can find a way to work. Using theater-related techniques in both group and individual settings, the clients work in improvisation, projective techniques (including puppetry, masks, video and audio recordings, sand play, and storytelling), and psychodramatic techniques.

Drama therapy is a language of metaphor, which children and young people find nonthreatening, easy, and fun. During the drama therapy process, the client and therapist work in tandem to create a hypothetical scene dealing with the group's particular situation. This dialect of metaphor allows the clients to create, investigate, manipulate, and recreate boundaries, roles, interpersonal relationships, personal histories, and futures, all in a safe and protected environment. It offers them a rehearsal for life situations in which they can play the role of a successful strategist or a problem solver. The client doesn't have to edit his or her responses, but instead is spontaneous in a role, which often produces surprising insight, for both the client and the group.

A DRAMA THERAPY MODEL

Many of us came up through the ranks of various aspects of working in the theater and/or educational theater and creative dramatics. In England, Peter Slade—whose book, *An Introduction to Child Drama* (1958), attempts to describe drama therapy as a method of therapy for educational purposes—takes his inspiration for the use of drama as therapy from the "free play" of children. His pamphlet, *Dramatherapy as an Aid to Becoming a Person,* prompted others, including Billie Lindkvist and Sue Jennings, to explore the connections with their own work. The British Drama Therapy Association began in 1976. Drama therapy, however, evolved gradually with a number of starting points. In the United States, Gert Shattner taught drama therapy courses in 1971 at Turtle Bay Music School in New York City. The National Association for Drama Therapy was incorporated in 1979.

Drama therapy, like most creative arts therapies, begins a session with a warm-up, a warm-up to action. The purpose is to get to know each other and create that comfortable, nonjudgmental environment so necessary for any therapy. Our warm-ups can be either affective or cognitive. If it is an affective warm-up, it can be as simple as a stretch up to the ceiling with a big yawn; then, trying it again, and this time throwing off any tension felt. Sometimes I give the group a simple task, such as passing an object from one to another while they are seated. The task has to be very simple, however, with no possibility of failure. The therapist must develop trust with the people in the group and insure that his or her drama therapy session is a safe place to try out new behaviors or deal with existing situations in a different way, without the fear of any negative consequences. Many drama therapists use name games. One favorite name game, which helps people to remember names, is to say the first name and something that describes that person, starting with the same first letter as the name. For example, "My name is *Pat* and I'm *pleasant.*" Of course, when working with the same group members, after a while one must create new ones. My favorite is, "I'm *Pat* and I'm *punctilious!*"

Drama therapy offers the opportunity to discuss feelings in a judgment-free environment. Perhaps one of its greatest assets is to help participants learn to identify their feelings and verbalize them. How many times do therapists hear, "What do you mean, what am I feeling? I don't know what I'm feeling, so how can I tell you." Then the therapist can interject, "You're right. We don't get enough practice in identifying our feelings and verbalizing them. That's one of the best ways we can learn to communicate, especially with the people we care about." After a while, most clients agree that it is important to be able to identify their own feelings and learn to verbalize what they are feeling. Those feelings must be validated and accepted, so another favorite line to use is, "Nobody else can tell you what you feel or what you should or shouldn't feel. You're the expert on your feelings!"

Many young people think they are the only ones who have such-and-such a problem, but they soon learn that they are not alone. The same issues come up over and over again. Through sharing and interaction, participants realize that their problems are not so different from others as they had thought. In fact, the people may change, but the problems do not.

There are ways to gain insight into the client's problems through certain activities, as well as to get them warmed up to action. Here is one that usually offers some insight. "Take a look at your watch." I have an old one that I pass around and ask the question, "If you could set time backwards or forwards, where would you set it and why?" The therapist can offer his or her own response first to get the group started. "I'd set it forward to the year 3000, because I think either we'll have our problems solved or the world won't be here." Of course, I don't need the watch to ask the question or to give the response, but it gives the participants something to focus on, and better yet, something to hold on to. Another favorite warm-up activity that also elicits information is an item most women carry (although I like to bring a large one in), and that is a mirror. The therapist can hold up the mirror to a client and say," Where would you like to see yourself a year from now and what would you be doing?" Of course, the mirror is just a symbol for the question, but somehow, by holding something in the hand, it makes the response more real. These are two objects that usually elicit some information about the client, that promote some interaction with the therapist. Sometimes, however, the therapist can get information he or she would rather not have. When using the mirror once with a severely depressed seventeen-year-old, her answer to where she would see herself in a year from now was, "All I see is black. I can't see anything else."

After the warm-up comes the action. Sometimes clients are already warmed up to action. At other times, the therapist must "prime the pump." Often participants are reluctant to get up or talk in front of others. They have trouble coming up with the words. Several techniques can ease them into dialogue without their realizing it. For example, one can tell them to decide who will be number one and who will be number two. Number one says the line, "I want it." Number two responds with, "You can't have it." Say those two lines several times and then let the dialogue take you where it will . . . and it will.

Drama therapists also use several short scripts with six or eight lines on the page, that have unfinished dialogues. Two volunteers read what is on the page and then improvise from there. Clients are amazed at how astute the therapist is in recognizing their problems. They say things like, "That's exactly what I'm going through." Or "How did you know that's just the way it is with my boyfriend?" Of course, what they do not realize is that they bring all of their own emotional baggage to the scene. They create the situation and the lines in the improvisation, not the therapist. Here are two examples of those dialogues:

#1: Why are you so mean to me?

#2: What are you talking about?

#1: When other people are around, you always put me down.

#2: I do not!

#1: You always criticize me in front of your friends.

#2: I do not. You're imagining things.

The participants continue the dialogue from there.

#1: Why won't you ever trust me?

#2: I don't know. It's just very hard for me to trust anybody.

#1: But, I'm not "anybody." I'm someone who cares about you.

#2: I'd like to believe that.

#1: Why can't you?
#2: I want to, but I . . .
#1: But what?

And again the players continue the dialogue, making up their own lines as they go. These few scripted lines give them a structure with which to begin. That makes it easier to get started and complete the scene than just setting it up cold.

When the group is already warmed up to an issue, listen carefully to their concerns and begin from there. Often substance abuse clients are angry about one thing or another that has occurred within the unit. As mentioned earlier, "People change but the problems don't." The same problems come up over and over again, and the number one problem within most groups is often anger. Anger is often the issue therapists deal with, whatever the population, especially with substance abuse clients and psychiatric patients. In fact, a list of the Big Five—the five most common problems dealt with in my experience in psychiatric hospitals and drug rehabilitation facilities—are, first, anger; second, trust ("I can't trust anybody anymore," and even more often is the reverse, "Nobody will ever trust me again"); third, communicating feelings ("It's just not a macho thing to talk about how you feel," "Guys don't do that!"); fourth, guilt ("I've done so many terrible things to the people I love, I can never forgive myself. How can they ever forgive me?"); and fifth, grief ("He died before I could tell him how much he meant to me," or "She left before I could tell her I was sorry for what I did").

Anger tops the list. It is way ahead of all the others. "I can't control my temper." "I go berserk and the rage takes over." "You don't want to be around me when I get mad. I go crazy." Of course, there is nothing wrong with anger, for we have all felt it. Anger is a perfectly natural emotion; it is how we deal with it that becomes the problem. There are a wide variety of ways to address anger. Ask yourself what three things make you most angry. Whatever they are, you are probably not alone with whatever you have listed. It is amazing how much more we are alike than we are different.

Drama therapists also frequently combine their talents with other creative-arts therapists in facilities where there are several different types of therapies offered. As another way of dealing with anger, the drama therapist can work with an art therapist to create a clay personification of anger. In one facility the art therapist helped the clients make a clay sculpture of their own anger during her art therapy session. When they came to drama therapy, the clients first introduced the anger sculpture and then explained it to us (i.e., how it controls them or takes over). After that, they decided what they wanted to do with it. Did they want to keep it, change it, or get rid of it altogether? Sometimes they wanted to smash it right there on the floor, which I encouraged. They verybalized what they were doing and how they were getting rid of their anger.

Often the art therapist asked the participants to draw a picture of their anger. One of the clearest descriptions of anger that I have ever seen was drawn in several panels. It depicted how this client started with drinking, and after two years ended up in a homeless shelter. By then his head was so messed up that he began using heroin, which he pictured with a needle in an arm. Next, he drew a razor blade, which signi-fied the time he tried to kill himself. After that, there was a big question mark, which for him illustrated the big question of why he did not die. From there he came into treatment, which he drew as a light in a dark room. He certainly had no doubts about what brought him to treatment. In drama therapy we focused on where he could go next, and he had the opportunity to practice role training in situations where one could stay away from drugs and prepare for a place in the workforce.

With some groups, the drama therapist is brought in to deal with a certain issue or offer training dealing with the specific needs of the group. For example, a drama therapist is contracted to work with a group of special education teachers on class-room management. All of the exercises, role plays, and explorations deal with bringing about a greater understanding and sensitivity to the individual student's needs versus those of the group. A wide range of disciplinary models is offered and various alternative methods are sought. Role play scenes are set up and played, dealing with as many different situations as the group can come up with.

Currently, drama therapists are working with every population that can benefit from any of the creative arts therapies, including special education classes, psychiat-ric patients, persons recovering from substance abuse, trauma victims, dysfunctional families, developmentally and physically disabled persons (including AIDS pa-tients), prisons and correctional facility inmates, anorexic and bulimic patients, the homeless, the elderly, children, and adolescents. These therapists provide services to individuals, groups, and families, in addition to conducting clinical research.

DIVERSITY IN DRAMA THERAPY

One of the beauties of drama therapy is the diversity in which it is practiced. A favorite approach relies heavily on sociodrama. Sociodrama is an outgrowth of psychodrama but concerns itself with the group problems, a central concern or common issue (not a personal one). It is a group action method in which partici-pants act out agreed-upon social situations spontaneously and discover alternative ways of dealing with the problem. There are key "alternative ways of dealing with a problem." The drama therapist tries to illustrate that there is never only one an-swer to a problem, that there are always alternatives. How often do people, and es-pecially young ones, get locked into that old feeling, "There's only one answer to my problem," or "I can't live without him." We should encourage participants to get in the habit of always finding alternative solutions to their problems. This mo-dality includes some exceptionally effective techniques, such as role reversal, dou-bling, and walk and talk. Sociodrama concerns itself with those aspects of a role that we share with others and helps people express their thoughts and feelings, solve problems, and clarify their values.

DRAMA THERAPY CONCLUSIONS

Drama therapy is an exploration of our strengths in order to discover ways to bring about change in our lives. It helps us learn to use the imagination as a problem-solving tool. It enables us to put ourselves in another person's shoes to understand how the other person feels. It offers us a rehearsal for life situations, a safe way to try on new behaviors or redefine old ones without the fear of any consequences and a safe way to create new behaviors and understanding of ourselves and others. Drama therapy affirms that the creative act can be a healing act. Drama therapy is many things to many people. Just as the art therapist uses a variety of different media and art supplies in his or her work, and the music therapist uses many different kinds of music, musical instruments, tapes, and vocals, so the drama therapist uses dramatic performance, role play, mime, masks, theater games, imagination exercises, and sensory awareness—whatever action methods he or she feels will best serve the clients. Drama therapy is a journey to new places, to new terrains, offering new ways of looking at things and seeing them in a new perspective.

There is a need for more drama therapy research and greater public awareness of the benefits it offers in both education and therapy. Educators and school personnel must be aided in overcoming their fear of the word "therapy" when it is used with drama in the classroom. A drama therapist is a recognized, registered professional, trained in using the many facets of drama/theater process and practices in problem solving and the art of healing human ills.

The challenge of educators today is to find ways to connect. Connections are no longer being made in many homes, in many families. Students often arrive at school disenfranchised and afraid. Their only connection is with their peers. They play out the role that is expected of them. For too many, their neighborhood or their street corner defines the boundaries of their existence. Drama educators can demonstrate ways to reach young people and reconnect them to the world. Through the process of drama we can teach across the curriculum and offer a big picture of the world, a world that is multicultural. We can take them somewhere else and safely explore life's possibilities.

In his book *Drama and Intelligence,* Richard Courtney (1990) revealed,

Our creative imagination and dramatic actions are experienced as a whole, and together they create meaning. They bring about the "as if" world of possibility (the fictional), which works in parallel with the actual world and is a cognitive tool for understanding it. Imagining and dramatic acts work by transformation; they change what we know. This change is learning, or a "knowing how to do." . . . The dramatic world we create is a significant element in a universe of cognitive meaning. (p. 9)

As educators and scientists, we must all safeguard the child's right to play. Dramatic play merges physical actions with the imagination and offers healing in action, as well as insight into the self and others.

BIBLIOGRAPHY

ASGPP (American Society for Group Psychotherapy and Psychodrama. (1942). Princeton, NJ: ASGPP.

Courtney, R. (1990). *Drama and Intelligence.* Montreal, Quebec: McGill–Queens University Press.

Landy, R. (1986). *Drama Therapy.* Springfield, IL: Chas. C. Thomas.

——— . (1994). *Persona and Performance.* London: Jessica Kingsley.

McCaslin, N. (1990). *Creative Dramatics in the Classroom and Beyond* (6th ed.). New York: Longman.

Moreno, J. L. (1975). *Psychodrama.* Vol. 3. Beacon, NY: Beacon House.

NADT (National Association for Drama Therapy). (2001–2002). *Membership Directory.* Pittsford, NY: NADT.

Slade, P. (1958). An Introduction to Child Drama. London: University of London Press.

Sternberg, P. (1998). *Theater for Conflict Resolution in the Classroom and Beyond.* Portsmouth, NH: Heinemann.

Sternberg, P., & A. Garcia. (2000). *Sociodrama: Who's in Your Shoes?* (2d ed.). New York: Praeger.

Way, B. (1972). *Development through Drama.* Atlantic Highlands, NJ: Humanities Press.

47

The Need for Action
Methods in Education

E. Paul Torrance

Action methods have been sadly neglected and are greatly needed in education. Such methods include role playing, improvisation, creative dramatics and sociodrama. They are ideal for use in groups of varied levels of ability and are effective at all ages and educational levels. At their best, these methods are creative problem-solving techniques. These methods aim to involve every member of a group at a deep level, and employ both hemispheres of the brain. Also involved are all of Howard Gardner's multiple intelligences, especially interpersonal and intrapersonal intelligences, developing self-concepts and self-confidence. Action methods are associated with experiential learning.

The action methods of learning and teaching incorporate the creative problem-solving process as deliberately and realistically as any other problem-solving process. The methods can be conducted in an ordinary classroom, theater, or any other physical setting. The director or teacher must create the proper atmosphere. A simple, single stage prop helps, but this is not necessary. The director or teacher must provide effective warm-up, as in any learning.

Most role playing and other action methods use only simple presentation techniques. However, a variety of production techniques can make the learning more powerful if appropriately used. These production techniques include soliloquy, future projection, role reversal, dream/fantasy, "Magic Shop," "Magic Net," and a variety of other techniques. Especially effective are audience techniques used in involving all members of a group. In addition to a simple presentation or a presentation of one of the production techniques, the entire audience (group) can be assigned a one-sided public opinion role or the roles of all those involved in the problem or conflict. Even more powerful is reality role playing in an entire class, school, or other organization. It can make use of the role-reversal technique to help the group learn how another person experiences the problem or conflict.

TRUE–FALSE ITEMS ABOUT IMPROVISATION AND OTHER ACTION METHODS

The following are assertions about improvisation, role-playing, sociodrama, and other action methods of teaching, learning, and thinking. Some of these statements are true and others are false. Indicate whether each statement is true or false.

1. Active participation in improvisation, role playing, and other action methods requirescreative thinking.   True_____   False_____

2. Active participation in action methods requires originality.   True_____   False_____

3. High fluency is usually accompanied by high originality.   True_____   False_____

4. It is not necessary to elaborate original ideas.   True_____   False_____

5. Fluency is always accompanied by flexibility.   True_____   False_____

6. Finding a problem is necessary in action methods.   True_____   False_____

7. Solutions always result from action methods.   True_____   False_____

8. Action methods are excellent for the development of empathy.   True_____   False_____

9. Emotions should be avoided when using action methods.   True_____   False_____

10. Fantasy has no place in action methods in schools.   True_____   False_____

11. All of the senses may be involved in action methods.   True_____   False_____

12. Laughter spoils the effectiveness of action methods.   True_____   False_____

13. Props are necessary in action methods.   True_____   False_____

14. Reversing roles in action methods is usually very effective in role playing.   True_____   False_____

15. Training improves the use of action methods.   True_____   False_____

16. Using techniques like asking individuals to imagine themselves as snowflakes or someone of a different race or sex is nonsense.   True_____   False_____

17. Original ideas should be welcome in the use of action methods.   True_____   False_____

18. Teachers or leaders should always be concerned with fluency when using action methods.   True_____   False_____

19. Hostility should always be avoided when using action methods.   True_____   False_____

20. Play has no place in action methods.   True_____   False_____

21. Action methods are fun because of the creativity, spontaneity, and the unexpectedness.   True_____   False_____

22. Action methods should not be used with the deaf.   True_____   False_____

23. Action methods are not appropriate in teaching a
    subject like history.   True_____   False_____
24. Action methods are useful in producing elaboration.   True_____   False_____
25. The use of techniques such as "Magic Net" is
    effective in teaching children to tell a story.   True_____   False_____

ANSWERS TO TRUE–FALSE ITEMS REGARDING ACTION METHODS OF TEACHING

1. True
2. False
3. True
4. False
5. False
6. True
7. False
8. True
9. False
10. False
11. True
12. False
13. False
14. True
15. True
16. False
17. True
18. False
19. False
20. False
21. True
22. False
23. False
24. True
25. True

REFERENCES

Gardner, H. (1983). *Frames of Mind: The Theory of Multiple Intelligences*. New York: Basic Books.
Torrance, E. P., M. Murdock, & D. Fletcher. (1996). *Creative Problem Solving through Role-Playing*. Pretoria, South Africa: Benedic Books.
Torrance, E. P., & D. A. Sisk. (1997). *Gifted and Talented Children in the Regular Class-room*. Buffalo, NY: Creative Education Foundation Press.

48

Nice Monsters, Sandcastles, and Soccer: A Thematic Analysis of Humor and Play

Howard R. Pollio and Marilyn R. Pollio

The weather is warm and the day clear. A father and his son are at the beach, looking up at the sky and inventing objects from clouds that hover over the ocean. "An enormous white alligator with a wide open mouth," says the father; "I can see it," says the son. "A pirate ship with a large sail," says the son; "I can see it," says the father. "Ah," says the father, "there's a bird; a white dove just like in Picasso's paintings." "I can see the bird, dad, but who is Picasso?" And so the game goes; the boy and his father share a few playful images that tell us something about the boy, the father, their relationship, and the game.

Suppose we shift to a similar game in a psychologist's office, and suppose we replace clouds with inkblot cards and the boy and his father with a professional comedian and a clinical psychologist, respectively; what sorts of things will now be seen and will the psychologist still be able to say "I see it" to the imaginative productions of his or her partner? When Seymour and Rhoda Fisher (1981) did this type of analysis on the responses of professional comedians to Rorschach inkblots, they found that comedians tended to describe four images considerably more frequently than was true of people in the general population. Specifically, their sample of thirty-five comedians reported seeing a significantly greater number of angels and devils, small or tiny things, objects or people falling down in unexpected ways, and something the comedians labeled "nice monsters." Although what "nice monsters" are might not be immediately clear, items falling in this category included things such as "sweet tarantulas," "funny devils," "cute pigs," and so on. In attempting to understand benign deceptions of this type, Fisher and Fisher pointed out that comedians also noted that "there's a little bit of lie in everything," thereby suggesting that they see things differently, often better, than most people.

Each of these categories not only relates to a major theme of comedy but also to a major theoretical principle. The tendency to be extremely sensitive to angels and/or devils suggests a concern with morality and, indeed, what comedian has not styled himself or herself as a teacher, priest, or doctor? The major theorist concerned with issues of morality—largely those surrounding the taboo topics of sex and aggression—was, of course, Sigmund Freud. For Freud (1905/1960), the issue was always one of controlling these impulses, and his theory dealt with society's attempt to keep issues of sex and aggression—including their scatological aspects—from unscheduled appearances in the social world. The dirty joke, by an ingenious use of an imaginary facade or clever verbal wordplay, masks the intention of the joke, which, of course, is to release control over the person's enjoyment of forbidden material.

The tendency to be hypersensitive to extremely small parts of the inkblot, to come now to the second category of comedian response, relates fairly directly to Hobbes's theory of humor as well as to issues of power and powerlessness. Hobbes (1651) called his theory "sudden glory" or superiority, and explained it in the following rather unappealing terms (leave it to Hobbes to see a nasty monster): "The passion of laughter is nothing else but sudden glory arising from a conception of some eminence in ourselves by comparison with the inferiority of others or with our own formerly" (p. 43). In short, we laugh at things that make us no longer feel small, but allow us to feel bigger and better than some one else. This feeling of superiority can also be equated with a laugh (or snarl) of triumph when we win some game or overcome some opponent. Every comic remark has this expectation, perhaps explaining why the last sentence in a joke is called the punch line.

The third category of image reported by Fisher and Fisher's (1981) comedians concerned objects or people that fall down unexpectedly. Although we may think of the classic stage bit in which an elegant gentleman slips on a banana peel or where an inelegant clown regularly falls, the major principle here was proposed by Bergson (1911), who noted that the essence of comedy concerns an experience of "the mechanical encrusted on the living." What this means is that there is a constant contrast between some event or being that is spontaneous, unpredictable, or free—in short, alive—and some other event or being that is predictable, repetitive, or rigid—in short, mechanical. The clown (or the dignified gentleman) simply reveals, in the comic moment, that what was alive can, at any time, become a thing having none of the spontaneity of a living being. The joke or comic performance is meant to teach us not to become mechanical, not to lose our spontaneity or originality, and thereby to help us remain human and alive. In the extreme, Bergson's contrast is one between the existence of thing and that of a living being, which in the final analysis captures the somber distinction between dead (a mechanical, nonliving body) and alive (a spontaneous, living being).

To come now to the final category, that of the little lie captured in the image of a "nice monster," we find issues of incongruity and dramatic change as the joke or conclusion pulls the listener unexpectedly from one category (monster) to another (nice). Incongruity describes a structural element in humor by conjuring up, in relatively rapid order, images that belong to two separate domains; for example: an adolescent male who described a virgin forest as one "in which the hand of man has never set foot." Although there are obvious Freudian overtones here, the crucial word play involves an ill-suited but comprehensible pairing of disparate body parts. Laughter simply acknowledges the sudden perception of incongruity; that is, the possibility of talking about forests and people in the same terms, no matter how poor the fit.

These considerations suggest that humor and metaphor have much in common and it is quite possible to argue that the difference between them concerns the author's intent in putting the images together: In the case of the poet, the purpose would seem to be change one or both of the concepts joined; in the case of the comic, the purpose may simply be to expose the contrast with no attempt to change either one of them (Pollio, 1997). In a sense, the four contrasts noted as crucial for each of the major themes—sacred/profane, superior/inferior, spontaneous/rigid, truthful/deceptive—represent significant antinomies used in comic art, and laughter would seem to represent the only possible human response to these continuing and unresolvable issues of human life.

This view of laughter, first proposed by Plessner (1941/1970), represents one of a number of different views as to the meaning of laughter. To a greater or lesser extent, all views imply release (or freedom) as an essential aspect. Thus, both Freud (1905/1960) and Lorenz (1958) viewed laughter from a Darwinian perspective and characterized it as a mechanism for working off excess aggressive and sexual energies in such a way as not to endanger other people. As Darwin (1872) himself noted, the sounds of normal laughter—which are broken and of relatively low frequency—are as different as possible from those of aggression, courtship, or distress. Darwin also noted that when laughter is extremely explosive, or continues for too long a period of time, we are likely to experience pain, thereby suggesting prolonged laughter has a built-in stopping mechanism: It hurts to laugh for too long, and we talk about "laughing till our sides hurt." Laughter thus seems to be a short-lived reaction, over and done within a brief period of time.

Hobbes (1651) described laughter as expressing power, and it is important to distinguish between two different types of power associated with human laughter: "laughing at" and "laughing with." The first, more derisive form of laughter, seems to express victory over an opponent; a not so sublimated snarl of triumph. A variant on this meaning includes submissive laughter at the boss's joke. Although laughter may signal being put down or in a one-down position, certain naturalistic observations of groups in which humorous targeting occurs suggest that laughter may serve to promote a perception of the person targeted as "someone who can take it" (Scogin & Pollio, 1980). Unfortunately, however, the meaning of laughter in hierarchical groups (Coser, 1960) does seem to indicate a situation of lesser power for the person laughed at. In any case, we can all agree with the idea that laughter serves to include or exclude an individual from full membership in some group. Lorenz (1963) put it quite well when he noted, "Laughter provides a strong fellow-feeling among participants and joint aggression against outsiders. . . . Laughter forms a bond and draws a line" (p. 253).

Laughter not only has the possibility of forming a bond, it also may indicate the presence or absence of a preexisting relationship among individuals in a group. A long series of observational studies (e.g., see an early summary in Pollio, 1983, and a more recent one in Pollio and Swanson, 1995) indicates that groups composed of friends laugh considerably more frequently at taboo jokes told by such comedians as Don Rickles, Richard Pryor, or George Carlin than do groups of strangers listening to the same comic performers. The effect of preexisting social relationships on laughter is no small effect, with mean values ranging from 14.5 to 3.6 for students listening to these comedians in groups composed of friends and strangers, respectively. There is always a social component to laughter, and more laughter occurs when participants share a common history and/or perspective.

Other issues still remain: Is a laugh simply a big smile (as the French word for smile, *sous-rire*, suggests), or are they two different behaviors having somewhat the same form? Most theories accept the first conclusion: Laughs and smiles are different levels of the same behavior. Despite this opinion, there are two compelling reasons to consider them as different: (1) They develop at different times in infancy, and (2) a smile renders the human face beautiful and inviting, whereas a laugh contorts the face and may even make it unpleasant looking. In addition, the laughing person is in no position to cooperate with others, however much he or she may feel related to them on the basis of communal laughter. In terms of development, it seems clear that a need to connect with the maternal person must precede an ability to appreciate nice monsters. While laughter may yield connection, it provides a much less powerful invitation than the angelic smile of an infant or young child.

Each theory, in addition to considering a specific set of thematic concerns, also specifies both a comic situation (or joke type) as prototypic as well as a specific experiential state both evoked and resolved by the comic act. So, for example, Hobbes's (1651) theory suggests the prototypic joke is the put-down and the correlated human experience that of feeling superior. For Freud (1905/1960), the essential joke type is the dirty or aggressive joke (both of which may include scatological content) and the correlated experience of momentary relief from the constraints of social prohibition. For incongruity theory the essential joke form is the pun, and the correlated human experience is that of feeling smart or "in the know," incapable, for the moment, of being deceived. This feeling may be similar to the one associated with superiority, albeit in an intellectual rather than a physical or political sense. Finally, for Bergsonian (1911) theory, the essential comic form is a jack-in-the-box or any repetitive and mechanical movement pattern such as those exhibited by the clown or the drunk. The correlated human experience here is one of feeling spontaneous, free, and alive; in other words, as unlike as possible from the jack-in-the-box, clown, or drunk. The experience of feeling free also relates to Freud's theory, where the person is thought to experience release (or freedom) from moral constraint.

Each of the various theories describes experiences that blend with one another, thereby revealing comedy as a complex patterned event, what psychologists usually call a *gestalt*. Considering humor in this way suggests that each theory captures only a single aspect of the total event greeted by laughter. In humor—as in perception more generally—the whole does not equal the sum of its parts, and perhaps the best way to capture this conclusion is to describe humor in terms of a geometric pattern, such as the one presented in Figure 48.1, in which all five themes are arranged into an overall pattern. In this figure, each of the external vertices connects to the core experience noted by each of the theories: a feeling of freedom from constraints imposed by society, intellect, morality, and power. Laughter allows for a moment of radical freedom from the unresolvable contrasts that bedevil human communal life, and in this way provides us with a feeling of being alive and vibrant. The experience of radical freedom is only short lived, and both the body and the social order call us back to our present situation in the world of everyday concern and reality. Such considerations are captured in Figure 48.1 by the large rectangle surrounding the central figure, which is meant to indicate that humorous events emerge from the context provided by other people and the social order.

One more implication remains to be noted: Each of the experiential meanings defining a successful humorous event has a shadow aspect, and the pattern of these darker themes defines the concerns and difficulties of noncomedic moments comprising much of contemporary life. Reversing the core elements of freedom and spontaneity yields experiences of feeling controlled and mechanical; a similar reversal for experiences of feeling connected produces experiences of being lonely and/or alienated. Considering the three remaining themes, feeling smart reverses itself into feeling confused or ignorant, feeling released reverses itself into feelings of paralysis brought about by moral sanctions, and feeling powerful reverses itself into feeling small, down, or weak. If humor does nothing other than reverse these polarities, it would seem an extremely significant aspect of healthy human life.

THEMES IN THE EXPERIENTIAL MEANING OF PLAY

A mother and her infant daughter are playing a game of peek-a-boo. The mother looks first at her young daughter and then hides her face behind her hands. Following this, she lowers her hands, looks out at the child and says, "Peek-a-boo, I see you!" The infant laughs with delight, and the game is repeated a few more times. Other mother–infant games follow roughly the same pattern: "kootchie-coo" works by tickling the baby, all the time having mother say "kootchie-coo." Both games involve surprise, repetition, laughter, and even a bit of aggression. Such mother–daughter games also invariably occur in relaxed conditions for both the infant and the mother.

This description of mother–infant games suggests that play and humor have many elements in common. In fact, both activities are often described as contrasting with the more serious work of survival in the case of nonhuman organisms and social productivity in the case of human beings. Such a characterization for either or both activities is easily undermined by considering their respective roles in promoting adaptation and/or viability. In this light, play affords a developmentally useful situation of encouraging new learning under low- or no-stress conditions, and humor serves as a method of promoting bodily health and/or recovering from

Figure 48.1
Themes Defining the Human Experience of
Humor and Laughter

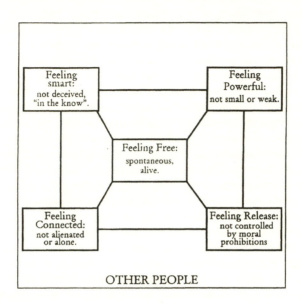

illness: "A merry heart doeth good like medicine," as both the book of Proverbs (17:22) and Norman Cousins (1979) have said.

To evaluate similarities and differences between humor and play in human life, it would seem necessary to determine what humor and play mean to, and for, human beings. The human meaning of humor has already been described in terms of issues uniquely significant to comedians and theorists of comic art and reaction. A different and considerably more direct strategy was followed in attempting to capture the experiential meanings of play: Here, two different groups of people were asked to provide examples of play and then to describe what stood out to them in these episodes. One group of participants was composed of fifteen volunteers at a national conference on imaginative play and brain research. A second group of participants was composed of thirty college students who volunteered to participate in a "descriptive study of play." In both cases, the task was the same: Each participant was requested "to list three situations in which you experienced yourself as playing." Following this, the participant was asked to "select one of (these) situations and describe in as much detail as you choose, what you were aware of during that experience."

After completing both tasks, all responses were typed and submitted to two different interpretive groups for thematic analysis. The first of these groups included both authors and three additional graduate students skilled in interpretive analysis. The second group also involved both authors as well as a different set of four graduate students skilled in this type of analysis. The specifics of the way in which thematic interpretation is accomplished in groups of this type is described in Pollio, Henley, and Thompson (1997) and consists primarily of reading each response aloud and having group members offer suggestions as to the thematic meaning(s) of the response. When everyone in the interpretative group is satisfied that a thematic understanding of the response has been reached, the same procedure is repeated for each of the remaining responses. No response is considered completely thematized until all members of the interpretive group agree with its suggested meaning.

Themes are always phrased in terms of specific words used by participants; no attempt is made to introduce technical language at any time in the analysis. Once an individual response protocol has been thematized to everyone's satisfaction, the process is continued for each of the remaining protocols to produce a thematic description of the overall meaning of play. As before, technical terms are not used to capture such meanings; only a subset of the specific words used by participants are selected to describe thematic meanings for the activity in question.

As an example of how the process works at the level of an individual protocol, consider the following essay written by a student (P12) in the second group: "When I played soccer I had a blast. No one cared if we won or lost. We just played for fun. We laughed at each other and helped one another. I would consider this playing, rather than one of my high school varsity games, because we weren't worried about the score or how well someone played; we just played for fun and felt free."

The major theme defining this protocol concerns an experiential contrast between "playing for fun" and playing in "high school varsity games." In the former case "we weren't worried about the score," and no one "cared if we won ... or ... how well someone played." Finally, interpersonal relationships were described in terms of "laughing at each other and helping one another." The experience of play for this participant involves little or no awareness of outcome (and a concomitant feeling of being free) and a much greater awareness of helping and fun. The two realms—of play and of varsity competition—are experientially quite distinct in this response.

As a second example, consider the following brief response from one of the participants (P13) at the national conference (the situation described was "role playing a character in a socio-drama in warm-up"): "The sense of freedom and fun; the increased energy I felt. The joy of playing a role so different from me."

Not much interpretive skill seems required for this case: First, a theme of freedom and fun; second, feelings of increased energy; third, playing a role different from me. The experience of play for this participant involved experiencing joy at being in a role different from the one ordinarily played combined with a sense of freedom and increased energy. To play means to try being something different, a situation yielding feelings of freedom, joy, and increased vitality. Although it might seem tempting at this point to coalesce both protocols—they do, after all, both stress freedom, fun, and an awareness of the difference between play and doing things as usual—the actual interpretative procedure used treated both sets of protocols separately so as to allow for cross-group comparisons.

All fifteen individuals at the national conference on play, with one exception, produced three play situations, yielding a total of forty-four episodes for this group of participants. These responses included items as diverse as "building sandcastles at the beach," "playing tennis," "running with my dogs," and "sex" (that was all that was written on the response sheet). Although there was some overlap in situations, especially if categories were made broad enough (e.g., board games, athletic activities), the overall set of situations was too diverse to categorize clearly. When two independent raters went through the list of situations looking for easily scorable characteristics, only two emerged: whether the activity took place indoors or outdoors (sex was coded, after discussions, as "indoors") and whether it involved being alone or with others (Sex, after consultation, was coded as "with others"). A characteristic that was attempted but could not be coded reliably by independent raters concerned whether or not the activity was structured or was better construed as spontaneous.

The results of a two-way categorization involving the factors of inside/outside and alone/with others is presented in Table 48.1, where it can be seen that thirty-three of forty-four total situations involved being with other people and that twenty-nine of forty-one situations involved being indoors. Since each participant contributed more than a single entry, it was not possible to evaluate the significance of this pattern; for this reason, the same categorization was done over the fifteen items described in detail by participants in response to the second request. The numbers in parenthesis present the relevant values for this analysis: Eleven of fifteen episodes occurred indoors, and twelve of fifteen episodes involved other people. A binomial test performed on these values indicated that for this group of respondents episodes of play usually involved other people ($p < 0.02$) and that they tended to take place indoors ($p < 0.06$).

Turning now to the question of experiential meanings, the present set of responses was interpreted to produce a five-theme pattern (see Figure 48.2). This pattern was described by almost all participants as taking place within a context of present and prior relationships with other people. Within this context, five themes were noted, either wholly or in part, by all fifteen participants: getting it, connecting, getting away, feeling free, and feeling good. Examples deriving from various protocols expressing each of these themes are as follows:

Theme I: Getting It

[The child] improved in skill . . . from game to game (P2).

[I had] pride in getting the . . . sequence correct (P7).

I was aware of his skill level now . . . how much he has improved since last time (P14).

Theme II: Connecting

It was the beginning of a wonderful friendship (P4).

I was feeling love as I caught her and hugged her (P15).

Adults and kids were willing to join in with us (P6).

Table 48.1
Characteristics of Situations Mentioned by Therapists

Geographic Location	Social Setting		
	Alone	With Others*	Totals
Inside (I)	7(2)	22(9)	29(11)
Outside (O)	4(1)	8(3)	12(4)
Sum: I + O	11(3)	30(12)	41(15)
Uncodable	0	3	3
Totals	11(3)	33(12)	44(15)

*Includes two situations with pets.

Figure 48.2
Themes Defining the Experience of Playing as Reported by Conference Participants

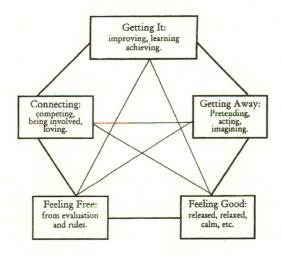

Theme III: Getting Away (Pretending, Acting, Imagining)

I didn't want to think about that—or the speech I was to work on, or the job left undone at home. . . . So I set my mind on something . . . totally unproductive, totally different, totally escapist (P10).

[I] just pretended to be a wealthy world traveler having a drink at the Plaza Hotel (P9).

We played a pretend game in which the child [client] was asked to help the [therapist] solve the child's problem—we reversed roles . . . [and] he comes up with a method to help him [me] with this problem (P12).

Theme IV: Feeling Free

. . . feeling free from evaluation; knowing others were jealous of . . . [us] (P5).

. . . taking time to read a novel—freeing myself of work (P8).

Theme V: Feeling Good

I was having fun, relaxed, enjoying myself (P8).

My awareness—how much fun we had doing it (P3).

The good feeling of doing [this] (P5).

The joy of . . . (P13).

Taking all of these themes into account suggests the following first-person description of how play was characterized by participants: Experiences of play emerge as a patterned *gestalt* against the background of present and prior relationships with other people and myself. Within these contexts, I am most keenly aware of feeling free and of experiencing change, accomplishment, or improvement in others or myself. I am also aware of connecting with people in terms of establishing new relationships or in terms of cooperating and/or competing with them. Situations of play are accompanied by feelings of joy, fun, and relaxation, as well as by those of overcoming feelings of anxiety, constraint, or guilt. Finally, I am aware of a pretend quality in playing that enables me to experience getting away from ordinary situations of doing, being, and feeling that define situations of nonplay: The play world is clearly different for me than the serious world of everyday life.

THEMATIC PATTERN FOR STUDENT PARTICIPANTS

The second group of participants contained thirty student volunteers from introductory classes at a large southeastern university. Protocols produced by this group of respondents were analyzed in accordance with the same procedures used for the first group and, as before, resulted in two complementary sets of data: (1) a descriptive enumeration of situations in which play was described as taking place, and (2) an interpretative analysis of themes. As in the case of the first group of respondents, college-age participants described a broad range of situations in which they experienced play. Since a sufficient number of situations were described in detail by participants in response to the second request, only these episodes were considered in detail for both analyses.

Of the thirty situations described, eight involved formal athletic games such as soccer, basketball, and so on. A smaller group of four situations concerned "playing with kids," whereas three respondents talked about performing music in a band or by oneself. The remaining fifteen situations described unique events, such as "trying on a

Halloween costume," "goofing off," "wrestling with friends," and so on. When all thirty situations were coded according to the two categories of alone/with others and inside/outside, results indicated that twenty-three of the thirty situations involved other people and that fourteen of the twenty-six situations took place inside. Four situations could not be coded in regard to inside or outside, although each of these situations could be coded as involving other people.

The total pattern of codings produced by this first analysis is presented in Table 48.2; results indicate that most play situations for this group of participants involved other people ($p < 0.01$). In contrast to results produced by conference participants, where twenty-nine of forty-one examples took place indoors, student respondents showed no clear preference for either location. On the basis of both sets of results, it seems clear that for students and therapists episodes of play take place in connection with other people. The preponderance of indoor situations reported by therapists seems easily understood, since they are likely to have many of their play episodes take place in classrooms or offices. Then, too, not too many students are likely to "pretend to be a wealthy traveler having a drink at the Plaza Hotel," as was the case of P9 in the professional group.

Turning now to student essays, it was possible to describe the experiential meaning of play in terms of four different and interrelated themes: freedom and control, release, different world, and connection. As in the case of conference participants, each of these specific terms occurred in the essays written by participants. Also in agreement with earlier results, the meaning of play invariably involved other people, either explicitly in the situation or as a memory from the participant's personal past. For participants in this group—as for conference participants—play episodes were primarily contexualized by other people, and each of the specific themes made either explicit or implicit reference to such conditions.

Examples deriving from various protocols expressing each of the major thematic meanings are as follows:

Theme I: Freedom and Control

My friend and I were stressed because of the pressures. We stopped typing and . . . just began to dance . . . while I was dancing I felt so free (P7).

When you're playing an instrument in a band you have to be aware of what others are doing. . . . The drummer . . . controls the tempo for what you are playing and you have to match his tempo. . . . I gave myself over to the music and felt very free (P1).

Hiking is a form of play . . . the only structure to hiking is the trail, which you are always free to go off of—otherwise you can set your own pace and pick your destination (P2).

Theme II: Release, Relief, Calm, Fun, Excitement

When I ran around campus, it was relieving my stress so I considered it fun like playing (P10).

To me, reading is a very enjoyable type of play . . . and for a few hours I leave the pain of this world (P18).

When I play the piano . . . I am in a zone. I block out all . . . frustration. I am at peace while my fingers stroke the keys (P26).

Table 48.2
Characteristics of Situations Described by Students

Geographic Location	Social Setting		
	Alone	With Others	Totals
Inside (I)	4	10	14
Outside (O)	3	9	12
Sum: I + O	7	19	26
Uncodable	0	4	4
Totals	7	23	30

Theme III: Different World

Quotes from both P18—"I leave the pain of this world"—and P26—"I am in a zone," also express this theme. Other examples are as follows:

I daydream a lot about . . . spinning records at a local club, bringing the electric scene to a mass audience. . . . Sure I dream a lot but for . . . now I will stick with my turntable mixing at home (P1).

People play games with each other. . . . It may not be fun and it may not be real, but by playing this game he might ask to be let back into this world (which he took for granted) (P3).

Our memories (of high school) went wild. . . . We were all being goofy and carefree of all our worries. This is what I call playing because you give your self over to your memories (P30).

Now I am not thinking about anything (but the game) and letting my body take over. . . . I am really in the game, and nowhere else (P8).

Theme IV: Connection

When playing with my kids at daycare I am aware of the innocence they have to almost everything in the world. . . . They are looking for someone to love them and share affection to them. . . . I feel as though I am playing when they smile (at me) and have a good time (P26).

There is a 17-year difference between me and my baby sister. . . . When I went to college, of course, I missed her. . . . Each time I have returned home I cannot quit playing with her. I fear she will not know me as well as I would like (P4).

Every now and then I would get in and swim with the kids. . . . I remember thinking I wish that I were still little like them (P11).

Although only a few excerpts have been presented, it seems clear that the various themes strongly interconnect with one another. It is almost impossible to read any given essay and not see two, three, or all four themes being described. When talking about freedom, for example, participants talked about being relaxed or calm and being in a different world, such as that of an athletic game. Although some participants described play as a solitary activity (such as reading a book or playing a piece of piano music), most reported that they were connected with other people who were crucial to their own experiences of play. In the most obvious sense of the term, all four themes defined a coherent pattern (see Figure 48.3). As in the earlier case, the experiential meaning of play is contextualized by other people and this aspect of present results is represented by the larger rectangle surrounding the central thematic figure.

Taking all themes and contexts into account suggests the following first-person description of the way in which play was characterized: Play is an experiential state in which I feel both free and controlled—free from the concerns of everyday life and controlled by the rules of an unfolding activity. Such rules are explicit in the case of a formal game and implicit in the case of ad hoc activities, such as wrestling with friends. If I do not let the game (or activity) control—as in the case where I am worried about the evaluation of my coach or some onlooker—I experience little or no freedom. Sometimes I am unsure as to whether to give myself over to the game and I experience an in-between state that affords neither freedom nor control: "You have to find a balance between a friendly game (of *Scrabble*) or a competitive one—[when I play with my girlfriend] it's a contest between [my] desire to win and [my] desire to keep her happy. It would be an easy decision if she weren't such a good player" (P18).

Since some players reported experiencing both freedom and control, the correlated emotional states were described in two different ways. For some respondents, total participation produced a feeling of "euphoria"—a "rush," "excitement," "fun"; for other participants, total participation produced an experience of relief or release. In both cases, participants reported a clear difference between being in the world of the game and being in the "real world." Most participants noted that other people were experienced as being significant to them, and that play not only affirmed relationships but also strengthened them. This aspect of play was rendered, most poignantly, in an the essay quoted earlier by the participant, seventeen years older than his baby sister, who "couldn't quit playing with her for fear she would not know me as well as I would like" (P4).

THE THEMATIC MEANINGS OF PLAY

Despite some significant differences in respondents—play therapists and college students—and some highly significant differences in the conditions under which they wrote their responses—one after a late-evening session of a national conference and the other in the quiet of a college research room—it was comforting to note significant similarity of results across groups. For both sets of respondents, issues of freedom, good feelings of peace and calm on one side and those of excitement and fun on the other, and the experience of getting away from the everyday world were all in evidence in the protocols. The one theme that was different concerned the issue of "getting it," emphasized by therapists. As may be recalled, this theme indicated an awareness of increased skill or improvement when both the therapist and his or her partner were engaged in play.

Figure 48.3
Thematic Meanings of Student Responses

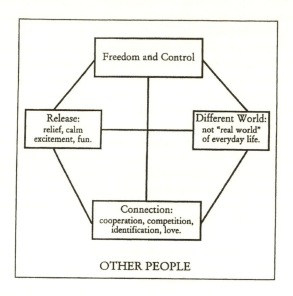

A more subtle difference concerned student descriptions of the relationship between freedom and control. While there was little difference across groups in the experience of "feeling free," there was some difference in how participants reported it was brought about. For therapists it was largely a matter of "escaping from" the constraints of one's job or responsibilities; for students it was not only possible to "get away" from the concerns of everyday life, it was also possible—to a degree considerably less emphasized by the therapists—to lose oneself in an ongoing activity. Students noted that giving oneself over to the constraints of a game or activity allowed them a measure of freedom from the ordinary concerns of everyday life. It seems fair to say that when the game played participants to the same degree as they played the game, release from daily constraint was complete. For this reason, students tended to emphasize their experiences of being in a "different" world or "zone" more strongly than their older compatriots.

This emphasis on a different mode of consciousness seems related to a more Zen-like understanding of the meaning of play. Whether concerned with an unsolvable problem such as a koan or with the practice of yoga or some martial art, the usual understanding is that such activities promote an experiential state in which the abstract functions of thinking are suspended. Under these conditions, the difference between mind and body is overcome and the person acts and experiences these acts as a unity. When this happens the dualism of mind/body or subject/object disappears, and the person experiences a more unified mode of being.

This mode of being not only allows more skillful performance (as stressed by the therapists); it also allows for a more integrated experience of world and self (as stressed by the students). Such moments not only instruct and release, they bring peace, communion, and the seemingly paradoxical experience of both freedom and control, themes all noted as aspects of play by student participants.

When we return, once more, to protocols produced by the play therapists, concerns over teaching and helping seemed to preclude a total commitment to the unfolding world of play. If the aim of play is to help someone, it falls upon the shoulders of the teacher or therapist to maintain a split mode of consciousness—one part being within the game and one part being an evaluator of its efficacy. To play completely means not to evaluate the game in terms of criteria external to it as a means of producing change either in one's clients or students. It is not so much that therapists are unable to play in this way, only that playing, for them, serves as a technique for facilitating a positive outcome in someone else. Although some participants described clear examples of entry into a "pretend world," many more examples were concerned with mastery than with immersion. Thematically they were concerned with helping someone "get it" by practicing under relaxed conditions rather than helping them "get it" by enabling them to "get away."

How do these results relate to humor? Here again there is a good deal of thematic and contextual similarity across both activities. For one, both humor and play take place within the context of other people. Although we may play solitaire or laugh alone at a humorous book, the more usual conditions for both humor and play are in the world with other people. In this context, both humor and play emphasize relationships as well as feelings of freedom from ordinary constraints around significant social and personal issues.

Play, however, gives a more realistic and usable experience of freedom than humor. In the case of humor we are left with a feeling of radical freedom, a situation with no constraints. Although this is a short-term possibility, the body, after prolonged laughter, has a way of calling us back to itself, in this situation, in this place. Within the context of play we learn that freedom is not only freedom from but also freedom to: We are always free to choose a new situation, a new set of constraints. What we are not free to do is not to engage in some situation. To be free is to choose one's constraints and supports, not to be independent of them.

This understanding accords rather well with the description of freedom experienced by engaging, full tilt, in a game. Only by committing ourselves to the control of a game or to the spontaneous pretending of the play world are we able to experience freedom from our present situation. Such freedom requires either discipline and/or practice in the case of a formal game or a commitment to imaginative creation in the case of spontaneous play. In neither case is freedom unconditional: Freedom is not only escaping from our present situation, it is also moving to engage more wholeheartedly in a new one.

Both activities also produce "good feelings"; in the case of humor, these derive from a momentary release from the darker and unresolvable forces at the heart of human social life. In the case of play, "feeling good" derives from an ability to immerse oneself totally in an ongoing activity, whether this activity concerns a formal game or the unfolding creation of an imaginary object or world. In both cases we are relatively unconcerned with the evaluations of other people not presently engaged with us in the activity. This state of affairs allow for two further possibilities: (1) we are able to attempt or practice new levels of skill, and (2) we are able to experience a more centered and integrated mode of being in which the ordinary distractions of everyday life are minimal. To hear a child laugh is to know he or she has experienced a feeling of release; to see a child play is to know not only that he or she is experiencing freedom but that he or she also is experiencing commitment to a more unified mode of awareness capable of facilitating new learning and personal change.

This same line of analysis also captures adult experiences of play. By immersing ourselves in a world different from that of everyday life, not only are we refreshed in terms of feeling free, we also are likely to gain new skills and/or a new perspective. While it is true that humor and laughter may also yield a changed perspective on reality—it was Freud who compared the logic of a joke to the structure of a dream—such changes are momentary, and a good joke works only once or twice as a source of relief or inspiration. By continuously engaging in the world of a game or of imagination, we come to achieve a mastery that would not be possible under the ordinary conditions of evaluation present in everyday life. While it is true that looser forms of spontaneous play also occur, their purpose would seem closer to that originally noted for humor by Bergson (1911): To provide a reminder of the spontaneity necessary for feeling alive.

One further conclusion seems to derive from the present analysis: Humor and laughter serve a brief segment of the present in the light of the past; play, on the other hand, serves the future by allowing a relatively safe context within which to achieve mastery over the world and ourselves. Far from being a luxury, play is a necessary condition for future possibilities. Although humor and laughter also are valuable in making life livable, they seem more concerned with allowing for a bit of space when in the vicinity of darker forces than with providing an opportunity for growth and development. In both cases, however, we must be quite clear about one thing: Humor and play are not only nice, they are absolutely necessary for a meaningful and productive human life.

REFERENCES

Bergson, H. (1911). *Laughter: An Essay on the Meaning of the Comic*. New York: MacMillan.

Coser, R. (1960). Laughter among Colleagues. *Psychiatry* 23: 81–95.

Cousins, N. (1979). *Anatomy of an Illness*. New York: Norton.

Darwin, C. (1872). *The Expression of Emotions in Man and Animals*. London: Murray.

Fisher, S., & R. Fisher. (1981). *Pretend the World Is Funny and Forever*. Mahwah, NJ: Erlbaum.

Freud, S. (1960). *Jokes and Their Relation to the Unconscious*. New York: Norton. (Original work published 1905.)

Hobbes, T. (1651). *The Leviathan*. London: Crooke.

Lorenz, K. (1963). *On Aggression*. New York: Harcourt, Brace and World.

Plessner, H. (1970). *Laughing and Crying*. Evanston, IL: Northwestern University Press. (Original work published 1941.)

Pollio, H. R. (1983). Notes toward a Field Theory of Humor. In P. E. McGhee & J. H. Goldstein (eds.), *Handbook of Humor Research*, vol I (pp. 213–230). New York: Springer Verlag.

————. (1997). Boundaries in Humor and Metaphor. In J. S. Mio & A. N. Katz (Eds.), *Metaphor: Implications and Applications* (pp. 231–254). Mahwah, NJ: Erlbaum & Associates.

Pollio, H. R., T. Henley, & C. Thompson. (1997). *The Phenomenology of Everyday Life*. London: Cambridge University Press.

Pollio, H. R., & C. Swanson. (1995). A Behavioral and Phenomenological Analysis of Audience Reactions to Comic Performance. *International Journal of Humor* 8: 5–28.

Scogin, F., & H. Pollio. (1980). Targeting and the Humorous Episode in Group Process. *Human Relations* 11: 831–851.

PART V

DECLARATION OF
THE CHILD'S RIGHT TO PLAY

WHAT IS PLAY?

Children are the foundation of the world's future.

Children have played at all times throughout history and in all cultures.

Play, along with the basic needs of nutrition, health, shelter, and education, is vital to develop the potential of all children.

Play is communication and expression, combining thought and action; it gives satisfaction and a feeling of achievement.

Play is instinctive, voluntary, and spontaneous.

Play is a means of learning to live, not a mere passing of time.

ALARMING TRENDS AFFECTING CHILDHOOD

IPA is deeply concerned by a number of alarming trends and their negative impact on children's development:

- Society's indifference to the importance of play.
- Over-emphasis on theoretical and academic studies in schools.
- Increasing numbers of children living with inadequate provisions for survival and development.
- Inadequate environmental planning, which results in a lack of basic amenities, inappropriate housing forms, and poor traffic management.
- Increasing commercial exploitation of children, and the deterioration of cultural traditions.

- Lack of access for third world women to basic training in childcare and development.
- Inadequate preparation of children to cope with life in a rapidly changing society.
- Increasing segregation of children in the community.
- The increasing numbers of working children, and their unacceptable working conditions.
- Constant exposure of children to war, violence, exploitation and destruction.
- Over-emphasis on unhealthy competition and "winning at all costs" in children's sports.

PROPOSALS FOR ACTION

The following proposals are listed under the names of government departments having a measure of responsibility for children.

Health

Play is essential for the physical and mental health of the child.

- Establish programmes for professionals and parents about the benefits of play from birth onwards.
- Ensure basic conditions (nutrition, sanitation, clean water and air) which promote the healthy survival and development of all children.
- Incorporate play into community programmes designed to maintain children's physical and mental health.
- Include play as an integral part of all children's environments, including hospitals and other institutional settings.

Education

Play is part of education.

- Provide opportunities for initiative, interaction, creativity and socialisation through play in formal education systems.
- Include studies of the importance of play and the means of play provision in the training of all professionals and volunteers working with and for children.
- Strengthen play provision in primary schools to enhance learning and to maintain attendance and motivation.
- Reduce the incompatibilities between daily life, work and education by involving schools and colleges, and by using public buildings for community play programmes.
- Ensure that working children have access to play and learning opportunities outside of the system of formal education.

Welfare

Play is an essential part of family and community life.

- Ensure that play is accepted as an integral part of social development and social care.
- Promote measures that strengthen positive relationships between parents and children.
- Ensure that play is part of community-based services designed to integrate children with physical, mental or emotional disabilities into the community.
- Provide safe play environments that protect children against abduction, sexual abuse and physical violence.

Leisure

Children need opportunities to play at leisure.

- Provide time, space, materials, natural settings, and programmes with leaders where children may develop a sense of belonging, self-esteem, and enjoyment through play.
- Enable interaction between children and people of all backgrounds and ages in leisure settings.
- Encourage the conservation and use of traditional indigenous games.
- Stop the commercial exploitation of children's play, and the production and sale of war toys and games of violence and destruction.
- Promote the use of co-operative games and fair play for children in sports.
- Provide all children, particularly those with special needs, with access to a diversity of play environments, toys and play materials through community programmes such as pre-school play groups, toy libraries and play buses.

Planning

The needs of the child must have priority in the planning of human settlements.

- Ensure that children and young people can participate in making decisions that affect their surroundings and their access to them.
- When planning new, or reorganising existing, developments, recognise the child's small size and limited range of activity.
- Disseminate existing knowledge about play facilities and play programmes to planning professionals and politicians.
- Oppose the building of high-rise housing and provide opportunities to mitigate its detrimental effects on children and families.
- Enable children to move easily about the community by providing safe pedestrian access through urban neighborhoods, better traffic management, and improved public transportation.
- Increase awareness of the high vulnerability of children living in slum settlements, tenements, and derelict neighborhoods.
- Reserve adequate and appropriate space for play and recreation through statutory provision.

AFFIRMATION

IPA is determined to sustain the momentum created by the International Year of the Child in 1979 to arouse world opinion for the improvement of the life of children, and:

Affirms its belief in the United Nations' Declaration of the Rights of the Child, which in Article 7 states, "The child shall have full opportunity to play and recreation, which should be directed to the same purposes as education; society and the public authorities shall endeavor to promote the enjoyment of this right"; and endorses its belief in Article 31 of the Convention on the Rights of the Child.

Recognises that the population of children in developing countries is three quarters of the world's total child population, and that efforts directed at the promotion of education and literacy, and the stopping of environmental deprivation would improve the capacities of the poorest.

Affirms its commitment to working with other national and international organisations to ensure basic conditions of survival for all children in order that they may fully develop as human beings.

Acknowledges that each country is responsible for preparing its own courses of public and political action in the light of its culture, climate and social, political and economic structure;

Recognises that the full participation of the community is essential in planning and developing programmes and services to meet the needs, wishes, and aspirations of children;

Assures its co-operation with U.N. agencies and other international and national organizations involved with children;

Appeals to all countries and organizations to take action to counteract the alarming trends which jeopardize children's healthy development and to give high priority to long-term programmes designed to ensure for all time: THE CHILD'S RIGHT TO PLAY.

NOTE

The IPA Declaration of the Child's Right to Play was produced in November 1977 at the IPA Malta Consultation held in preparation for the International Year of the Child (1979). It was revised by the IPA International Council in Vienna, Austria, in September 1982 and Barcelona, Spain, in September 1989. It should be read in conjunction with Article 31 of the U.N. Convention on the Rights of the Child (adopted by the General Assembly of the United Nations, November 20, 1989), which states that the child has a right to leisure, play, and participation in cultural and artistic activities.

In 1971 the IPA Board decided that it was important to cooperate with the U.N. organizations. IPA is recognized by UNESCO, ECOSOC (Economic and Social Council), and UNICEF, and works in agreement with their principles, which give a context to the work of IPA, as follows:

1. A focus on human rights, specifically the Child's Right to Play as stated in the U.N. Declaration of the Rights of the Child, and now embodied in the Convention on the Rights of the Child.

2. A feeling of solidarity with children all over the world.

3. An involvement in peace education. IPA has been appointed as a Messenger of Peace by the United Nations.

4. A commitment to the development of each individual to the maximum of their potential, the protection and enhancement of their culture, and the importance of the family and the community.

Index

About the Editors and Contributors

RAQUEL ARY-DE ROZZA is a children's center teacher and part-time professor of child development at Chaffey College, Rancho Cucamonga, California. She writes original stories and songs and performs lectures on play and integrated learning theories.

BRIAN ASHLEY is an educational sociologist and works as a freelance consultant in community development and community education in Stockholm, Sweden. Educated in London University as a sociologist, he has subsequently trained and practiced as a social worker, a guidance counselor, and a teacher, and he is an author of books on educational sociology, community development, and social policy. At present, he is the editor of *Playrights*, the international journal of the theory and practice of play.

LOIS A. BERGGREN has been an artist-teacher, community organizer, program consultant, and curriculum developer for the past thirty years. She is committed to including individuals with disabilities in multicultural communities. She has brought up her own four children on three continents with four changes of language. This has informed her practice in diverse ethnic, racial, and cultural communities. Currently, she works as a lead teacher in an arts and play-based infant–toddler program serving mixed-income families in transition at Paige Academy, Roxbury (Boston), Massachusetts, the only African-American private school in New England.

KATE BISHOP is a Churchill Fellow and currently a research student in the Department of Education at James Cook University in Townsville, Australia. Through her workshop, Play for All, she custom designs and builds play equipment and indoor play environments for children with the total range of abilities. Principally, she works with special schools, hospitals, and early intervention services. In 1995 she completed the first playroom in Australia for children who are vision impaired for the Royal Blind Society, Sydney, New South Wales.

MAC H. BROWN is a prolific writer, national presenter, and a professor of early childhood education at the University of South Carolina in Columbia. Author of two books, he has recently published in the areas of curriculum and child care and maintains play as a primary research interest.

PEI-SAN BROWN is a founding member of the Children's Institute for Learning and Development and a doctoral student in early childhood education at the University of Texas at Austin. She has conducted research with the Consumer Products Safety Commission, the National Institute of Child Health and Human Development, the National Aeronautics and Space Association, the University of California at Irvine, and several departments at the University of Texas.

GORDON M. BURGHARDT is currently alumni distinguish professor in the departments of Psychology and Ecology and Evolutionary Biology at the University of Tennessee. An internationally recognized expert in ethology, specializing in behavioral development and learning, he has lectured extensively and has authored or edited several books.

CHRISTINA CARLUCCI has been a research associate at the University of Maryland, an education consultant with Jostens Learning Corporation, and a teacher at the School for the Deaf in Tucson, Arizona. For the past three years she has been program coordinator for the Supervised Parenting and Play Program at the Arsenal Family and Children's Center.

JOHN CASTRONOVA is director of the Committee on Preschool Special Education and the Committee on Special Education for the Uniondale Union Free School District on Long Island, New York. He is also a Certified Image Relationship therapist in private practice.

PEI-YU CHANG is an assistant professor at the Center for Teacher Education at National Taipei College of Nursing. Her research interests include children's play and artistic representations.

RHONDA L. CLEMENTS is a professor at Hofstra University, and the author of seven books and numerous articles on the topic of play, games, and movement activities for preschool and elementary school age children. She is also a consultant to several major toy and child product manufacturers, and is currently the president of the American Association for the Child's Right to Play (IPA/USA).

MARK COTTER is a volunteer advocate for children in foster care, has coached emotionally disturbed foster children in Future Problem Solvers Programs, and has taught creative drama techniques and given workshops in creative problem solving.

LINDSAY C. DAVIS is an instructor at Ryerson University, Toronto, Ontario, Canada, where she teaches courses in intergenerational programming to early childhood education students. She also sits on the board of directors of United Generations Ontario, a nonprofit group of individuals and organizations promoting intergenerational programs and issues.

GEORGIANNA DUARTE is a professor in early childhood education and the coordinator of the Graduate Early Childhood Education Program at the University of Texas at Brownsville. She is the author of numerous articles on play, literacy, and migrant education issues. She is a national consultant for the Bureau of Youth and Families for Migrant and Seasonal Farm Workers and early, regional, and Indian Head Start Programs. She is an advocate for best practices for multilingual children.

JANET EDWARDS, an ordained Presbyterian minister, is a parent mentor at the Arsenal Family and Children's Center.

LEAH HOLLAND FIORENTINO is a professor in the Department of Movement Sciences and Physical Education at Adelphi University in Garden City, New York. She is the author of several articles on the implementation of technological applications to the teacher/coach preparation system. Her research using technology is aimed at improving the quality of work that teachers and play specialists will conduct in their work settings.

GILBERT M. FOLEY is an associate professor in the School/Child Clinical Psychology program at Ferkauf Graduate School of Psychology, Yeshiva University, New York City. He also serves as senior clinical supervisor at the Pediatric Resource Center, Bellevue Hospital Center, and maintains a private practice. He has lectured widely and is coauthor of three books.

NANCY K. FREEMAN is an assistant professor of early childhood education and the research director of the Children's Center at the University of South Carolina in Columbia. She has published books and articles that explore the ethical dimensions of teaching, and has served on the National Association for Educating Young Children Ethics panel.

JOE FROST has focused on play leadership and play design for more than twenty years. He is best known, however, for his investigations and presentations that focus on playground safety. The author of numerous articles and books, his recent works have conceptualized play as important as any other human need and writes that play deprivation is a real concern of all civilized countries.

MELISSA GEMEINHARDT is a Ph.D. candidate in early childhood education at the University of New Orleans and teaches at Newcomb College Nursery School for Tulane University. She uses relevant principles of art history and theory to support a meaningful art curriculum for children.

NEIL GREENBERG is a professor of ecology and evolutionary biology at the University of Tennessee and a well-known researcher and scholar in the neural and endocrine background to behavior, specializing in causes and consequences of stress, including its influence in social behavior and creativity. He is also a member of the University Studies Colloquy on Creativity at the University of Tennessee, where he is researching the ethology of creativity.

BRUCE D. GROSSMAN is a professor of education and early childhood and a teaching fellow at New College at Hofstra University. He has taught developmental psychology at Hofstra for thirty-six years, including a course titled "Play and Imagination," and has published numerous articles on play theories.

SUSAN HUDSON is the education director of the National Program for Playground Safety and the McElroy Professor of Youth Leadership Studies at the University of Northern Iowa. She is considered one of the leading experts in the field of playground safety in the United States. She has co-authored more than sixty-five articles in the area of playground safety.

JOANNE HYNES-DUSEL is an assistant professor of physical education at Towson University in Towson, Maryland. She has presented over fifty papers at international, national, state, and district conferences, and has written twenty articles published in journals, as well as six chapters in books. She is currently writing two books on play and physical activity.

FREDERICK JOHNSON has a acrobatics background and has worked for many years in youth centers in low-income, minority neighborhoods. He has a master's degree in social work and is the author of *The Tumbleweeds: Somersaulting Up and Out of the City Streets.*

JAMES E. JOHNSON is a professor on the faculty of the Curriculum and Instruction Department in the College of Education at Pennsylvania State University. His research interests are in the areas of children's play, culture, and parent–child relations. He is the author of eight books on early childhood education.

KAREN MCCHESNEY JOHNSON is an adjunct professor in early childhood education at Pennsylvania State University and a therapist for Northwestern Human Services, Lewistown, Pennsylvania. Her research interests are in the areas of play and special education.

GUSTAVE T. JUHLIN teaches physical education at Chapel of the Redeemer in Bayside, New York. He is a frequent visitor to the Scandinavian countries because of his Swedish descent and the many relatives he has there.

YVONNE E. KEAIRNS has been director of the Arsenal Family and Children's Center for twenty years. She is a licensed child psychologist in the Commonwealth of Pennsylvania. Currently she is head researcher at the Quaker United Nations office, conducting a study of the demobilization and reintegration of female child soldiers in four conflict areas around the world.

MEI-CHUN LIN is an associate professor on the faculty of the Early Childhood Education Department of the National Tainan Teachers College in Taiwan. Her research interests are in creative drama and play. She has been a featured speaker at numerous conferences.

IVANA LISUL is a doctorate student in psychology at the University of Novi Sad, Yugoslavia. She completed educational training in crisis intervention organized by UNICEF during NATO's bombing of Yugoslavia in the spring of 1999 in Novi Sad, Yugoslavia. She has since worked as a volunteer with children ages six and seven at one of Novi Sad's largest primary schools, which itself had been heavily damaged during the bombing.

LISA HERMINE MAKMAN is an assistant professor of English at William Paterson University. She specializes in the history and culture of childhood, and nineteenth- and twentieth-century literature for children and adolescents. She has published articles on children's writers such as George MacDonald, Edward Lear, Beatrix Potter, and Roald Dahl, and is currently working on a book, *Childhood Lost and Found: Locating Children in British Culture, 1870–1920*.

MARILENA FLORES MARTINS is a social worker and the founder and president of Promove Habilitation Center in Brazil, which provides services to children and adolescents who are at high risk and have special needs. She is also the cofounder and first president of the International Play Association in Brazil, and is currently the International Association's vice president for Latin America.

ROISIN McCOOEY teaches early childhood studies at Stranmillis University College in Belfast, Northern Ireland, and is currently a doctoral student at the Graduate School of Education, Queens University, Belfast. Her research interests include childhood socialization, peer interaction, peer acceptance, play in early education, and quality of early childhood programs.

CHARLIE McCORMICK is an assistant professor of English and communications at Cabrini College in Radnor, Pennsylvania. He studies unofficial youth culture and rites of passage in the contemporary world. He is currently completing a manuscript on adolescent cruising on the commercial strip.

MONICA McHALE-SMALL has been a school psychologist in Pennsylvania for more than twelve years. Currently she is Pupil Services Coordinator in the West Chester Area School District and also a part-time faculty member at Immaculata College.

CHRISTOPHER M. NUNES is an assistant professor of recreation and program coordinator of recreation at Ashland University in Ashland, Ohio. His interest in youth sports is the result of working with community recreation and parks departments as a coach, official, and supervisor of youth sports programs.

RIKUKO OKUDA is president of Japan's International Association for the Child's Right to Play. A scholar and distinguished researcher, her expertise is on the Japanese parenting culture, play spaces, and social movements.

CAROLYN M. PATTERSON is the assistant director of the Grove City College Early Childhood Lab School in Grove City, Pennsylvania. With more than thirteen years of teaching in the field of early childhood, she is currently responsible for the daily operations of the Lab School, which includes mentoring approximately twenty preservice teachers and being a full-time instructor in preschool classes.

JANICE H. PATTERSON is currently on the faculty of Curriculum and Instruction at the University of Alabama at Birmingham. She has conducted research on resilience for teachers and schools, conducted workshops and presentations throughout the United States, and published widely in her field. She has also trained teachers in Israel and Ecuador.

JOANNA PAYNE-JONES is a professor of child development at Chaffey College and a part-time professor with the Sociology Department at Mount Soc Community College. She is an advocate for children's play and is the past chairperson for the Cultural Arts Community in Pomona, California.

BEATRIZ PEREIRA is a professor at the University of Minho, Institute of Childhood Studies, Department of Arts and Physical Education, in Braga, Portugal. She is an author of a book aimed at children at risk, has written chapters for several books, and has presented papers at conferences. Her studies have focused primarily on game activities for preschool and elementary school-age children.

EVA PETERSON learned to play in the wilds of her native Arizona desert before she organized community-built playgrounds on a Sioux reservation in 1971. Since then she has done extensive teaching, staff development, and research for numerous institutions, museums, and universities regarding playful behaviors, play apparatus, and investigative processes. She currently writes and teaches in Washington, DC.

HOWARD R. POLLIO is a member of the faculty of psychology at the University of Tennessee at Knoxville. He is the author of eight books, a fellow of the American Psychological Association, and an acknowledged world expert in the phenomenology of metaphor and humor.

MARILYN R. POLLIO is currently in independent practice in Knoxville, Tennessee. Previously she taught at Maryville College, where she was a founding director of a learning center for children with educational problems. She is the author of a number of papers on metaphor and creativity in children.

LYNDA REEVES is currently the managing editor of Research in Action for P.E. Central, the most comprehensive Web site for physical educators.

ELIZABETH RIKE received the first American Association for the Child's Right to Play "Doctor of Play" award for her lifelong contribution to promoting imaginative play. She has presented at numerous conferences, and has been a keynote for many creative drama workshops. Her research has been used by many play and brain and learning specialists, and she is the author of several works on imaginative play.

ANNE M. ROTHSCHADL is an associate professor of recreation and tourism at Springfield College in Springfield, Massachusetts. Her interest in intrinsic motivation as a means to sustain long-term involvement in youth sports and physical activity is the result of several years of research on the effects of competition and cooperation.

AMANDA E. SCHWEDER is currently a doctoral student in developmental psychology at Yale University. In her dissertation she will examine the influence of risk and protective factors on the development of behavioral problems among maltreated children. She has previously evaluated the effectiveness of play training given to parents and teachers on indices of children's school readiness.

JEROME L. SINGER is professor of psychology and child study in the Department of Psychology at Yale University. With Dorothy Singer he is codirector of the Yale University Family Television Research and Consultation Center, and their most recent publications are *Make-Believe: Games and Activities for Imaginative Play* and *The Handbook of Children and the Media.*

DOROTHY G. SINGER is senior research scientist in the Department of Psychology and Child Study Center at Yale University. With Jerome Singer she is codirector of the Yale University Family Television Research and Consultation Center, and their most recent publications are *Make-Believe: Games and Activities for Imaginative Play* and *The Handbook of Children and the Media.*

PARAMVIR SINGH is an assistant professor at the Punjabi University in Punjab, India. He is presently vice president of the Sport Sciences Society and is the author of one book.

AUDREY SKRUPSKELIS is an associate professor of early childhood education at the University of South Carolina at Aiken. She is an ardent advocate for the child's right to play and serves as secretary on the IPA board of directors. During the summer she teaches graduate courses at Vytautas Magnus University in Kaunas, Lithuania, and serves as consultant to the Lithuanian Ministry of Education for Early Childhood. Her principal interests are open-ended play and its relationship to cognitive development, language development, and historical perspectives in education.

CONNIE STEELE is currently chairperson of Child Watch at the University of Tennessee Knoxville's Promise Advocacy for Quality Childcare through use of developmentally appropriate books and materials during infant's and children's play. Her research has investigated how play impacts the young child's cognitive constructs.

PATRICIA STERNBERG is a full professor in the Theatre Department at Hunter College, New York, where she also teaches and directs the Hunter College Mad Hatters, a group of college students who perform for young audiences. She has had four plays published and numerous others produced. A practicing drama therapist, lecturer, and workshop leader, she is also the author of eight books.

VICKI L. STOECKLIN is the education and child development director of the White Hutchinson Leisure and Learning Group, a Kansas City, Missouri, firm specializing in the design and development of family and children's leisure and learning venues worldwide. She has twenty-eight years' experience in the early childhood education and play, and has coauthored (with Randy White) more than fifty published articles on all aspects of family and children's leisure and play.

JOHN A. SUTTERBY is a cofounder of the Children's Institute for Learning and Development (CHILD). He is a doctoral candidate at the University of Texas and has been an instructor there for the last three years. He has worked as a field researcher for university-, industry-, and government-sponsored projects, taught courses on children's play and play environments, and served as an editor for several journals. He is also a volunteer member of SafeKids and the Pillow Elementary Campus Advisory Committee.

DONNA THOMPSON, founder and director of the National Program for Playground Safety, a professor in the School of Health, Physical Education, and Leisure Services at the University of Northern Iowa. A national and international expert in the field of safety and playgrounds, she has appeared on *Good Morning America* and *Later Today* addressing the importance of playground safety.

CANDRA D. THORNTON is a founding member of CHILD and currently an early childhood education doctoral candidate at the University of Texas at Austin, with a research emphasis on children's agency in gender construction. She has been an early childhood educator for many years, and currently teaches and supervises preservice elementary school teachers in the field.

MARIANNE TORBERT is a professor of kinesiology and director of the Leonard Gordon Institute for Human Development through Play at Temple University, Philadelphia, Pennsylvania. She is the author of *Follow Me: A Handbook of Movement Activities for Children* and *Secrets to Success in Sport and Play*, and coauthor of *Follow Me Too: A Handbook of Movement Activities for Three- to Five-Year-Olds*.

E. PAUL TORRANCE is director of Georgia Studies of Creative Behavior. He is renowned throughout the world and has made a significant impact in the field of creativity research as the creator of the Torrance Tests of Creative Thinking, which have greatly advanced the science of creativity. In 1974 he founded the Future Problem Solving Program to encourage the growth of creative problem solving and futurism in tomorrow's leaders. He has done extensive work incorporating sociodrama and role-playing techniques as part of creative problem solving, and has published more than 90 books and 400 articles in professional and research journals.

TABATHA A. UHRICH has taught elementary physical education for eleven years at the Union Canal Elementary School in Lebanon, Pennsylvania. She is currently pursing a doctorate degree at Temple University.

ELAINE M. VAN LUE is a program professor of early childhood at Nova Southeastern University in Orlando, Florida. She was a kindergarten and primary classroom teacher for twenty-five years and presently teaches graduate early childhood and elementary education courses. She is a practicum advisor and is also currently designing and writing curriculum for graduate early childhood programs.

BETTY J. WAGNER is director of the Chicago Area Writing Project and an internationally recognized authority on composition and instruction and the educational uses of drama. Her most recent book is *Educational Drama and Language Art*, a comprehensive overview of major research in the field, highlighting the effects of drama on thinking, oral language, reading, and writing.

RANDY WHITE is chief executive officer of the White Hutchinson Leisure and Learning Group, a Kansas City, Missouri, firm that specializes in the design and development of family and children's leisure and learning venues worldwide. He has coauthored (with Vicki L. Stoecklin) more than fifty articles on all aspects of family and children's leisure and play.

JOYCE A. WILKINSON is a professor of aesthetic education at the University of Toronto. An author, presenter, and award winner for creative drama, she has lectured extensively and has served as a special guest researcher to the Shanghai Education Commission to Develop English Literacy through Drama in China. She is presently a consultant and English editor for the national college on-line language project of the Chinese Ministry of Education.